Gerhard Altenbourg

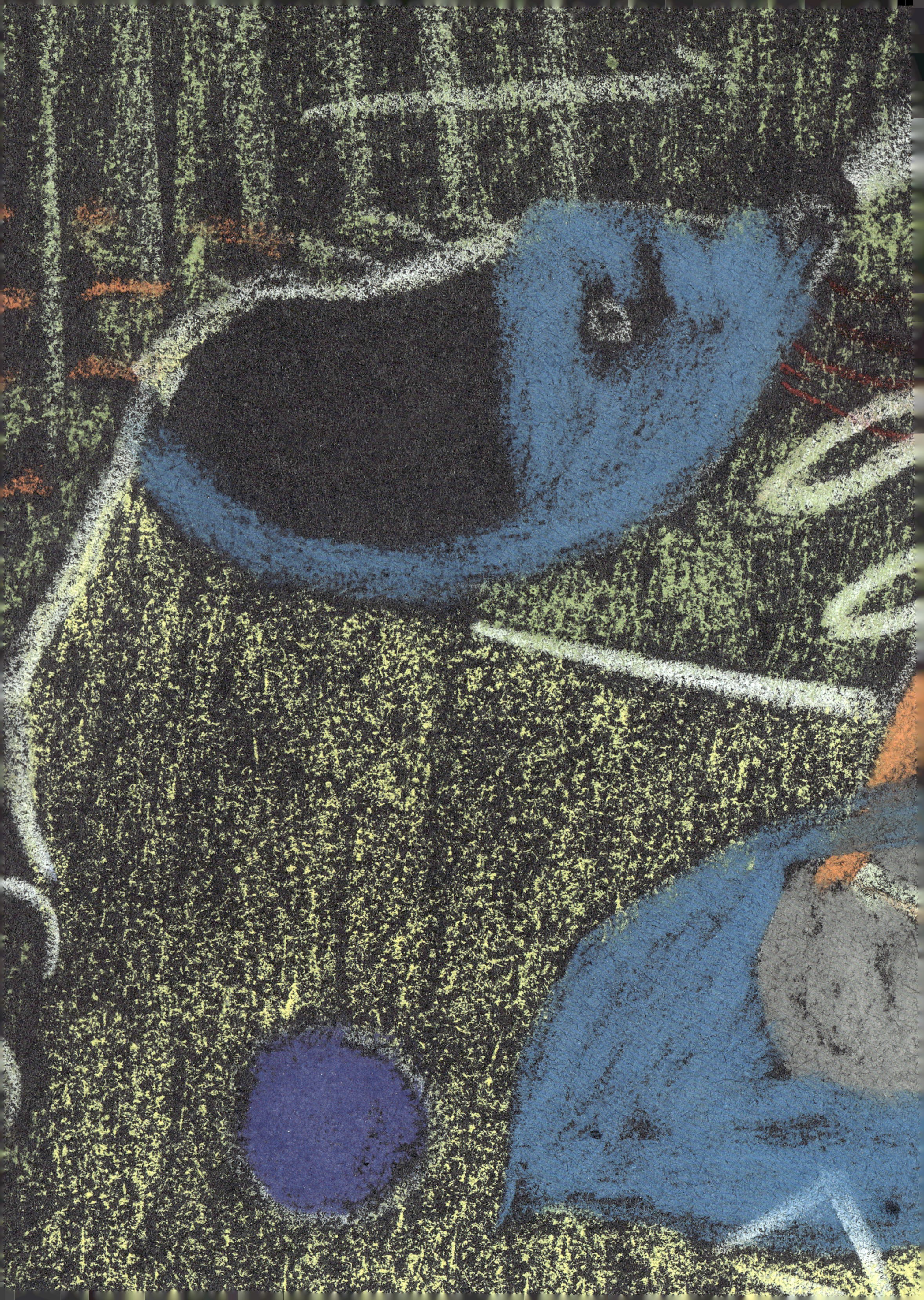

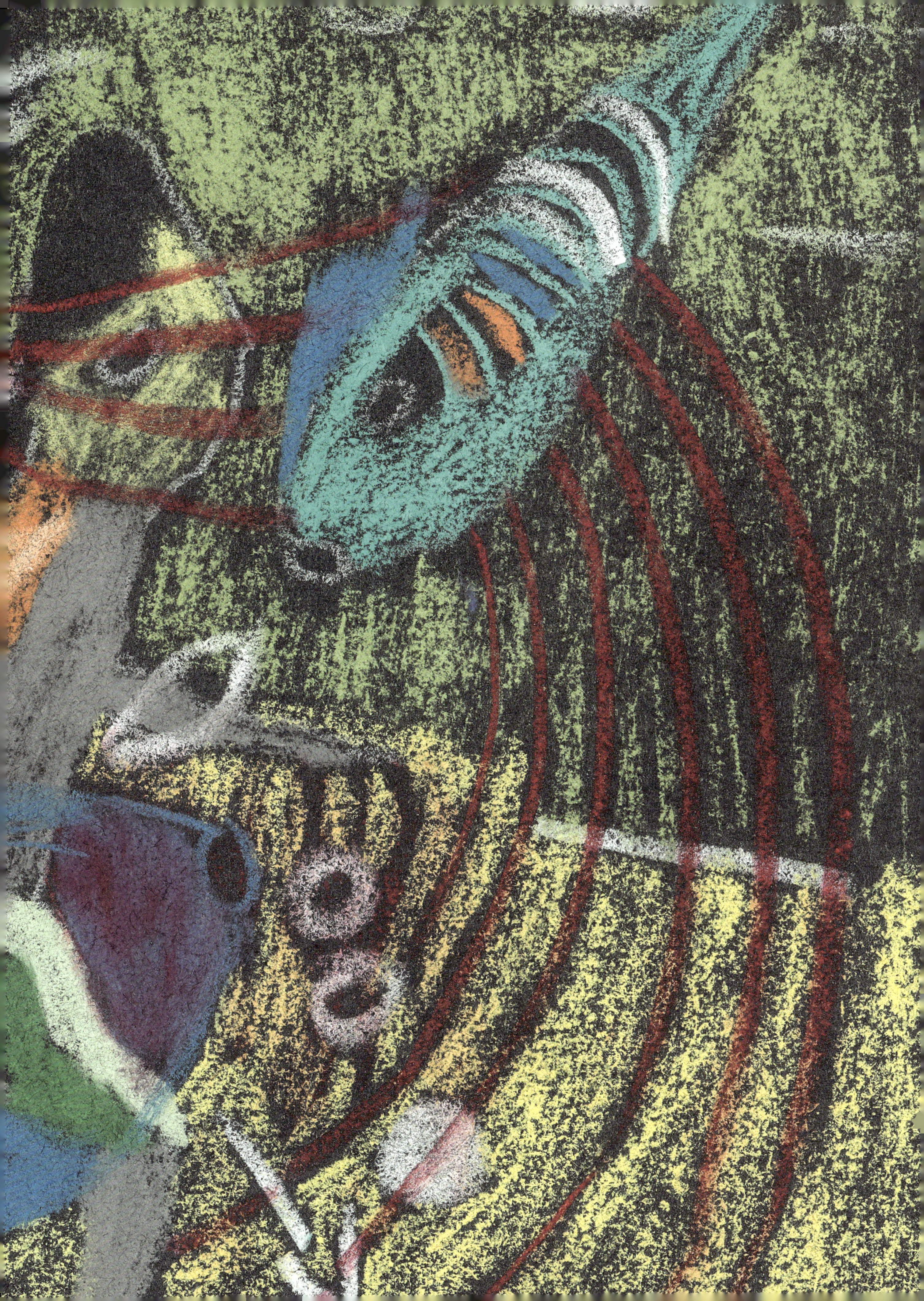

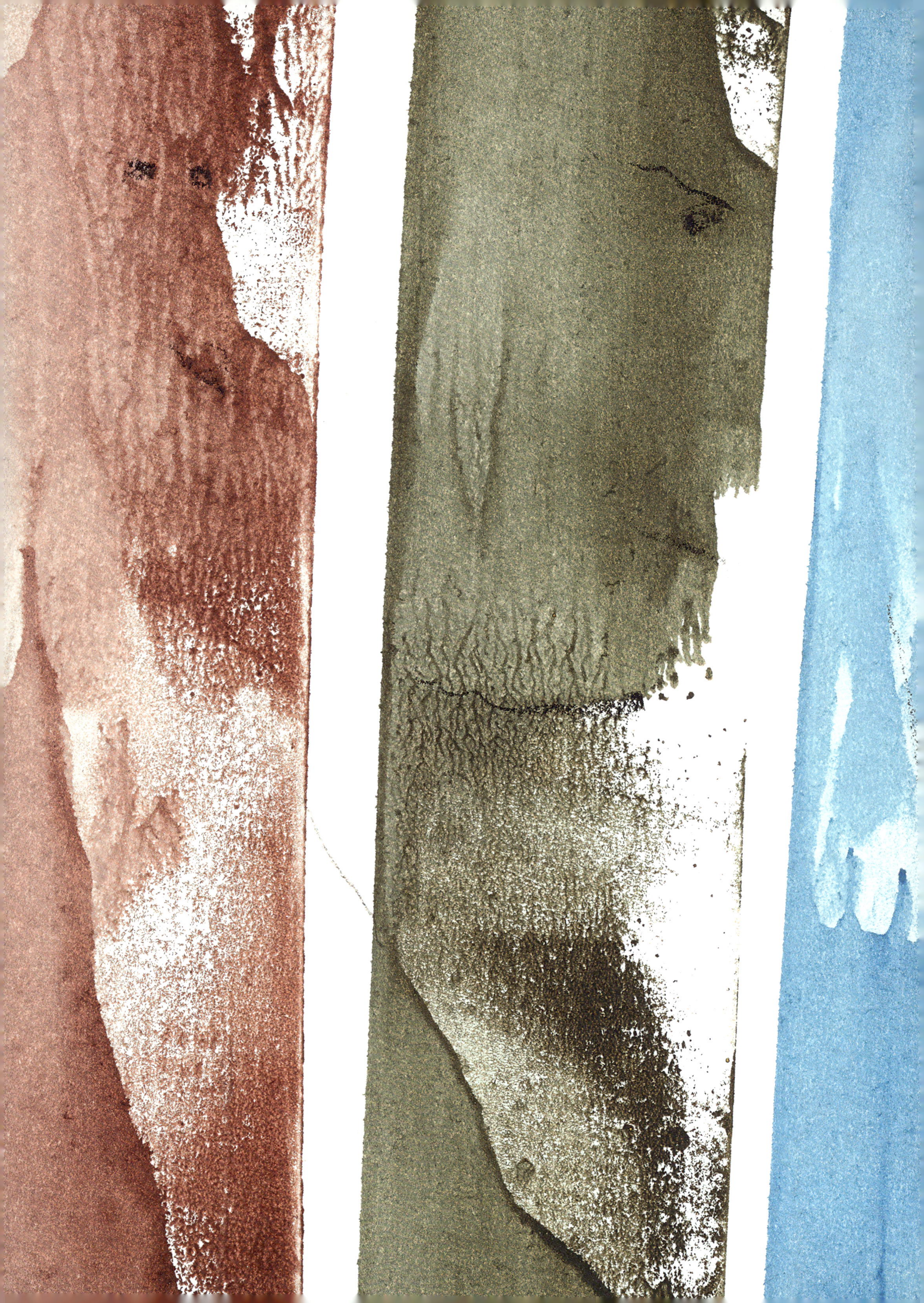

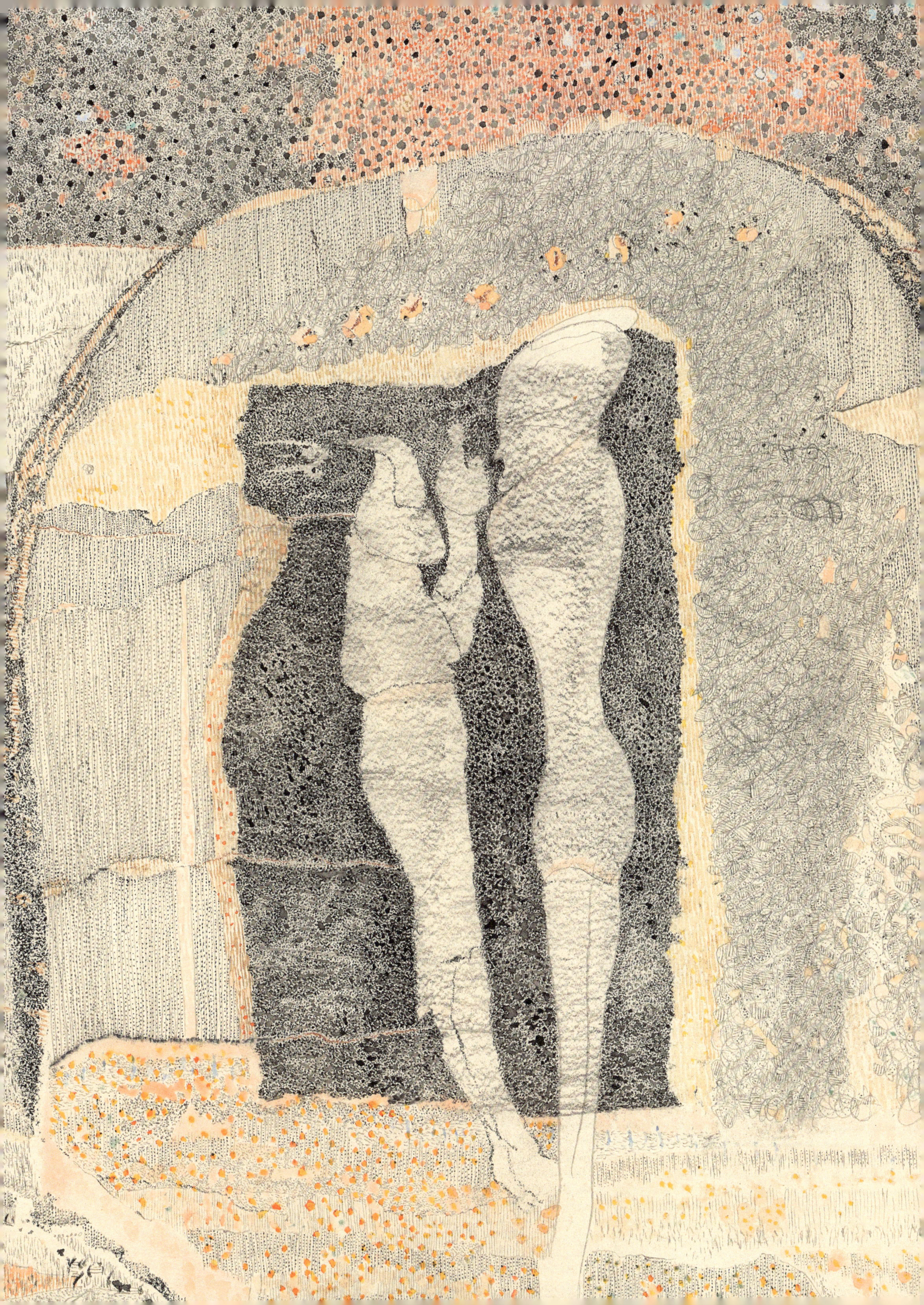

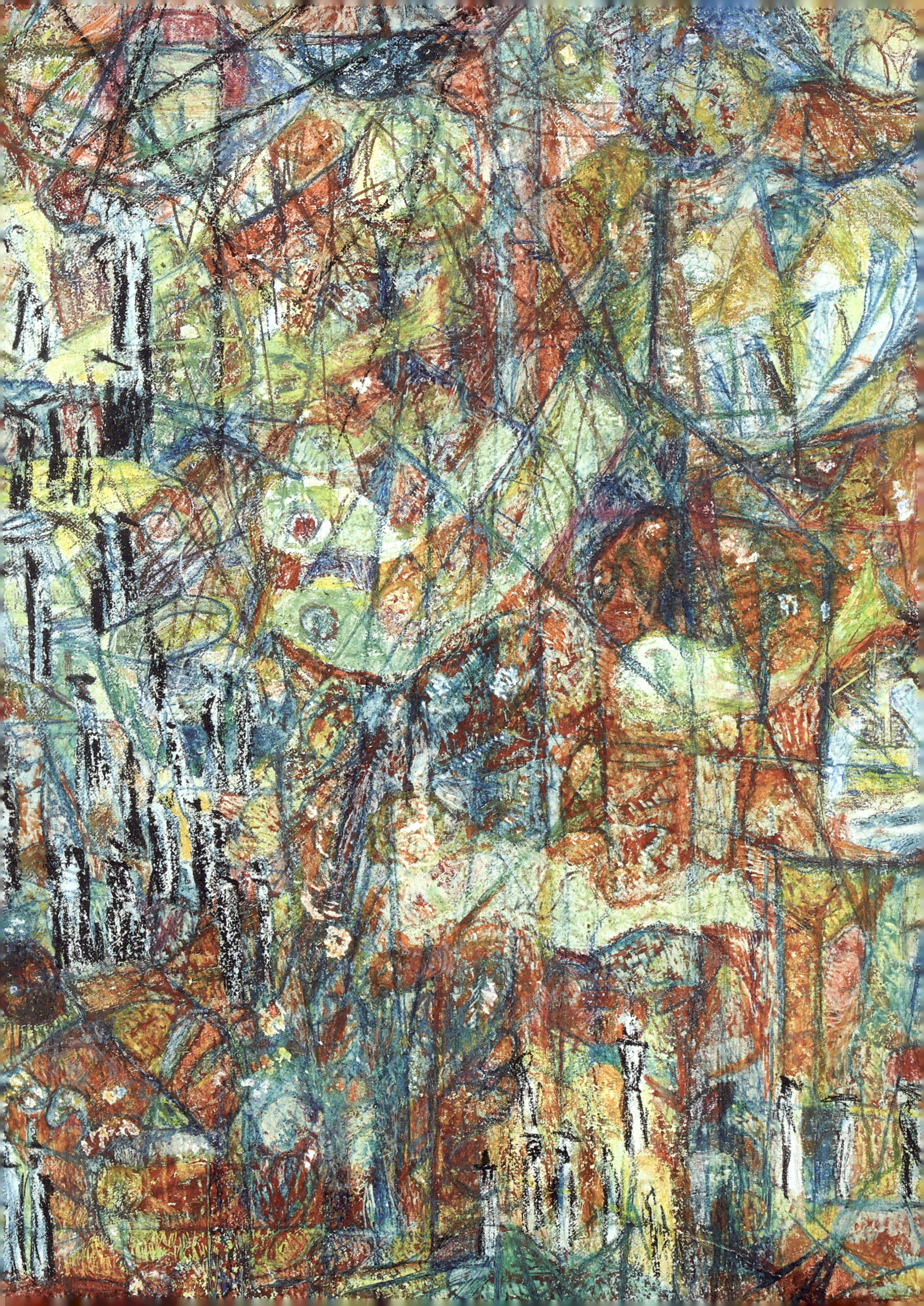

The Fantastic Der fantastische Gerhard Altenbourg

The Centennial Zum 100. Geburtstag

Hrsg. v. / Ed. by Roland Krischke
für das / for the Lindenau-Museum Altenburg

Mit Beiträgen von / With Contributions by
M. Büchting, S. Fischer, M. Heuß, T. R. König,
S. Krautzig, R. Krischke, S. Schmitt-Maaß

LINDENAU-MUSEUM ALTENBURG

HIRMER

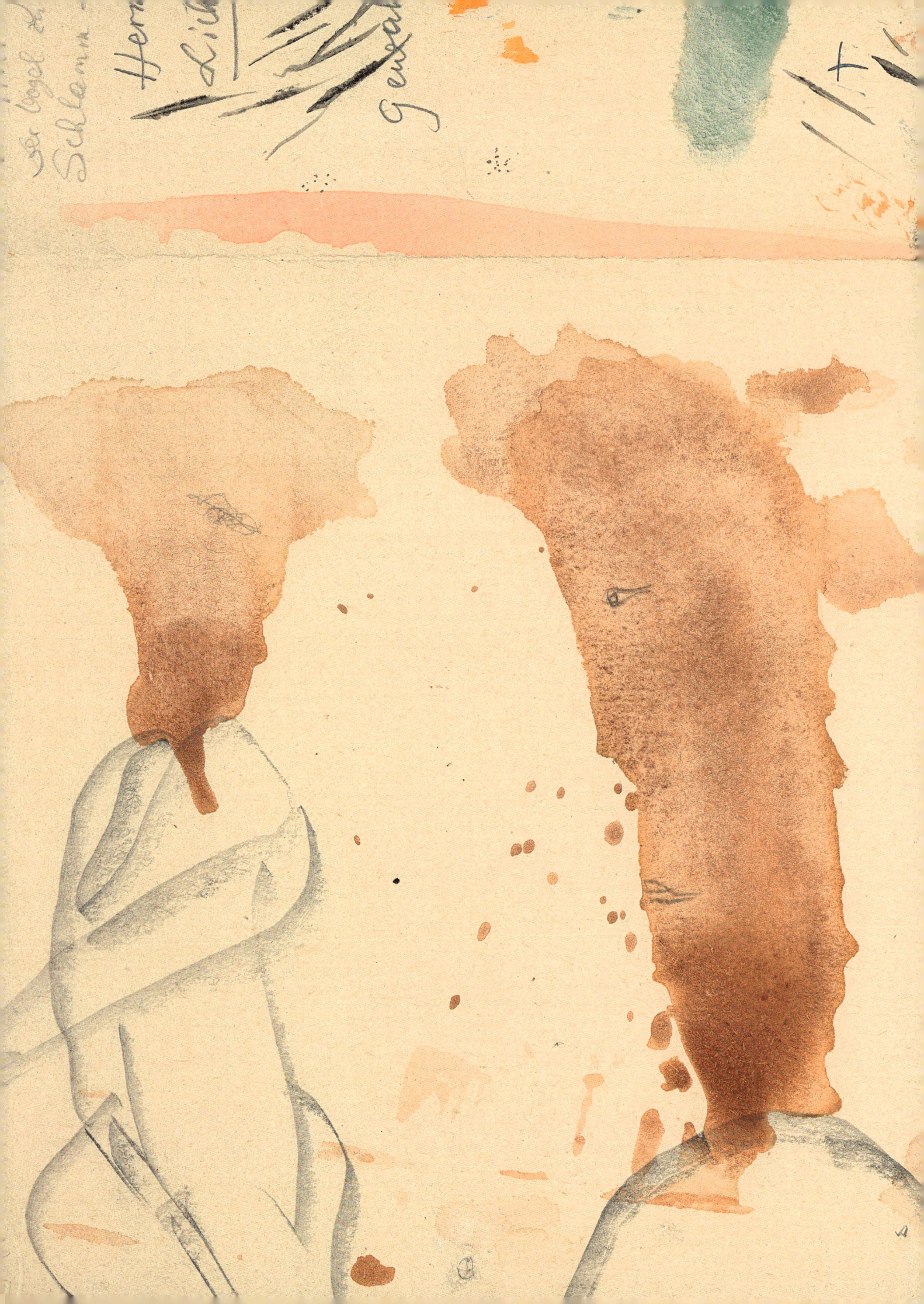

Inhalt | Contents

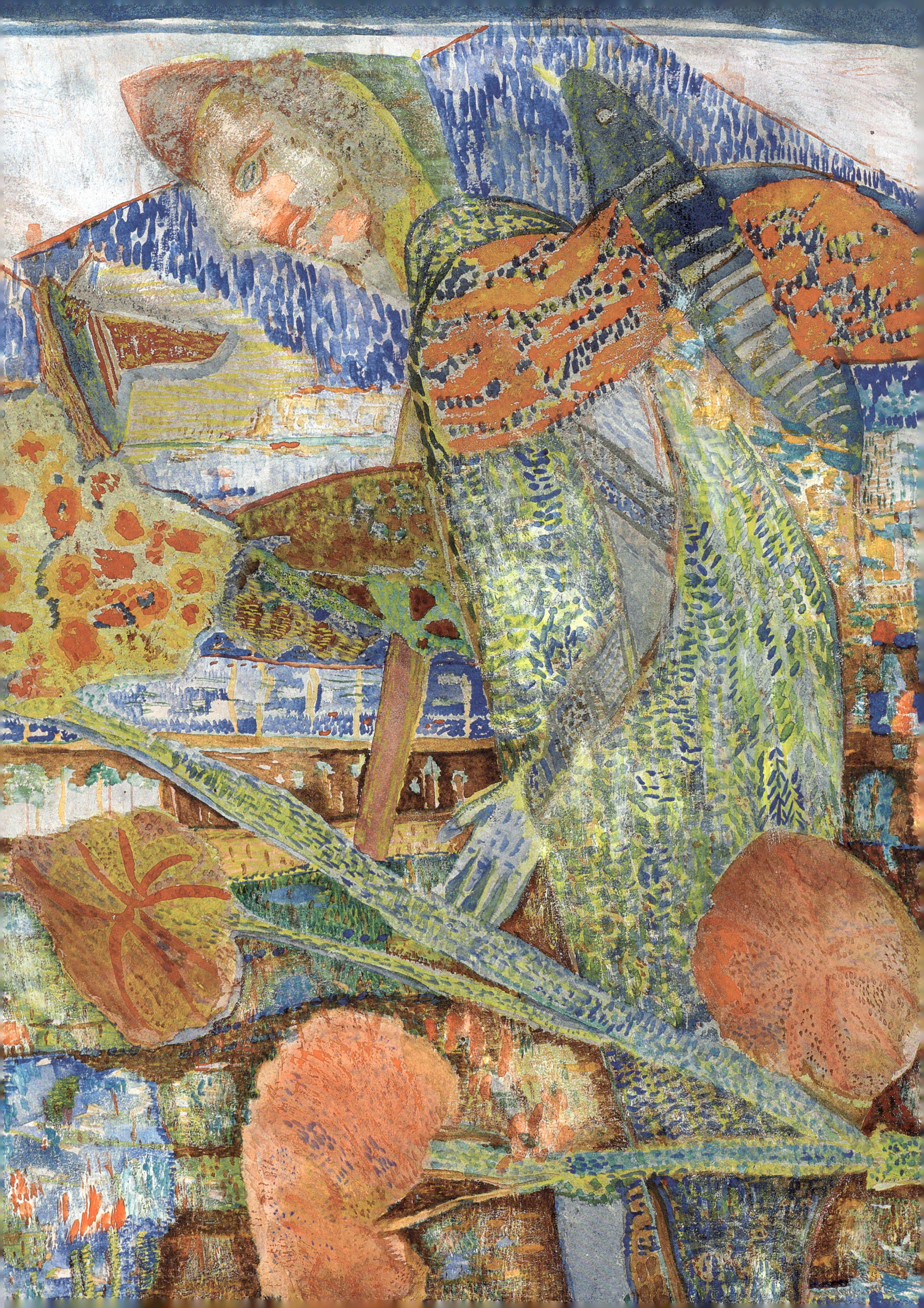

Grußwort des Landtagspräsidenten

Sehr geehrte Gäste der Altenburger Museen,

als ehemalige Thüringer Residenzstadt kann Altenburg mit vielen Pfunden wuchern, von den »Roten Spitzen« aus der Zeit Kaiser Barbarossas über das majestätische Residenzschloss mit seinen Museen inmitten weitläufiger Parkanlagen bis hin zu dem nach seinem Stifter benannten Lindenau-Museum. In der an kulturellen Schätzen nicht gerade armen Kulturlandschaft Thüringen hütet letzteres einen besonderen Schatz: die größte Sammlung von Werken des Malers, Grafikers und Lyrikers Gerhard Altenbourg. 2026 begehen die Altenburger Museen dessen 100. Geburtstag mit einem Jubiläumsjahr und der Ausstellung *Der fantastische Gerhard Altenbourg*.

Das Jubiläumsjahr ist ein Baustein einer umfassenden Strategie, um Altenburg mit seinen Sammlungen als kulturellen Leuchtturm in Thüringen zu etablieren. Durch ihr anspruchsvolles Ausstellungsprogramm haben die Altenburger Museen in den vergangenen Jahren bereits wichtige Schritte in diese Richtung unternommen. Um Gerhard Altenbourg und weitere Sammlungen künftig in einem angemessenen Rahmen präsentieren zu können, wird das Lindenau-Museum Altenburg dank einer großzügigen Unterstützung durch den Bund und den Freistaat Thüringen umfassend saniert und erweitert. Die Neugestaltung des Museums bildet den Auftakt zur Umsetzung eines neuen Masterplans: Der Schlossberg mit all seinen Gebäuden soll zu einer musealen Bildungslandschaft von überregionaler Bedeutung weiterentwickelt werden.

Ausstellungen wie *Der fantastische Gerhard Altenbourg* mit regionalem Bezug und von nationaler Tragweite sind ein wichtiger Teil dieser Strategie, weshalb ich gern die Schirmherrschaft übernommen habe. Ich lade Sie ein, einen großartigen Künstler und ein einzigartiges kulturelles Ensemble (wieder) zu entdecken. Mein Dank gilt den Altenburger Museen sowie dem Beauftragten der Bundesregierung für Kultur und Medien und dem Thüringer Ministerium für Bildung, Wissenschaft und Kultur, die diese Ausstellung ermöglicht haben.

Dr. Thadäus Rudolf König

Präsident des Thüringer Landtags

President of the Thuringian State Parliament

Greeting from the President of the Thuringian State Parliament

Dear guests of the Altenburger Museen,

As the former Thuringian ducal capital, Altenburg has much to boast about, from the “Red Towers” dating from the time of Emperor Frederick Barbarossa, to the majestic ducal castle with its museums set amidst extensive parkland, to the Lindenau-Museum, named after its founder Bernhard August von Lindenau. Within Thuringia’s cultural landscape, rich in cultural treasures of all kinds, the Lindenau-Museum preserves a special gem: the largest collection of works by the painter, graphic artist and poet Gerhard Altenbourg. In 2026 the Altenburger Museen will celebrate his centennial with a year of special programmes including the exhibition *The Fantastic Gerhard Altenbourg*.

The anniversary year is one component of a comprehensive strategy that aims to make Altenburg, with its many art collections, into a cultural beacon for Thuringia. Thanks to their ambitious programme of exhibitions, the Altenburger Museen have taken decisive steps toward this goal in recent years. In order to house the Gerhard Altenbourg collection and other collections appropriately, the Lindenau-Museum Altenburg will be thoroughly renovated and expanded, thanks to the generous support of the German federal government and the Free State of Thuringia. The museum’s new appearance will mark the first step in implementing a new master plan: the castle hill with all its buildings will be further developed into a museum and educational complex of national significance.

Exhibitions such as *The Fantastic Gerhard Altenbourg*, with a regional theme but national import, are an important part of this strategy, which is why I have gladly assumed the patronage of this show. I invite all of you to (re-)discover this extraordinary artist and a unique destination. I would like to express my gratitude to the Altenburger Museen, to the Federal Commissioner for Culture and the Media, and to the Thuringian Ministry for Education, Science and Culture for making this exhibition possible.

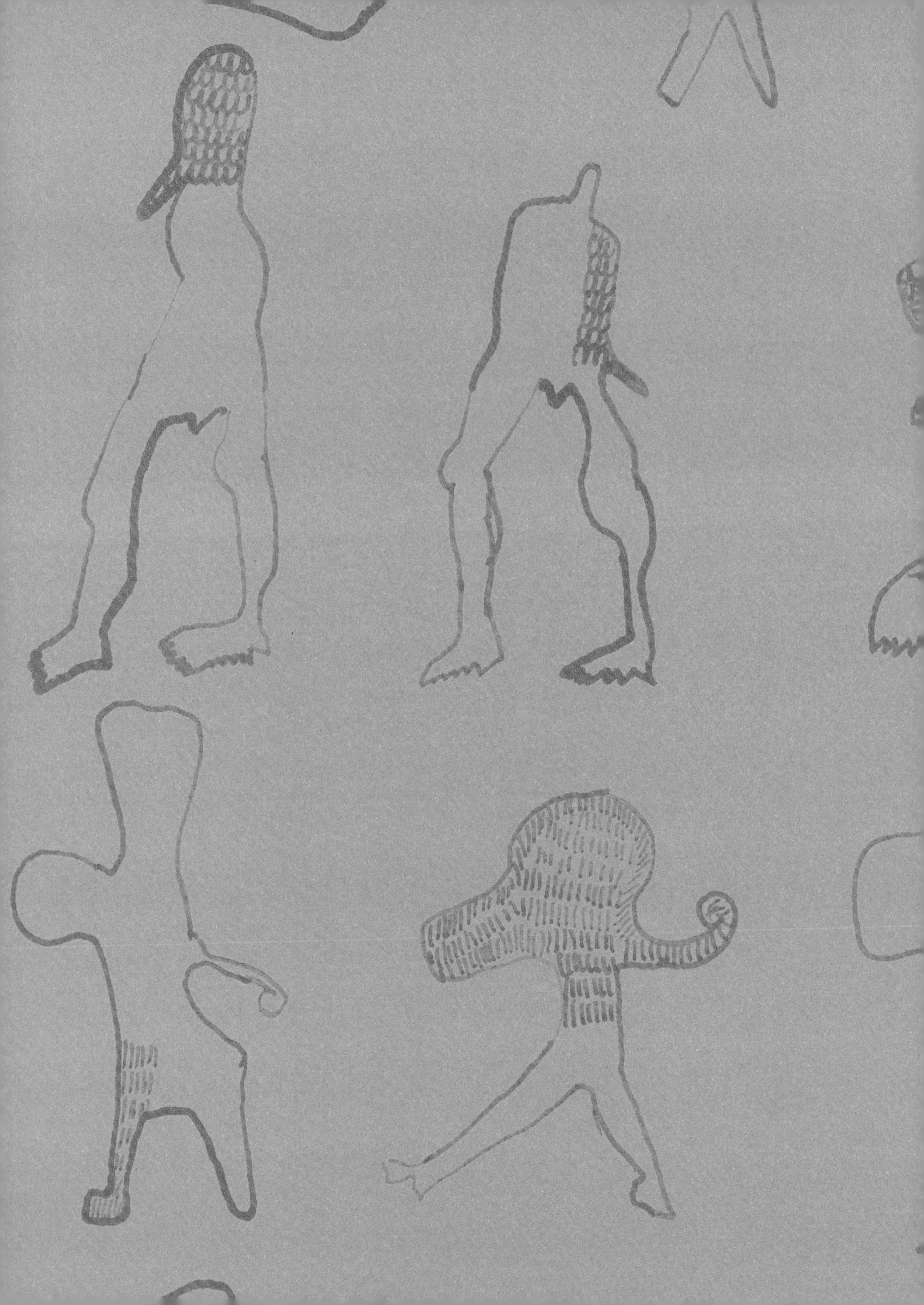

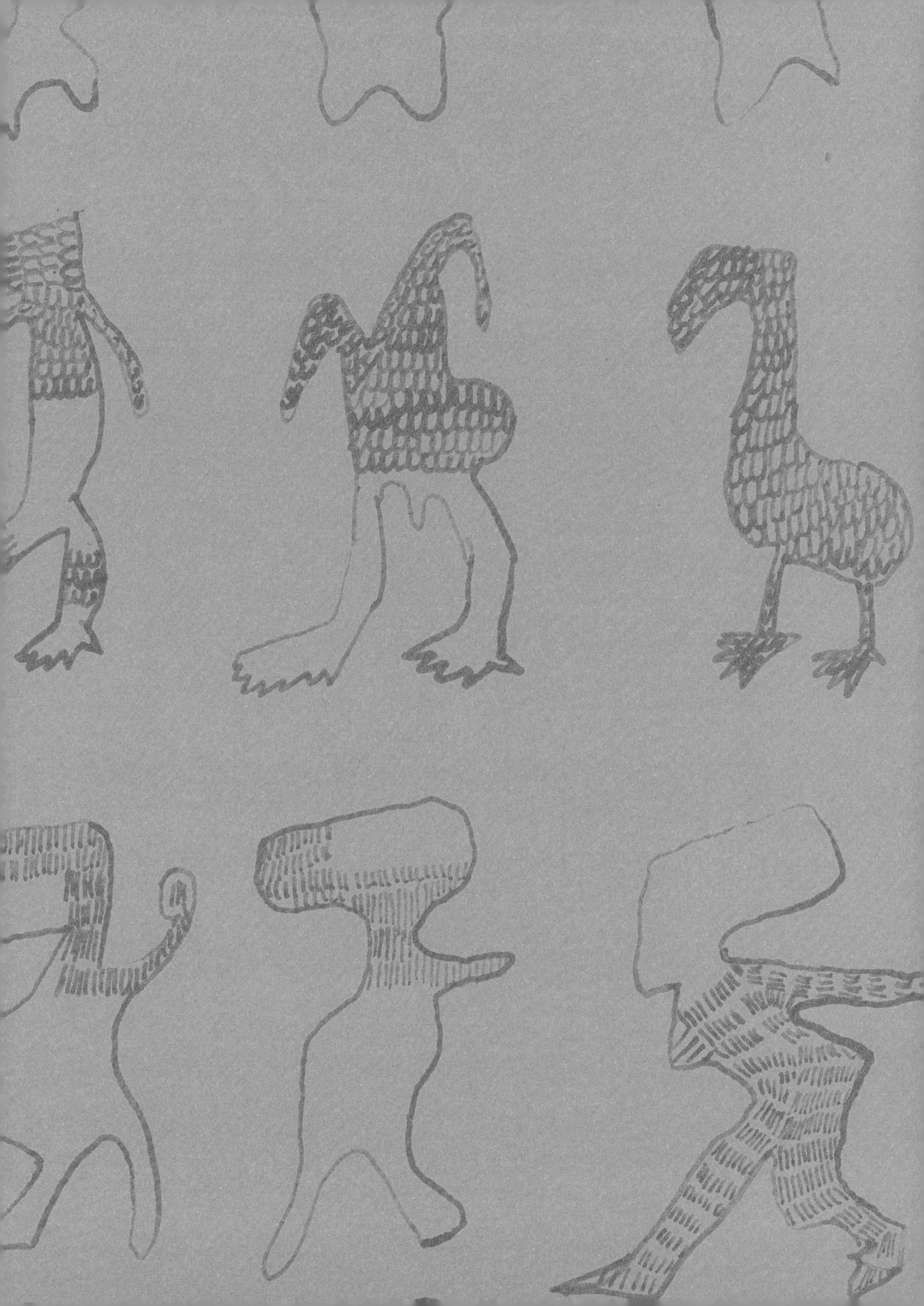

1 Katalog für Schweripel hat

Dr. Klaus Seyffarth hat * Werner Hofmann

* Pinzens hat

Ingrid 2 X

Bloß hat

Heyne hat

Krinhke hat

Anneliese hat

Hans Werner hat Berlin

...ke hat gedankt

...Wolf hat ...lin

Dr. Falke hat

franke Rat

hat Dr. Arzt Aachen

hat Kubow : ~~muß haben~~ neu

1 Erich Sietz hat

...log für ...* Eggers Hamburg hat

Hans-Peter Schulz, Leipzig

...eiten 1x Glück Dr. Geitel 1x 2x (farbig + einfarbig)

K. K. Dresden Werner Schmidt 1x ... 1x

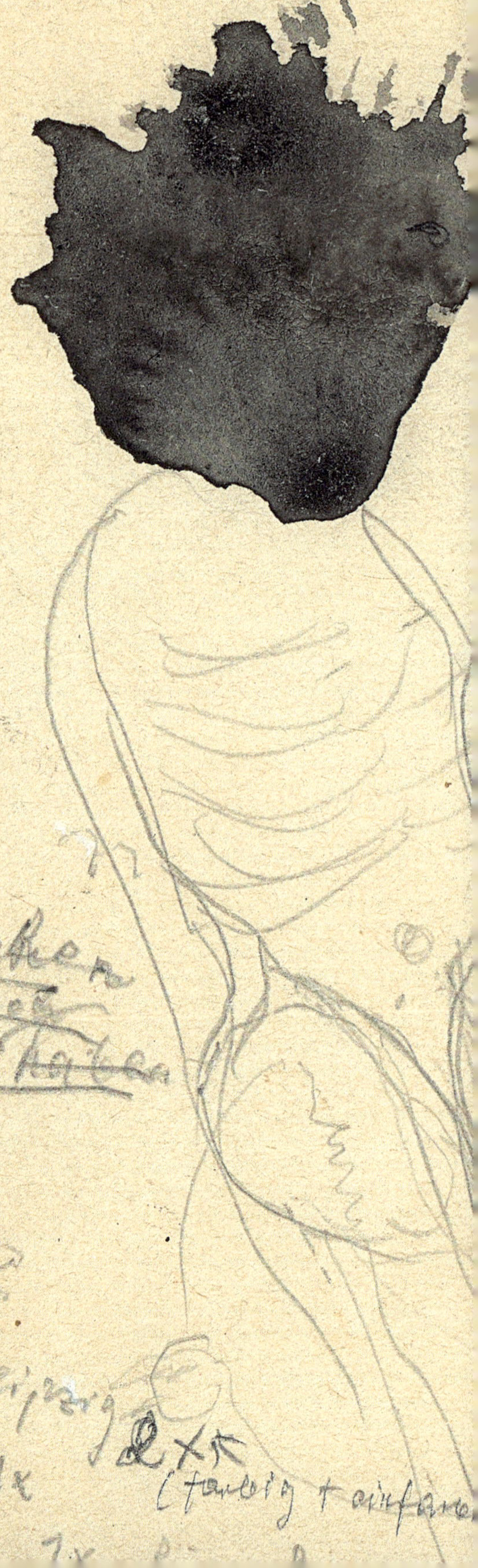

Roland Krischke

Zitronenfalter im Reich des Fantastischen

Gerhard Altenbourg im Jahr seines 100. Geburtstages

In der ehemaligen DDR bis in die 1980er-Jahre blockiert, von Weggefährten verehrt und als Geheimtipp gehandelt, wurde Gerhard Altenbourg (1926–1989), der »Zitronenfalter im Hauptbahnhof«,[1] im »Westen« bereits hochgeschätzt **(Abb. 1)**. Der Grafiker, Zeichner und Dichter hinterließ ein umfangreiches Œuvre, das in großen Teilen im Lindenau-Museum Altenburg und in der Stiftung Gerhard Altenbourg bewahrt wird, die seinen Nachlass verwaltet. 2026 wäre er 100 Jahre alt geworden. Das Lindenau-Museum Altenburg begeht ihm zu Ehren ein Jubiläumsjahr mit einem beachtlichen Programm, dessen Höhepunkt die Ausstellung *Der fantastische Gerhard Altenbourg* ist, zu welcher dieser Katalog erscheint. Die Ausstellung stellt eine häufig nebenbei thematisierte Facette der Arbeiten des Künstlers ins Rampenlicht und zeigt einen Querschnitt seiner fantastischen Drucke, Metallarbeiten und Zeichnungen **(Kat. 3, 4)**.

In seiner Anthologie *Malerei und Graphik in der DDR* formulierte Lothar Lang: »Altenbourgs Kunst (…) ist in ihrer poetischen Einheit von Naturbeobachtung, Gedachtem, Gefühltem und Traumhaftem ein wichtiger Beitrag zum ›phantastischen Realismus‹.«[2] Es mag so aussehen, als habe der Kunsthistoriker, Kritiker, Kurator und ehemalige Direktor von Museum Schloss Burgk die Wirkung des im »ländlichen Raum« (wie man heute sagen würde) lebenden Künstlers damit nivelliert. Vor allem aber ordnete er Altenbourg Strömungen fantastischer Kunst zu, die in der DDR durchaus als subversiv angesehen worden waren.[3] 1992 formulierte Eduard Beaucamp »Altenbourgs Kunst, die sich über Jahrzehnte in der puren Phantastik eingerichtet hatte, bannte, begeisterte (Erhart) Kästner und ließ seine Sprache aufblühen«.[4] Genau genommen war Altenbourg selbst aber nie ein aktiver Anhänger oder gar ein Angehöriger des sogenannten Phantastischen Realismus.[5] Vielmehr hatte er sich in einem Gespräch mit Friedhelm Mennekes davon zurückhaltend distanziert: »Das hat ja sogar ein Kritiker geschrieben:

A Brimstone Butterfly in the Realm of the Fantastic

Gerhard Altenbourg on His Centennial

Suppressed until the 1980s in the former GDR, where he was admired by his contemporaries and spoken of as an insider tip, Gerhard Altenbourg (1926–1989) – the "brimstone butterfly in the train station"[1] – was highly regarded in Western Germany early on **(fig. 1)**. The graphic artist, draughtsman and poet left behind an immense body of work, the greater part of which is preserved in the Lindenau-Museum Altenburg and in the Gerhard Altenbourg Foundation. In 2026 he would have been 100 years old. To commemorate the occasion, the Lindenau-Museum Altenburg is celebrating an anniversary year with an extensive programme of events, culminating in the exhibition *The Fantastic Gerhard Altenbourg. 100th Birthday Exhibition*, which is accompanied by this catalogue. The show spotlights an often-marginalised aspect of the artist's work: his fantastic prints, works in metal and drawings **(cats. 3–4)**.

In his anthology *Malerei und Graphik in der DDR* (Painting and Graphic Arts in the GDR), Lothar Lang declared that "Altenbourg's art … is in its poetic fusion of the observation of nature, of what is imagined, felt and dreamed, an important contribution to 'fantastic realism'."[2] It almost sounds as though the art historian, critic, curator and former director of the

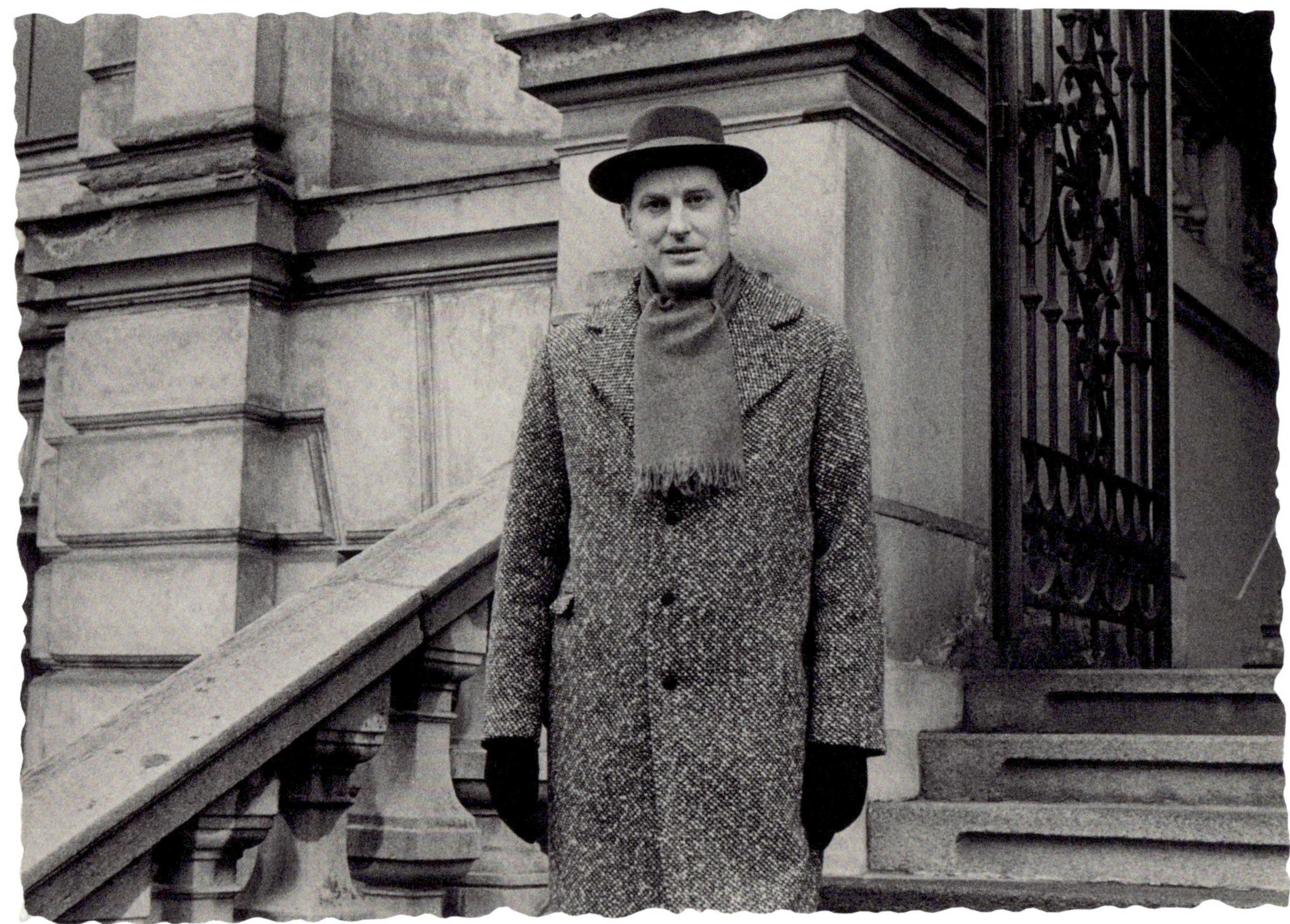

Abb. 1 Gerhard Altenbourg vor dem Lindenau-Museum, 1964, Schwarz-Weiß-Fotografie, Stiftung Gerhard Altenbourg, Inv.-Nr. SGA F1576
Fig. 1 Gerhard Altenbourg in front of the Lindenau-Museum, 1964, black-and-white photograph, Gerhard Altenbourg Foundation, inv. no. SGA F1576

ich wäre im Gegensatz zu den fantastischen Wienern (…) einer von denen, die noch das Ganze sehen.«[6]

Tatsächlich hatten sich nach dem Zweiten Weltkrieg in den bildenden Künsten unterschiedliche Tendenzen durchgesetzt. Neben einer erstarkenden Neigung zum Ungegenständlichen und zur Abstraktion wurden auch figürliche Kompositionen umgesetzt. Künstler und Künstlerinnen dieser Schule orientierten sich besonders am Surrealismus, der wiederum aus dem Dadaismus entstanden war, wie auch am Magischen Realismus der 1920er- und 1930er-Jahre.[7] In Deutschland machte Wieland Schmied, damals Direktor der Kestnergesellschaft in Hannover, auf die Entwicklung aufmerksam, indem er die Künstler in Hannover und Recklinghausen ausstellte.[8] Auch in Frankreich und Italien war man auf das Thema aufmerksam geworden: »Die junge

Museum Schloss Burgk underappreciates the contribution of the artist who lived in a "rural area" (as it would be called today). Above all, he groups Altenbourg together with movements of fantastic art that were considered subversive in the GDR.[3] In 1992, Eduard Beaucamp wrote that "Altenbourg's art, which for decades has moved in the purest fantasy, captivated and inspired (Erhart) Kästner and allowed his language to blossom".[4] Strictly speaking, however, Altenbourg was never an active proponent or even a member of the so-called Fantastic Realism movement.[5] In fact, in an interview with Friedhelm Mennekes, he distanced himself from this style: "A critic once even wrote that, in contrast to the fantastic Viennese … I was one of those who still saw the whole."[6]

After the Second World War, various movements arose in the visual arts in Europe. Along with a growing trend towards non-figurative art and abstraction, many also turned to figurative compositions. Artists of this school followed Surrealism in particular, which in turn had arisen

österreichische Malerei macht aus dem Phantastischen eine lebendige Kunst«,[9] schrieb etwa Pierre Cabanne, während der Festwochenausstellung des Jahres 1962 über die breit rezipierte Ausstellung *Surrealismus – phantastische Malerei der Gegenwart*, die Surrealisten und Phantastische Realisten erstmals zusammen präsentierte, während Alfred Kubin 1963 in Rom in Gegenüberstellung mit den »phantastischen« Wienern sehr erfolgreich ausgestellt wurde.[10] Grundlegend grenzten sich die »Phantastischen Realisten« vor allem von einem intuitiven Zugang der Surrealisten ab – etwa hervorgerufen durch Rauschmittel und Trance. Sie setzten vielmehr auf einen zielgerichteten und durchdachten Schöpfungsakt, der sich durch eine subtile Ausarbeitung manieristisch wirkender, grotesk-figürlicher Motive auszeichnete.[11]

Gustav René Hocke stellte die damaligen, figurativ-surrealen Tendenzen schließlich in den Kontext neomanieristischer Kunst.[12] Er spannte den Bogen von Fabrizio Clerici bis hin zu Gerhard Hoehme.[13] Die Künstler versuchten das grundsätzlich Immaterielle, Meditative zu erfassen, indem sie sich auf den künstlerischen Schöpfungs- und Arbeitsprozess fokussierten, der seine eigene Dynamik entfaltete. Zuweilen habe sich dies in einer feinmalerischen, häufig kleinteiligen Bildsprache geäußert, aber auch in der zyklischen Überlagerung von Linien, Farben und Figuren, die über unterschiedliche Zeitspannen hinweg entstanden seien. Dem Liebhaber der Arbeiten von Gerhard Altenbourg mag diese Beschreibung durchaus bekannt vorkommen, und so ist es nicht überraschend, wenn Altenbourgs Name auch in Hockes Buch genannt wird.[14]

Lother Lang hob Gerhard Altenbourg treffend als Bild-Dichter hervor: »Hier ist (…) eine Nachbarschaft zu Paul Klee. Das Groteske, Ironische und Komische hat einen tiefen Sinn – und durchaus einen Zeit-Sinn bei beiden Künstlern. Die poetisch-hintersinnige Kauzerei, geformt aus verspielt dahingleitenden Linien, nicht abstrakt, doch auch nicht exakt die Dinge beschreibend, naiv und phantastisch in einem, ist Bildwelt aus einem ›Zwischenreich‹ von Realität und Phantasie.«[15]

Gerhard Altenbourgs Zwischenreich besteht nicht allein aus Landschaften und einer künstlerischen Rezeption antiker Mythen und Philosophien, die seine Belesenheit, seine Bibliophilie und Materialbesessenheit belegen. Es speist sich aus der Fantasie, der Freude an Farben, Formen und ihren Variationen am werkpraktischen Vorgehen, am Verstecken und Entdecken: »Schon vom reinen Machen her, d. h. von der Kreide gehen auf mich wie magische Kräfte über, vom Geruch der Kreide und von der Fläche des Steines. Das ist wie eine Hochzeit.«[16]

Im Jubiläumsjahr 2026 zum 100. Geburtstag des Künstlers präsentiert unsere Ausstellung *Der fantastische Gerhard Altenbourg* neben Zeichnungen und Drucken erstmals auch skizzenhafte Werke mit fantasievollen und skurrilen Szenen von Gerhard Altenbourg. In seinen »fantastischen Figurationen« tummeln sich bizarre Monster und andere seltsame Wesen (Abb. 2),

from Dada, leading for example to the Magical Realism of the 1920s and 1930s.[7] In Germany, Wieland Schmied, then director of the Kestner Gesellschaft art center in Hanover, drew attention to this tendency by exhibiting these artists in Hanover and Recklinghausen.[8] In France and Italy, the movement likewise garnered attention. During the Vienna Festwochen exhibition in 1962, Pierre Cabanne wrote, "Young Austrian painting has made a living art out of the fantastic",[9] referring to the well-received exhibition *Surrealismus – phantastische Malerei der Gegenwart* (Surrealism – Fantastic Painting of Today), which presented Surrealists and Fantastic Realists together for the first time. In 1963, Alfred Kubin had a successful exhibition of his works in Rome along with the "fantastic" Viennese painters.[10] In essence, the Fantastic Realists set themselves apart from the intuitive approach of the Surrealists – who were often stimulated by drugs or trance states. The Fantastic Realists relied much more on a deliberate and thought-out act of creation, characterised by a subtle working out of mannerist, grotesque and figurative motifs.[11]

Gustav René Hocke situated the figurative-surrealist movements of the times within the context of neo-Mannerist art.[12] He traced a line from Fabrizio Clerici to Gerhard Hoehme.[13] Such artists, according to Hocke, strove to capture what was essentially immaterial and meditative by focussing on the artistic process of creation and execution, which unfolded through its own dynamics. This was at times expressed in a delicate painterly technique and an often extremely detailed visual language, but also in the cyclical overlapping of lines, colours and figures made over different periods of time. For those who admire the work of Gerhard Altenbourg, this description by Hocke may indeed sound familiar, so it is not surprising that Altenbourg's name is mentioned in Hocke's book.[14]

Lothar Lang rightly characterised Gerhard Altenbourg as an image-poet: "There is … a proximity to Paul Klee. The grotesque, ironic and comic has profound meaning – and certainly a time-meaning in both artists. The poetic-cryptic eccentricities, formed from delicate lines gliding along the page, not abstract, yet not depicting things precisely, naive and fantastic at the same time, delineate a visual world that arises from an 'intermediary realm' between reality and fantasy".[15]

Gerhard Altenbourg's "intermediary realm" consists not merely of landscapes and the

die eine intensive künstlerische Auseinandersetzung mit Kunstströmungen der Moderne nahelegen. Das Lindenau-Museum Altenburg und die Stiftung Gerhard Altenbourg entführen Besucherinnen und Besucher in die fantastische Welt von Gerhard Altenbourg.

*

Jubiläumsjahr und Ausstellung treffen das Lindenau-Museum im Verbund der Altenburger Museen und die Stiftung Gerhard Altenbourg in einer sehr besonderen Situation an. Das Lindenau-Museum wird saniert und voraussichtlich 2029 neu eröffnet. Die Jubiläumsausstellung findet deshalb – wie alle Sonderausstellungen des Museums in den Jahren des Interims – im Prinzenpalais des Residenzschlosses Altenburg statt, einem charmanten Ausweichquartier, dessen Einrichtung durch die großzügige Projektförderung Lindenau21^PLUS des Beauftragten der Bundesregierung für Kultur und Medien möglich geworden ist, aber auch durch die Kooperation zwischen Lindenau-Museum und dem Eigenbetrieb Residenzschloss Altenburg im Rahmen der Kommunalen Arbeitsgemeinschaft Altenburger Museen. Die beiden seit 2020 nach Beschluss ihrer Träger Landkreis Altenburg Land und Stadt Altenburg lose verbundenen Kultureinrichtungen werden nach weiteren Gremienbeschlüssen nun ab 2027 in einem Zweckverband Altenburger Museen zusammengeschlossen, welcher der in den letzten Jahren wachsenden Bedeutung der Museums- und Bildungslandschaft Altenburg Rechnung trägt. Zwei Masterpläne – *Der Leuchtturm an der Blauen Flut – Das Lindenau-Museum und die Altenburger Trümpfe* (2017) und *Prinzen im Dornröschenschloss – Die Altenburger Museen im Aufbruch zur Bildungslandschaft* (2025) – haben die mögliche Entwicklung des zur Konferenz Nationaler Kultureinrichtungen zählenden Lindenau-Museums und der bislang zu wenig beachteten Sammlungen und Liegenschaften des Residenzschlosses Altenburg aufzuzeigen versucht. Die Bundesrepublik Deutschland und der Freistaat Thüringen haben die Pläne mit zwei bedeutenden Förderungen für die Sanierung und Erweiterung des Lindenau-Museums (2018) sowie eine Projektförderung des Bundes für das Lindenau-Museum und die Lindenau'schen Sammlungen im Schlossmuseum (2020) kräftig unterstützt. Landkreis Altenburger Land und Stadt Altenburg haben nun mit der Gründung des Zweckverbandes Altenburger Museen die Voraussetzungen für eine weitere Profilierung der Museumslandschaft Altenburg geschaffen. Nach der Eröffnung des »neuen« Lindenau-Museums bedarf es eines weiteren Schrittes, um einen Ort zu schaffen, der die Werkstätten der Restauratoren, die Depots für die Sammlungen der Altenburger Museen, die Büros der Mitarbeiterinnen und Mitarbeiter, Räume für die Arbeit der Kunst- und Kulturvermittlung, Veranstaltungsbereiche und Ausstellungsräume für die Grafische Sammlung, darunter besonders auch das Werk von Gerhard Altenbourg, aufnehmen kann. Dafür ist schon lange der Herzogliche Marstall im Schlossgarten im

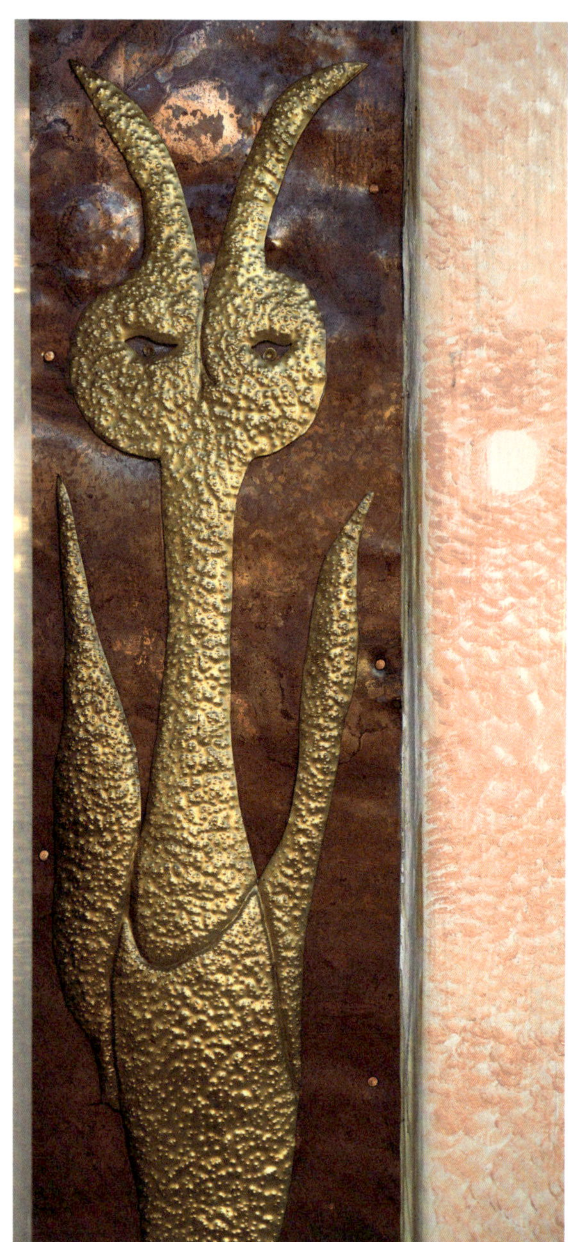

Abb. 2 Gerhard Altenbourg, Metallarbeit *Mit den grazilen Hüften* (1973) im Flur seines Künstlerhauses (Detail), 2013
Fig. 2 Gerhard Altenbourg, metal work *Mit den grazilen Hüften* (With the Svelte Hips), 1973, in the hall of his house (detail), 2013

artistic adoption of the myths and philosophies of antiquity, which attest to his erudition, his passion for books and his obsession with materials. It is also nurtured by his imagination, his delight in colours, forms and variations in the processes of creative work, in veiling and in discovering. "Just by simply making, that is, the crayon, the smell of crayon and the surface of

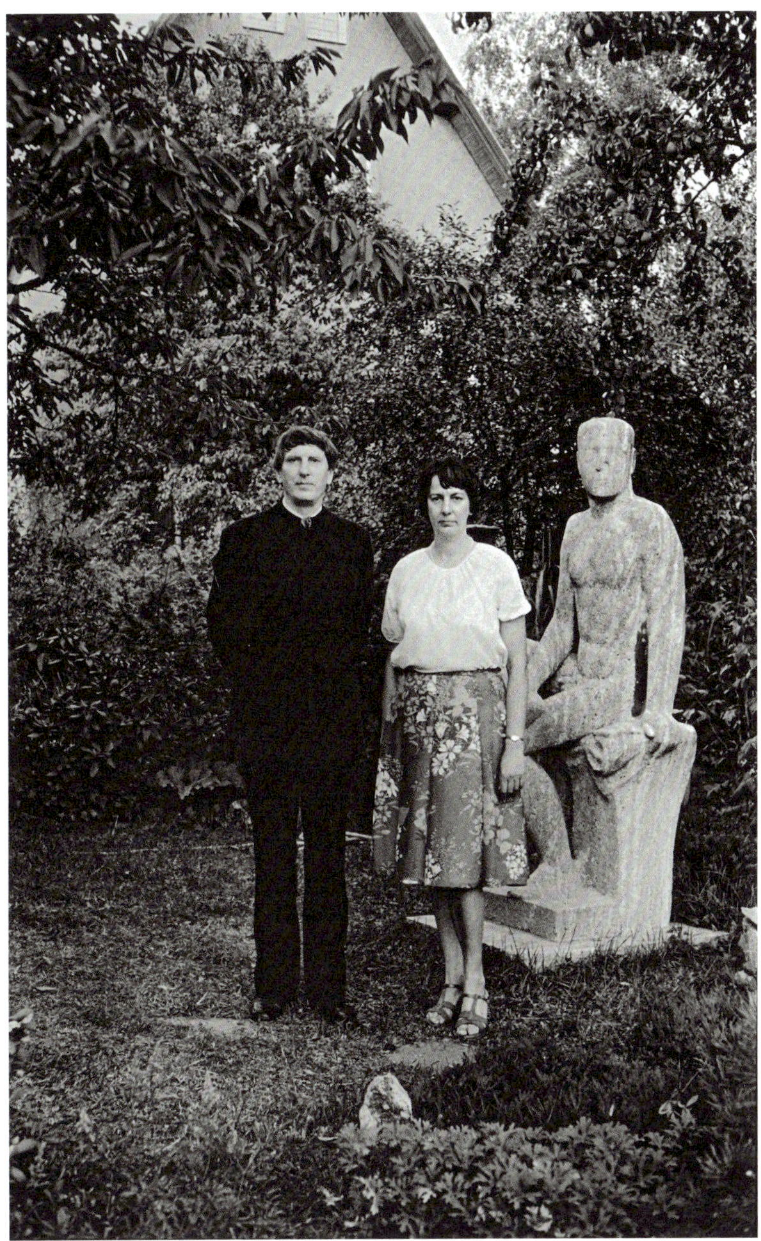

Abb. 3 Christian Borchert, *Gerhard Altenbourg und seine Schwester Anneliese Ströch im Garten des Künstlerhauses neben einer Skulptur von Hans Mettel (1936)*, 1978, Schwarz-Weiß-Fotografie, Stiftung Gerhard Altenbourg, Inv.-Nr. SGA F0837
Fig. 3 Christian Borchert, *Gerhard Altenbourg and His Sister Anneliese Ströch in the Garden of the Artist's House Next to a Sculpture by Hans Mettel (1936)*, 1978, black-and-white photograph, Gerhard Altenbourg Foundation, inv. no. SGA F0837

Gespräch, aus Platzgründen aber auch ein Erweiterungsbau wie die »Neue Remise« oder vielleicht sogar die Gebäude der Alten Spielkartenfabrik, die sich unweit des Lindenau-Museums befinden.

Der neue Zweckverband Altenburger Museen bindet auch die eigenständige Stiftung Gerhard Altenbourg enger ein. Die Stiftung war von Anneliese Ströch, der Schwester des Künstlers, gegründet worden **(Abb. 3)**, hat aber außer

the stone almost have a magical effect on me. It is like a wedding."[16]

For the anniversary year of 2026, on the occasion of the artist's centennial, our exhibition *The Fantastic Gerhard Altenbourg* displays drawings and prints and, for the first time, also sketch-like works with fantastic and quirky scenes by Gerhard Altenbourg. Bizarre monsters and other strange creatures populate his "fantastic figurations" **(fig. 2)**, which testify to an intensive study of the artistic movements of modernism. The Lindenau-Museum Altenburg and the Gerhard Altenbourg Foundation will transport visitors away, taking them to the fantastic world of Gerhard Altenbourg.

*

The anniversary year and exhibition occur at a very special moment for the Lindenau-Museum as part of the Altenburger Museen and the Gerhard Altenbourg Foundation. The Lindenau-Museum's building is currently being restored and is scheduled to reopen in 2029. The centennial exhibition will take place – like all of the museum's special exhibitions when it is closed – in the Prinzenpalais of the ducal castle Altenburg. This charming temporary venue has been made possible by generous funding for the Lindenau21[PLUS] project from the Federal Government Commissioner for Culture and the Media, but also through a collaboration between the Lindenau-Museum and the Residenzschloss Altenburg municipal enterprise, within the framework of the Altenburger Museen municipal consortium. The two cultural institutions have been loosely joined together since 2020 according to the decision of their maintaining authorities, the district of Altenburg Land and the city of Altenburg. After further resolutions by these authorities, they will now be fused together into the special purpose association Altenburger Museen in 2027, an initiative that takes into account the growing importance of Altenburg's museum and educational landscape in recent years. Two master plans, *The Lighthouse on the Blaue Flut – The Lindenau-Museum and Altenburg's Trump Cards* (2017) and *Princes in Sleeping Beauty's Castle – The Altenburger Museen on the Road to Becoming an Educational Landscape* (2025), have shown the opportunities for the Lindenau-Museum, which is included in the German Conference of National Cultural Institutions, and the collections and properties

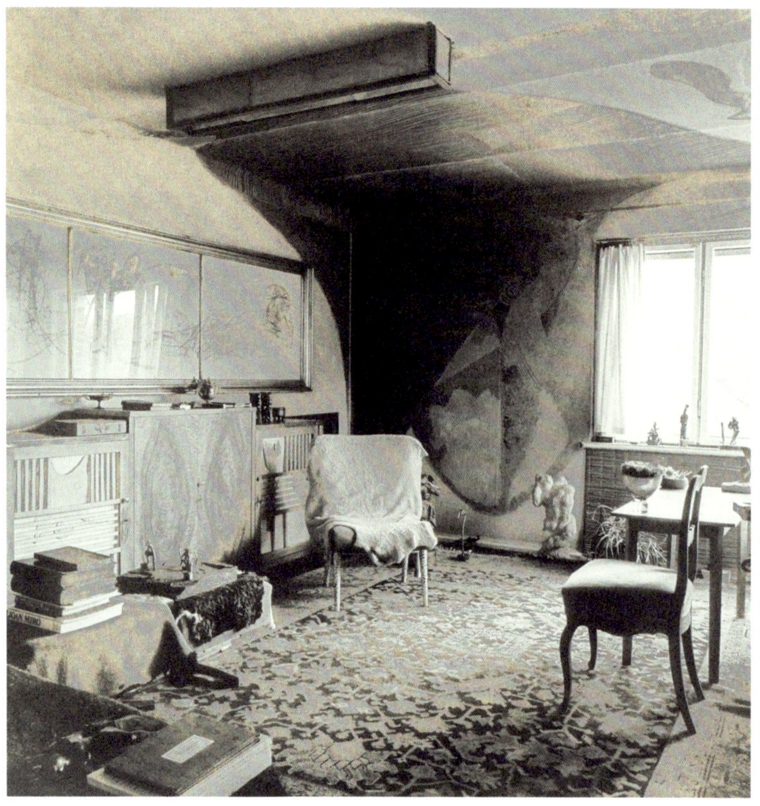

Abb. 4 Ulrich Lindner, *Das sogenannte »Atelier« im Künstlerhaus von Gerhard Altenbourg*, Schwarz-Weiß-Fotografie, 1990, aus: Ulrich Lindners Mappe *Gerhard Altenbourg. »Dies Haus als Aufgabe«*, 1991, Stiftung Gerhard Altenbourg, Inv.-Nr. SGA 6095-14-Ks
Fig. 4 Ulrich Lindner, *The So-Called "Studio" in Gerhard Altenbourg's House*, black-and-white photograph, 1990, from Ulrich Lindner's portfolio *Gerhard Altenbourg. "Dies Haus als Aufgabe"* (This House as Purpose, 1991), Gerhard Altenbourg Foundation, inv. no. SGA 6095-14-Ks

den Einnahmen durch die Bildrechte an Gerhard Altenbourg keine Absicherung, sodass die finanzielle Situation in den letzten Jahren bereits prekär war. Anspruchsvolle Aufgaben wie die Unterhaltung des einzigartigen Künstlerhauses und des Künstlergartens im Braugartenweg oder auch erste Untersuchungen und Maßnahmen zu einer grundlegenden Sanierung des Gebäudes und der kontinuierlichen Pflege des Gartens konnten nur dank großzügiger Förderung der Deutschen Stiftung Denkmalschutz und des Thüringer Landesamtes für Denkmalpflege und Archäologie sowie der 2018 eigens gegründeten Gerhard Altenbourg Gesellschaft begonnen werden. Der Zweckverband kann nun in Form eines Geschäftsbesorgungsvertrages einen Schutzschirm bilden, die laufenden Kosten übernehmen, vor allem aber die Fachexpertise der Belegschaft der Altenburger Museen noch stärker für die anstehenden Maßnahmen und die Vorbereitung einer behutsamen Öffnung von Haus und Garten für die Öffentlichkeit nutzen **(Abb. 4)**.

So ist das Jubiläumsjahr zugleich ein Jahr des Übergangs in Vorbereitung der Gründung des Zweckverbandes

of the ducal castle Altenburg, which have – for too long – not received the attention they deserve. The Federal Republic of Germany and the Free State of Thuringia have vigorously supported the plans with two major funding projects for the restoration and expansion of the Lindenau-Museum (2018), as well as financing from the federal government for the Lindenau-Museum and the Lindenau Collections in the Altenburg Palace Museum (2020). The district and city of Altenburg have now created the optimal conditions for further raising the profile of Altenburg's museum landscape by establishing the special purpose association Altenburger Museen. After the opening of the "new" Lindenau-Museum, it will be necessary in a further phase to create spaces for a variety of functions: the workshops of the conservators, the storage rooms for the collections of the Altenburger Museen, offices for our staff, rooms for the activities of art and culture outreach, administrative areas and exhibition rooms for the graphic collection, in particular for the work of Gerhard Altenbourg. The Marstall (ducal stables) building in the castle gardens has long been in discussion as a possible site for this purpose, but for reasons of space there is also the option of an annex, such as the Neue Remise (New Coach House), or perhaps even the buildings of the Alten Spielkartenfabrik, the former playing-card factory located close to the museum.

The new Altenburger Museen special purpose association has also integrated the independent Gerhard Altenbourg Foundation more closely. It was founded by the artist's sister, Anneliese Ströch **(fig. 3)**, but had little revenue aside from the sale of image rights to Gerhard Altenbourg's works, so that its financial situation in recent years had become increasingly precarious. Major undertakings – such as the maintenance of the artist's house and his garden in the Braugartenweg, the first steps for a fundamental restoration of the building and the continuous maintenance of the garden – could only be carried out thanks to the generous support of the Deutsche Stiftung Denkmalschutz (German Foundation for Monument Conservation) and the Thuringian Regional Office for Monument Conservation and Archaeology, as well as the Gerhard Altenbourg Gesellschaft, founded in 2018 precisely for this purpose. The Altenburger Museen special purpose association can offer the foundation a protective shield in the form of a

Altenburger Museen, aber auch der weiteren Arbeiten für das neue Lindenau-Museum, dessen Sammlungen künftig nicht mehr allein im historischen Gebäude an der Gabelentzstraße präsentiert werden. Für das Werk von Gerhard Altenbourg kann der geplante neue Ausstellungsort für die Grafische Sammlung im Marstall einen Aufmerksamkeitsschub bedeuten. Das Team der Altenburger Museen steht mitten in den Planungen und sieht dem Jubiläumsjahr und seinen möglichen Impulsen gespannt entgegen.

*

Das umfangreiche Rahmenprogramm des Jubiläumsjahres und die Ausstellung *Der fantastische Gerhard Altenbourg* entstehen in gemeinsamer Arbeit im Team der Altenburger Museen. Ein besonderer Dank gilt dem Team der Kunst- und Kulturvermittlung unter der kommissarischen Leitung von Jacqueline Glück für ein Begleitprogramm, das über die Dauer der Ausstellung hinausgeht. Das Team Restaurierung und Technik unter der Leitung von Johannes Schaefer trug die Verantwortung für Transporte und den Ausstellungsaufbau. Der Leihverkehr wurde von Anna Lutz verantwortet.

Ausstellungen der Altenburger Museen werden seit einiger Zeit von einem Kuratorenteam geleitet, das den wichtigen Beitrag der Vermittlung schon in der Planung berücksichtigt. So hat Manuela Büchting kontinuierlich den kreativen Impuls eingebracht und auch einen Beitrag zu diesem Katalog verfasst, während Dr. Silvia Schmitt-Maaß das Ausstellungsprojekt initiiert und es mit großer Verve und Herzblut kuratiert hat. Auch die Planung des Katalogs, zu welchem sie einen einleitenden Aufsatz beigetragen hat, oblag ihr, dessen Redaktion dankenswerterweise Karoline Schmidt übernommen hat.

Wir danken Dr. Sören Fischer, Dr. Marit Heuß und Steffen Krautzig für ihre Recherchen und ihre sehr gelungenen Beiträge, die zu diesem Band entstanden sind.

Ein großer Dank geht an die Staatlichen Kunstsammlungen Dresden, das Kupferstich-Kabinett, namentlich an Dr. Stephanie Buck und Martin Buhlig, für ihre Bereitschaft, uns Werke von Gerhard Altenbourg auszuleihen. Außerdem danken wir Felix Brusberg, Ulf Drechsel, Willi Heining sowie Anemone Kramer für ihre hilfreichen Unterstützungen.

Auch dem Hirmer Verlag sei für die angenehme und gute Zusammenarbeit gedankt, insbesondere Sophie Friederich, Judith Kárpáty und Lutz Stirl. Die Printmedien hat das Stabsreferat Kommunikation zusammen mit dem Grafikbüro GRÜTZNER TRIEBE aus Berlin und Leipzig erstellt.

Es ist uns eine besondere Freude, dass der Präsident des Thüringer Landtages, Dr. Thadäus R. König, die Schirmherrschaft für das Jubiläumsjahr übernommen hat. Wir danken herzlich für diesen Vertrauensbeweis.

Wir danken dem Beauftragten der Bundesregierung für Kultur und Medien für die großzügige Förderung zur

business management contract, assume its fixed costs and especially benefit from the expertise of the Altenburger Museen's staff in taking steps towards a limited public opening of the artist's house and garden (fig. 4).

Consequently, this anniversary year also represents a year of transition, towards the preparation for the founding of the Altenburger Museen special purpose association, but also for further measures for the new Lindenau-Museum, whose collections in the future will not only be shown in the historical building in the Gabelentzstraße. For Gerhard Altenbourg's oeuvre the planned new exhibition space for the Graphic Collection in the Marstall will certainly bring increased attention. The team at the Altenburger Museen is now in the midst of a planning process, eagerly looking forward to the anniversary year and all the inspiration it can bring.

*

The extensive event programme for the anniversary year and the exhibition *The Fantastic Gerhard Altenbourg* have been put together by the combined efforts of the Altenburger Museen team. Special thanks go to the art and culture education staff under the interim leadership of Jacqueline Glück for an accompanying programme that will last beyond the duration of the exhibition. The conservation and technical staff led by Johannes Schaefer was responsible for transport and setting up the exhibition. Anna Lutz organised the loan arrangements.

For some time now, exhibitions at the Altenburger Museen have been managed by a team of curators who take into account the important role of communications, even in the early planning stages. Manuela Büchting has been a constant source of creative ideas while also contributing an essay to this catalogue, while Dr Silvia Schmitt-Maaß initiated the exhibition project and curated it with great verve and passion. She was also responsible for planning the catalogue, to which she contributed an introductory essay, and we thank Karoline Schmidt for her role as editor.

We would like to thank Dr Sören Fischer, Dr Marit Heuß and Steffen Krautzig for their research and their incisive contributions to this volume.

Our sincere thanks go to the Staatliche Kunstsammlungen Dresden, Kupferstich-Kabinett (Dresden State Art Collections, Print Cabinet),

Einrichtung der Ausstellungsräume, aber auch zur Ermöglichung dieser Publikation.

Mit diesem Katalog wollen wir das bildkünstlerische und literarische Erbe von Gerhard Altenbourg einmal mehr in den Mittelpunkt der Aufmerksamkeit stellen, zugleich aber darauf hinweisen, dass noch große Anstrengungen unternommen werden müssen, um das von ihm gestaltete Gesamtkunstwerk aus Haus und Garten langfristig zu sichern und einer interessierten Öffentlichkeit zugänglich zu machen. Hierfür bitten wir auch auf diesem Weg herzlich um Ihre Unterstützung! Erfreuen Sie sich aber zunächst an diesem ganz besonderen Katalog, der ihnen einen fantastischen Zugang zu einem der außergewöhnlichsten deutschen Künstlerpersönlichkeiten des 20. Jahrhunderts eröffnet.

Altenburg, im Januar 2026

Dr. Roland Krischke
Direktor der Altenburger Museen

1 Vgl. Brusberg, Dieter: Die Fahrt hinaus. Gerhard Altenbourg und Erhart Kästner. Eine Begegnung, in: (Altenbourg, Gerhard/Kästner, Erhard:) Das dritte Auge. Ein Dialog der Freunde Gerhard Altenbourg und Erhart Kästner. Mit einem Geleitwort von Eduard Beaucamp und Texten von Dieter Brusberg, Dieter Hoffmann, Roland Jäger, Werner Schmidt und Bernard Schultze, Frankfurt a. M./Leipzig 1992, S. 17–23, hier S. 20. Brusberg erläutert, dass Eberhard Roters Altenbourg während einer Eröffnungsrede in der Kunsthalle Düsseldorf so genannt hatte.
2 Vgl. Lang, Lothar: Malerei und Graphik in der Deutschen Demokratischen Republik, Leipzig 1983, S. 270.
3 Vgl. Berendse, Gerrit-Jan: Surrealismus in der DDR. Kampfansage an den sozialistischen Realismus in der ostdeutschen Literatur 1945–1990, Göttingen 2022.
4 Vgl. Beaucamp, Eduard: Geleitwort, in: Altenbourg/Kästner 1992 (wie Anm. 1), S. 5–8, hier S. 6.
5 Vgl. Muschik, Johann: Die Wiener Schule des Phantastischen Realismus, München/Gütersloh/Wien 1974, S. 59–67; ders.: Wiens »Phantastische Realisten«, in: Alte und moderne Kunst. Österreichische Zeitschrift für Kunst, Kunsthandwerk und Wohnkultur, 12 (1959), 4. Jg., S. 18–21; ders.: Wohin man sieht: die Wiener Schule, in: Neues Österreich, 24. Januar 1960.

namely to Dr Stephanie Buck and Martin Buhlig, for their willingness to lend us works by Gerhard Altenbourg. We would also like to thank Felix Brusberg, Ulf Drechsel, Willi Heining and Anemone Kramer for their valuable support.

We are also grateful to Hirmer Verlag for their pleasant and productive collaboration, in particular Sophie Friederich, Judith Kárpáty and Lutz Stirl. The print media for the exhibition was produced by our communications department in collaboration with the graphic design agency GRUETZNER TRIEBE from Berlin and Leipzig.

We are particularly pleased that the President of the Thuringian State Parliament, Dr Thadäus R. König, has agreed to be the patron of our anniversary year. We are very grateful for this vote of confidence.

We would like to thank the Federal Government Commissioner for Culture and the Media for generous support in setting up the exhibition rooms as well as for making the publication of this catalogue possible.

With this catalogue we wish to showcase the artistic and literary legacy of Gerhard Altenbourg, while also making clear that great efforts will have to be made in order to preserve the house and garden that he designed as a *Gesamtkunstwerk* and to make it accessible to the public. For this we would like to ask you to support us! But first, enjoy this very special catalogue, which opens up an extraordinary portal to one of the most remarkable German artists of the twentieth century.

Dr Roland Krischke
Director of the Altenburger Museen
Altenburg, January 2026

1 See Dieter Brusberg, "Die Fahrt hinaus. Gerhard Altenbourg und Erhart Kästner. Eine Begegnung", in Gerhard Altenbourg and Erhard Kästner, *Das dritte Auge. Ein Dialog der Freunde Gerhard Altenbourg und Erhart Kästner. Mit einem Geleitwort von Eduard Beaucamp und Texten von Dieter Brusberg, Dieter Hoffmann, Roland Jäger, Werner Schmidt und Bernard Schultze* (Frankfurt am Main/Leipzig: Insel, 1992), pp. 17–23, here p. 20. Brusberg explains that Eberhard Roters referred to Altenbourg as the "Zitronenfalter im Hauptbahnhof" during an opening speech at the Kunsthalle Düsseldorf; the *Zitronenfalter* (lit. lemon butterfly) is known in English as the brimstone butterfly.
2 Lothar Lang, *Malerei und Graphik in der Deutschen Demokratischen Republik* (Leipzig: Reclam, 1983), p. 270.
3 Gerrit-Jan Berendse, *Surrealismus in der DDR. Kampfansage an den sozialistischen Realismus in der ostdeutschen Literatur 1945–1990* (Göttingen: Wallstein, 2022).

6 Gerhard Altenbourg, in: (Altenbourg, Gerhard/Mennekes, Friedhelm:) Im Gespräch (Interview mit Friedhelm Mennekes), in: Grinten, Franz Joseph von der/Mennekes, Friedhelm: Abstraktion – Kontemplation. Auseinandersetzung mit einem Thema der Gegenwartskunst,
Stuttgart 1987, S. 234–241, hier S. 241. Altenbourg bezieht sich damit allerdings auf Lothar Lang, der unter dem Pseudonym Ludwig Last schlussfolgerte: »Diese Sicht auf das Ganze ist heute selten geworden.« Vgl. Lang, Lothar (Last, Ludwig): Ironie bei Altenbourg, in: Brusberg, Dieter (Hrsg.): Gerhard Altenbourg. Werk-Verzeichnis 1947–1969, unter Mitarbeit von Annegret Janda, zugl. Ausst.-Kat. Berlin / Baden-Baden / Hannover / Düsseldorf, Hannover 1969, S. 15 f., hier S. 15.

7 Vgl. Muschik 1974 (wie Anm. 5), S. 61.

8 Vgl. Vgl. Schmied, Wieland/Kestner-Gesellschaft (Hrsg.): Die Wiener Schule des phantastischen Realismus. Brauer, Fuchs, Hausner, Hutter, Lehmden, Ausst.-Kat. Kestner Gesellschaft, Hannover, Hannover 1965; Ders./Städtische Kunsthalle Recklinghausen (Hrsg.): Reiche des Phantastischen: Ruhrfestspiele Recklinghausen. Ausst.-Kat. Kunsthalle Recklinghausen, Recklinghausen 1968.

9 Vgl. Pierre Cabane, in: Pariser Kunstzeitschrift: Arts, 11. Juli 1962. Zit. nach: Muschik 1974 (wie Anm. 5), S. 65.

10 Alfred Kubin ed i pittori fantastici Viennesi, eingeleitet von Gustav René Hocke, Ausst.-Kat. Galleria Il Bilico, Rom, Rom 1963.

11 Vgl. die Ausstellung *Surrealismus – phantastische Malerei der Gegenwart*, Wien 1962.

12 Vgl. Hocke, Gustav René: Malerei der Gegenwart. Der Neo-Manierismus. Vom Surrealismus zur Meditation, Wiesbaden/München 1975.

13 Vgl. ebd., S. 190 f.

14 Vgl. ebd., S. 271–273 sowie S. 303, Anm. 10 mit einer Auflistung der ausgestellten Künstler u. Künstlerinnen. Der Autor bezieht sich auf: Deutsche Gesellschaft für Bildende Kunst/Akademie der Künste (Hrsg.): Labyrinthe. Phantastische Kunst vom 16. Jahrhundert bis zur Gegenwart, zusammengestellt von Eberhard Roters, Ausst.-Kat. Kunstverein und Akademie der Künste, Berlin / Staatliche Kunsthalle Baden-Baden / Kunsthalle Nürnberg, Berlin 1966, S. 64, Nr. 156. Ausgestellt war: Gerhard Altenbourg, *Ecce homo*, 1949, Kreidezeichnung auf Packpapier, 2042 x 1220 mm, damals mit Provenienz Galerie Springer, aktuell: Kolumba, Erzbischöfliches Diözesanmuseum Köln (erworben 1995). Vgl. Janda, Annegret: Gerhard Altenbourg. Monographie und Werkverzeichnis, 3 Bde., Bd. 1, 1937–1958, S. 247, Nr. 49/141. Vgl. auch den Beitrag von Silvia Schmitt-Maaß in diesem Band.

15 Lang, Lothar: Altenbourg, Der Bilddichter (1987), in: (Altenbourg, Gerhard/Lang, Lothar:) Gerhard Altenbourg / Lothar Lang – Briefwechsel 1965–1988, bearb. u. komm. v. Katrin Roth, hrsg. von Christa Grimm, Leipzig 2008, S. 183–187, hier S. 186.

16 Vgl. Gerhard Altenbourg. Zit. nach: Janda, Annegret: Altenbourg im »Hügelgau«, in: Brusberg 1969 (wie Anm. 6), S. 12–15, hier S. 13.

4 Eduard Beaucamp, "Geleitwort", in Altenbourg and Kästner, *Das dritte Auge* (n. 1 above), pp. 5–8, here p. 6.

5 See Johann Muschik, *Die Wiener Schule des Phantastischen Realismus* (Munich/Gütersloh/Vienna: Bertelsmann, 1974), pp. 59–67; Johann Muschik, "Wiens 'Phantastische Realisten'," *Alte und moderne Kunst. Österreichische Zeitschrift für Kunst, Kunsthandwerk und Wohnkultur* 12 (1959), vol. 4, pp. 18–21; Johann Muschik, "Wohin man sieht: die Wiener Schule", *Neues Österreich* (24 January 1960).

6 Gerhard Altenbourg, in Gerhard Altenbourg and Friedhelm Mennekes, "Im Gespräch (Interview mit Friedhelm Mennekes)", in Franz Joseph von der Grinten and Friedhelm Mennekes, *Abstraktion – Kontemplation. Auseinandersetzung mit einem Thema der Gegenwartskunst* (Stuttgart: Verlag Katholisches Bibelwerk, 1987), pp. 234–41, here p. 241. Altenbourg is referring here to Lothar Lang, who under the pseudonym Ludwig Last had declared that "This view of the whole has become seldom today". See Lothar Lang (Last, Ludwig), "Ironie bei Altenbourg", in Dieter Brusberg (ed.), *Gerhard Altenbourg. Werk-Verzeichnis 1947–1969, unter Mitarbeit von Annegret Janda*, exh. cat. Berlin / Baden-Baden / Hannover / Düsseldorf (Hanover: Verlag der Galerie Brusberg, 1969), pp. 15f., here p. 15.

7 Muschik, *Die Wiener Schule* (n. 5 above), p. 61.

8 Wieland Schmied and Kestner Gesellschaft (eds.) *Die Wiener Schule des phantastischen Realismus. Brauer, Fuchs, Hausner, Hutter, Lehmden*, exh. cat. Kestner Gesellschaft, Hanover (Hanover: Kestner Gesellschaft, 1965); Wieland Schmied and Städtische Kunsthalle Recklinghausen (eds.), *Reiche des Phantastischen: Ruhrfestspiele Recklinghausen*, exh. cat. Kunsthalle Recklinghausen (Recklinghausen: Städtische Kunsthalle, 1968).

9 See Pierre Cabane in the Paris journal *Arts*, 11 July 1962; quoted in Muschik, *Die Wiener Schule* (n. 5 above), p. 65.

10 *Alfred Kubin ed i pittori fantastici Viennesi*, introduction by Gustav René Hocke, exh. cat. Galleria Il Bilico, Rome (Rome: Galleria Il Bilico, 1963).

11 See the exhibition *Surrealismus – phantastische Malerei der Gegenwart* (Vienna: Künstlerhaus Wien, 1962).

12 See Gustav René Hocke, *Malerei der Gegenwart. Der Neo-Manierismus. Vom Surrealismus zur Meditation* (Wiesbaden/Munich: Limes, 1975).

13 Ibid., pp. 190ff.

14 Ibid., pp. 271–73 and p. 303, note 10, with a list of the exhibited artists. The author draws on Deutsche Gesellschaft für Bildende Kunst/Akademie der Künste, Eberhard Roters (eds.), *Labyrinthe. Phantastische Kunst vom 16. Jahrhundert bis zur Gegenwart*, exh. cat. Kunstverein und Akademie der Künste, Berlin / Staatliche Kunsthalle Baden-Baden / Kunsthalle Nürnberg (Berlin: Deutsche Gesellschaft für Bildende Kunst, 1966), p. 64, no. 156. The exhibition included Gerhard Altenbourg's *Ecce homo*, 1949, chalk drawing on packing paper, 2042 × 1220 mm, then belonging to the Galerie Springer, today to Kolumba, Erzbischöfliches Diözesanmuseum Köln (acquired in 1995). See Annegret Janda, *Gerhard Altenbourg. Monographie und Werkverzeichnis*, 3 vols. (Cologne: Wienand, 2004–10), vol. 1, 1937–1958, p. 247, no. 49/141. See also the essay by Silvia Schmitt-Maaß in this volume.

15 Lothar Lang, "Altenbourg, Der Bilddichter (1987)", in Gerhard Altenbourg and Lothar Lang, *Gerhard Altenbourg / Lothar Lang – Briefwechsel 1965–1988*, transcribed and commented by Katrin Roth, ed. by Christa Grimm (Leipzig: Lehmstedt, 2008), pp. 183–87, here p. 186.

16 Gerhard Altenbourg, quoted in Annegret Janda, "Altenbourg im 'Hügelgau'," in Brusberg, *Gerhard Altenbourg. Werk-Verzeichnis* (n. 6 above), pp. 12–15, here p. 13.

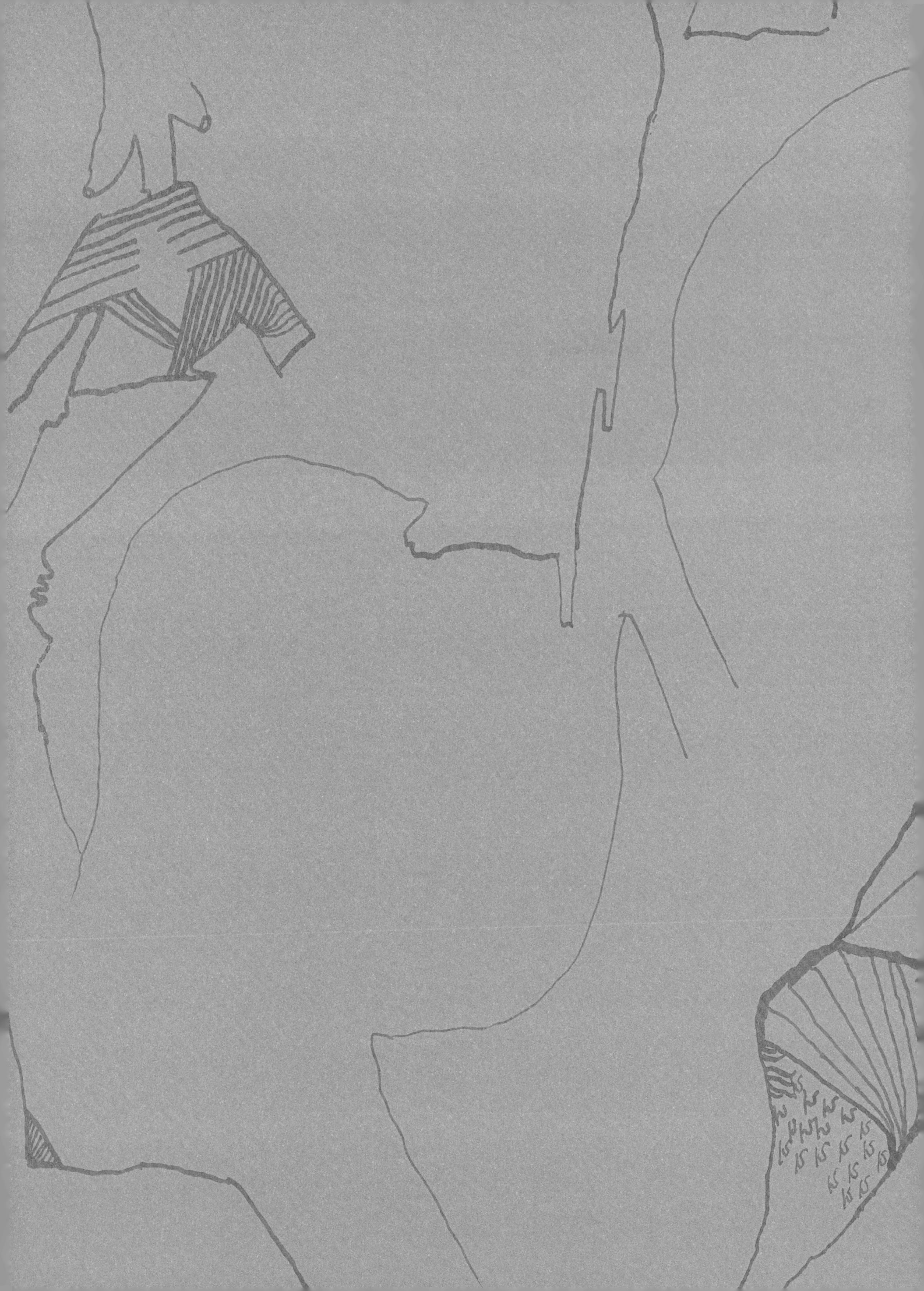

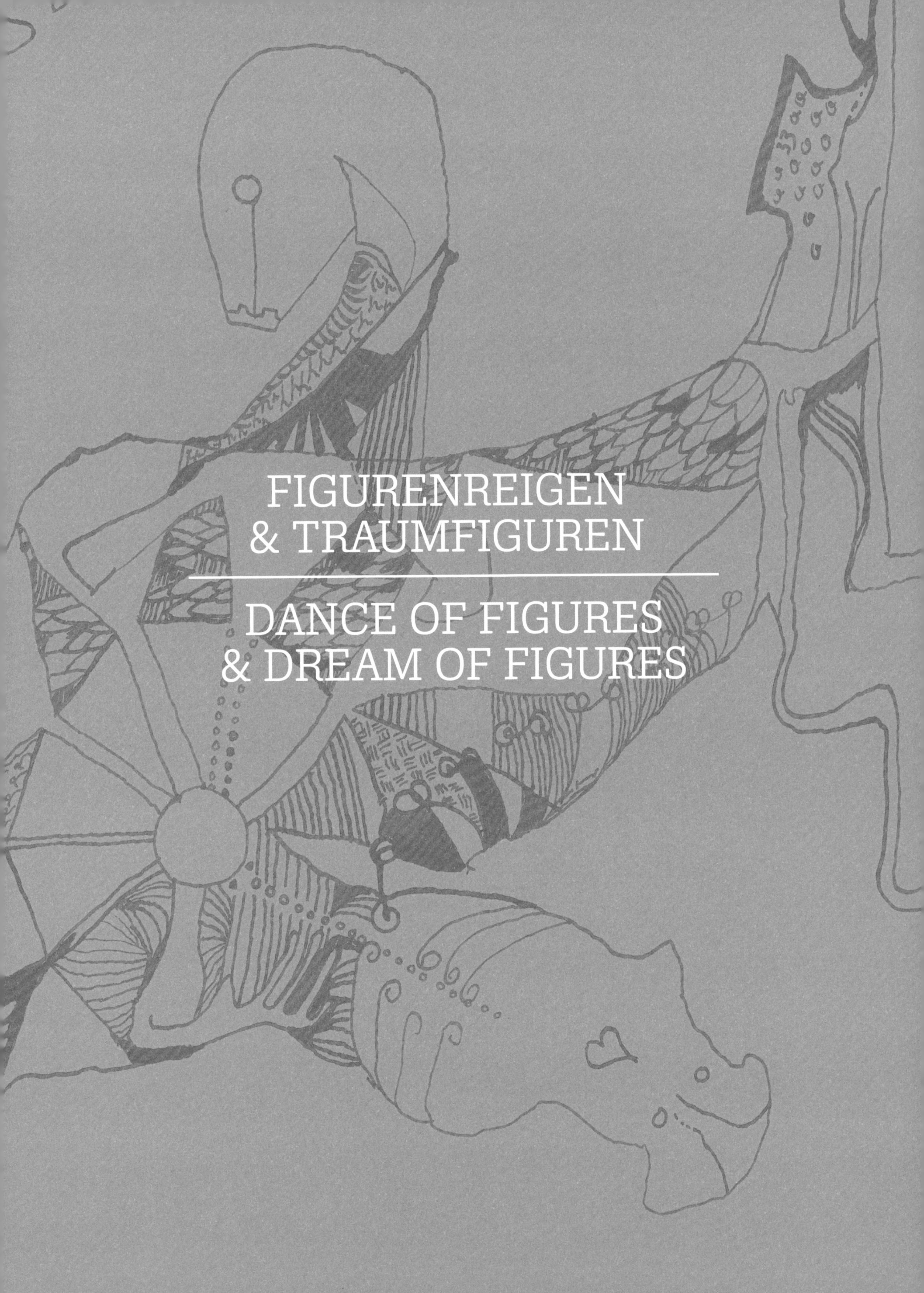

FIGURENREIGEN & TRAUMFIGUREN

DANCE OF FIGURES & DREAM OF FIGURES

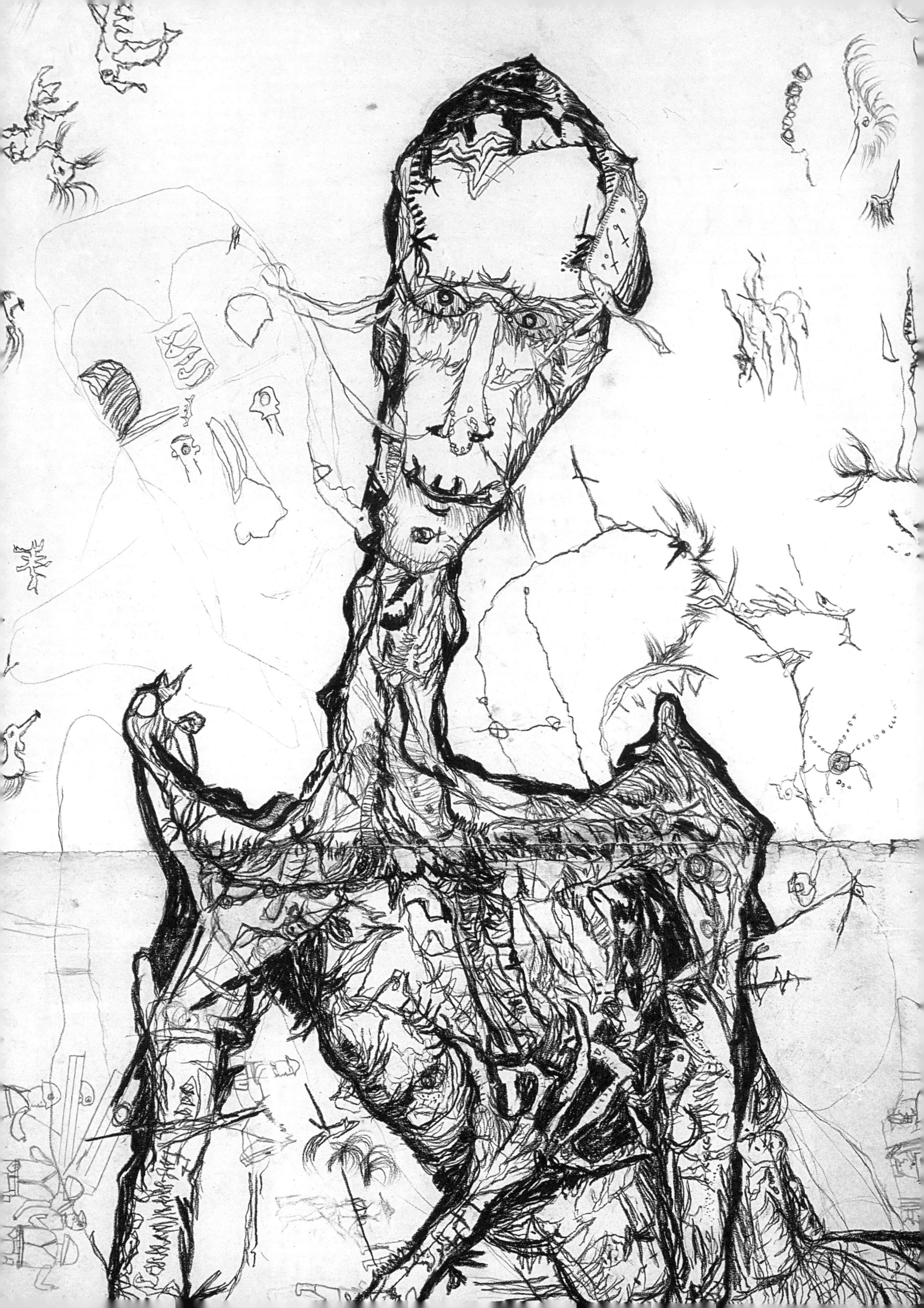

Silvia Schmitt-Maaß

Labyrinthe, skurrile Gestalten

Fantastische Figurationen

»Absurdes ist allen diesen Szenen gemeinsam. Es sind sanft Besessene, die da auftreten; Rätselhaftes geschieht.«
Erhart Kästner, 1969[1]

Gerhard Altenbourg gelang es, »ein künstlerisches Werk zu schaffen, das sein Wesen vollkommen ausdrückte und das sich seiner Eigenart und Qualität neben den Werken der großen Meister behaupten konnte«.[2] Nach 1945 setzte sich Altenbourg mit unterschiedlichen Kunstströmungen auseinander. Er entwickelte nicht nur eine starke Neigung zum Ungegenständlichen und zur Abstraktion, sondern setzte auch die figürlichen Tendenzen der Moderne fort, die sich bei anderen Künstlern dieser Generation ganz ähnlich nachvollziehen lassen **(Abb. 1)**. Werner Schmidt, der als einer der Ersten Gerhard Altenbourgs Werke in einer Ausstellung des Kupferstich-Kabinetts der heutigen Staatlichen Kunstsammlungen Dresden präsentierte, stellte das Anknüpfen des Künstlers an dadaistische Tendenzen heraus und ergänzte: »Die Künstlergeneration, deren Jugend von Faschismus und Krieg überschattet war und die nach 1946 ihr Studium aufnahm, stand vor dem Neubeginn. Die Wege der Überlieferung waren verschüttet oder fragwürdig, die Verbindung mit der internationalen Entwicklung abgebrochen. Die Vorstöße in künstlerisches Neuland zwischen Kubismus und Surrealismus waren nur sporadisch bekannt und galten nach der historischen Katastrophe der Hitlerära als eher überholte Sonderfälle.«[3]

In Österreich hatte sich Ende der 1950er-Jahre der sogenannte Phantastische Realismus herausgebildet. Künstler und Künstlerinnen dieser Schule waren zweifellos von surrealistischen Themen inspiriert.[4] Und auch Gerhard Altenbourg knüpfte an diese an; natürlich hatte er während seiner Auseinandersetzung mit dem Dadaismus für sich bereits entsprechende Entwicklungen erschlossen, auch die Aufspaltung der Gruppierungen nachvollzogen.[5] Aber Altenbourg war von unterschiedlichsten Künstlern und Strömungen beeinflusst. Vor allem Paul Klee und Wols

Labyrinths, Bizarre Figures

Fantastic Figurations

"The absurd pervades all of these scenes. Figures appear that are gently obsessed; puzzling things occur."
Erhart Kästner, 1969[1]

Gerhard Altenbourg was able to "create an artistic oeuvre that expressed his being entirely and that can hold its own in comparison with the works of the great masters, thanks to its singular nature and quality."[2] Engaging with various art movements in the postwar period, Altenbourg developed not only a strong inclination towards the non-objective and abstract, but also continued modernist figurative trends, as can be observed in many other artists of his generation. Werner Schmidt, one of the first to exhibit Altenbourg's works in a show at the Kupferstich-Kabinett (Collection of Drawings and Prints) of the present-day Staatliche Kunstsammlungen (State Art Collections) in Dresden, emphasised how the artist connected with Dadaist traditions. Schmidt also observed that "the generation of artists whose youth has been overshadowed by fascism and war, who began their studies after 1946, stood before a completely new beginning. The channels that had previously transmitted art traditions were blocked, the links with international developments cut off. Advances into uncharted artistic territories lying between Cubism and Surrealism were, after the historical catastrophe of the Hitler era, little known and regarded as outdated exceptions."[3]

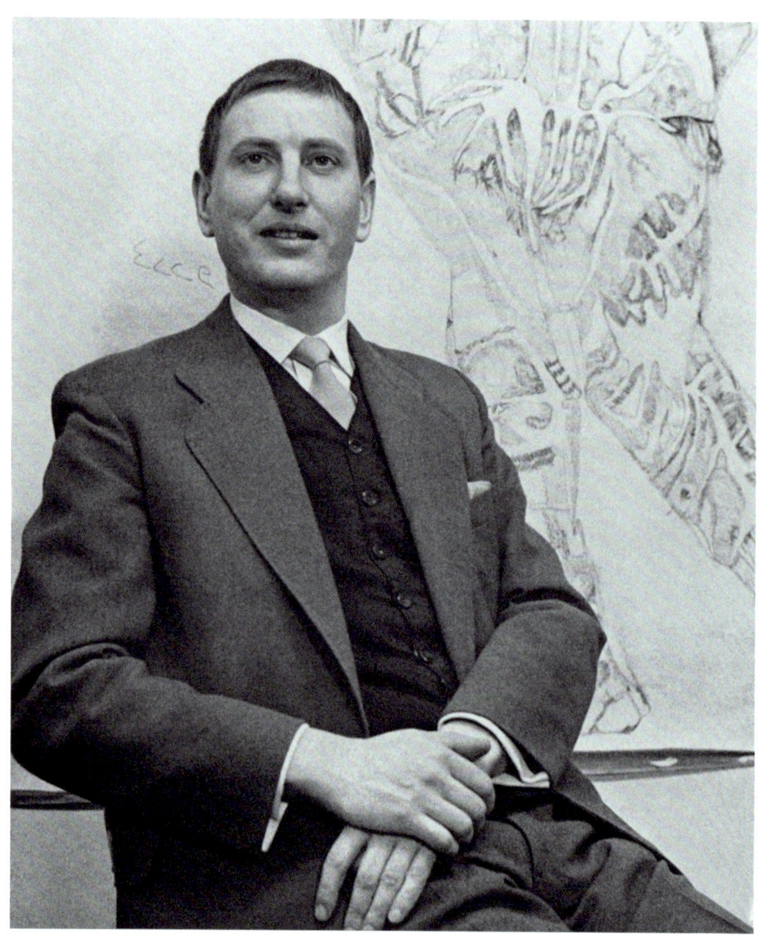

Abb. 1 Gerhard Altenbourg vor seiner Zeichnung *Ecce homo*, 1950, Schwarz-Weiß-Fotografie aus dem Ausstellungskatalog *Phantastische Figuration*, 1966
Fig. 1 Gerhard Altenbourg in front of his drawing *Ecce homo* (1950), black-and-white photograph from the exhibition catalogue *Phantastische Figuration*, 1966

werden als seine Vorbilder angesehen.[6] Klee ist wiederum von den Surrealisten verehrt worden.[7] Die Surrealisten Hans Bellmer, Salvador Dalí und Max Ernst schätzte Altenbourg außerordentlich und verfolgte interessiert ihre Ausstellungen. Zeugnis geben davon Monografien, Ausstellungs- und Werkkataloge in seiner Privatbibliothek. Auch besaß Altenbourg selbst einzelne surrealistische Kunstwerke **(Abb. 2, 3)**.

Altenbourgs frühe Werke wurden zudem im Kontext fantastischer Kunst präsentiert, sodass seine Selbstverortung innerhalb der Strömung nicht von der Hand zu weisen ist. 1966 geschah dies insbesondere in den Ausstellungen *Phantastische Figuration*[8] im Haus am Waldsee in Berlin-Zehlendorf sowie *Labyrinthe. Phantastische Kunst vom 16. Jahrhundert bis zur Gegenwart.*[9] Weitere Veranstaltungen in den ehemaligen westdeutschen Bundesländern lassen sich ergänzen. Etwa die Nürnberger Ausstellung *Ars phantastica – deutsche Kunst des Magischen Realismus, Phantastischen Realismus und Surrealismus seit 1945.*[10] Noch Johannes Gachnangs Ausstellung *Der gekrümmte Horizont.*

The movement known as Fantastic Realism arose in Austria at the end of the 1950s. Artists of this school were undeniably influenced by Surrealist themes.[4] Altenbourg likewise drew on Surrealism, naturally developing corresponding ideas for himself during his engagement with Dada and studying how it split into separate factions.[5] Yet he was influenced by a variety of other artists and movements as well. His models were above all Wols and Paul Klee,[6] and Klee in turn was venerated by the Surrealists.[7] Altenbourg especially admired the Surrealists Hans Bellmer, Salvador Dalí and Max Ernst and followed their exhibitions with interest. The monographs, exhibition catalogues and catalogues raisonnés in his private library testify to this, as do the several Surrealist artworks that he owned **(figs. 2–3)**.

Altenbourg's early works were moreover presented in the context of what was defined as fantastic art, so that his personal self-identification with this tendency should not be dismissed too quickly. This occurred especially in the 1966 exhibitions *Phantastische Figuration*[8] (Fantastic Figuration) at the Haus am Waldsee in Zehlendorf (Berlin) and *Labyrinthe. Phantastische Kunst vom 16. Jahrhundert bis zur Gegenwart* (Labyrinths: Fantastic Art from the Sixteenth Century to the Present).[9] Further similar events in the former West German states can be cited, such as the Nuremberg exhibition *Ars phantastica – deutsche Kunst des Magischen Realismus, Phantastischen Realismus und Surrealismus seit 1945* (Ars Phantastica: German Art of Magical Realism, Fantastic Realism and Surrealism since 1945).[10] Even as late as 1980, Johannes Gachnang's exhibition *Der gekrümmte Horizont. Kunst in Berlin 1945–1967* (The Curved Horizon: Art in Berlin 1945–1967) displayed works by Gerhard Altenbourg alongside those of Wols and Max Ernst.[11]

Altenbourg was therefore publicly perceived under the "fantastic" label for the first time in the spring of 1966.[12] The arts section of the Berlin newspaper *Tagesspiegel* reported on "painting designed to shock";[13] Gerhard Altenbourg was, it claimed, "an excellent … colourist" but occasionally became entangled in "mystifications".[14] By contrast, Will Grohmann in the *Frankfurter Allgemeine Zeitung* praised the "successful exhibition for taking stock of the future in the realm of unwavering contemporary fantasy, the opposite of the 'Viennese School', to put it bluntly".[15] Grohmann was amazed by Altenbourg's "eccentric power

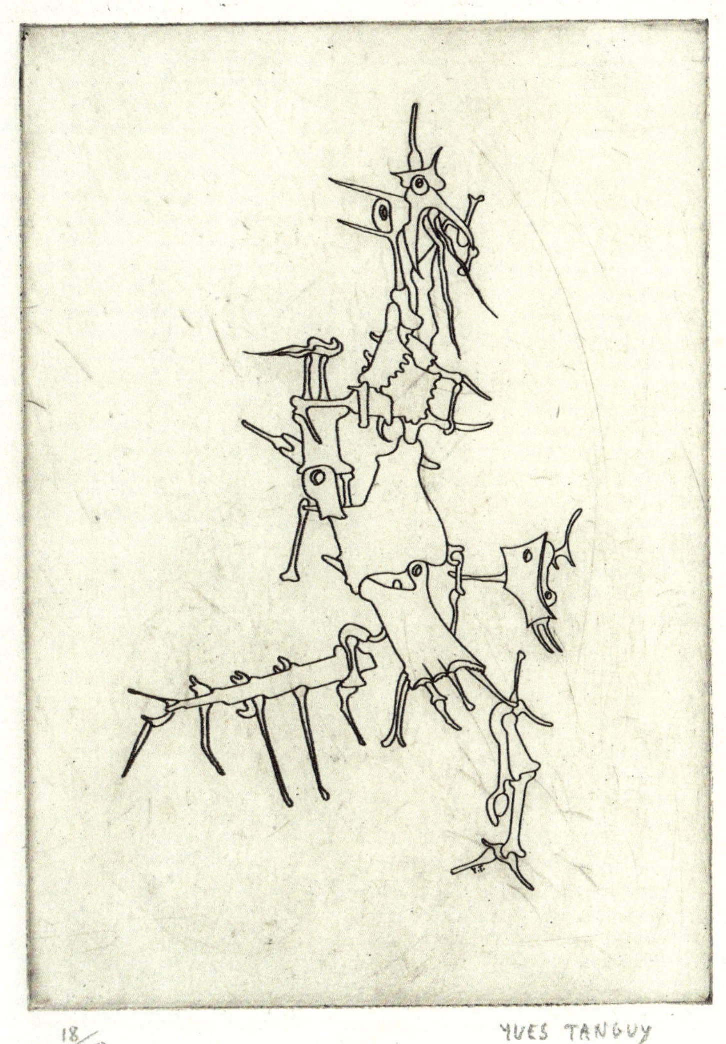

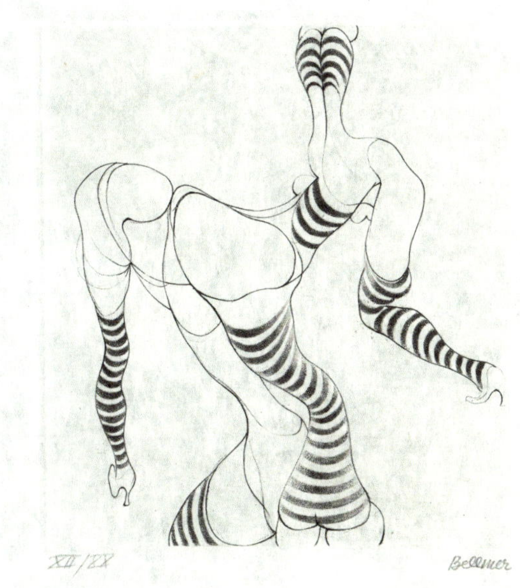

Abb. 2 Yves Tanguy, *zu Yvan Goll »Le Mythe de la Roche percée«*, 1947, Radierung, Blattmaß: 255 × 205 mm, sign. u. re.: YVES TANGUY, numm. u. li.: 18/100, Stiftung Gerhard Altenbourg, Inv.-Nr. SGA 5262-Ks
Fig. 2 Yves Tanguy, after Yvan Goll, *Le Mythe de la Roche percée* (The Myth of the Pierced Rock), 1947, etching, 255 × 205 mm, signed bottom right: YVES TANGUY, numbered bottom left: 18/100, Gerhard Altenbourg Foundation, inv. no. SGA 5262-Ks

Abb. 3 Hans Bellmer, *Ohne Titel* [Liegende in Strümpfen, auch: *Spektakel und Orakel*], 1967, Radierung auf Japanpapier, Blattmaß: 320 × 250 mm, sign. u. re.: Bellmer, numm. u. li.: XII/XX, Stiftung Gerhard Altenbourg, Inv.-Nr. SGA 5263-Ks
Fig. 3 Hans Bellmer, *Untitled* (Reclining in Stockings, also known as *Spectacle and Oracle*), 1967, etching on Japan paper, 320 × 250 mm, signed bottom right: Bellmer, numbered bottom left: XII/XX, Gerhard Altenbourg Foundation, inv. no. SGA 5263-Ks

Kunst in Berlin 1945–1967 stellte 1980 neben Wols und Max Ernst auch Werke von Gerhard Altenbourg aus.[11]

Unter dem Begriff des Fantastischen wird Altenbourg somit erstmals im Frühjahr 1966 öffentlich wahrgenommen.[12] Im Feuilleton des *Tagesspiegels* las man von »Bürgerschreck-Malerei«.[13] Gerhard Altenbourg sei »als Kolorist (…) hinreißend«, verstricke sich jedoch »zuweilen in Mystifikation«.[14] Will Grohmann hob in der *Frankfurter Allgemeinen Zeitung* hingegen hervor, dass »eine Ausstellung gelungen (sei), die so etwas wie eine Bestandsaufnahme des Kommenden im Reiche der unbeirrbaren zeitgemäßen Phantasie bedeutet, das Gegenteil der ›Wiener Schule‹, um es ganz klar zu sagen.«[15] Altenbourg erstaune allerdings »durch seine abseitige Erfindungskraft und durch die skurrile, dabei aber überlegene Linienführung. Diese Linien sind mehr Nerven als Grenzen, in allen Fällen aber bedeuten sie ein Innen und Außen, sind Anschauungsbild und gleichzeitiger

of invention and by his bizarre yet outstanding use of line. These lines are more nerves than boundaries, in any case they represent an inside and an outside, they are simultaneously visual image and commentary."[16] Together with the works of Hans Bellmer, Richard Oelze, Ursula Schultze-Bluhm, Paul Wunderlich and Friedrich Schröder-Sonnenstern, he claimed, Gerhard Altenbourg's art represented the psychological profile of an entire generation of artists.[17]

The catalogue to *Phantastische Figuration* augured a "new German painting", which derived its "powerful impact from the nightmarish memories of the recent German past".[18] This art movement was above all heir to Max Ernst, for his "visionary art represented only the concluding point of a development … that rested

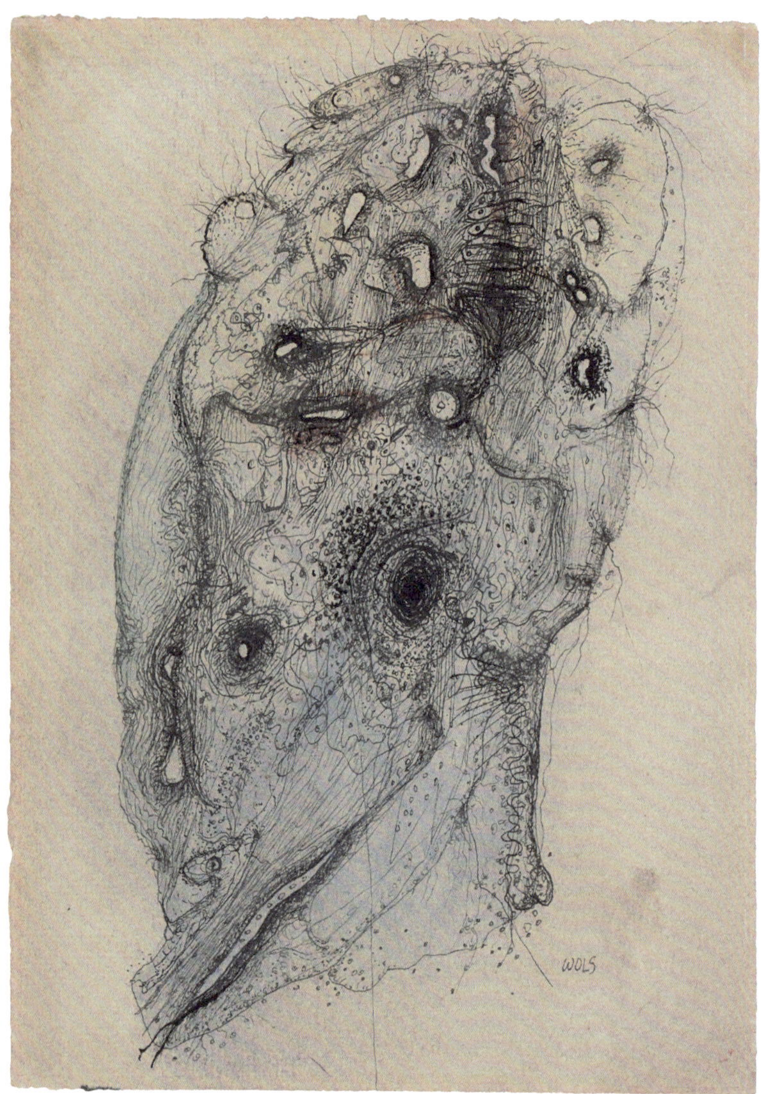

Abb. 4 Wols, *Tête abîmée [Verletzter Kopf]*, um 1944, Feder in schwarzer Tusche, Aquarell und weiße Lasur auf rosa meliertem Vergé-Papier, Spuren einer Umfassungslinie in weißer Kreide, 170 x 123 mm, Städel Museum, Frankfurt am Main, Inv.-Nr. SG 3385
Fig. 4 Wols, *Tête abîmée* (Injured Head), ca. 1944, pen and black ink, aquarelle and white glaze on mottled pink laid paper, traces of an edging line in white chalk, 170 x 123 mm,Städel Museum, Frankfurt am Main, inv. no. SG 3385

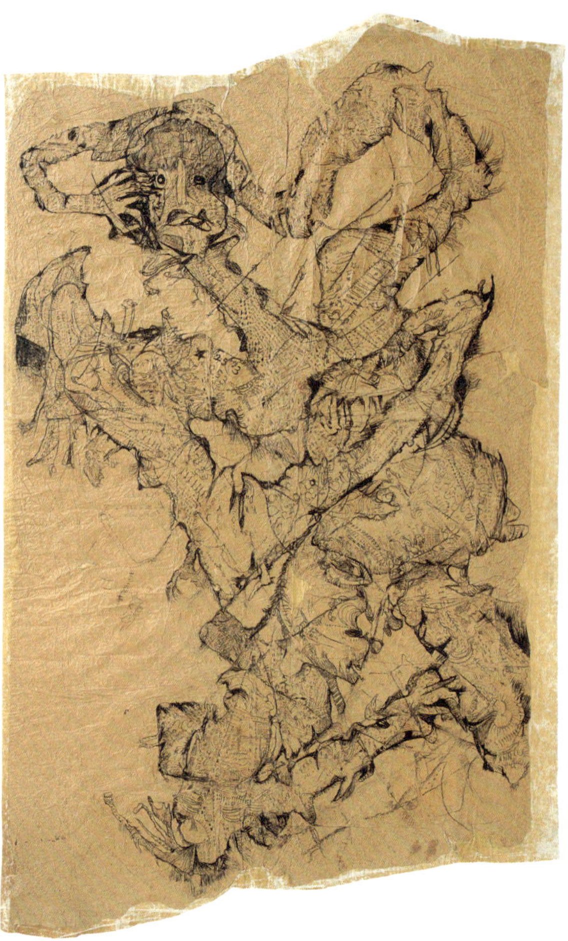

Abb. 5 Gerhard Altenbourg, *Ecce homo*, 1949, Kreidezeichnung auf Packpapier, 2042 × 1220 mm, Kolumba, Erzbischöfliches Diözesanmuseum Köln, Inv.-Nr. 1995/0044
Fig. 5 Gerhard Altenbourg, *Ecce homo*, 1949, chalk drawing on packing paper, 2042 × 1220 mm, Kolumba, Erzbischöfliches Diözesanmuseum Köln, inv. no. 1995/0044

Kommentar.«[16] Zusammen mit Werken von Hans Bellmer, Richard Oelze, Ursula Schultze-Bluhm, Paul Wunderlich und Friedrich Schröder-Sonnenstern bildete Gerhard Altenbourgs Kunst ein Psychogramm einer ganzen Künstlergeneration ab.[17]

Im Katalog *Phantastische Figuration* von 1966 wurde noch »neue deutsche Malerei« in Aussicht gestellt, die »ihre Eindruckskraft aus alptraumhaften Erinnerungen an die unmittelbare deutsche Vergangenheit«[18] bezogen habe. Diese Kunst sei vor allem auf Max Ernst zurückzuführen, denn dessen »visionäre Kunst (habe) nur den Endpunkt einer Entwicklung« dargestellt, »die auf einer langen und reichen

on a long and rich tradition. From Caspar David Friedrich and the Romantics, its roots lead to the apocalyptic art of the German renaissance and Middle Ages".[19]

Altenbourg's portrait photograph in this publication shows part of a drawing from his *Ecce homo* cycle **(fig. 1)**, which, just like the version in the Lindenau-Museum Altenburg **(cat. 1)**, was not exhibited at the Haus am Waldsee.[20] For the photo, he positioned himself in front of the drawing, sitting between the word "Ecce" and the abdomen of the drawn figure. This was his way of referring to the war trauma mentioned above. The word "Ecce" standing

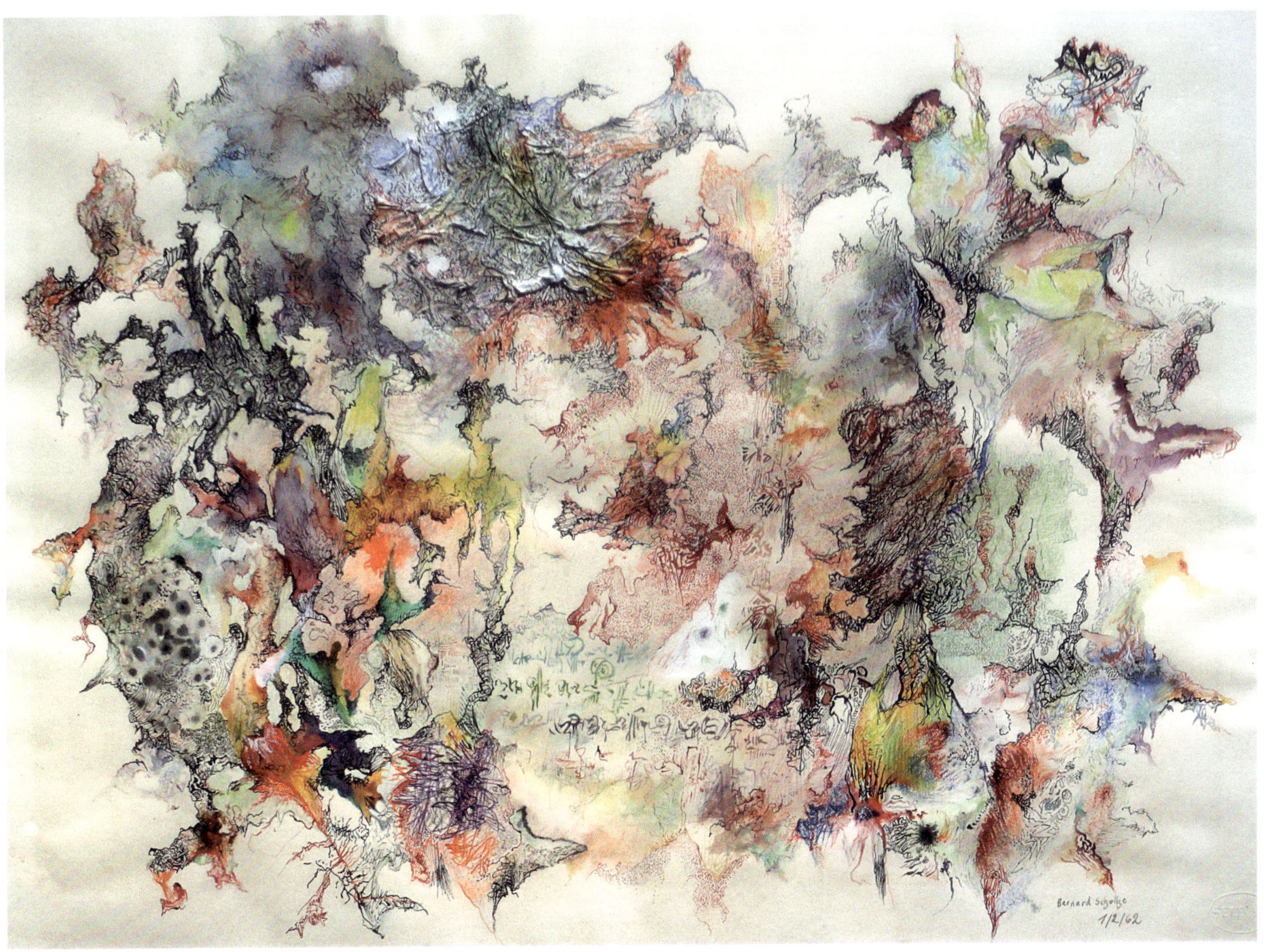

Abb. 6 Bernard Schultze, *1/2/62*, 1962, Mischtechnik auf weißem Karton, 435 × 665 mm, Museum Bochum, Inv.-Nr. 989
Fig. 6 Bernard Schultze, *1/2/62*, 1962, mixed technique on white cardboard, 435 × 665 mm, Museum Bochum, inv. no. 989

Tradition beruht (habe). Über Caspar David Friedrich und die Romantiker führ(t)en ihre Wurzeln zur apokalyptischen Kunst der deutschen Renaissance und des Mittelalters.«[19]

Altenbourgs Porträtfoto in dieser Publikation gab den Blick auf eine Zeichnung aus dem *Ecce homo*-Zyklus frei **(Abb. 1)**, die ebenso wie das Exemplar des Lindenau-Museums Altenburg **(Kat. 1)** im Haus am Waldsee gar nicht zu sehen war.[20] Für das Foto hatte Altenbourg derart vor dem exponierten Werk posiert, dass er zwischen dem Schriftzug »Ecce« und dem Unterleib der gezeichneten Gestalt sitzend abgelichtet wurde. Es war seine Art und Weise, auf das genannte Kriegstrauma einzugehen. Das neben die eigene Person gerückte »Ecce« verweist in diesem Fall auf ihn: diesen Altenbourg! Zugleich ruft er damit Bilder der Surrealisten aus der Zeit der Internierung im südfranzösischen Les Milles in

over him points in this case to himself: behold Altenbourg! At the same time, he alludes to pictures by Surrealists from the period who faced imprisonment in Les Milles in southern France, who created similarly amorphous structures. Wols, for example, visualises such a process of physical dissolution in *Tête abîmée (Verletzter Kopf)* (Injured Head; **fig. 4**).[21] The *Phantastische Figuration* exhibition, however, also displayed fifteen drawings by Altenbourg that did not fit this characterisation, among them *Der Gärtner* (The Gardener), 1954 (cat. 2) and *GING GANZ* (WENT COMPLETELY), 1958 (cat. 3).[22]

In 1966, the same year as *Phantastische Figuration*, the exhibition *Labyrinthe. Phantastische Kunst vom 16. Jahrhundert bis zur Gegenwart* was shown at the Kunstverein Berlin, proposing the labyrinth as a metaphor for the exploration of the unconscious. Of Altenbourg's works it only showed *Ecce homo* (1949), a monumental chalk drawing on packing paper that captures the horrors of the war and its

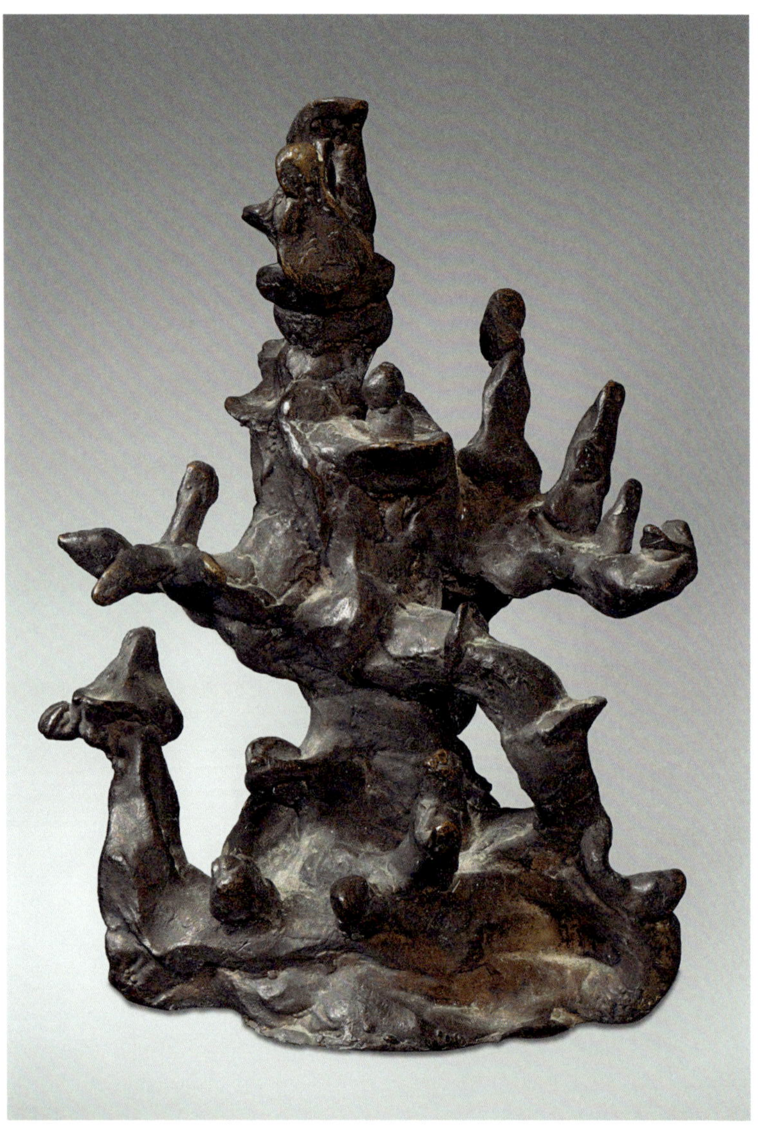

Abb. 7 Bernard Schultze, *Turm-Migof*, 1966, gegossene Bronze, 16 × 11,5 × 11 cm, Stiftung Gerhard Altenbourg, Inv.-Nr. SGA 5059-Ks
Fig. 7 Bernard Schultze, *Turm-Migof* (Migof Tower), 1966, cast bronze, 16 × 11.5 × 11 cm, Gerhard Altenbourg Foundation, inv. no. SGA 5059-Ks

Erinnerung, die ähnlich amorphe Strukturen aufweisen. Eindrucksvoll führt etwa Wols *Tête abîmée (Verletzter Kopf)* einen solchen körperlichen Auflösungsprozess vor Augen **(Abb. 4)**.[21] In der Ausstellung wurden von Gerhard Altenbourg allerdings 15 Zeichnungen präsentiert, die diesem Charakter wiederum nicht entsprechen; darunter: *Der Gärtner*, 1954 **(Kat. 2)** und *GING GANZ*, 1958 **(Kat. 3)**.[22]

Die Ausstellung *Labyrinthe. Phantastische Kunst vom 16. Jahrhundert bis zur Gegenwart*, die im Kunstverein Berlin im selben Jahr (1966) zu sehen war, zielte auf das Labyrinth als Metapher für die Erkundung des Unbewussten. Sie präsentierte von Altenbourg ausschließlich *Ecce homo*, 1949,

psychological consequences on the surface (fig. 5).[23] Such scenes were also depicted in the works of Bernard Schultze (fig. 6). His deformed – and, in their physical structure, apparently maimed – objects reflect the perplexingly "labyrinthine",[24] which he developed further in fantastic environments. Such formations became the sites of riddles, of disorientation and frightening excrescences. Altenbourg later acquired a small bronze sculpture by him, which can be seen in his house today (fig. 7). The Nuremberg exhibition showed his drawing *Achtung!* (cat. 4) and *Ein Kinderspiel* (A Child's Game), which has come down to us as a later lithograph (cat. 5). Later, Altenbourg competed for the Premio Marzotto, a prize in Italy that had last been awarded to figurative painting in 1968 (cat. 34).[25]

According to Erhart Kästner, Altenbourg's art production can be divided into three thematic blocks: 1. landscapes as the poetic transformation of nature; 2. heads that often contain landscapes or could be constructed from these; and 3. bizarre or grotesque figurative compositions.[26] Naturally, this categorisation might not apply to all of the works. Altenbourg himself defined the figurative compositions as "groups of figures and ambiguous transformation scenes". Their actions remain enigmatic, even when the fanciful titles of the works at times offer explanations and allusions to antiquity or world literature. In the case of the drawing *Verständigung der Auguren über ein Geschick* (Agreement Among the Augurs About a Fate; cat. 6) the title superficially refers to the officials of ancient Rome who interpreted natural phenomena in order to predict the future. Yet Altenbourg also mentioned as the subject the confrontation between his gallerists Rudolf Springer and Dieter Brusberg, who at that time were negotiating over representing him. The humorous title *Echse mit Blumenstrauß, der kleine Werner, Ungeheuer mit Regenschirm und Applaudierende* (Lizard with Bouquet of Flowers, Little Werner, Monster with Umbrella and Applauding Figures; cat. 7) might clarify the depiction somewhat, but ultimately does not offer any clear explanation of the scene. Altenbourg's figurations emerge as head shapes (cats. 8, 43) or as interacting clusters of figures and dream figures arranged in groups and pairs (cats. 9–13), who sometimes appear human, sometimes monstrous or related to mythical creatures (cats. 18–24).[27] Often these figural scenes are embedded in a landscape (cats. 33, 38). Altenbourg's obsession with tiny

eine monumentale Kreidezeichnung auf Packpapier, welche den Schrecken des Kriegs und seiner seelischen Folgen in die Fläche bannte **(Abb. 5)**.[23] Auch Bernard Schultzes Arbeiten knüpften an derartige Szenarien an **(Abb. 6, 7)**. Schultzes deformiert und in ihrer körperlichen Struktur versehrt wirkende Objekte spiegeln das verwirrend »Labyrinthische«[24] wider, das er in fantastischen Environments entwickelte. Solche Gebilde wurden zu Orten des Rätselns, des Verirrens und der beängstigenden Wucherungen. Altenbourg erwarb später eine kleine Bronzeplastik von ihm, die bis heute in seinem Künstlerhaus zu sehen ist **(Abb. 7)**. Die Nürnberger Ausstellung präsentierte von ihm dagegen die Zeichnung *Achtung!* **(Kat. 4)** und *Ein Kinderspiel*, das als spätere Lithografie überliefert ist **(Kat. 5)**. Später nahm Altenbourg am Wettbewerb um den Premio Marzotto teil, einem Kunstpreis der in Italien zuletzt 1968 für figürliche Malerei vergeben wurde **(Kat. 34)**.[25]

Altenbourgs Œuvre ließe sich – laut Erhart Kästner – in drei Themenblöcke unterteilen: 1. Landschaften als poetischen Umwandlungen der Natur, 2. Köpfe, die häufig auch Landschaften enthalten oder aus diesen gebildet sein können, und 3. skurril oder grotesk wirkende figürliche Kompositionen.[26] Freilich vermag diese Kategorisierung nicht in jedem Fall zu überzeugen. Altenbourg selbst definierte die figürlichen Kompositionen als »Figurenensembles, (und) doppeldeutige(n) Verwandlungsszenen«. Ihre Handlungen bleiben rätselhaft, wenn die fantasievollen Werktitel auch zuweilen Erklärungen bieten oder Brücken in antike oder weltliterarische Gefilde bauen mögen. Im Fall der Zeichnung *Verständigung der Auguren über ein Geschick* **(Kat. 6)** nimmt der Titel etwa vordergründig auf Beamte des antiken Roms Bezug, die Naturphänomene interpretieren und die Zukunft vorhersagen konnten. Allerdings benannte Altenbourg die Auseinandersetzung seiner Galeristen Rudolf Springer und Dieter Brusberg, die seinerzeit über ihn verhandelten, ebenso. Der lustige Titel des Holzschnitts *Echse mit Blumenstrauß, der kleine Werner, Ungeheuer mit Regenschirm und Applaudierende* **(Kat. 7)** mag die Darstellung erhellen, doch bietet der Titel letztlich keine wegweisende Erklärung dieser Szene.

Altenbourgs Figurationen begegnen als Kopfgestalten **(Kat. 8, 43)** oder als interagierende, zu Gruppen und Paaren arrangierte Figurenreigen und Traumfiguren **(Kat. 9–13)**, die mal menschlich, mal monströs wirken, oder mit Fabelwesen verwandt zu sein scheinen **(Kat. 18–24)**.[27] Häufig sind diese figürlichen Szenen zugleich in eine Landschaft eingebunden **(Kat. 33, 38)**. Altenbourgs Begeisterung für winzige Strukturen – Linien, Tupfen, Striche und Punkte – ist bemerkenswert, denn aus diesen entwickelte er bizarre Kulissen, die an verborgene zelluläre Muster erinnern und doch auch figürliche Szenen oder Kopfbilder enthalten. Häufig wirken diese übervollen Zeichnungen wie mikroskopische Abbilder, denen der Künstler manchmal Rätselhaftes hinzugab: »Wenn man in die Gewebe (der Zeichnungen) eindringt, kann man spitzbübische

structures – lines, spots, dashes and dots – is remarkable, since from these he evolved bizarre scenery that recall hidden cellular patterns and yet contain figurative scenes or shapes of heads. These overfull drawings frequently appear like microscope images, to which the artist sometimes appended puzzling comments: "If you penetrate the tissue (of the drawing) you can make impish discoveries. The draughtsman has concealed many things with a mischievous delight in playing hide-and-seek."[28]

Altenbourg composed the majority of these works in mixed techniques, but also produced delicate sketches and graphic prints (cat. 18). Independent of categorisation according to motifs, the artist placed special emphasis on colours, pigments, paper types and drawing materials. He was just as fussy in his graphic works in regard to paper and colours, which he tested in protracted operations in serial printing proofs.[29] He employed a similar procedure in the metal works (cats. 9, 19, 21, 27), which he had executed by befriended craftsmen according to his drafts and ideas (cats. 22, 26, 76). Altenbourg usually marked his finished works with the date, annotations, texts, often with his initials, his artist's monogram and frequently – and this sometimes several times – with his signature as well as his embossing stamp.

For his artist's books and series, whether drawn or printed in limited editions, he always had elaborately designed boxes, slip cases and bindings made – in the case of the *Bobrowski-Mappe* with copper reliefs especially produced from his designs.[30] Several selected copies or single printings from these artist's books and series are presented in this catalogue (cats. 28–31, 39). Even ceramic vessels (cat. 28) and other groups of works such as sketches, metal works and even pieces of furniture for his house are to be included here, as mentioned in the foreword by Roland Krischke. The interior of the house was designed by Altenbourg as a "walk-in picture" and *Gesamtkunstwerk*, "in which the artistic fantasies of Gerhard Altenbourg are present in an incomparable manner."[31]

The present publication presents highlights from Gerhard Altenbourg's art production, focussing on figurative representations. The catalogue is divided into three parts: 1. dance of figures and dream of figures; 2. bizarre landscapes and microcosms; and 3. colour frenzy and studio frenzy. A chronology is avoided. Following on this introduction, the panorama

Entdeckungen machen. Der Zeichner hat vieles versteckt, mit einer diebischen Freude am Versteckspiel.«[28]

Altenbourg komponierte diese Werke zumeist als Mischtechniken, doch auch zarte Skizzen und Druckgrafiken sind überliefert **(Kat. 18)**. Unabhängig von einer motivischen Einordnung legte Altenbourg besonderen Wert auf Farben, Pigmente, Papiersorten und Zeichenmaterialien. Genauso wählerisch war er bei Druckgrafiken im Hinblick auf Papier und Farben, die er in langwierigen Operationen mit seriellen Probedrucken austestete.[29] Ähnlich verfuhr er mit Metallarbeiten **(Kat. 9, 19, 21, 27)**, die er von befreundeten Handwerkern nach seinen Entwürfen und Vorstellungen ausarbeiten ließ **(Kat. 22, 26, 76)**. Fertig gestellte Werke kennzeichnete Altenbourg in der Regel mit Datierungen, Bezeichnungen, Beschriftungen, häufig noch mit seinen Initialen, dem Künstlermonogramm und zumeist (und dies gelegentlich mehrfach) mit seiner Signatur wie auch mit seinem Prägestempel.

Für seine gezeichneten oder in geringen Auflagen gedruckten Künstlerbücher und Serien, von denen in diesem Katalog ausgewählte Exemplare bzw. Einzeldrucke präsentiert werden **(Kat. 29–31, 39)**, ließ er stets aufwendig gestaltete Schuber, Kassetten und Einbände fertigen – im Falle der Bobrowski-Mappe sogar mit eigens nach seinen Entwürfen gearbeiteten Kupferreliefs.[30] Selbst keramische Gefäße **(Kat. 28)** und weitere Werkgruppen wie Entwürfe, Metallarbeiten und sogar Möbel für sein Künstlerhaus können hier angeführt werden, wie im Vorwort von Roland Krischke angeklungen. Das Innere dieses Hauses gestaltete Altenbourg zu »einem begehbaren Bild« und Gesamtkunstwerk, »in dem die künstlerischen Fantasien Gerhard Altenbourgs in unvergleichlicher Weise präsent sind«.[31]

Der vorliegende Katalog bietet eine Auswahl von Glanzlichtern aus dem Schaffen von Gerhard Altenbourg, die sich auf figürliche Darstellungen fokussiert. Er ist in drei Teile untergliedert: 1. Figurenreigen & Traumfiguren, 2. bizarre Landschaften & Mikrokosmen sowie 3. Farben- & Werkstattrausch. Eine Chronologie wird vermieden. Im Anschluss an diese Einleitung fächert sich das Panorama figürlicher, grotesk anmutender und schillernder Gestalten Altenbourgs zunächst mit Figurenreigen & Traumfiguren auf. Da sich figurale Szenen sogar unter den Künstlerbüchern ausmachen lassen, analysiert Marit Heuß in diesem Kontext das Künstlerbuch *Salutation* **(Kat. 29)** aus literaturwissenschaftlicher Perspektive und zeigt auf bild-poetischer Ebene spannende, surreale Bezüge auf.

Der zweite Katalogteil präsentiert Altenbourgs bizarre Landschaften & Mikrokosmen. Sören Fischer wirft hierfür einen Blick auf die prozesshaften zeichnerischen Operationen Altenbourgs. Er vergleicht dessen Zeichnungen mit zeitgenössischen Werken von Ursula, Unica Zürn und weist Altenbourgs inspirierendes und damit zukunftsweisendes (Ein-)Wirken auf Gabriela Oberkofler, Sebastian Rug und Egbert Kasper nach. Im Anschluss wird der Blick auf opulente Werkbeispiele eröffnet.

of figurative, seemingly grotesque and colourful figures unfolds initially with a dance of figures and a dream of figures. Since figurative scenes even appear in the artist's books, Marit Heuß analyses the artist's book *Salutation* **(cat. 29)** in this context from a literature studies perspective, revealing fascinating, surreal references at the level of image and poetry.

The second part of the catalogue presents Altenbourg's bizarre landscapes and microcosms. Sören Fischer takes a look at Altenbourg's processual drawing operations, comparing the artist's drawings with contemporary works by Ursula and Unica Zürn, pointing out Altenbourg's inspiring and pioneering influence and impact on Gabriela Oberkofler, Sebastian Rug and Egbert Kasper. Finally, the essay examines opulent examples of Altenbourg's works.

The part of the catalogue dedicated to colour frenzy and studio frenzy is dedicated to the little-known, sketch-like and sometimes unfinished works from the artist's estate **(cats. 49–52, 63, 67–73)**,[32] comparing these to several prints, some made in serial procedures. Referring to a few selected examples, Steffen Krautzig demonstrates how Altenbourg resorted to aleatoric, surrealist practices in these works as well. Manuela Büchting further develops this from the perspective of the museum education work in the "studio" at the Lindenau-Museum Altenburg. She approaches Altenbourg's art production through drawings, woodcuts and lithographs, presenting his fantastic works as important sources of inspiration for visitors to the museum.

In spite of the enthusiasm for and fascination with the fantastic character of his works, Altenbourg's art should not be "exclusively interpreted as fantastic, playful, bizarre", for, as Lothar Lang observed, "one should not forget the realistic foundation from which the artist's figures derive. This fantastic realist is a magnificent magician on paper, who forces colours and lines into figurations that have never been seen before in art."[33] While Max Ernst preferred "the riddle as the central characteristic of the fantasy piece, yet shifted it close to the fairy tale with a dash of irony",[34] Altenbourg drew on the wealth of knowledge in his private library, weaving together something new out of fragments taken from antiquity, philosophy, art history and theology. Altenbourg's work consequently contains an enormous potential that extends far beyond the category of the fantastic. This song to the freedom of art, to the freedom of forms, colours and imagination tied to the soul,

Der Katalogteil Farben- & Werkstattrausch widmet sich den bislang wenig beachteten, skizzenhaft anmutenden, manchmal unvollendeten Werken, die aus dem Nachlass des Künstlers stammen **(Kat. 49–52, 63, 67–73)**,[32] und stellt diese einigen druckgrafischen Werken gegenüber, die teils in seriellen Prozeduren entstanden sind. Anhand ausgewählter Beispiele weist Steffen Krautzig nach, dass Altenbourg auch bei diesen auf aleatorische, surrealistische Praktiken zurückgriff. Manuela Büchting spinnt hiervon ausgehend den Faden aus der Perspektive der musealen Vermittlungsarbeit des *studio* am Lindenau-Museum Altenburg weiter. Sie nimmt eine Annäherung an Altenbourgs Kunst am Beispiel von Zeichnungen, Holzschnitten und Lithografien vor und stellt die fantastischen Werke Altenbourgs als wichtige Inspirationsquellen für Museumsbesucher und -besucherinnen heraus.

Bei aller Begeisterung und Faszination am Fantastischen sollte Altenbourgs Kunst gleichwohl nicht »als (ausschließlich; Anm. der Autorin) phantastisch, verspielt, skurril« ausgelegt werden. Denn, so stellte Lothar Lang heraus, »man darf (…) nicht diesen realistischen Fundus vergessen, aus dem die Gebilde des Künstlers kommen. Dieser phantastische Realist ist ein großer Zauberer auf dem Papier, der Farben und Linien zu Figurationen zwingt, die so in der Kunst noch nicht zu sehen waren«.[33] Während Max Ernst das »zentrale Merkmal des Phantasiestücks, die Verrätselung (bevorzugte), es aber mit einer Prise Ironie, in die Nähe des Märchens (versetzte)«,[34] schöpfte Gerhard Altenbourg aus dem reichen Wissensschatz seiner Privatbibliothek, ersann aus antiken, philosophischen und kunsttheoretischen wie auch theologischen Versatzstücken Neues.

Gerhard Altenbourgs Œuvre entfaltet demnach ein enormes Potenzial, das weit über das Fantastische hinausgeht. Dieser Gesang an die Freiheit der Kunst, an die Freiheit der Formen, der Farben und der an den Geist geknüpften Fantasie, die auch (aber nicht allein) vom Leid und der Vergänglichkeit des menschlichen Daseins geformt wird, wird getragen von einem akribischen Wesen, einem strebsamen Arbeitsethos. Eklektisch nahm Altenbourg Strömungen der klassischen Moderne wie den Surrealismus auf, entwickelte diese jedoch zugleich weiter und verfremdete sie. Seine mal abstrakt wirkenden, mal zum Informel tendierenden Arbeiten, ganz besonders aber seine figurativen fantastisch oder surreal anmutenden bizarren Szenen, die der vorliegende Katalog beispielhaft versammelt, eröffnen einen einzigartigen Kosmos: den des fantastischen Gerhard Altenbourg.

shaped as well – but not only – by the suffering and the transitoriness of human existence, is sustained by a meticulous being, by an ambitious work ethic. Altenbourg adopted currents of modernism such as Surrealism eclectically while evolving and transforming them. His works sometimes seem abstract, sometimes tending more to the Art Informel movement. But in particular his figurative fantastic or surreally bizarre scenes, presented in this catalogue in selected examples, open up a singular cosmos: that of the fantastic Gerhard Altenbourg.

1 Erhard Kästner, "Für Altenbourg", in Gerhard Altenbourg and Erhard Kästner, *Das dritte Auge. Ein Dialog der Freunde Gerhard Altenbourg und Erhart Kästner. Mit einem Geleitwort von Eduard Beaucamp und Texten von Dieter Brusberg, Dieter Hoffmann, Roland Jäger, Werner Schmidt und Bernard Schultze* (Frankfurt am Main/Leipzig: Insel, 1992), pp. 43–48, here p. 45.

2 Annegret Janda, "Gerhard Altenbourg. Chronik eines Künstlerlebens im 20. Jahrhundert. Zweiter Teil 1959–1976", in idem, *Gerhard Altenbourg. Monographie und Werkverzeichnis*, 3 vols. (Cologne: Wienand, 2004–10), vol. 2, 1959–1976, pp. 8–25, here p. 9.

3 Werner Schmidt, "Gerhard Altenbourg. Zeichnungen und Graphik aus drei Jahrzehnten", in Staatliche Kunstsammlungen Dresden (eds.), *Gerhard Altenbourg. Zeichnungen und Graphik aus drei Jahrzehnten. Kupferstich-Kabinett der Staatlichen Kunstsammlungen Dresden*, exh. cat. Staatlichen Kunstsammlungen, Dresden (Dresden: Kupferstich-Kabinett, 1979), pp. 1–3, here p. 1.

4 Johann Muschik, *Die Wiener Schule des Phantastischen Realismus* (Munich/Gütersloh/Vienna: Bertelsmann, 1974), pp. 59–67.

5 His private library, for example, included William Rubin, *Dada und Surrealismus* (Stuttgart, 1972). In the chapter "Die Problematik der phantastischen Kunst" (The Problems of Fantastic Art), the author states that Surrealist art is "a means of expression, a tool for self-discovery, but is not made to be enjoyed"; see p. 122.

6 Gerhard Altenbourg, "'Jeder Satz zu seinem Aufschein gelangt'. Für Erhard Kästner (6. November 1978)", in Altenbourg and Kästner, *Das dritte Auge* (n. 1 above), pp. 9–16.

7 See Michael Baumgartner, Nina Zimmer, Zentrum Paul Klee Bern (eds.), *Paul Klee und die Surrealisten*, exh. cat. Zentrum Paul Klee Bern (Berlin: Hatje Cantz, 2017).

8 *Phantastische Figuration. Altenbourg, Bellmer, Oelze*, exh. cat. Haus am Waldsee, Berlin (Berlin, 1966), n.p., nos. 1–15.

9 Deutsche Gesellschaft für Bildende Kunst/ Akademie der Künste (eds.), *Labyrinthe. Phantastische Kunst vom 16. Jahrhundert bis zur Gegenwart, zusammengestellt von Eberhard Roters*, exh. cat. Kunstverein and Akademie der Künste, Berlin / Staatliche Kunsthalle Baden-Baden / Kunsthalle Nuremberg (Berlin, 1966), p. 64, no. 156.

10 Albrecht-Dürer-Gesellschaft e.V. (eds.), *Ars phantastica – deutsche Kunst des Magischen*

1 Vgl. Kästner, Erhard: Für Altenbourg, in: (Altenbourg, Gerhard/Kästner, Erhard:) Das dritte Auge. Ein Dialog der Freunde Gerhard Altenbourg und Erhart Kästner. Mit einem Geleitwort von Eduard Beaucamp und Texten von Dieter Brusberg, Dieter Hoffmann, Roland Jäger, Werner Schmidt und Bernard Schultze, Frankfurt a. M./Leipzig 1992, S. 43–48, hier S. 45.
2 Vgl. Janda, Annegret: Gerhard Altenbourg. Chronik eines Künstlerlebens im 20. Jahrhundert. Zweiter Teil: 1959–1976, in: dies.: Gerhard Altenbourg. Monographie und Werkverzeichnis, 3 Bde., Bd. 2, 1959–1976, Köln 2007, S. 8–25, hier S. 9.
3 Vgl. Schmidt, Werner: Gerhard Altenbourg. Zeichnungen und Graphik aus drei Jahrzehnten, in: Staatliche Kunstsammlungen Dresden (Hrsg.): Gerhard Altenbourg. Zeichnungen und Graphik aus drei Jahrzehnten. Kupferstich-Kabinett der Staatlichen Kunstsammlungen Dresden, Ausst.-Kat. Staatliche Kunstsammlungen, Dresden, Dresden 1979, S. 1–3, hier S. 1.
4 Vgl. Muschik, Johann: Die Wiener Schule des Phantastischen Realismus, München/Gütersloh/Wien 1974, S. 59–67.
5 In seiner Privatbibliothek findet sich etwa: Rubin, William: *Dada und Surrealismus,* Stuttgart 1972. Im Kapitel »Die Problematik der phantastischen Kunst« hält der Autor fest, dass surrealistische Kunst ein »Ausdrucksmittel, ein Instrument Selbstentdeckung darstellen, nicht aber zum Zweck des Genusses geschaffen« sei, vgl. ebd., S. 122.
6 Vgl. Altenbourg, Gerhard: »Jeder Satz zu seinem Aufschein gelangt«. Für Erhard Kästner (6. November 1978), in: Altenbourg/Kästner 1992 (wie Anm. 1), S. 9–16.
7 Vgl. Baumgartner, Michael/Zimmer, Nina/Zentrum Paul Klee Bern (Hrsg.): Paul Klee und die Surrealisten, Ausst.-Kat. Zentrum Paul Klee Bern, Bern/Berlin 2017.
8 Vgl. Phantastische Figuration: Altenbourg, Bellmer, Oelze, Ausst.-Kat. Haus am Waldsee, Berlin, Berlin 1966, o. S., Nr. 1–15.
9 Vgl. Deutsche Gesellschaft für Bildende Kunst/Akademie der Künste (Hrsg.): Labyrinthe. Phantastische Kunst vom 16. Jahrhundert bis zur Gegenwart, zusammengestellt von Eberhard Roters, Ausst.-Kat. Kunstverein und Akademie der Künste, Berlin / Staatliche Kunsthalle Baden-Baden / Kunsthalle Nürnberg, Berlin 1966, S. 64, Nr. 156.
10 Vgl. Albrecht-Dürer-Gesellschaft e.V. (Hrsg.): Ars phantastica – deutsche Kunst des Magischen Realismus, Phantastischen Realismus und Surrealismus seit 1945, Ausst.-Kat. Schloss Stein, Nürnberg, Nürnberg 1967, o. S., Nrn. 12–17, darunter die Lithografie *Ein Kinderspiel* (Kat. 5), allerdings datiert auf 1955.
11 Vgl. Penndorf, Jutta: »Ein Gehen der Wege, ein Schweben …«, in: Janda 2007 (wie Anm. 2), S. 26–31, hier S. 31; Gachnang, Johannes/Akademie der Künste (Hrsg.): Der gekrümmte Horizont. Kunst in Berlin 1945–1967, Ausst.-Kat. Akademie der Künste, Berlin, Berlin 1980, Abb. S. 72–75, Verzeichnis S. 114. Ausgestellt wurden *Ecce homo,* 1950, vgl. Janda, Annegret: Gerhard Altenbourg. Monographie und Werkverzeichnis, 3 Bde., Bd. 1, 1937–1958, Köln 2004, Nr. 50/66 (vgl. dazu unten Anm. 20), sowie die Zeichnungen *Knabentorso,* 1956; *Das schweinische Lächeln,* 1957; *Ach, diese Verstrickungen,* 1958.
12 Vgl. Ausst.-Kat. Berlin 1966 (wie Anm. 8); vgl. Tobben, Irene: Das Haus wächst. Thomas Kempas Standortbestimmungen, in: Blomberg, Katja (Hrsg.): 68 Jahre Haus am Waldsee, internationale Kunst in Berlin. Geschichte einer Institution, 2. Aufl., Köln 2013, S. 54–65, hier S. 54 f.
13 Vgl. Buesche, Albert: Eine neue Romantik. »Phantastische Figuration« im Haus am Waldsee, in: Der Tagesspiegel (Nr. 6252), 1966, S. 4.
14 Ebd.
15 Vgl. Grohmann, Will: Sieben Outsider werden Meister. »Phantastische Figuration« im »Haus am Waldsee« – Berlin, in: Frankfurter Allgemeine Zeitung, 20. April 1966. Den leider um die Seitenangabe gekürzten Zeitungsausschnitt erhielt Altenbourg von Horst Magold. Er hat sich im Nachlass erhalten.
16 Ebd.
17 Betrachtern und Betrachterinnen boten sich »Inhalte, (die) dem persönlichsten der Psyche des Künstlers entrissen« schienen, vgl. Tobben 2013 (wie Anm. 12), S. 54.
18 Vgl. Roditi, Edouard: Vorwort, in: Ausst.-Kat. Berlin 1966 (wie Anm. 8), o. S.
19 Ebd.
20 Janda 2004 (wie Anm. 11), S. 262, Nr. 50/66, *Ecce homo,* 1950, Kreide auf Papier auf Leinwand aufgezogen, 2810 x 1580 mm, Staatliche Museen zu Berlin, Preußischer Kunstbesitz (Inv.-Nr. FV 81), vgl. dazu Anm. 11.
21 Hans Bellmer war 1939 – ebenso wie Max Ernst – im Lager Les Milles interniert worden. Ferdinand Springer und Wols (i. e. Alfred Otto Wolfgang Schulze) ereilte dasselbe Schicksal. Trotz der menschenunwürdigen

Realismus, Phantastischen Realismus und Surrealismus seit 1945, exh. cat. Schloss Stein, Nuremberg (Nuremberg 1967), n.p., nos. 12–17, especially the lithograph *Ein Kinderspiel* (cat. 10), but here dated to 1955.
11 See Jutta Penndorf, "Ein Gehen der Wege, ein Schweben …", in Janda, *Monographie und Werkverzeichnis* (n. 2 above), vol. 2, pp. 26–31, here p. 31; Johannes Gachnang and Akademie der Künste (eds.), *Der gekrümmte Horizont. Kunst in Berlin 1945–1967*, exh. cat. Akademie der Künste, Berlin (Berlin, 1980), figs. on pp. 72–75, list on p. 114. *Ecce homo* (1950) was exhibited there; see Annegret Janda, *Gerhard Altenbourg. Monographie und Werkverzeichnis*, 3 vols. (Cologne: Wienand, 2004–10), vol. 1, 1937–1958, no. 50/66 (n. 20 below), as well as the drawing *Knabentorso* (Boy's Torso; 1956); *Das schweinische Lächeln* (The Swinish Smile; 1957); *Ach, diese Verstrickungen* (Oh These Entanglements; 1958).
12 See exh. cat. *Phantastische Figuration* (n. 8 above); Irene Tobben, "Das Haus wächst. Thomas Kempas Standortbestimmungen", in Katja Blomberg (ed.), *68 Jahre Haus am Waldsee, internationale Kunst in Berlin. Geschichte einer Institution*, 2nd ed. (Cologne, 2013), pp. 54–65, here pp. 54ff.
13 See Albert Buesche, "Eine neue Romantik. 'Phantastische Figuration' im Haus am Waldsee", *Tagesspiegel, no. 6252 (1966)*, p. 4.
14 Ibid.
15 See Will Grohmann, "Sieben Outsider werden Meister. 'Phantastische Figuration' im 'Haus am Waldsee' – Berlin", *Frankfurter Allgemeine Zeitung* (20 April 1966). The newspaper clipping, missing the page numbers, was given to Altenbourg by Horst Magold. It is preserved in the Altenbourg estate.
16 Ibid.
17 Observers found "content that seemed torn from the most personal part of the artist's psyche", see Tobben, "Das Haus wächst" (n. 12 above), p. 54.
18 See Edouard Roditi, "Vorwort", in exh. cat. *Phantastische Figuration* (n. 8 above), n.p.
19 Ibid.
20 Janda, *Monographie und Werkverzeichnis* (n. 11 above), vol. 1, p. 262, no. 50/66, *Ecce homo* (1950), chalk on paper mounted on canvas, 2810 × 1580 mm, Staatliche Museen zu Berlin, Preußischer Kunstbesitz (inv. no. FV 81); on this, see n. 11 above.
21 In 1939 Hans Bellmer was, just like Max Ernst, interned in the Les Milles prison camp. Ferdinand Springer and Wols (that is, Alfred Otto Wolfgang Schulze) met the same fate. Despite the inhuman conditions, they continued to practice art. See Juliette Laffon, "Quatre artistes au camp des Milles", in Fondation du Camp des Milles – mémoire et éducation (ed.), *Hans Bellmer, Max Ernst, Ferdinand Springer, Wols – au camp des Milles*, exh. cat. Camp des Milles (Paris, 2013), pp. 21–24.
22 See the list in exh. cat. *Phantastische Figuration* (n. 8 above): Gerhard Altenbourg, *Dahinter der Hund* (The Dog Behind; 1952); *Im Fenster* (In the Window; 1952); *Auch einer* (Also One; 1954); *Meiner Großmutter ihr Geburtstagsgeschenk* (For My Grandmother Her Birthday Gift; 1954); *Der Gärtner* (The Gardener; 1954); *Der Mann und vier Frauen* (The Man and Four Women; 1955); *Hart auf Hart* (Hard; 1956); *Seine Mission?* (His Mission?; 1956); *Kleiner Grenzverkehr* (Little Border Traffic; 1956); *Geselle* (Journeyman; 1956); *Ach, diese Tiere in uns* (Oh, These Animals in Us; 1956); *Phallus, Dunkel; Eva!* (Phallus, Darkness; Eva!; 1957); *Heiratsannonce: Dame Mitte dreißig* (Marriage Announcement: Woman Mid-Thirties; 1957); *Karussell – Zigarre* (Carrousel – Cigar; 1958);

Umstände waren sie weiterhin künstlerisch tätig. Vgl. Laffon, Juliette: Quatre artistes au camp des Milles, in: Fondation du Camp des Milles – mémoire et éducation (Hrsg.): Hans Bellmer, Max Ernst, Ferdinand Springer, Wols – au camp des Milles, Ausst.-Kat. Camp des Milles, Paris 2013, S. 21–24.
22 Vgl. die Auflistung in: Ausst.-Kat. Berlin 1966 (wie Anm. 8): Gerhard Altenbourg, *Dahinter der Hund*, 1952; *Im Fenster*, 1952; *Auch einer*, 1954; *Meiner Großmutter ihr Geburtstagsgeschenk*, 1954; *Der Gärtner*, 1954; *Der Mann und vier Frauen*, 1955; *Hart auf Hart*, 1956; *Seine Mission?*, 1956; *Kleiner Grenzverkehr*, 1956; *Geselle*, 1956; *Ach, diese Tiere in uns*, 1956; *Phallus, Dunkel; Eva!*, 1957; *Heiratsannonce: Dame Mitte dreißig*, 1957; *Karussell – Zigarre*, 1958; *GING GANZ*, 1958.
23 Gerhard Altenbourg, *Ecce homo*, 1949, Kreidezeichnung auf Packpapier, 2042,1 x 1220 mm (damals mit Provenienz: Galerie Springer), Kolumba, Erzbischöfliches Diözesanmuseum Köln (erworben 1995). Vgl. Janda 2004 (wie Anm. 11), S. 247, Nr. 49/141. Das monumentale Blatt wurde in der Abteilung »20. Jahrhundert« u. a. zusammen mit Werken von Georg Baselitz, Hans Bellmer, Giorgio de Chirico, Salvador Dalí, Ernst Fuchs, René Magritte und Arnulf Rainer ausgestellt.
24 Vgl. Santarcangeli, Paolo: Il Libro dei Labirinti, Florenz 1967.
25 Vgl. Premio Marzotto (…). La pittura figurativa in Europa (…), Valdagno 1968, S. 33–35, Kat. 6. Altenbourg hatte folgende Zeichnungen eingereicht: *Wie es um den grossen Pilzgott lebendig ist*, 1966; *Laban auf den Spuren der Erinnerung*, 1967; *Der grinsende Cäsar, die kleine Knolle*, 1967; *Variatio delectat*, 1968 (Kat. 34); Spiel auf zweierlei Ebenen (Kat. 33). Vgl. Janda 2007 (wie Anm. 2), S. 202–211, Nrn. 66/42, 67/17, 67/25, 68/1. Der Preis wurde Altenbourg nicht verliehen.
26 Vgl. Kästner 1992 (wie Anm. 1), S. 45–47.
27 Vgl. ebd.
28 Vgl. Lang, Lothar (Last, Ludwig): Ironie bei Altenbourg, in: Brusberg, Dieter (Hrsg.): Gerhard Altenbourg. Werk-Verzeichnis 1947–1969, unter Mitarbeit von Annegret Janda, zugl. Ausst.-Kat. Berlin / Baden-Baden / Hannover / Düsseldorf, Hannover 1969, S. 15 f., hier S. 15.
29 Vgl. Lang, Lothar: Annotation zum Holzschnitt-Werk von Gerhard Altenbourg, in: Museum und Kunstsammlung Schloss Hinterglauchau/ (Ullmann, Günter) (Hrsg.): Gerhard Altenbourg: Holzschnitte. (…), Ausst.-Kat. Museum und Kunstsammlung Schloss Hinterglauchau, Glauchau 1976. Lothar Lang übersandte das Manuskript des Textes als Anlage zu seinem Brief an Gerhard Altenbourg vom 21. März 1976; vgl. (Altenbourg, Gerhard/Lang, Lothar:) Gerhard Altenbourg / Lothar Lang – Briefwechsel 1965–1988, bearb. u. komm. v. Katrin Roth, hrsg. von Christa Grimm, Leipzig 2008, S. 179–188.
30 Vgl. Barbarino, Christin: Das Buchkunstwerk von Gerhard Altenbourg, Berlin 2018, S. 212–270.
31 Vgl. Blume, Dieter: Ein Engel im Atelier. Zu Gast bei Gerhard Altenbourg, hrsg. v. Roland Krischke, Göttingen 2021, S.14.
32 Vgl. Janda, Annegret: Gerhard Altenbourg. Monographie und Werkverzeichnis, 3 Bde., Bd. 3, 1977–1989, Köln 2010, S. 315. Anhand von Notizen Altenbourgs von Janda rekonstruierte Titel hat sie durch eckige Klammern markiert. Diese konstruierten Titel geben wir im Verzeichnis der ausgestellten Werke durch die Angabe »O. T.« an, setzen ihre Titel aber in eckigen Klammern dazu.
33 Lang, Lothar: Ein Souverän der Graphik – Gedanken zu einem bedeutenden Werk, unveröff. Typoskript (Schenkung von Elke Lang, 2023).
34 Vgl. Hofmann, Werner: Phantasiestücke. Über das Phantastische in der Kunst, München 2010, S. 284.

GING GANZ (WENT COMPLETELY; 1958).
23 Gerhard Altenbourg, *Ecce homo*, 1949, drawing, chalk on packing paper, 2042.1 × 1220 mm (then belonging to Galerie Springer), Kolumba, Erzbischöfliches Diözesanmuseum Köln (purchased in 1995). See Janda, *Monographie und Werkverzeichnis* (n. 11 above), vol. 1, p. 247, no. 49/141. The monumental work was exhibited in the "20th century" section together with works by Georg Baselitz, Hans Bellmer, Giorgio de Chirico, Salvador Dalí, Ernst Fuchs, René Magritte and Arnulf Rainer, among others.
24 See Paolo Santarcangeli, *Il Libro dei Labirinti* (Florence: I Libri Illustrati, 1967).
25 See *Premio Marzotto (…). La pittura figurativa in Europa (…)* (Valdagno, 1968), pp. 33–35, cat. 6. Altenbourg submitted the following drawings: *Wie es um den grossen Pilzgott lebendig ist* (How the Great Mushroom God Lives On; 1966); *Laban auf den Spuren der Erinnerung* (Laban in the Footsteps of Memory; 1967); *Der grinsende Cäsar, die kleine Knolle* (The Grinning Caesar, the Little Bulb; 1967); *Variatio delectat* (1968; cat. 34); *Spiel auf zweierlei Ebenen* (Game on Two Levels; cat. 33). See Janda, *Monographie und Werkverzeichnis* (n. 2 above), vol. 2, pp. 202–11, nos. 66/42, 67/17, 67/25, 68/1. Altenbourg did not win the prize.
26 See Kästner, "Für Altenbourg" (n. 1 above), pp. 45–47.
27 Ibid.
28 See Lothar Lang (Ludwig Last), "Ironie bei Altenbourg", in Dieter Brusberg (ed.), *Gerhard Altenbourg. Werk-Verzeichnis 1947–1969, unter Mitarbeit von Annegret Janda*, exh. cat. Berlin / Baden-Baden / Hanover / Düsseldorf (Hanover, 1969), pp. 15ff., here p. 15.
29 See Lothar Lang (Ludwig Last), "Annotation zum Holzschnitt-Werk von Gerhard Altenbourg", in Museum und Kunstsammlung Schloss Hinterglauchau / Günter Ullmann (eds.), *Gerhard Altenbourg Holzschnitte. (…)*, exh. cat. Museum und Kunstsammlung Schloss Hinterglauchau (Glauchau, 1976). Lothar Lang sent the manuscript of his article enclosed with a letter to Gerhard Altenbourg on 21 March 1976; see Gerhard Altenbourg and Lothar Lang, *Gerhard Altenbourg / Lothar Lang – Briefwechsel 1965–1988*, transcribed and commented by Katrin Roth, ed. by Christa Grimm (Leipzig: Lehmstedt, 2008), pp. 179–88.
30 See Christin Barbarino, *Das Buchkunstwerk von Gerhard Altenbourg* (Berlin: Bachmann, 2018), pp. 212–70.
31 See Dieter Blume, *Ein Engel im Atelier. Zu Gast bei Gerhard Altenbourg*, ed. Roland Krischke (Göttingen: Wallstein, 2021), p. 14.
32 See Janda, *Monographie und Werkverzeichnis* (n. 2 above), vol. 3, p. 315. Drawing on Altenbourg's notes, Janda reconstructed the titles of artworks and listed these in square brackets. In the "List of Illustrated Works" in this volume, her reconstructed titles are listed in parentheses after the label "Untitled".
33 Lothar Lang, "Ein Souverän der Graphik – Gedanken zu einem bedeutenden Werk", unpublished typescript, gift of Elke Lang, 2023.
34 See Werner Hofmann, *Phantasiestücke. Über das Phantastische in der Kunst* (Munich: Hirmer, 2010), p. 284.

1 *Ecce homo I (Sterbender Krieger)*, 1949 | *Ecce homo I (Dying Warrior)*, 1949

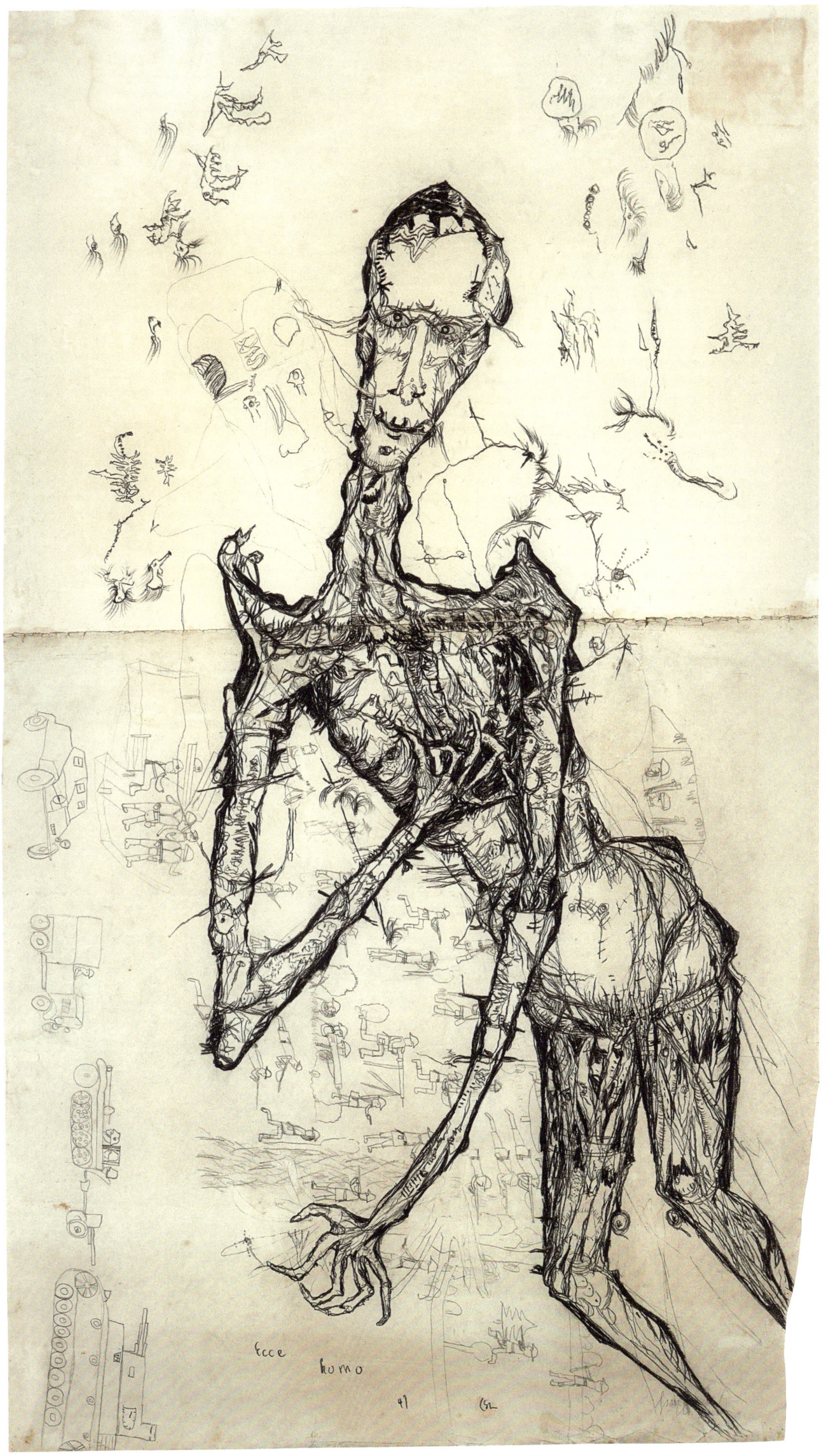
Ecce
homo
41

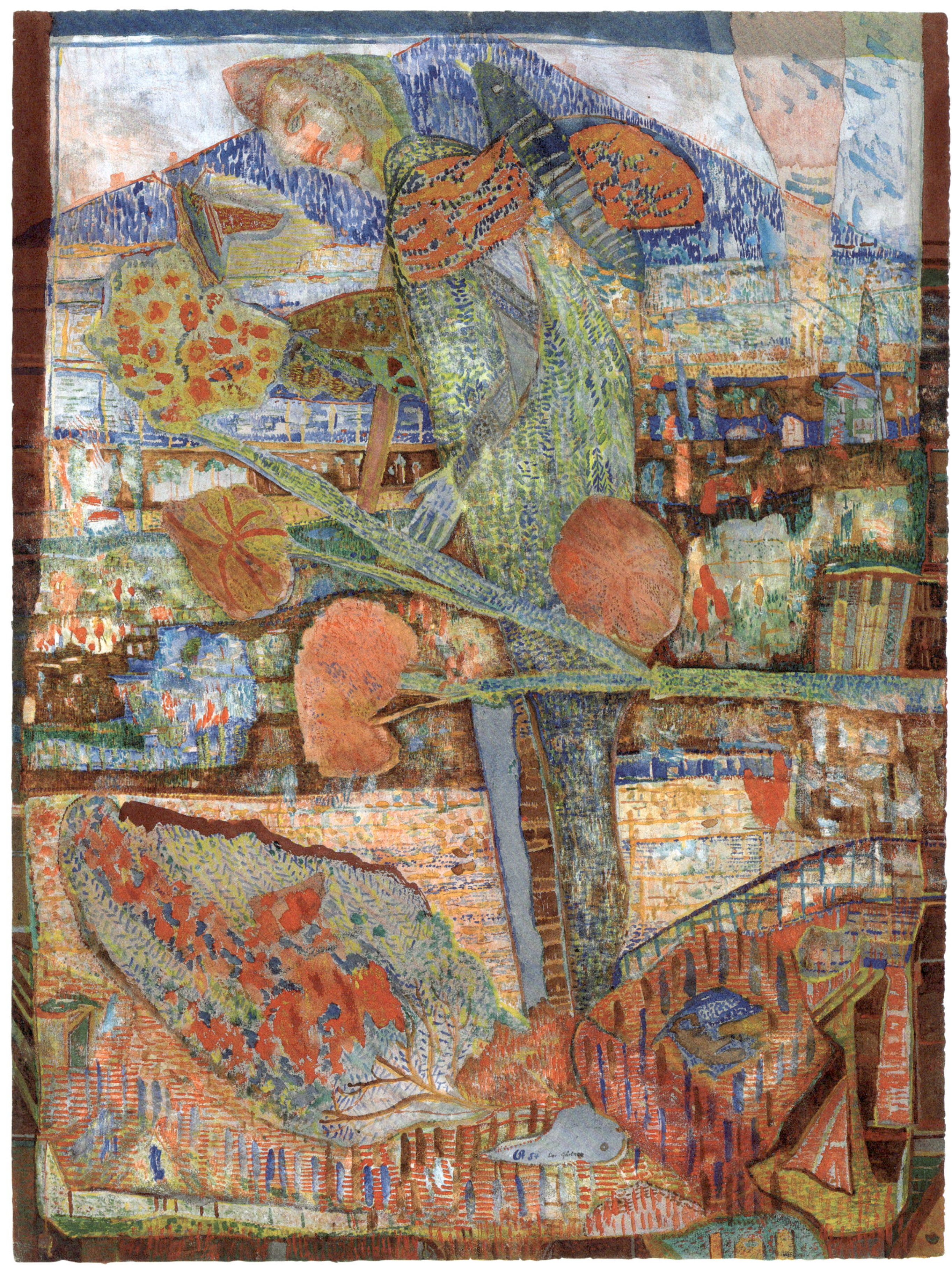

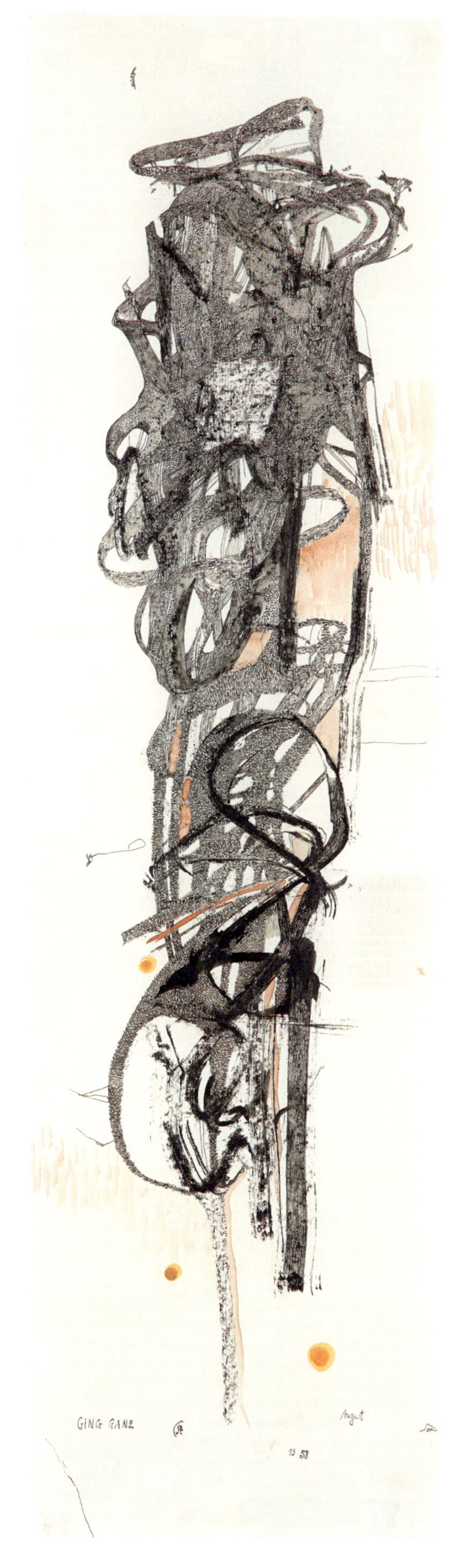

2 *Der Gärtner*, 1954 |
The Gardener, 1954

3 *GING GANZ*, 1958 |
WENT COMPLETELY, 1958

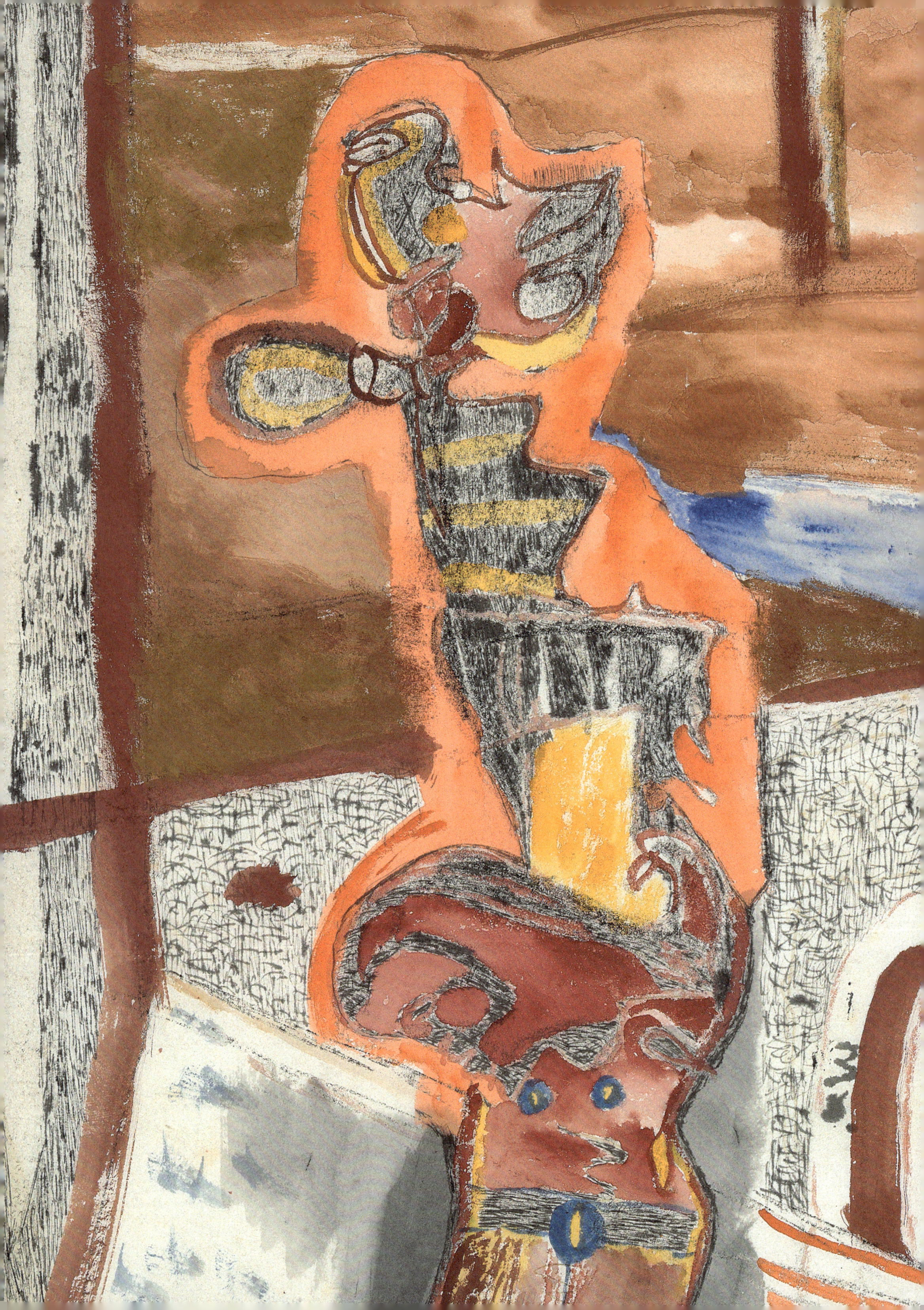

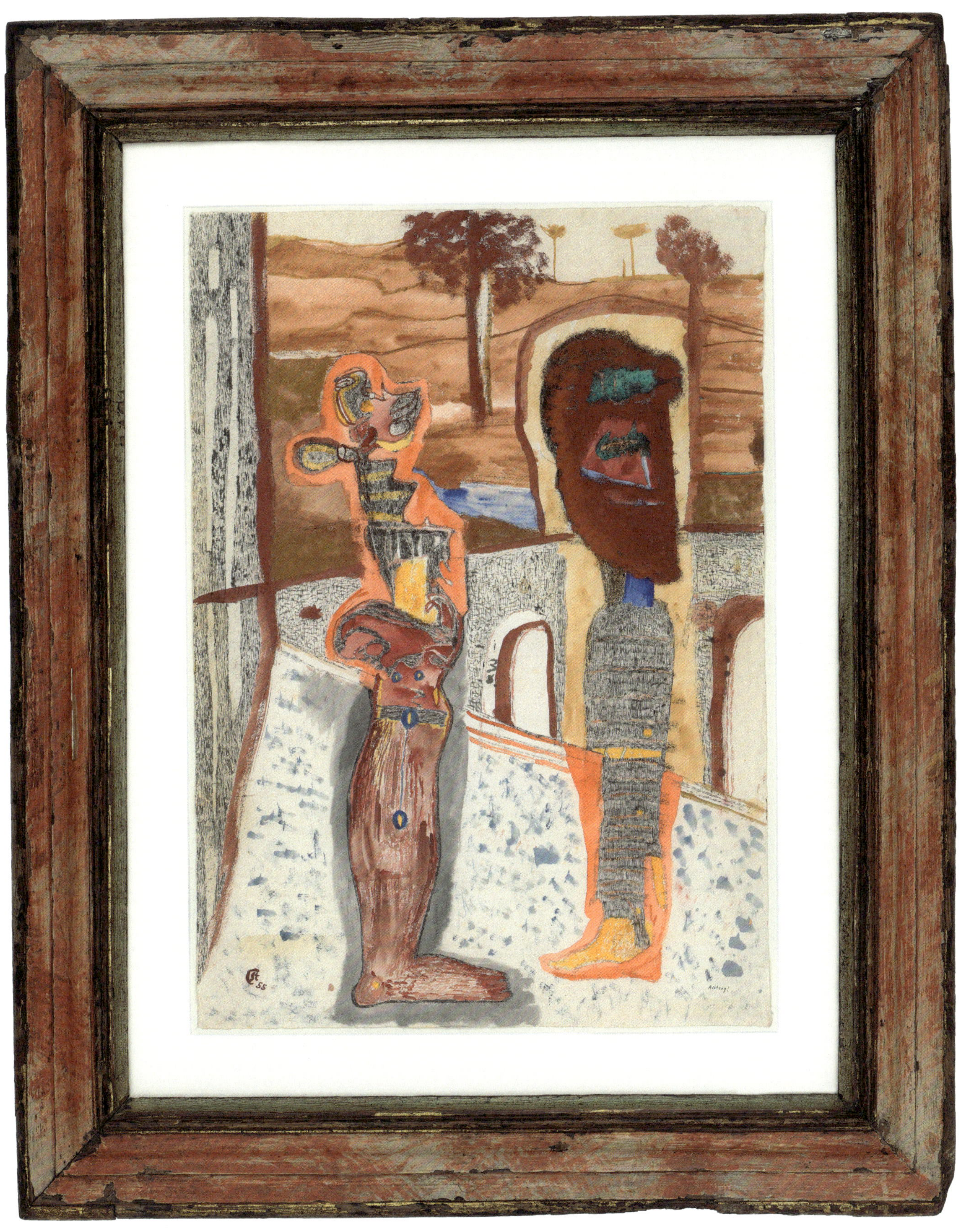

4 *Achtung!*, 1955 | *Attention!*, 1955

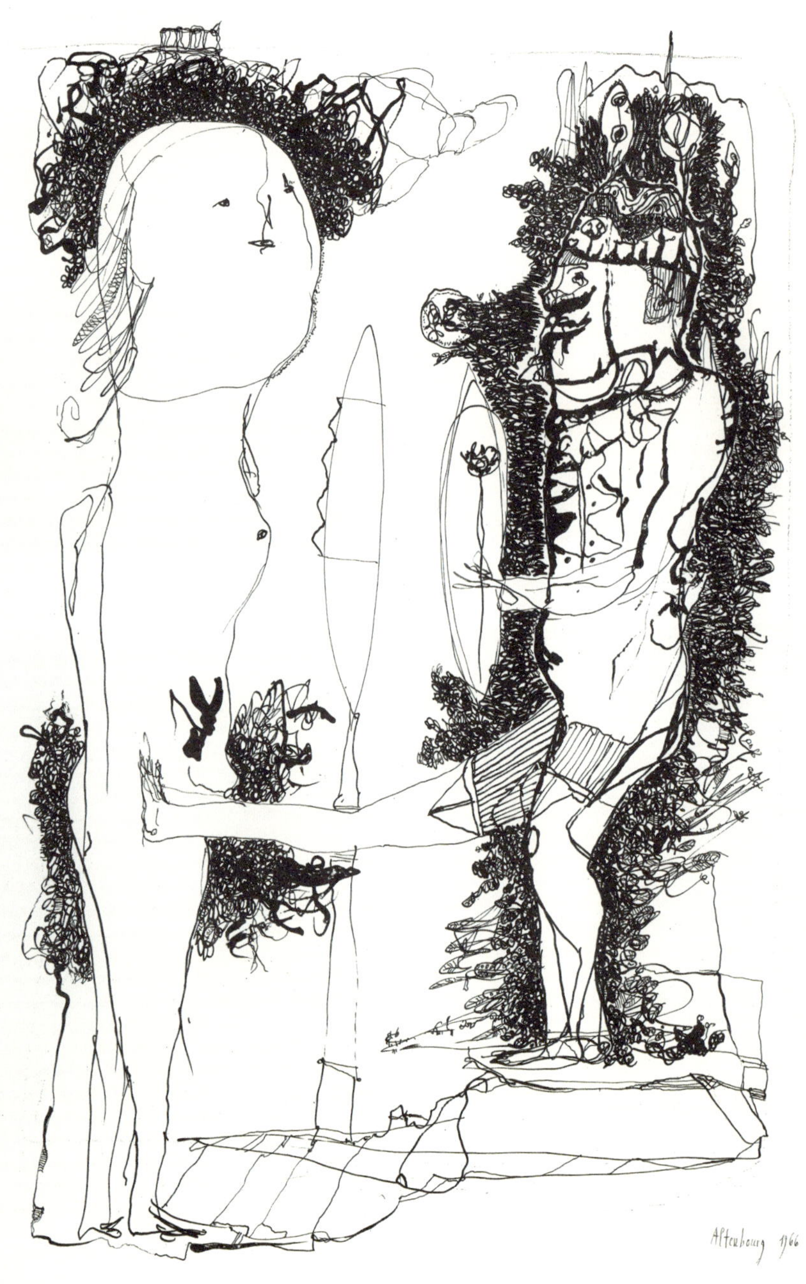

5 *Ein Kinderspiel*, 1966 |
A Child's Game, 1966

6 *Verständigung der Auguren über ein Geschick*, 1969 | *Agreement Among the Augurs About a Fate*, 1969

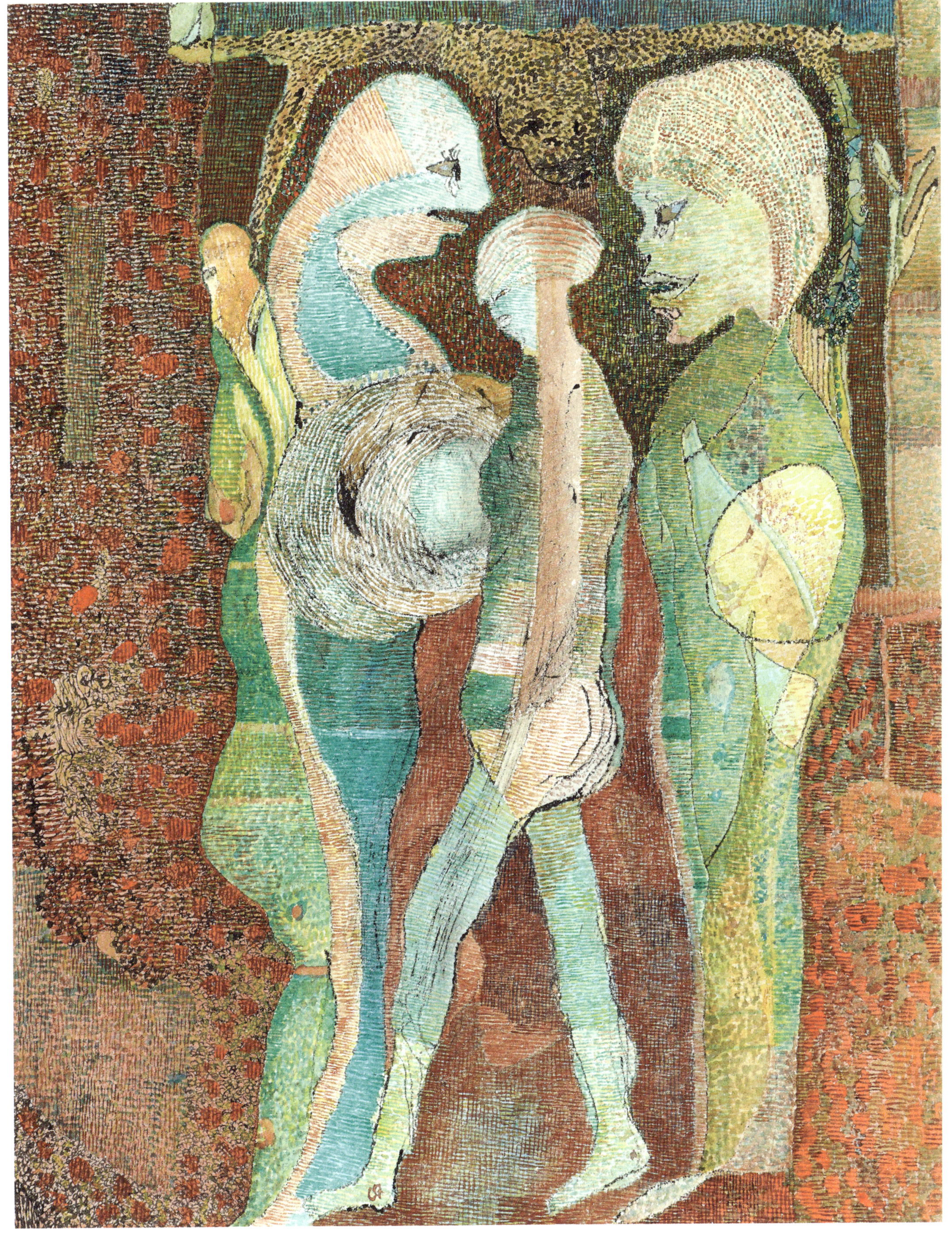

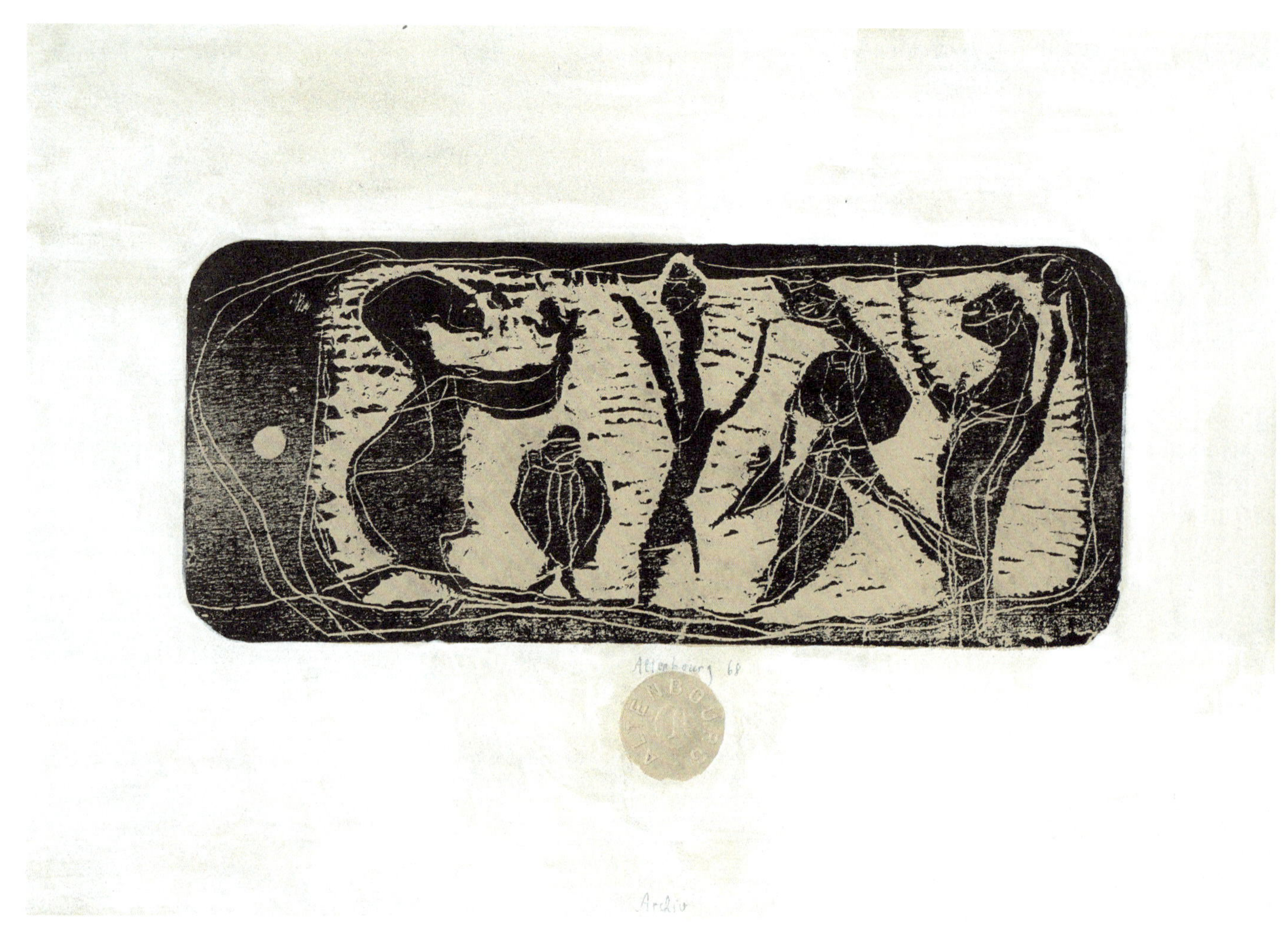

7 *Echse mit Blumenstrauß, der kleine Werner, Ungeheuer mit Regenschirm und Applaudierende*, 1968 | *Lizard with Bouquet of Flowers, Little Werner, Monster with Umbrella and Applauding Figures*, 1968

8 *Kwanon mit dem Wiesenblick*, 1973 | *Kwanon with Meadow-Gaze*, 1973

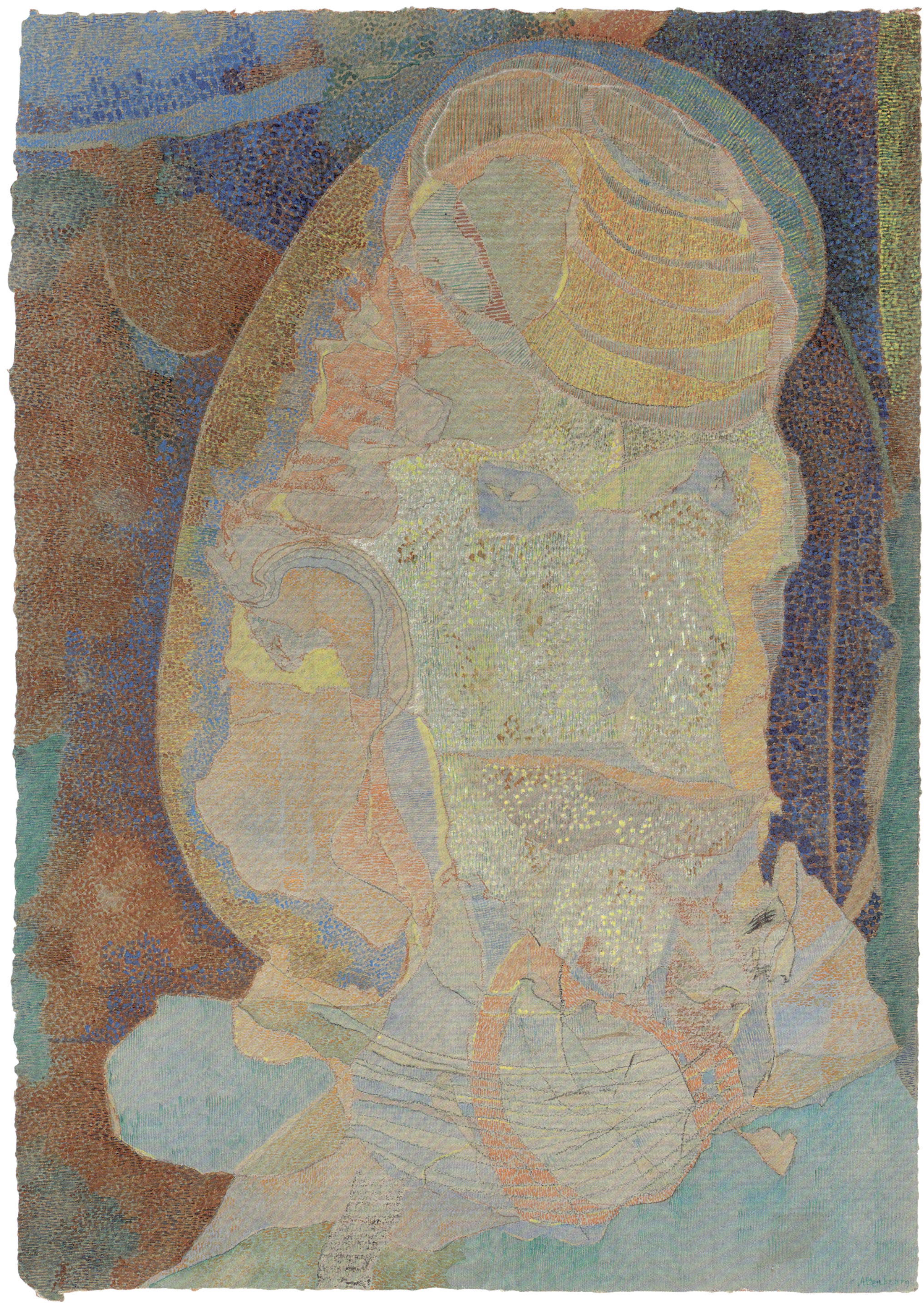

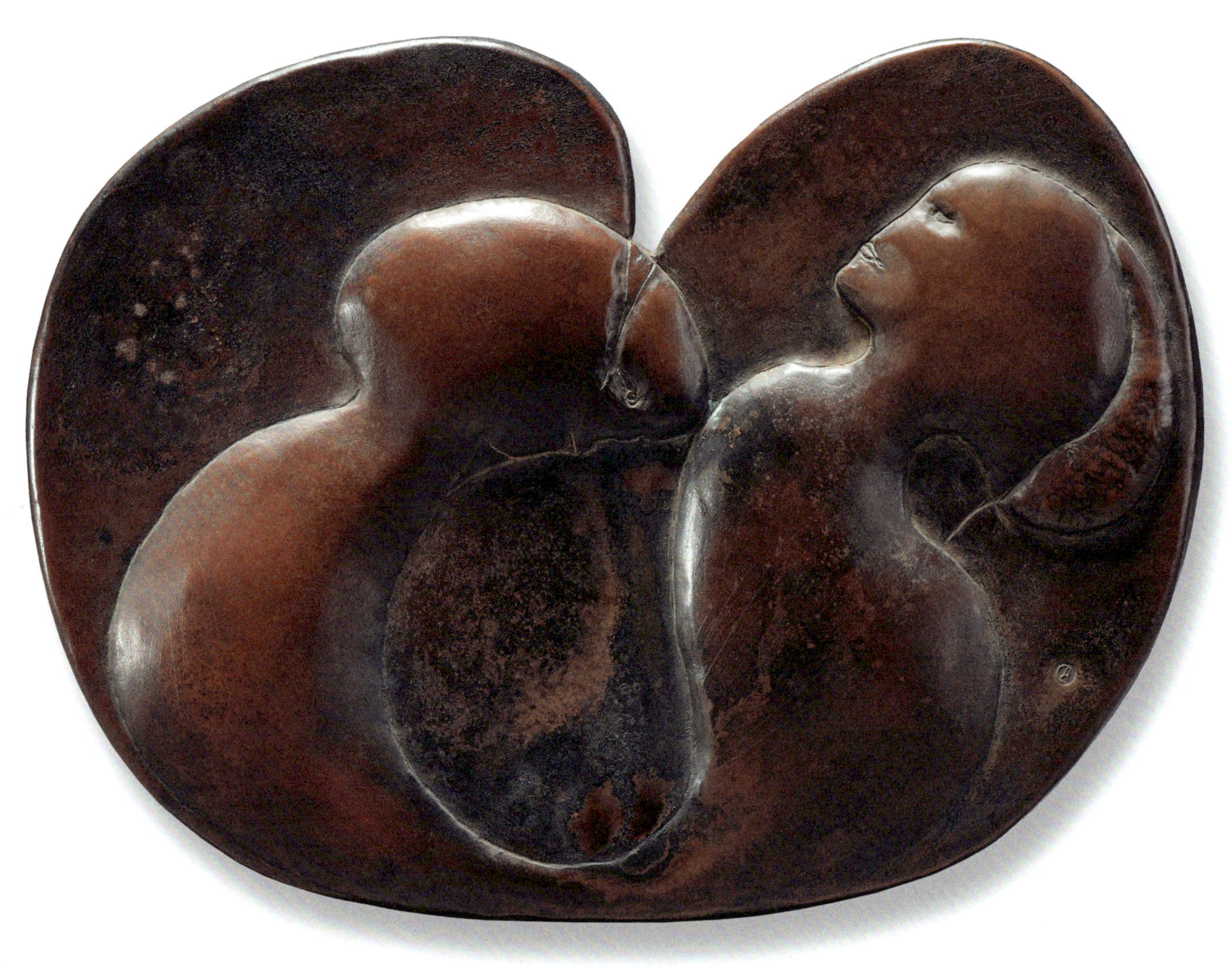

9 *Einung*, 1978 | *Union*, 1978

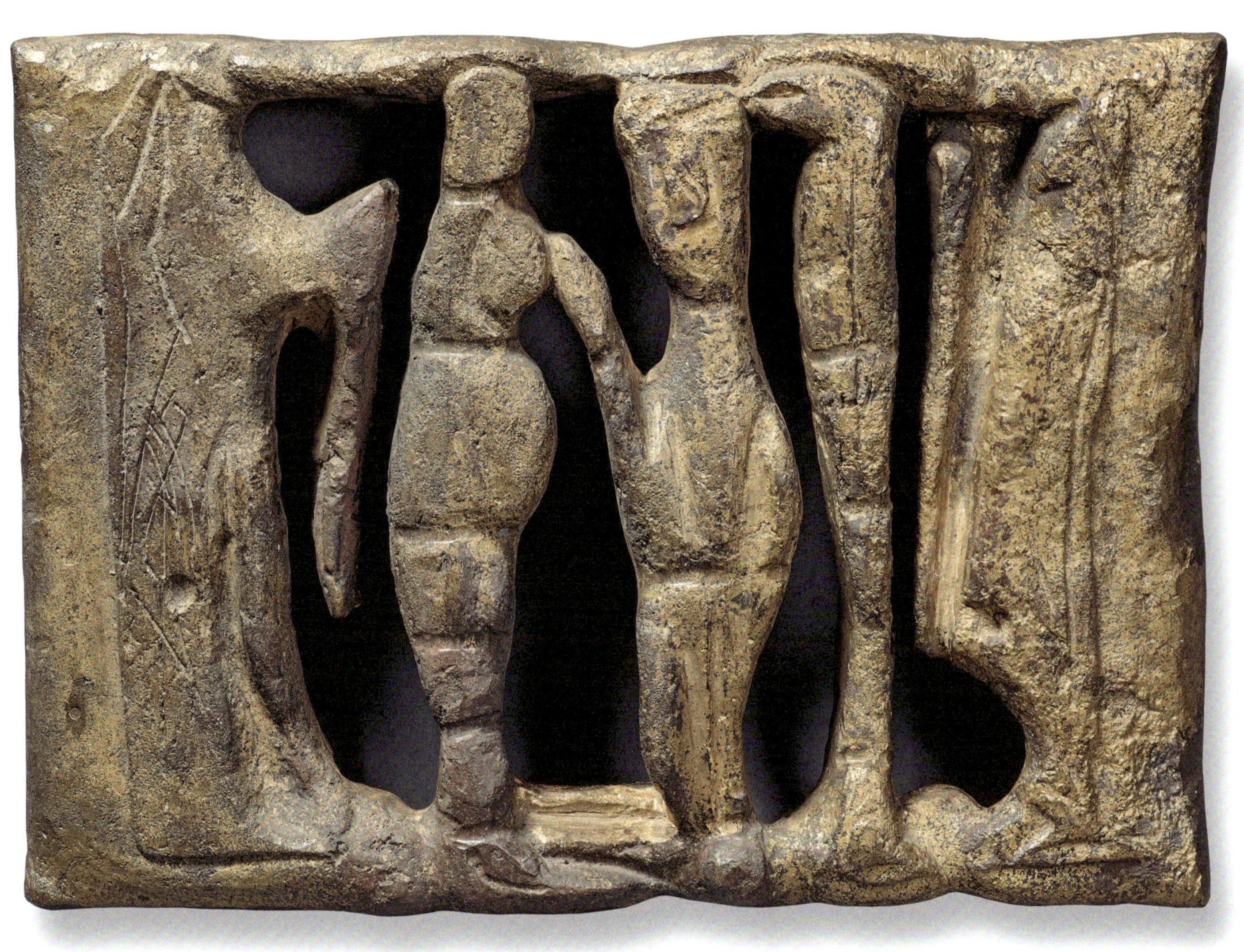

10 *Figuren*, 1983 | *Figures*, 1983

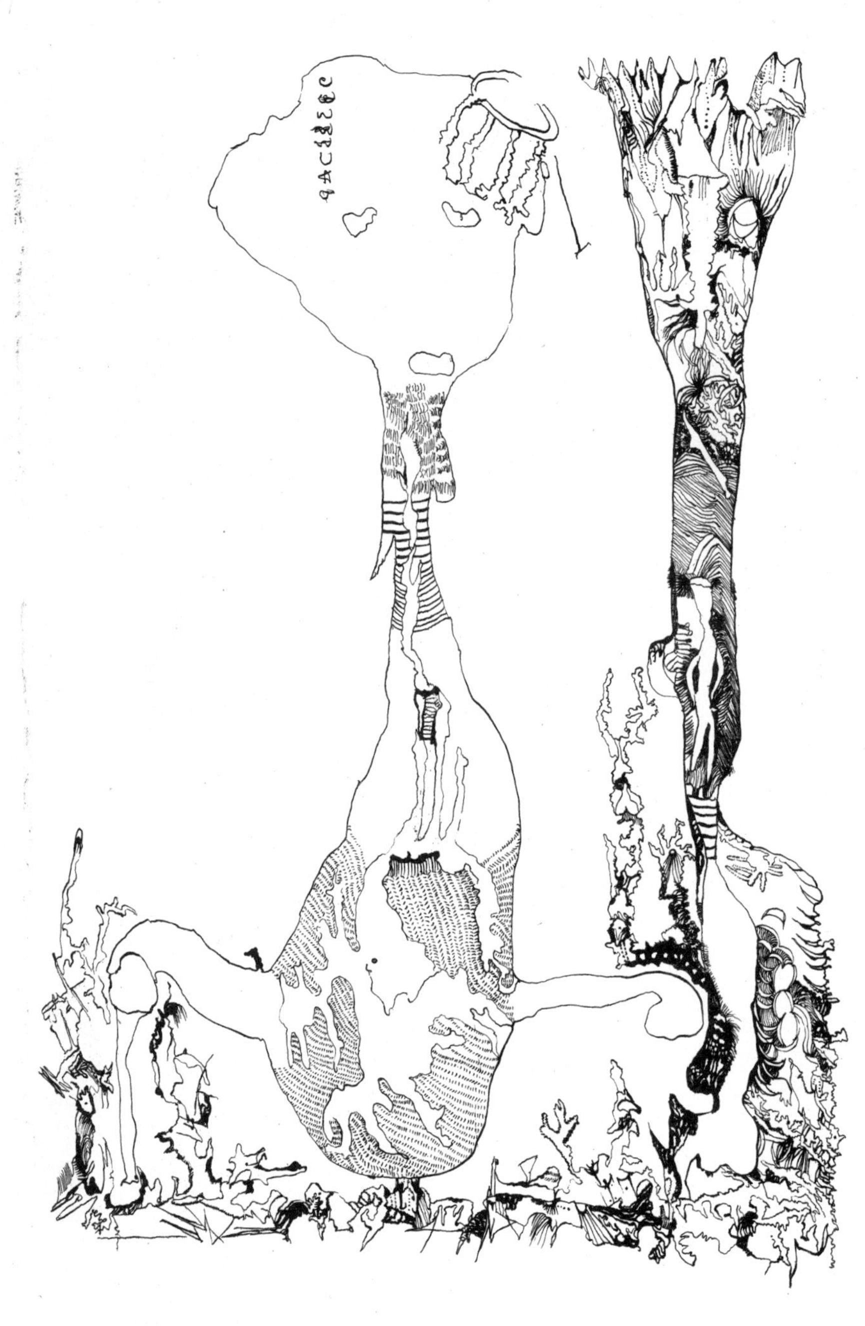

11 *nympha*, 1949

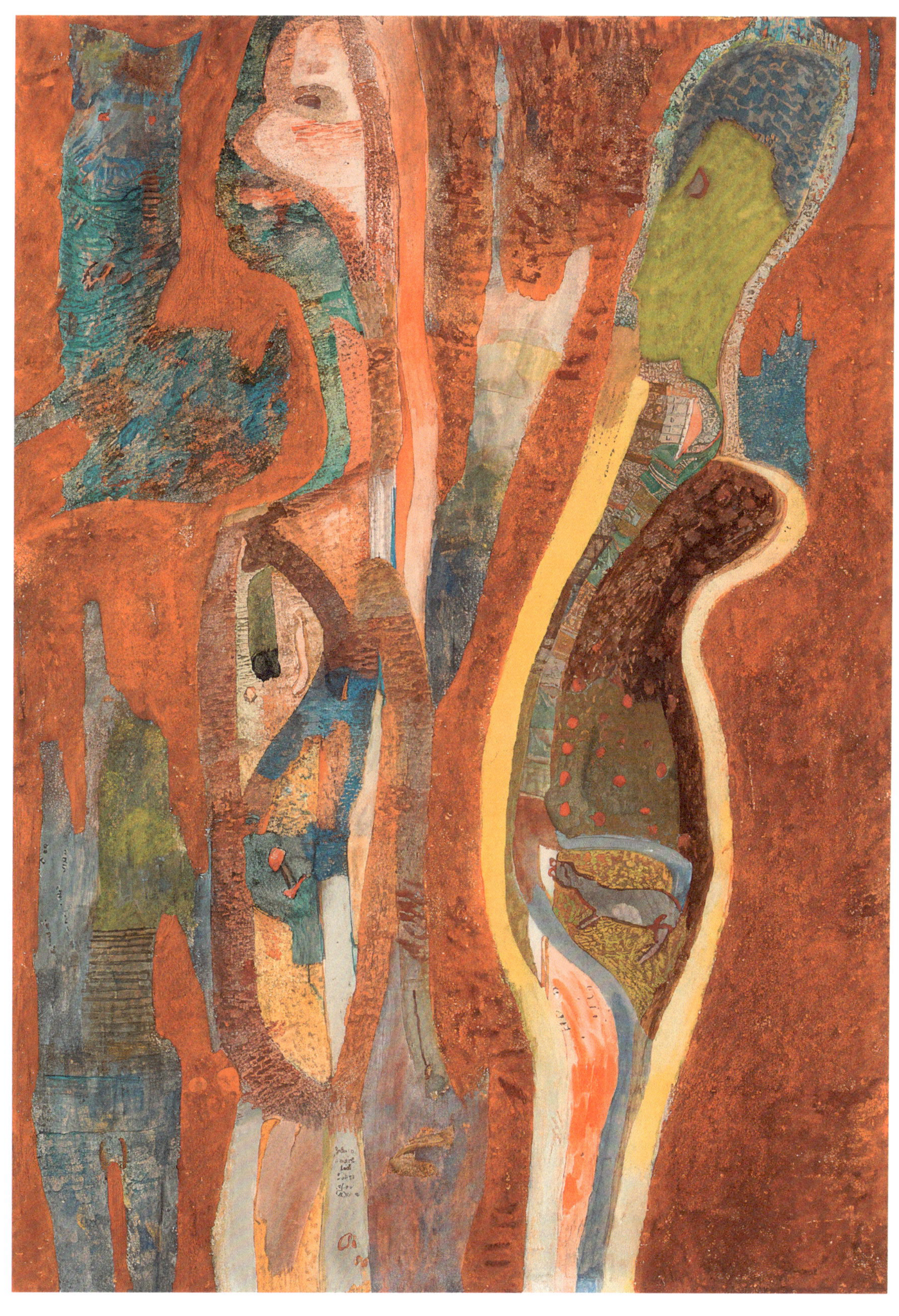

12 *Johanna wendet sich lieber ihrem Kater zu*, 1956 | *Johanna Prefers to Turn to Her Cat*, 1956

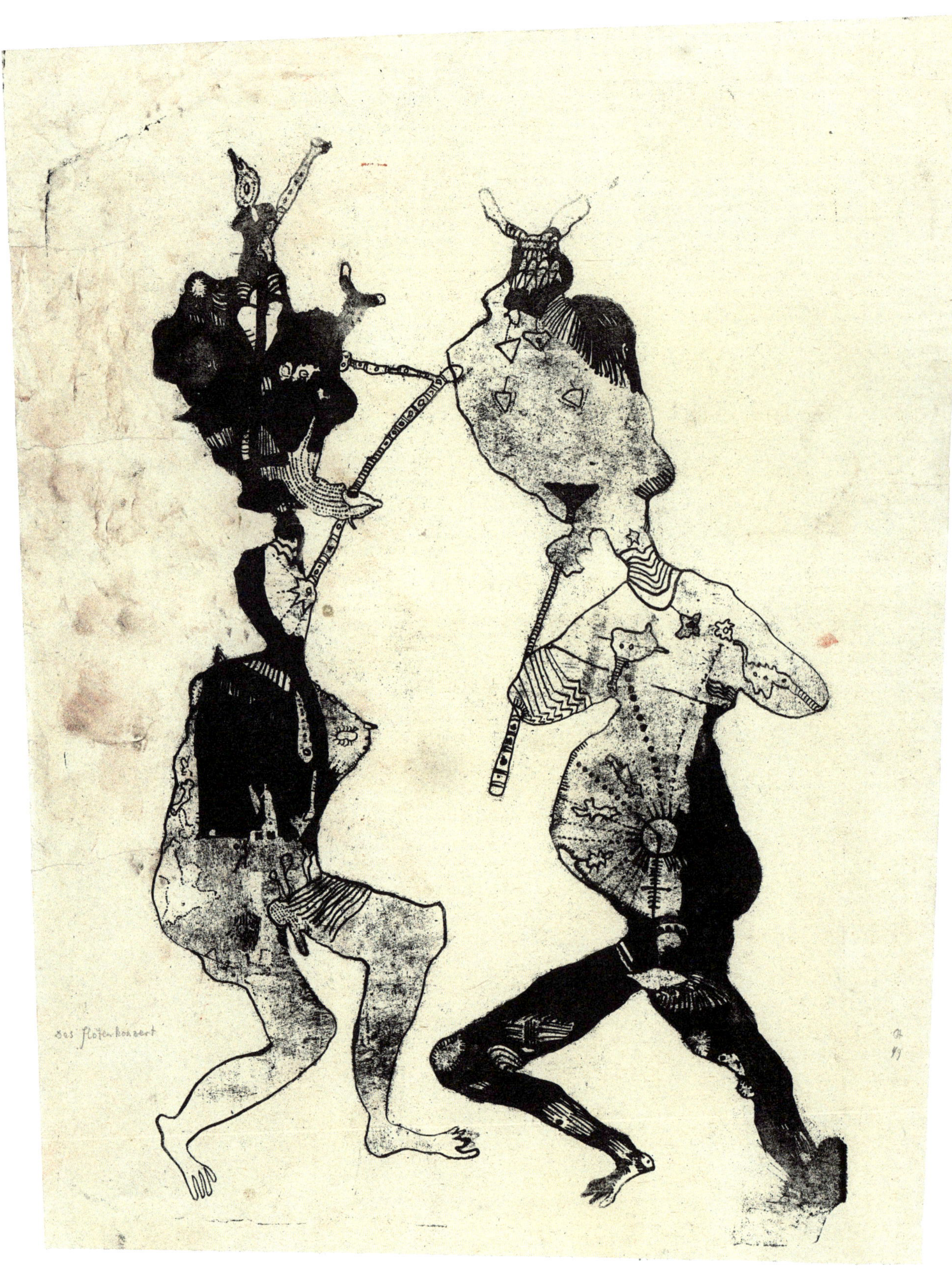

13 *Das Flötenkonzert*, 1949 |
The Flute Concert, 1949

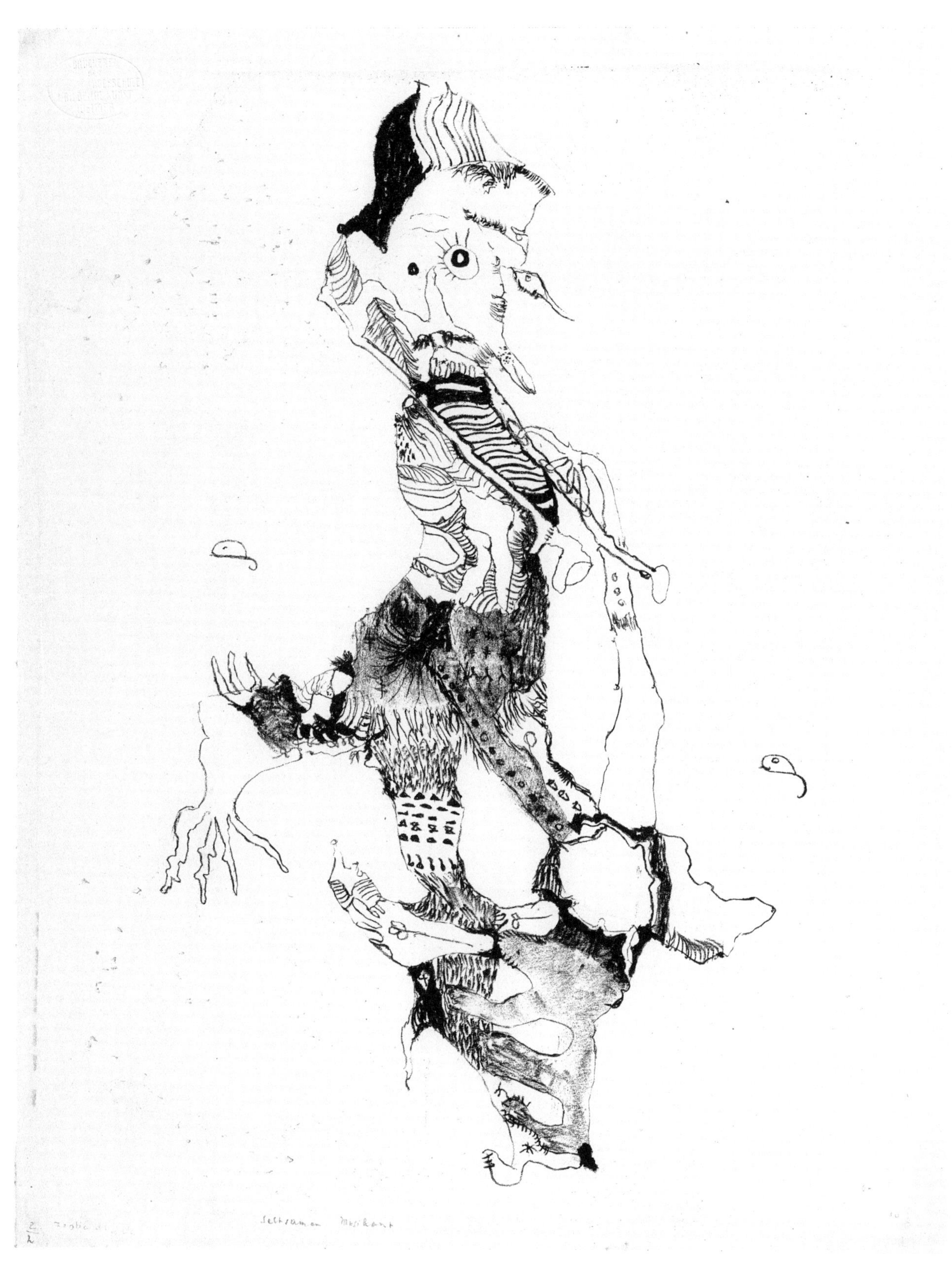

14 *Seltsamer Musikant*, 1950 |
Strange Musician, 1950

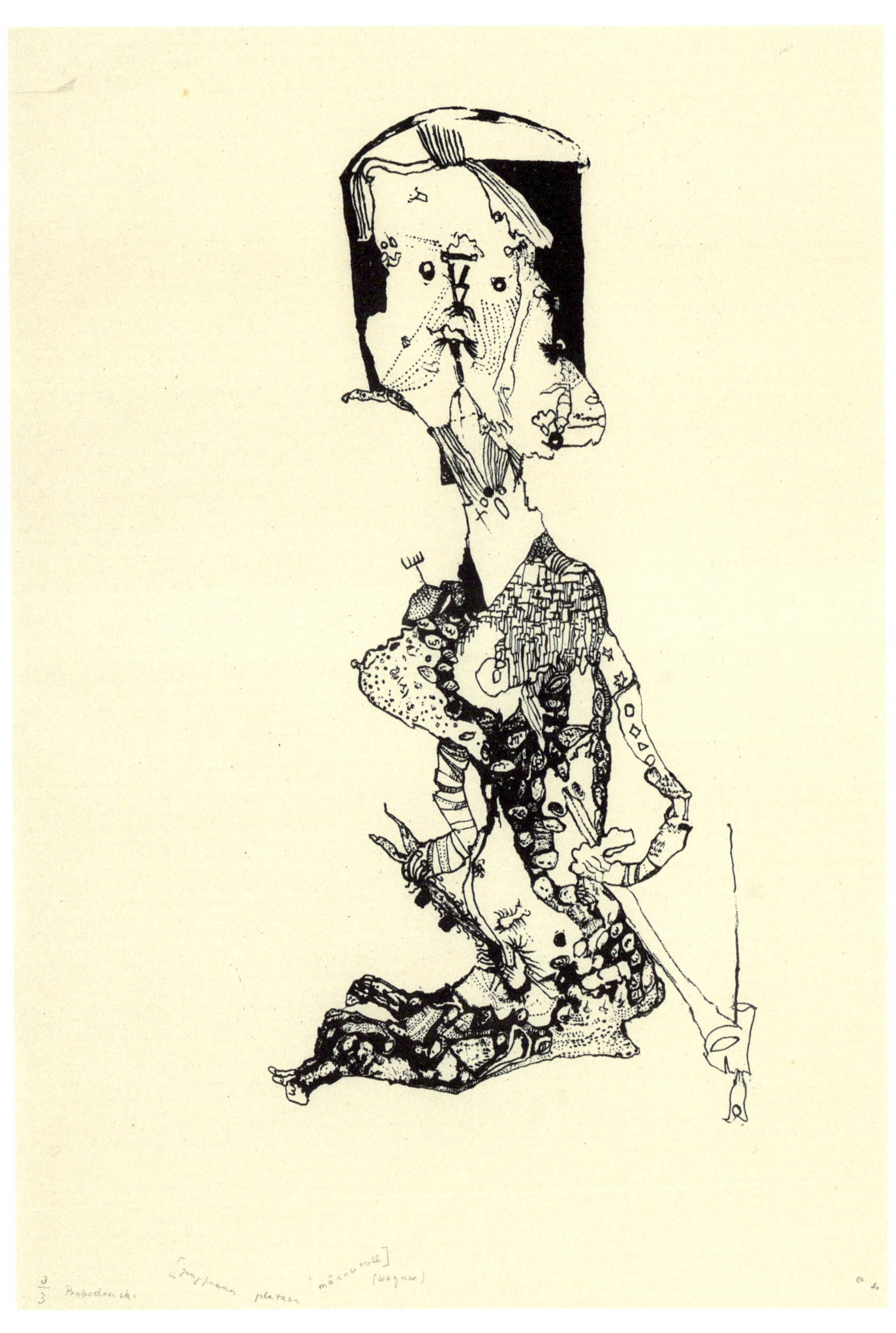

15 *Jungfrauen platzen männertoll (Wagner)*, 1950 | *Maidens Burst Man-Mad (Wagner)*, 1950

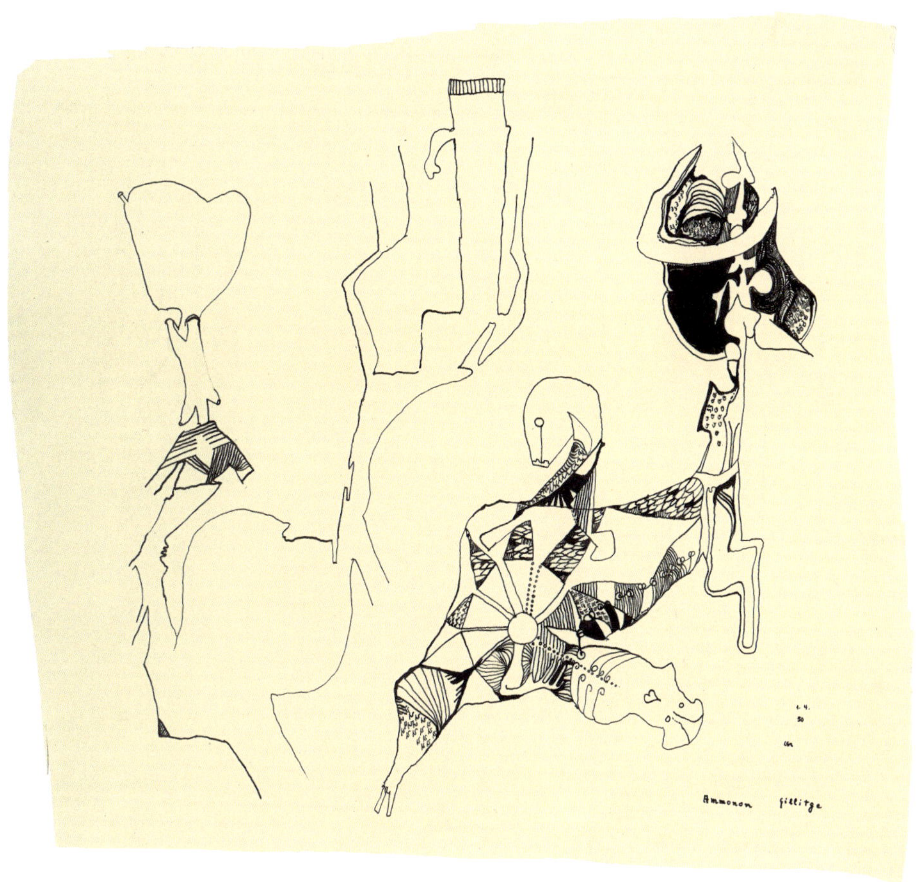

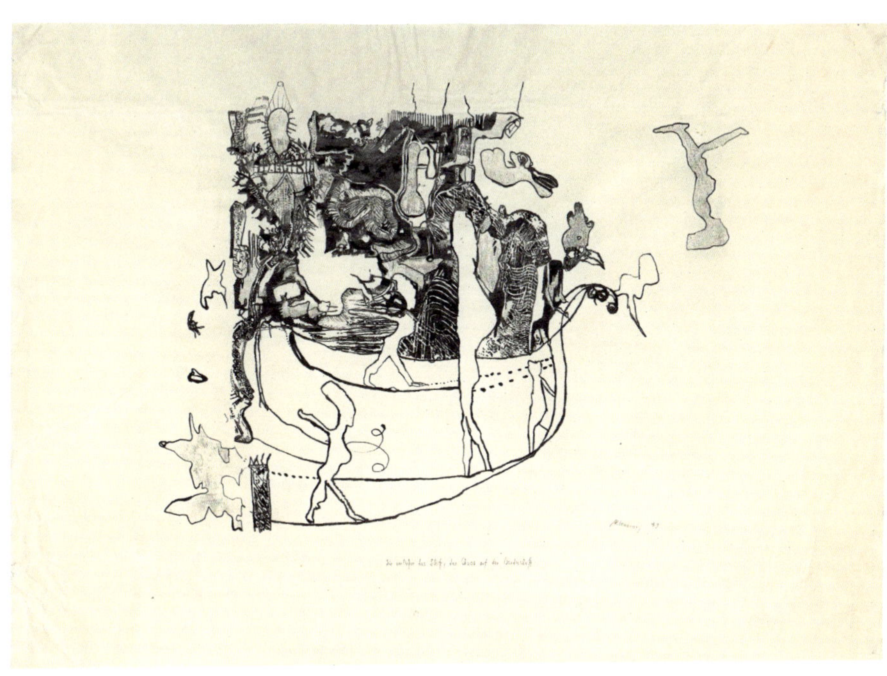

16 *Ammonon Gillitge*, 1949

17 *Sie verließen das Schiff; Chaos auf der Wanderschaft*, 1949 | *They Left the Ship; Chaos on the Wanderings*, 1949

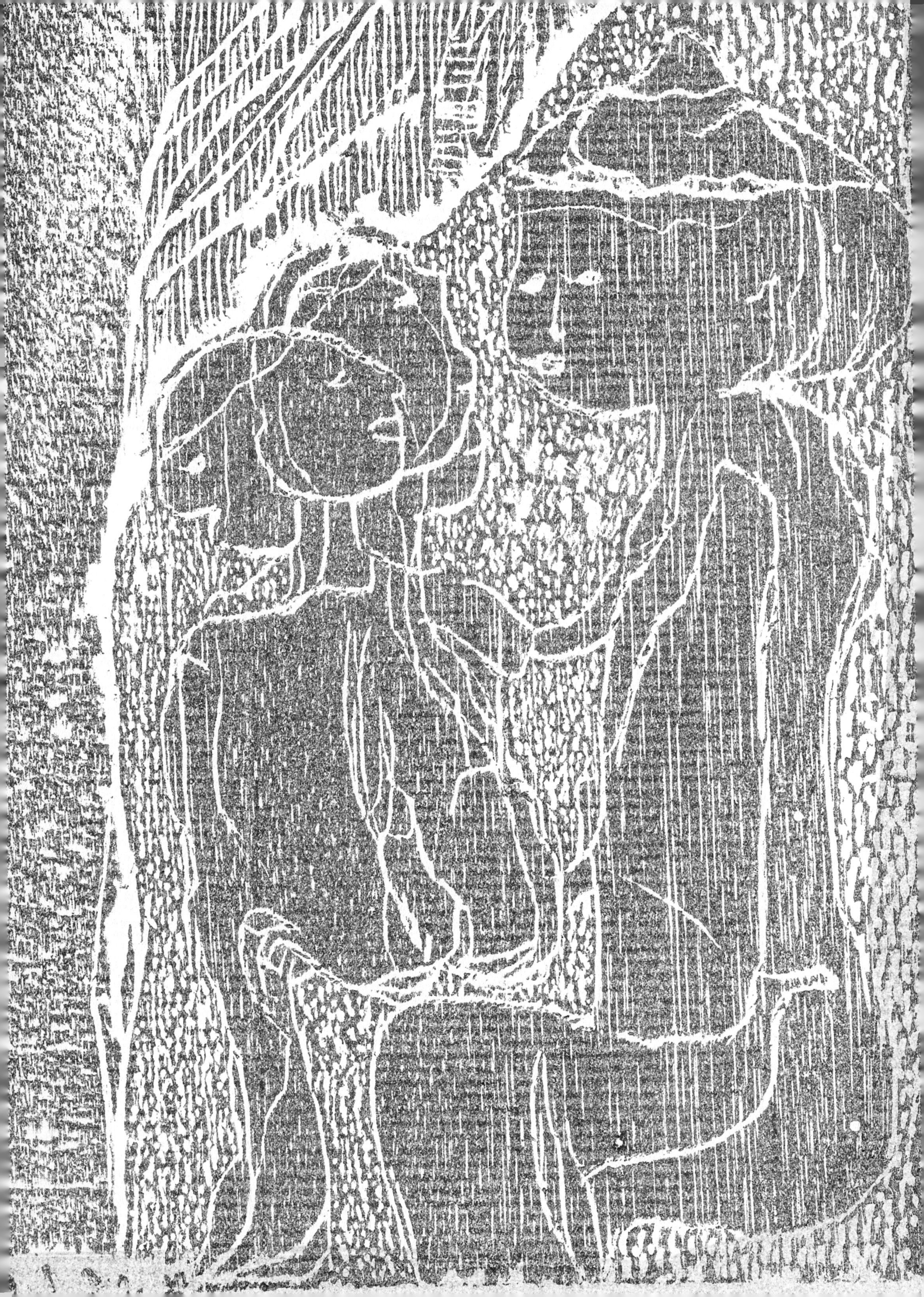

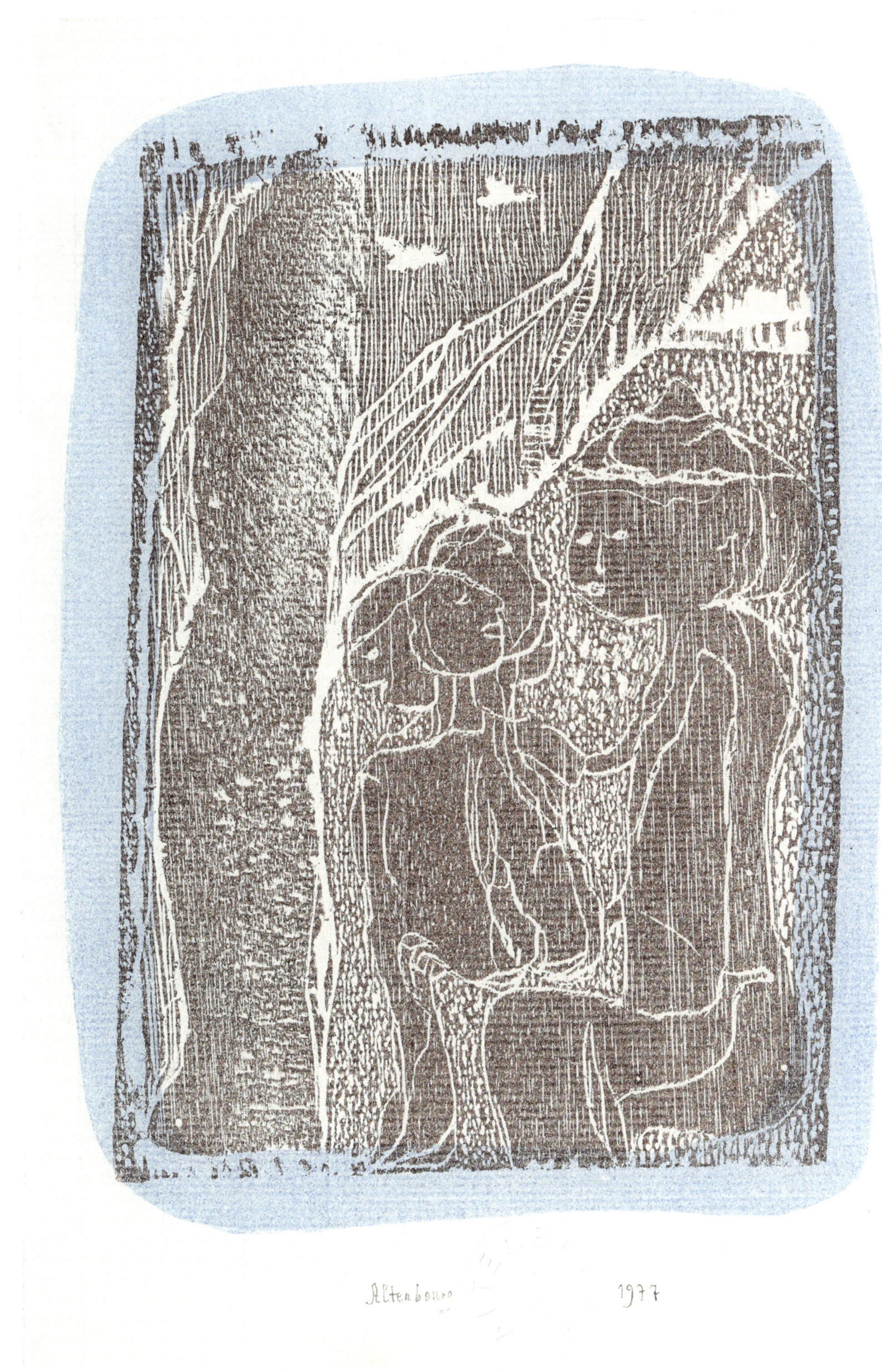

18 *Da sitzen sie in ihrer Frühlingsfrühe die Gedanken*, 1977 | *The Thoughts, They Sit There in Their Spring Morning*, 1977

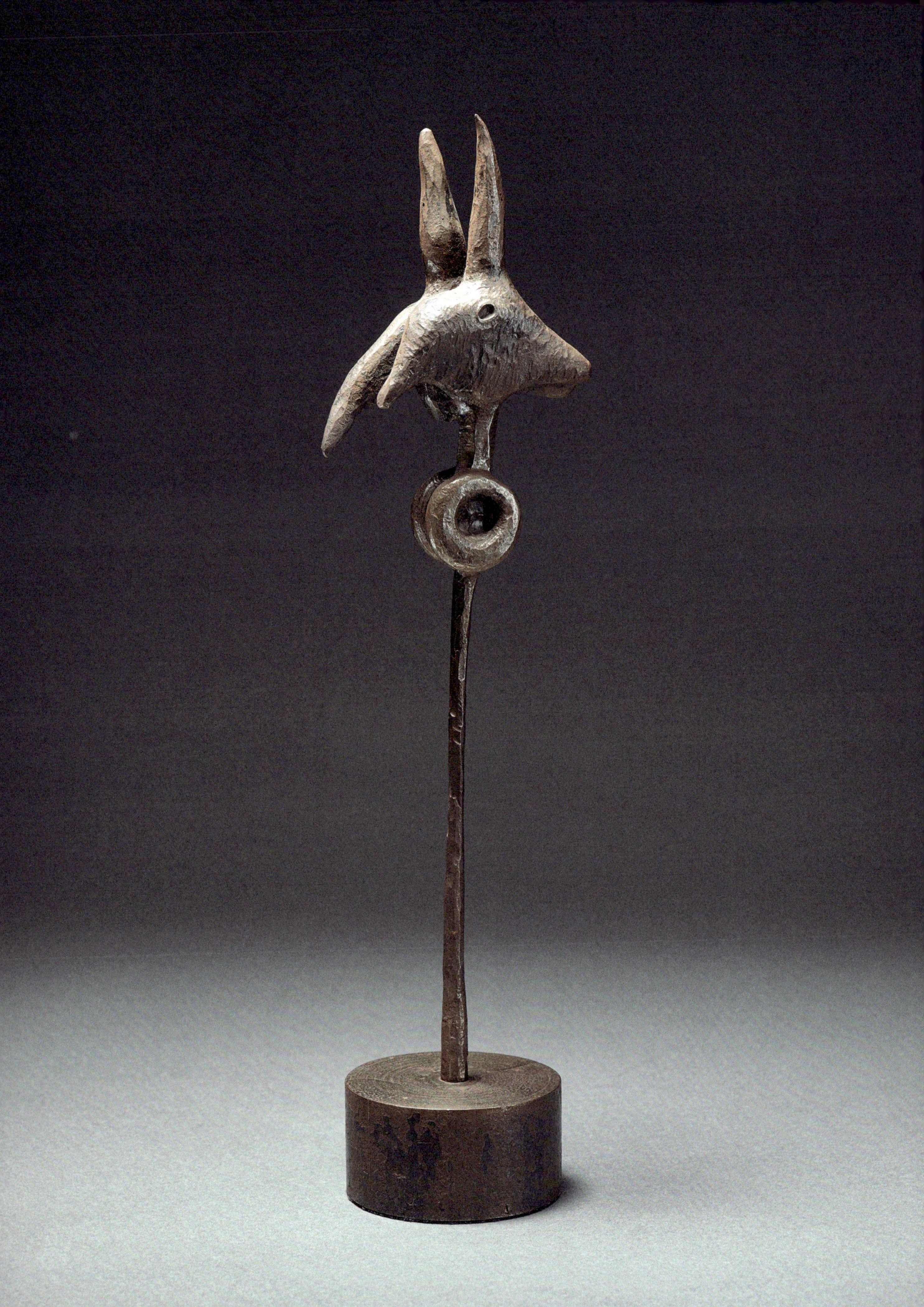

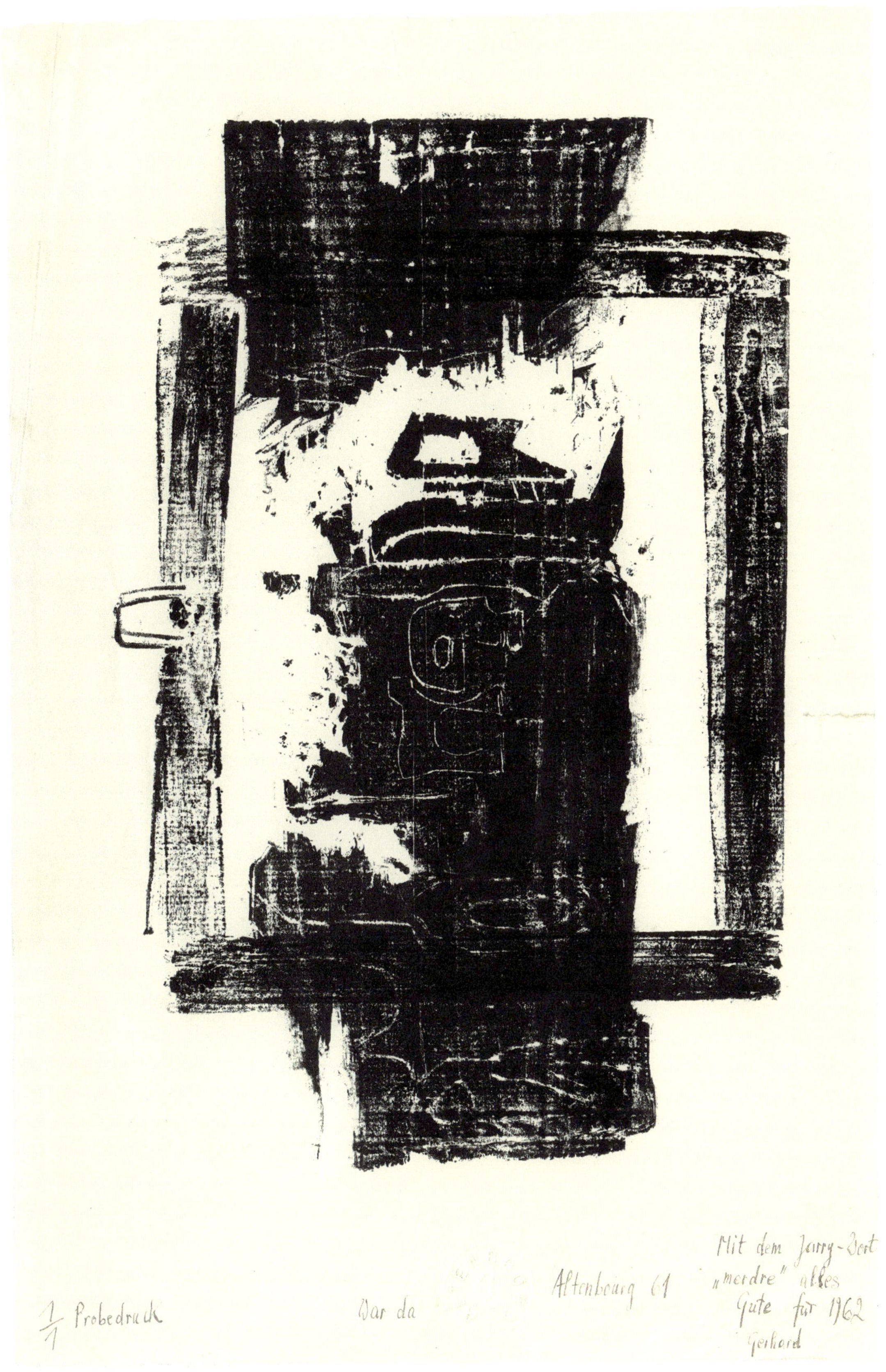

19 *Die Hörner*, 1972 | *The Horns*, 1972

20 *War da*, 1963 | *Was There*, 1963

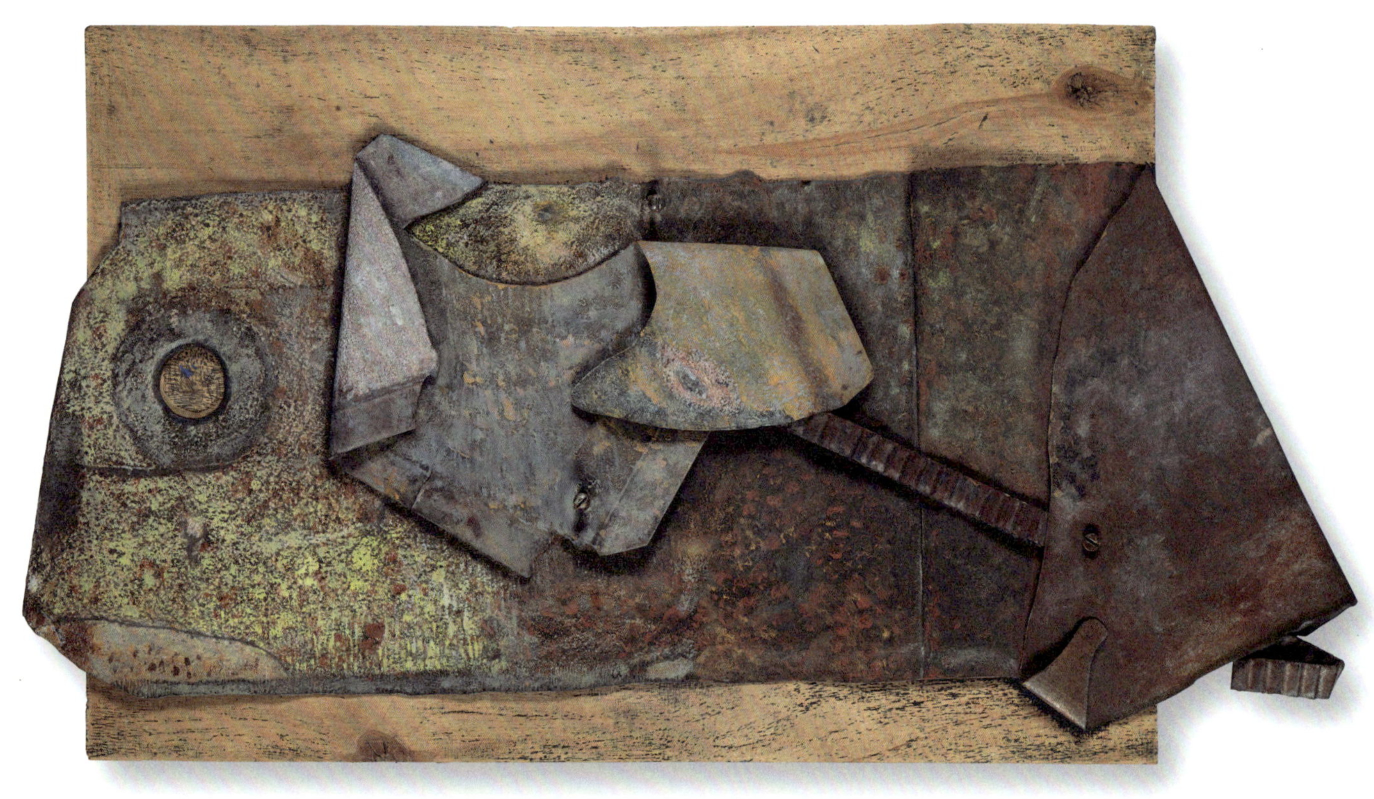

21 *Der uralte Moby*, 1961 |
The Ancient Moby, 1961

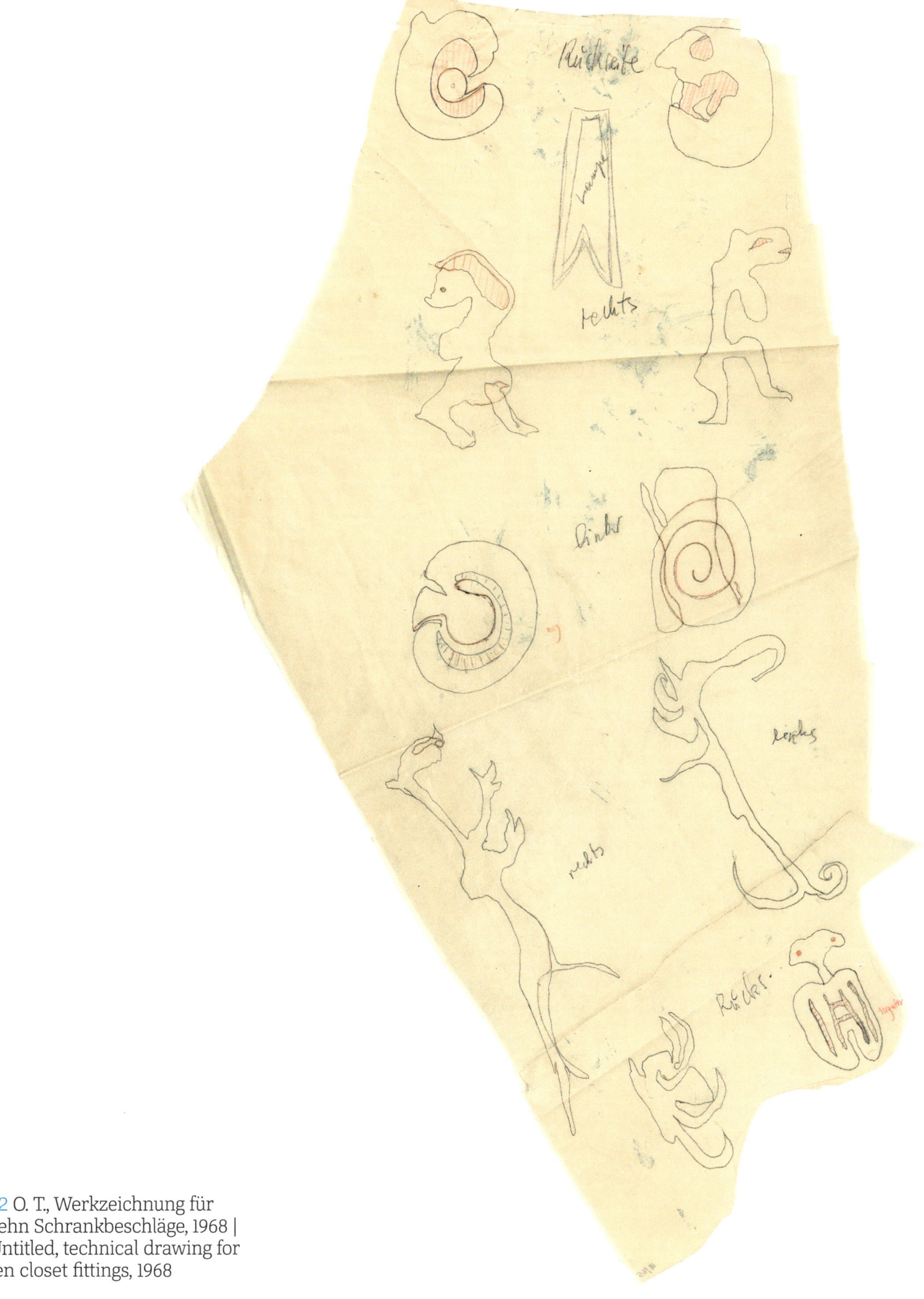

22 O. T., Werkzeichnung für zehn Schrankbeschläge, 1968 | Untitled, technical drawing for ten closet fittings, 1968

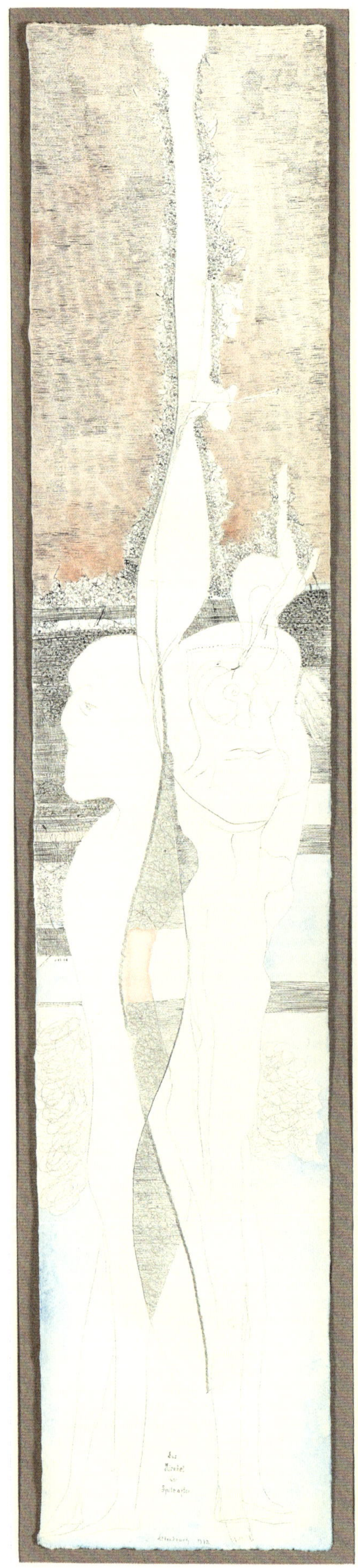

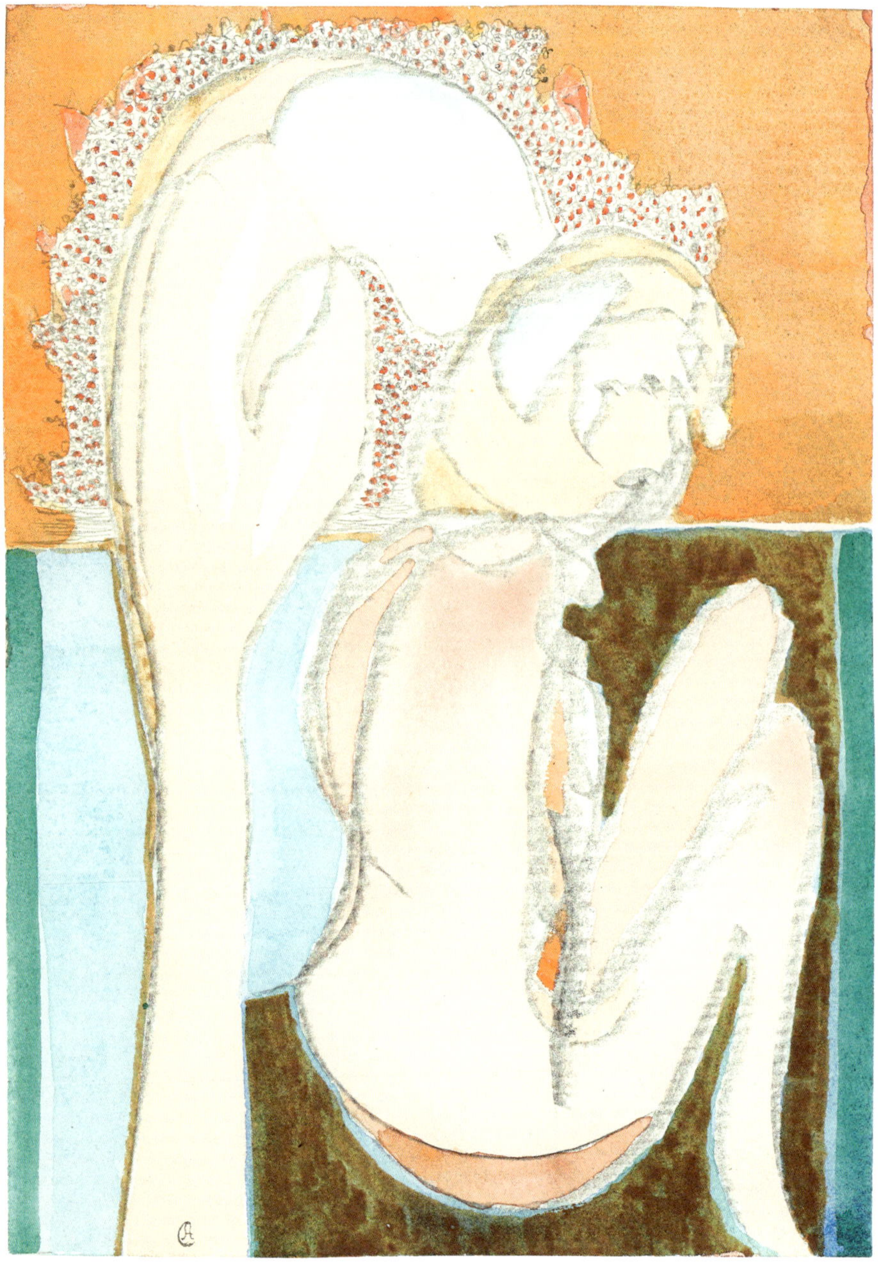

23 *Das Mirakel der Spitzafter*, 1972 | *The Miracle of the Pointed Anus*, 1972

24 *Verklärte Eingebung*, 1974 | *Transfigured Inspiration*, 1974

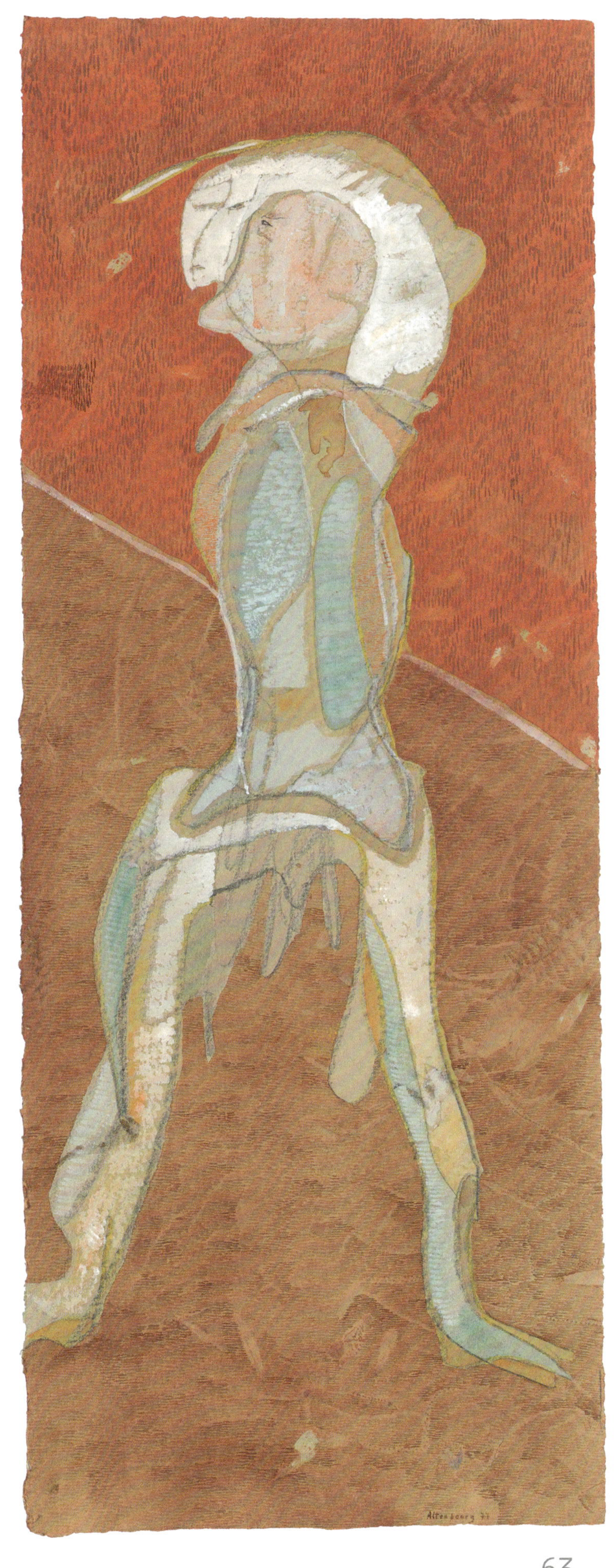

25 *Ritter ohne Furcht*, 1977 |
Fearless Knight, 1977

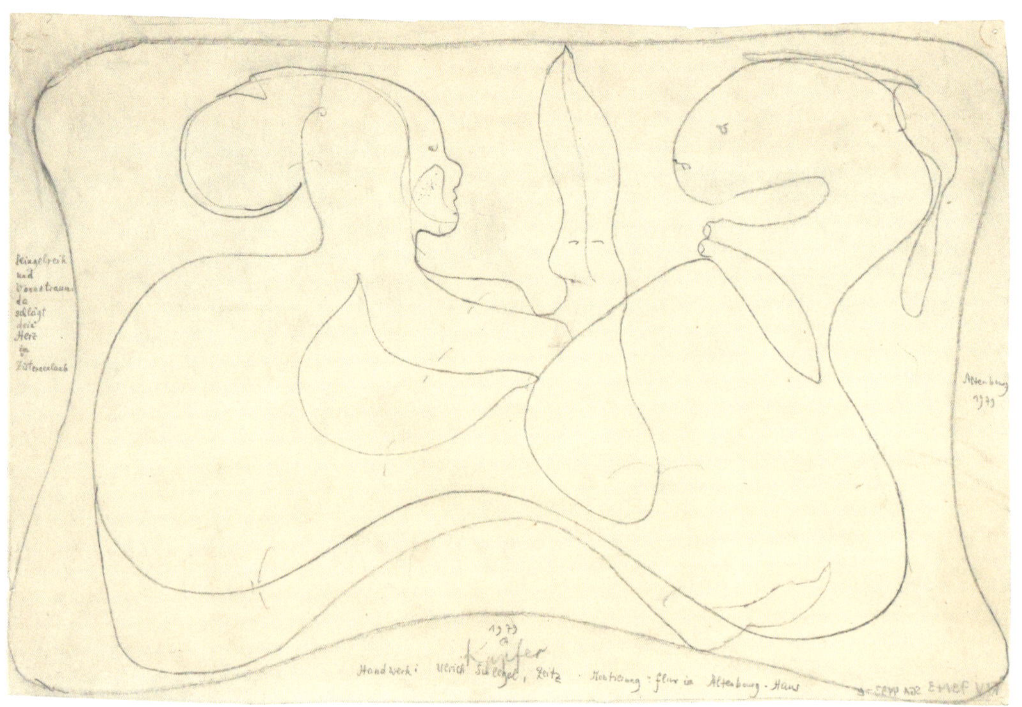

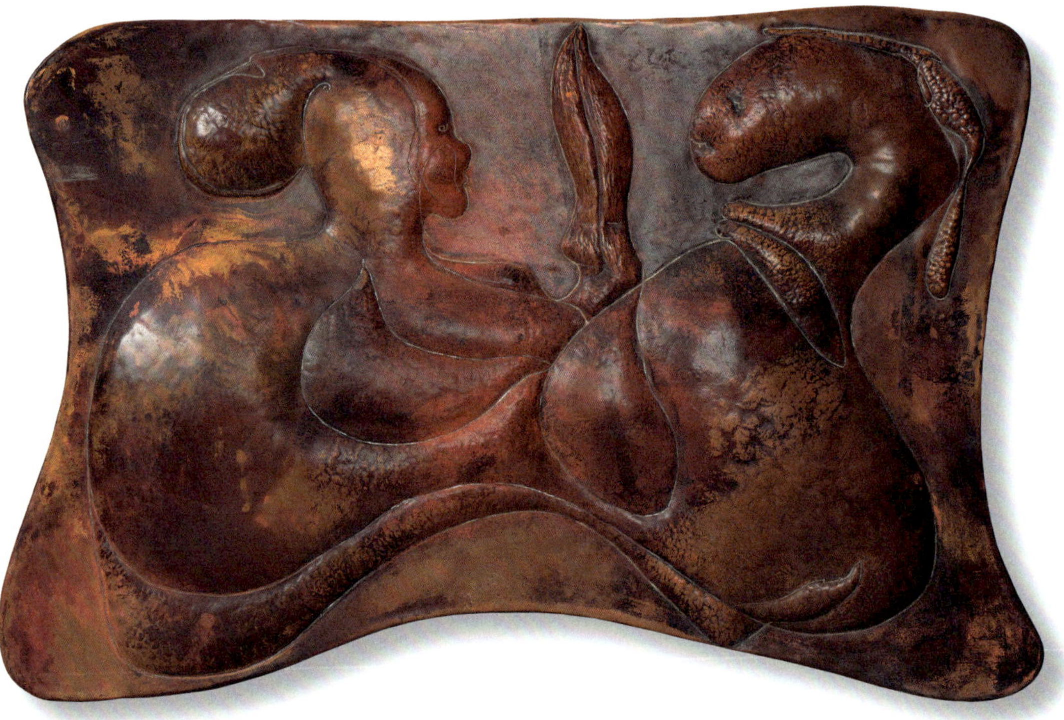

26 Werkzeichnung für das Relief *Ringelreih und Wonnetraum: da schlägt dein Herz im Zisternenlaub*, 1979 | Technical drawing for the relief *Circle Dance and Bliss Dream, Your Heart Beats in Cistern Leaves*, 1979

27 *Ringelreih und Wonnetraum: da schlägt dein Herz im Zisternenlaub*, 1979 | *Circle Dance and Bliss Dream, Your Heart Beats in Cistern Leaves*, 1979

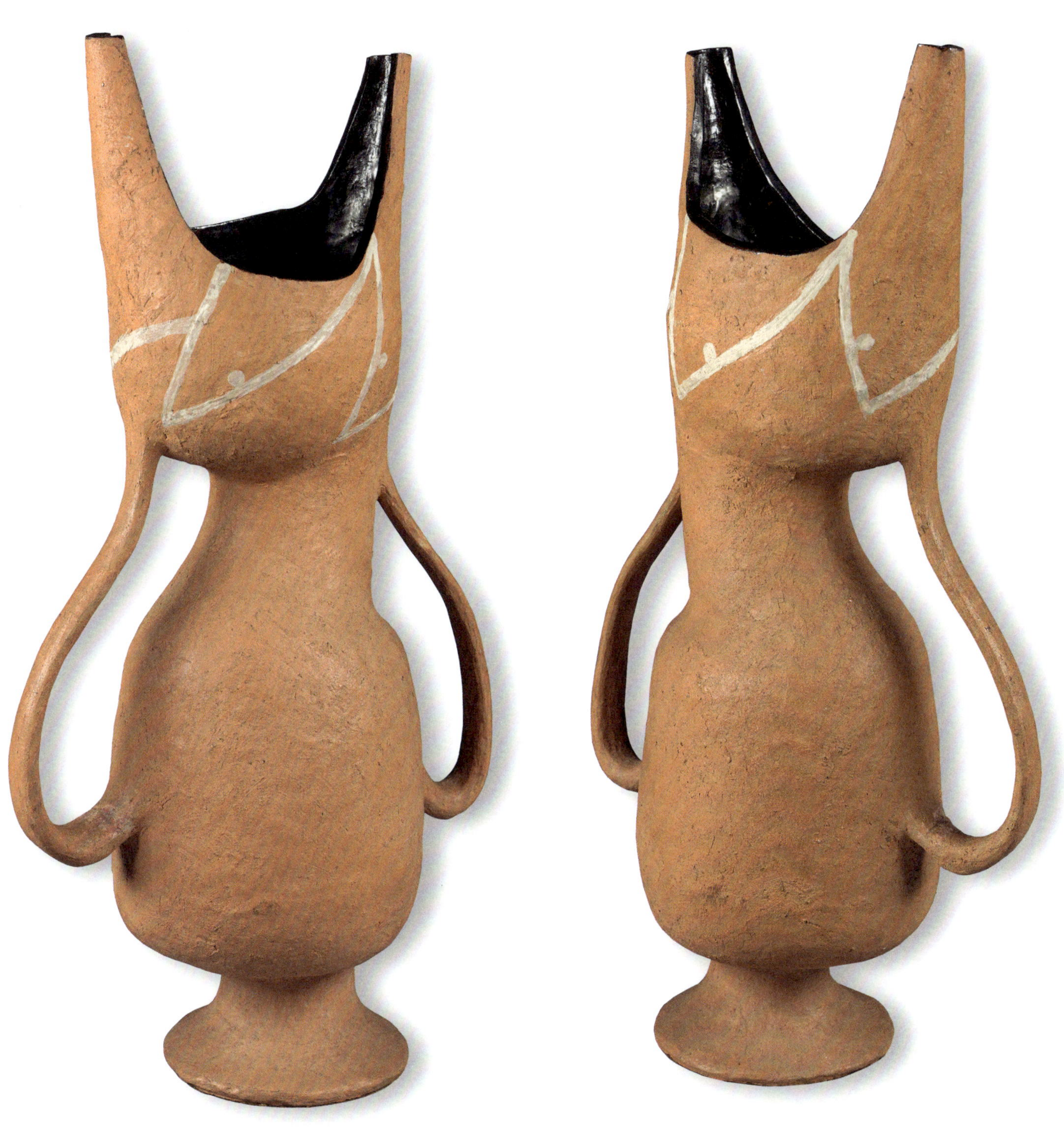

28 Vogelähnliches Tongefäß, 1958 |
Bird-Like Clay Vessel, 1958

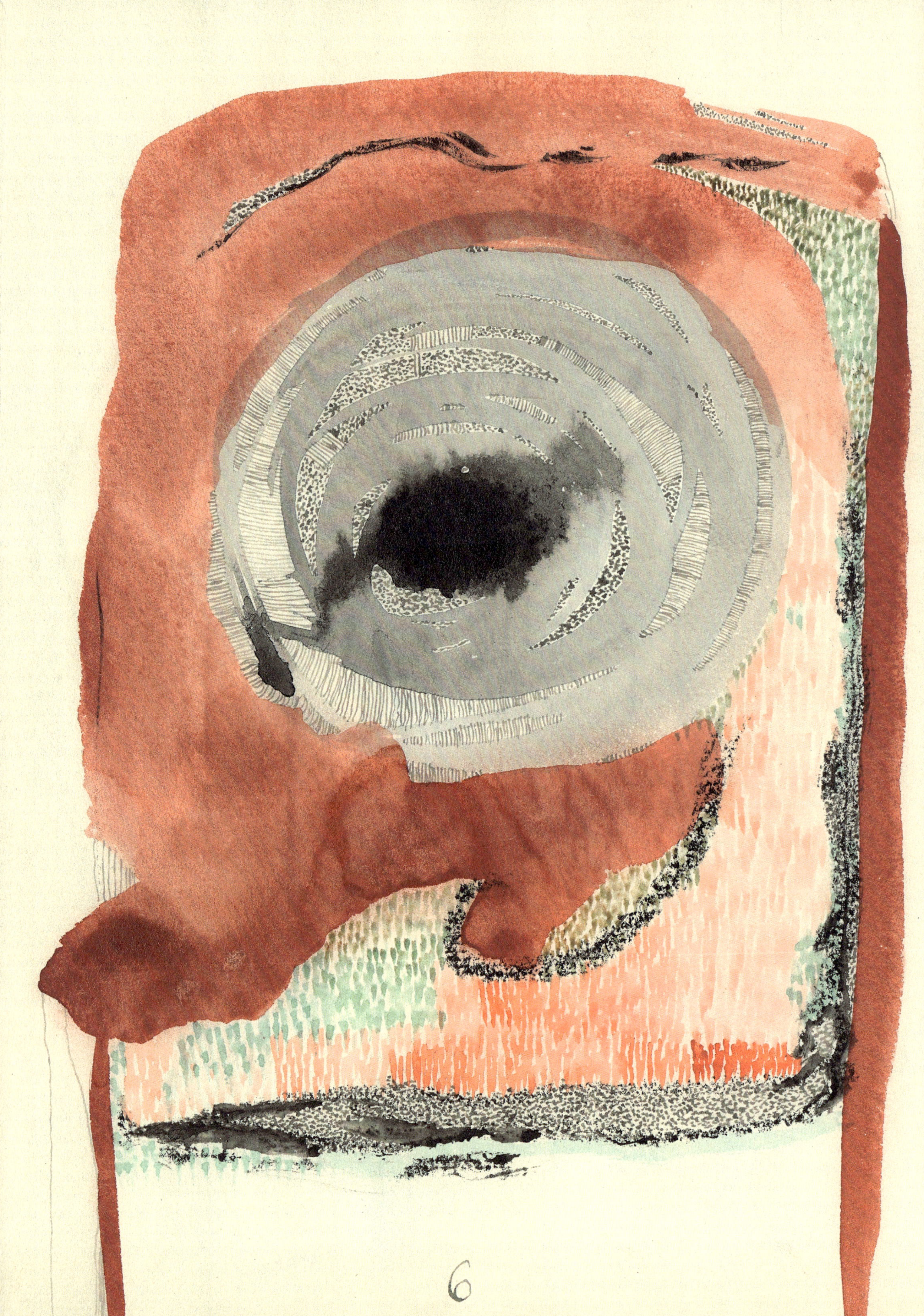
6

Marit Heuß

»Erotischer Surrealist«

Zu Gerhard Altenbourgs Künstlerbuch *Salutation*

»Es war an einem Abend, es hatte lange geregnet – und regnete noch in mir, als ich mir bewußt wurde, daß ich allein sei, in einer Schärfe, die mich erschrecken ließ und mir unwiderlegbar zeigte wie einsam.«[1] Gerhard Altenbourg beschrieb im autobiografischen Prosastück *Erlebnis 1959* die Erfahrung rückhaltlosen Alleinseins. Der Künstler und Schriftsteller sah sich in seinem Wohnhaus im Altenburger Braugartenweg wie auf eine lebensfeindliche Mondlandschaft versetzt, Augenblicke der Liebe und des resonanzreichen Gesprächs waren fern; die künstlerische Arbeit und die Lektüre blieben die einzigen Anhaltspunkte. »Allein in deinem Stuhl, allein in deinen Büchern, allein unter Bildern.«[2] Altenbourgs sublimes Schriftzeugnis existenzieller Einsamkeit – es gehörte zum Grunderlebnis der vom Krieg erschütterten europäischen Gesellschaft, philosophisch fundiert durch die französische Existenzphilosophie – birgt das Begehren nach einer Überwindung derselben.

Von der zeitweisen Auflösung dieser Isolation und Vereinzelung, von hellen Augenblicken des Gesprächs und der Freundschaft zeugt eine Sammlung von Gedichten und Bildern, die Gerhard Altenbourg im August 1960 in dem Künstlerbuch *Salutation* zusammengestellt hatte – das verrät bereits der Titel, das französische Wort *salutation* bedeutet »Gruß«. Dieser galt der Malerin und Bildhauerin Eva Schwalbe (1919–1972), ihr widmete Altenbourg das unikale Künstlerbuch, ihr waren die acht handgeschriebenen Gedichte und die dazugehörigen zehn Aquarelle zugeeignet:[3] »Das Buch wurde geschaffen / als Huldigung für / Frau / Eva Schwalbe«[4] **(Abb. 1)**, eine »Huldigung« für die Freundin, die dem Künstler bei persönlichen Begegnungen und vor allem in Briefen eine Möglichkeit zur Entäußerung der im Verschlossenen ruhenden Gedanken bot. Die erste Begegnung zwischen Altenbourg und der mit Mann und Kindern in Merseburg lebenden, belesenen und feingeistigen Frau auf einem literarischen Abend 1959 kam durch den Altenburger Maler Erich Dietz (1903–1990) zustande.[5] Die seltenen Zusammenkünfte mit Schwalbe waren nur bis zu ihrer Ausreise in die Bundesrepublik 1961 möglich,[6] zugleich waren diese

"Erotic Surrealist"

On Gerhard Altenbourg's Artist's Book *Salutation*

"It was one evening, it had been raining for a long time – and it still rained in me – when I became aware that I was alone, with an intensity that frightened me and showed me how undeniably alone I was."[1] In this autobiographical prose text, "Erlebnis 1959" (Experience 1959), Gerhard Altenbourg described the experience of absolute solitude. The artist and author saw himself in his home in the Braugartenweg in Altenburg as though transported to a hostile lunar landscape; moments of love and of conversation rich in resonances were distant; the only points of reference remained artistic labour and reading. "Alone in your chair, alone in your books, alone with pictures."[2] Altenbourg's sublime written testimony of existential solitude – part of the fundamental experience of a European society devastated by war and philosophically grounded in French existentialism – harbours the desire to overcome it.

The intermittent surmounting of this isolation and solitude, the bright moments of discussion and friendship, are captured in the collection of poems and pictures that Gerhard Altenbourg assembled in August 1960 in the artist's book *Salutation*. This unique artwork is dedicated to the painter and sculptor Eva Schwalbe (1919–1972); for her were the eight handwritten poems, for her the ten accompanying watercolours:[3] "The book was made / as a homage to / Ms. / Eva Schwalbe"[4] **(fig. 1)**. A "homage" to the friend who, in personal meetings and above all in letters, made it possible for him to externalise the thoughts slumbering in his being. The first

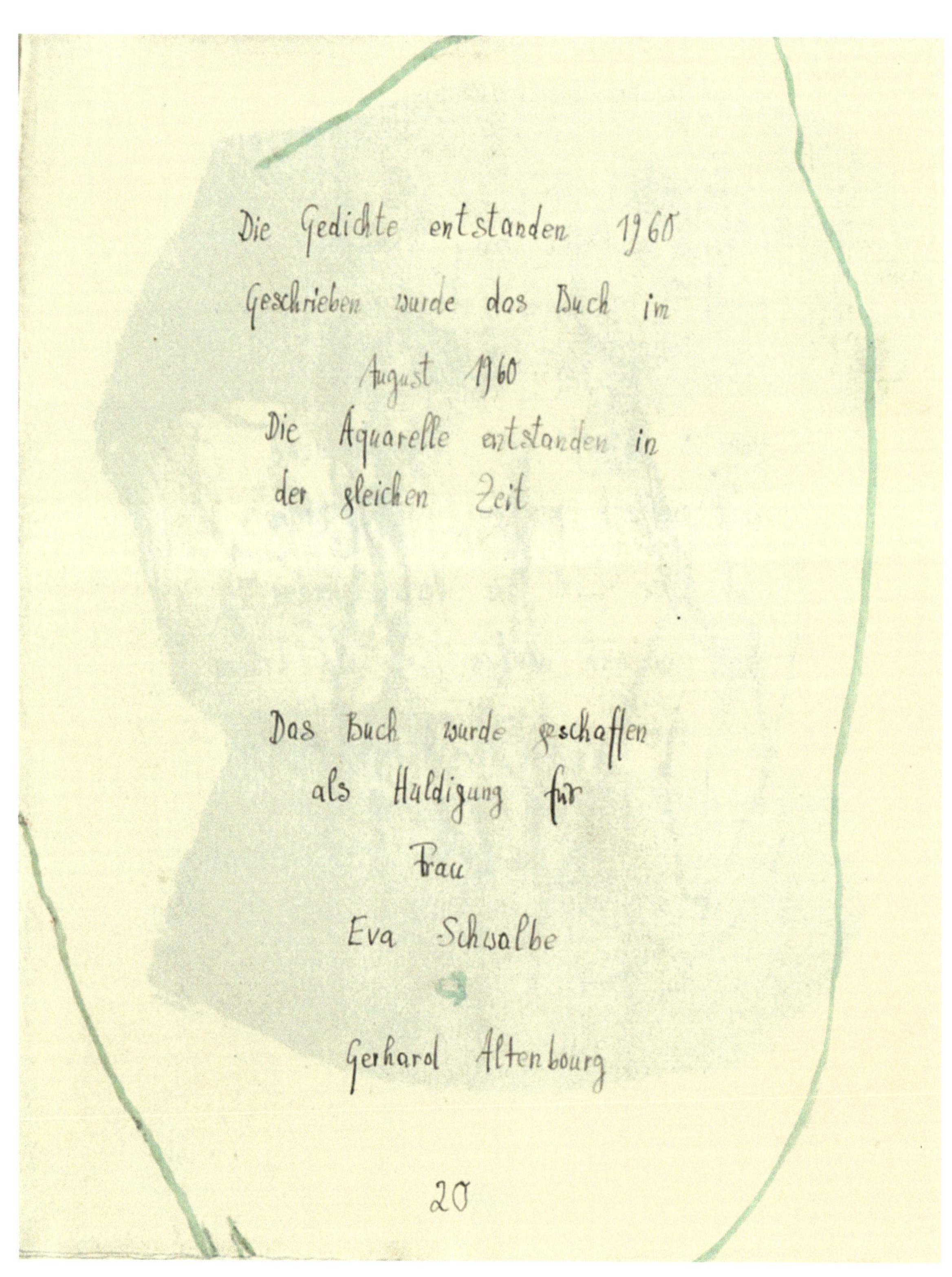

Abb. 1 Gerhard Altenbourg, Widmung an Eva Schwalbe im Künstlerbuch *Salutation*, 1960, S. 20
Fig. 1 Gerhard Altenbourg, dedication to Eva Schwalbe in the artist's book *Salutation*, 1960, p. 20

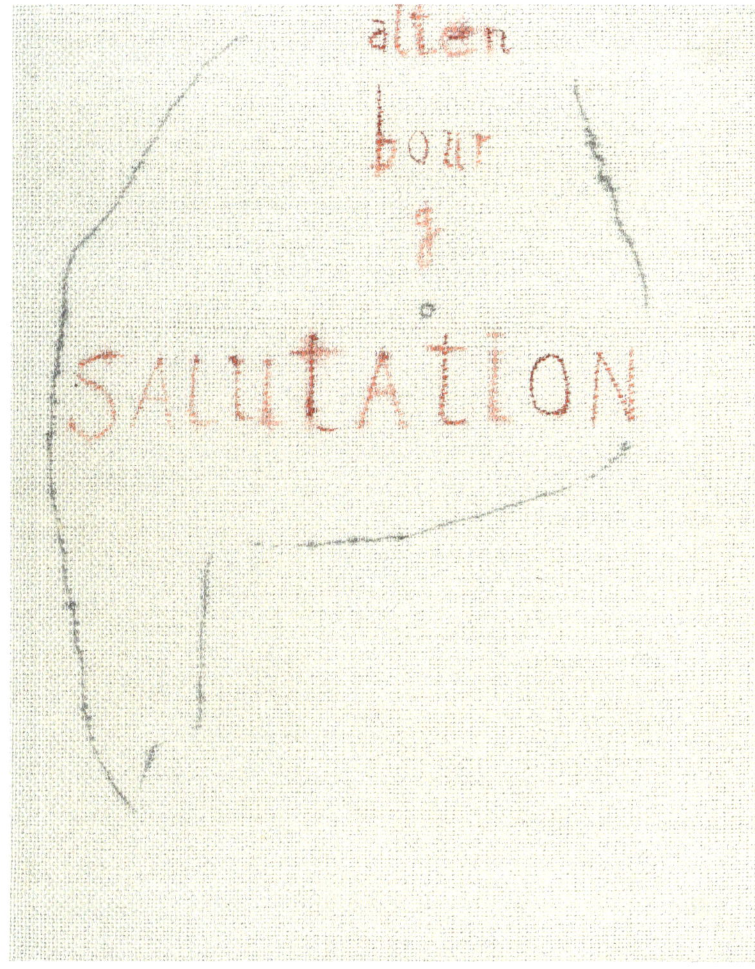

Abb. 2 Gerhard Altenbourg, Titel auf dem Deckel des Künstlerbuches *Salutation* 1960
Fig. 2 Gerhard Altenbourg, title on the cover of the artist's book *Salutation*, 1960

zwei Jahre die intensivste Zeit der Freundschaft. Die von Eva Schwalbe erhaltenen Briefe zeugen von Altenbourgs regen Ausstellungsbesuchen in der Bundesrepublik vor dem Mauerbau, etwa der documenta 2 (1959),[7] an der er selbst beteiligt war **(Kat. 30)**, vermitteln sein Interesse an informeller Malerei[8] und an der Kunst und Literatur der Moderne. In Lektüre- und Leseempfehlungen zirkulieren Namen wie Proust,[9] Camus,[10] Benn,[11] van Hoddis,[12] Emmy Hennings,[13] Alberti,[14] van Gogh[15] oder die der Pariser Surrealisten.[16] In dieses geistige Umfeld ist Altenbourgs Künstlerbuch *Salutation* zu verorten.

Bereits das Titelblatt von *Salutation* ist eine Reminiszenz an die Kunstströmung des europäischen Informel. Im Innenraum des im »linkischen Gestus«,[17] im Stil der »Ausgeschlossenen, der Außenseiter«[18] gezeichneten Umrisses einer Gedankenblase befindet sich der in roten Majuskeln geschriebene Titel sowie der in Minuskeln wie nachlässig

encounter between Altenbourg and this erudite and sophisticated woman, who lived with her husband and children in Merseburg, took place at a literary soirée in 1959 and came about through the Altenburg painter Erich Dietz (1903–1990).[5] The infrequent encounters with Schwalbe that followed were only possible until she left for West Germany in 1961,[6] yet these two years were the most intensive period of their friendship. The surviving letters from Schwalbe testify to Altenbourg's many visits to exhibitions in West Germany before the construction of the Wall, such as to *documenta 2* (1959),[7] in which he participated **(cat. 30)**, as well as demonstrate his interest in Art Informel painting[8] and modernist art and literature. Names such as Proust,[9] Camus,[10] Benn,[11] van Hoddis,[12] Emmy Hennings,[13] Alberti,[14] van Gogh[15] or the Paris Surrealists[16] circulate through their reading and literary recommendations. This is the intellectual and artistic setting in which Altenbourg's artist's book *Salutation* was created.

The cover of *Salutation* itself is already reminiscent of the European movement of Art Informel. Within the outline of the thought bubble, drawn with an "awkward gesture"[17] in the style of the "excluded, the outsider",[18] the title is lettered in red capital letters and the artist's name set almost carelessly in lowercase at the upper edge of the sheet **(fig. 2)**.[19] The writing here is "action" and the title *Salutation*, in a visual idiom of red warning letters, and the fleeting handwriting on terrifyingly empty paper, resound as a cry for help. The nervous performativity of the writing on the back cover of the artist's book has a comparable impact, with a similar motif in the same colours, but solely with the initials of Gerhard Altenbourg and of the title **(fig. 3)**.[20] In this manner, Altenbourg encloses within the book's covers – inscribed with the insignia of modernism's existential angst in the lettering's design – the book's interior, which is all the more fragile, tender and different: the wonder of an amorous encounter in word and image set in a blaze of colour and feverish red in the face of the violence of history.

This is expressed in the motto for *Salutation*, taken from the poem "Lettera amorosa" (1954) by René Char: "J'ai hâte de tenir dans mes mains la joie des tiennes"[21] (I long to hold in my hands the joy of yours; **cat. 29 a**).[22] Char's cycle of prose poems is the speech of a lover in which the experiences of previous pain are enfolded, the testimony of a lone artist's love, in which Altenbourg might have seen his own situation reflected: "You

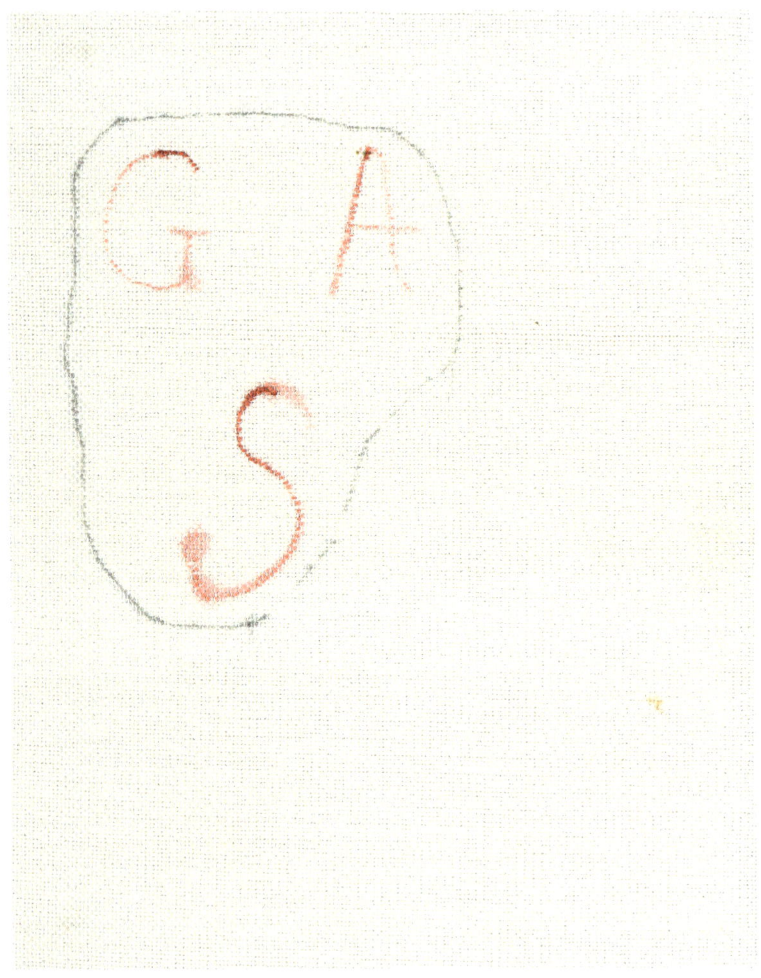

Abb. 3 Gerhard Altenbourg, Beschriftung auf dem Rücken des Künstlerbuches *Salutation* 1960
Fig. 3 Gerhard Altenbourg, writing on the back of the artist's book *Salutation*, 1960

an die obere Kante des Blattes gesetzte Künstlername **(Abb. 2)**.[19] Die Schrift ist hier Aktion, und der Titel *Salutation* in der Formsprache der roten warnenden Lettern und der flüchtigen Schrift auf dem erschreckend leeren Grund eher ein Hilferuf. Gleichermaßen wirkt die nervöse Performanz der Schrift auf der Rückseite des Künstlerbuches, auf der ein ähnliches Motiv in der gleichen Farbgestalt zu sehen ist, nur dass nunmehr lediglich die Initialen Altenbourgs und des Titels lesbar bleiben **(Abb. 3)**.[20] So umhüllt Altenbourg in der Schriftgestalt des Buchumschlags, welchem die Insignien der existenziellen Angst der Moderne aufgeprägt sind, das umso fragilere, zartere, andersartige Innere des Buches: das in Wort und Bild in Farbenpracht und fieberndes Rot gebannte Wunder einer Liebesbegegnung im Angesicht der Gewaltgeschichte.

Dazu passt das Motto von *Salutation*, das dem Gedicht *Lettera amorosa* (1954) von René Char entnommen ist:

are gone, yet you remain in the surging tide of circumstances, for we feel pain, the land and I."[23] René Char, a member of the Surrealists before he joined the French resistance, had put his "aesthetics of resistance"[24] into verse with his collection of prose poems *Feuillets d'Hypnos*, those "Notes from the Maquis" written in 1943–44 and dedicated to Albert Camus. The copy of René Char's *Poésies* in Altenbourg's personal library, published by S. Fischer Verlag in 1959, bears the marks of an intensive reading of the *Feuillets d'Hypnos* poems,[25] which Altenbourg surely read with sympathy after his experience serving as a conscripted soldier.[26] What connected him with Char was not least the poet's Surrealist beginnings, the escape from bourgeois narrow-mindedness via Eros, via love,[27] as is expressed in the motto, poetry and images of *Salutation*.

Salutation performs not just a *paso doble* between two lovers, but also between word and image, a dramolette of the arts in ten scenes corresponding to the book's double pages. Except for the first four pages **(cats. 29 a–b)**, the image-poem folios feature a picture on the left and a poem on the right. One is reminded of that clever and amusing game of references between words and image, a game that since René Magritte's *La trahison des images* (The Treachery of Images, 1929), and Michel Foucault's much later text "Ceci n'est pas une pipe" (This Is Not a Pipe, 1973), has shattered the relationship between media, dissolving the distinction between language and image into hybrid forms. For the poems written in Altenbourg's distinct handwriting are certainly also "images", while some of the abstracted figures in the watercolours possess the qualities of "writing". Although the number of images in *Salutation* surpasses that of the poems, one cannot speak of the text being subordinated to the image, nor of a commenting function of the poems vis-à-vis the watercolours.[28] In fact, are there eleven or twelve images? The first poem in particular is part of an image, embedded in a dark oval on an ochre, then orange-yellow, intricately engraved background: "Zärtlich ist das Blau der Stunde / in dem Gaumen von Opal / werden werden ach gesunden / doch nun endlich von der Qual // Leise Stunde aus dem Munde / Gras und Flimmerhaar von Draht / steigen wiegen leicht umrunden / still geeint zur grünen Saat"[29] (Tender is the blue of the hour / in the palate of opal / become become oh healthy / but now finally free from the torment // Quiet hour from the mouth / grass and

»J'ai hâte de tenir dans mes mains la joie des tiennes«[21] (Kat. 29 a), in der Übersetzung von Jean-Pierre Wilhelm, »Es drängt mich, in meinen Händen die Freude der deinigen zu halten.«[22] Chars Zyklus von *Poèmes en prose* sind Ansprachen einer Geliebten, in der die Erfahrungen von vergangenem Schmerz eingeschlossen sind, Zeugnisse der Liebe eines künstlerischen Solitärs, in denen Altenbourg seine eigene Situation wiedergefunden haben mochte: »Fort bist du, doch du verharrst im wogenden Gang der Verhältnisse, da wir Schmerz verspüren, das Land und ich.«[23] René Char, der vor seiner Zeit in der Résistance zum Kreis der Pariser Surrealisten zählte, hatte mit seiner Prosagedichtsammlung *Hypnos*, den 1943/44 entstandenen und Albert Camus gewidmeten *Aufzeichnungen aus dem Maquis*, seine »Ethik und Ästhetik des Widerstands«[24] versifiziert. Das Exemplar der 1959 im S. Fischer Verlag erschienenen *Poésies* von René Char aus Altenbourgs Privatbibliothek zeugt von einer intensiven Lektüre der *Hypnos*-Gedichte,[25] die gewiss die Zustimmung des Soldaten wider Willen,[26] der Altenbourg gewesen war, gefunden hatten. Und nicht zuletzt verbindet ihn mit Chars surrealistischen Anfängen der Weg aus bürgerlicher Enge über den Eros, über die Liebe,[27] was sich in Motto, Lyrik und Bild von *Salutation* zeigt.

Salutation erscheint dann auch als *Paso doble* nicht nur zweier Liebender, sondern auch von Wort und Bild, ein Dramolett der Künste in zehn Szenen, welche den Doppelseiten des Buches entsprechen – bis auf die ersten vier Seiten (Kat. 29 b–c) steht auf diesen Bild-Gedicht-Seiten immer links das Bild, rechts das Gedicht. Unweigerlich drängt sich der Gedanke an jenes listige wie lustige Verweisspiel zwischen Sprache und Bild auf, das seit René Magrittes *La trahison des images* (1929) und Michel Foucaults viel später erschienener Schrift *Ceci n'est pas une pipe* (1973) das Verhältnis zwischen den Medien erschütterte, die Distinktion zwischen Sprache und Bild hin zu hybriden Formen auflöste. Denn ganz sicher sind die in Altenbourgs exklusiver Handschrift geschriebenen Gedichte auch Bilder, besitzen manche der abstrahierten Figuren der Aquarelle den Charakter einer Schrift. Und wenn auch die Anzahl der Bilder die der Gedichte in *Salutation* übersteigt, kann von einer Unterordnung des Textes gegenüber dem Bild, einer Kommentarfunktion der Gedichte keine Rede sein.[28] Sind es eigentlich elf oder zwölf Bilder? Gerade das erste Gedicht ist Bestandteil eines Bildes, eingebettet in ein dunkles Oval auf ockerfarbenem, bald orangegelbem fein ziseliertem Grund: »Zärtlich ist das Blau der Stunde / in dem Gaumen von Opal / werden werden ach gesunden / doch nun endlich von der Qual // Leise Stunde aus dem Munde / Gras und Flimmerhaar von Draht / steigen wiegen leicht umrunden / still geeint zur grünen Saat«[29] (Kat. 29 d). Im Gedicht spricht hier weder ein Ich noch ein Wir, sondern es artikuliert sich ein Textsubjekt[30] – ja es wirkt, als würde das Gedicht sich hier selbst aussprechen und seine dynastische Macht behaupten: Der Gaumen und das Flimmerhaar der Nase, Organe und Instrumente verbalen Ausdrucks, werden im Symbol des

shimmering hair of wire / rise sway gently circle / silently united to green seed) (cat. 29 c). Neither an I nor a We speaks in this poem, rather it is a text-subject that articulates itself[30] – it even seems as though the poem speaks itself and claims its dynastic power: the palate and the nose's shimmering hair, organs and instruments of verbal expression, are ennobled in the symbol of the precious gemstone, the opal. An instance of harmony occurs through speech and poem during the blue hour – an hour dedicated to togetherness, as the watercolour on the poem-image folio depicts: two figures that appear like black letters against a blue background, their bodies smouldering red (cat. 29 b).

Salutation narrates the story of a lover and perhaps, *comme il faut*, the story of a young artist who fights for a place not only in the heart of his beloved, but also in the heart of art history. In *Salutation*, Altenbourg plays with the composition and themes of the "elders", plays around with them using an expressive brushstroke and cheekily sticks his tongue out at them as avant-garde artists do. The introductory picture recalls, in its positioning of the horned figure at a balustrade before a blue sea, those "portraits of young men" painted by Raphael, even citing the classic colour configuration of blue, red and green, but tinged with the fantastic.[31] Or is the figure with horns perhaps the Greek god Pan, who leads us to the monstrous abysses of Eros? The subject is counteracted by the childishly gestural quality of its modern execution, as a stick figure in broad black brushstrokes. The second watercolour in *Salutation* has a horizontal format and depicts a pastoral scene of two lovers on a green idyllic meadow, a shepherd with a staff in his hand and a reclining Venus.[32] Their harmony is threatened by an ominous approaching shadow that transforms the image into a pyramidal, triangular composition. In all three of Altenbourg's images, amorphous figures catch the eye of the observer, figures that set the rigid form into motion, like in Salvador Dalí's Surrealist pictures: whether in the lascivious horned figure, the rapacious shadow in the pastoral scene or the Bordeaux-coloured serpent that encircles the title. In this manner Altenbourg has introduced motifs and themes in *Salutation*, has created a tribute to love and artistry poised between tradition and modernism, as is expressed by the magnificent title page against a gold-red shimmering background.

The serpent in *Salutation* becomes a cryptogram for desire, but also for being engulfed and for hopelessness in the dialogue between the

wertvollen Edelsteins, des Opals, nobilitiert. Durch Gespräch und Gedicht ereignet sich ein Augenblick der Harmonie zur blauen Stunde – diese ist der Zweisamkeit gewidmet, so zeigt es wiederum das Aquarell der Bild-Gedicht-Seite. Hier sind zwei wie schwarze Schriftzeichen wirkende Figuren vor blauem Grund zu sehen: Ihre Körper glühen rot **(Kat. 29 b)**.

In *Salutation* wird die Geschichte eines Liebenden beschrieben und vielleicht auch, *comme il faut*, die Geschichte eines jungen Künstlers, der um seinen Platz nicht nur im Herzen der Angebeteten, sondern auch um den in der Geschichte der Kunst kämpft. Altenbourg spielt in *Salutation* auf Kompositionen und Sujets der *Alten* an, umspielt sie mit expressivem Pinselstrich und streckt ihnen nach der Manier der Avantgarden frech die Zunge heraus. Bereits das Eingangsbild erinnert in der Situiertheit der gehörnten Figur an einer Balustrade vor blauem Meer an jene Bildnisse junger Männer wie sie Raffael malte, dazu noch in der klassischen Farbkomposition aus Blau, Rot und Grün, doch ins Fantastische gewendet.[31] Oder ist die Figur mit Hörnern gar der griechische Gott Pan, der in die monströsen Abgründe des Eros führt? Konterkariert wird das Sujet von der modernen Ausführung der Figur, dem mit breitem schwarzen Pinsel in kindlicher Geste bedeuteten Strichmännchen. Das zweite Aquarell von *Salutation,* im Querformat betrachtet, zeigt eine pastorale Szene zweier Liebender auf grüner Au – ein Hirte mit dem Stab in der Hand und eine ruhende Venus.[32] Deren Eintracht zeigt sich durch einen herannahenden, sonderbaren Schatten gefährdet, durch den sich das Bild zu einer pyramidalen Dreieckskomposition fügt. Auf den drei Motiven Altenbourgs springen zudem amorphe Figuren ins Auge, die wie auf surrealistischen Bildern Salvador Dalís starre Formen zum Fließen bringen: sei es der wollüstige Gehörnte, der raubgierige Schatten in der Pastorale oder jene bordeauxfarbene Schlange, die das Titelsignet umschlingt. Damit hat Altenbourg Motivik und Thema von *Salutation* eingeführt, ein Gruß im Zeichen der auf dem Spiel stehenden Liebe und Künstlerschaft zwischen Tradition und Moderne – das prachtvolle Titelblatt vor im Goldrot flimmernden Grund bringt das zum Ausdruck.

Die Schlange wird in *Salutation* zur Chiffre für Begehren, aber auch für Verschlungensein und Ausweglosigkeit in der Zwiesprache der Liebenden. So korrespondiert das abstrahierte, rote Reptil, das auf einem Aquarell spiralenförmig eine schwarze Mitte umfasst, mit dem Gedicht *Schlangenhaft umwunden*, in dem die Existenzweise der Schlange metaphorisch für die symbiotische Beziehung eines Paares steht: »Schlangenhaft umwunden dies im / Schlangesein verloren / Biß in uns verloren / Was uns dann gebissen / auf der Wanderschaft des Fleisches (…)«[33] **(vgl. Detail, S. 66).** Währenddessen verwandelt sich die Schlange hin zum Ende von *Salutation* von der erotischen Umarmung in den Irrweg eines Labyrinths durch grünende, das Unterbewusstsein umfassende Wildnis – so zeigt es das Aquarell –, das der Ausweglosigkeit der Liebe im Gedicht *Wo sich das Auge*

lovers. Thus, the abstract red reptile that, in one watercolour, spirally encircles a black core corresponds to the poem "Schlangenhaft umwunden" (Serpent-like Entwined), in which the serpent's manner of existence stands metaphorically for the symbiotic relationship of a couple: "Schlangenhaft umwunden dies im / Schlangesein verloren / Biß in uns verloren / Was uns dann gebissen / auf der Wanderschaft des Fleisches"[33] (Serpent-like entwined this / lost in snake being / lost in the bite in us / What then bit us / on the flesh's wanderings; **see p. 66**).

In the meantime, the serpent metamorphoses at the end of the artist's book, from erotic embrace into the deceptive paths of a labyrinth through a verdant wilderness embracing the subconscious – as the watercolour shows us. It embodies the hopelessness of love expressed in the poem "Wo sich das Auge breitet" (Where the Eye Roams): a melancholy disgruntlement becomes palpable **(cat. 29 d)**.[34] In contrast to Char's modernist prose poems, Altenbourg's poetry adheres to more conventional lyrical forms – often in strophic verses with frequently alternating accented and unaccented syllables, even rhymed in one case.[35] Yet unusual compounds bordering on the absurd, like "Schneckenpein" (snail pain),[36] and abstract nouns alluding to existential struggles, such as "Anderssein" (otherness),[37] render the advanced, surreal aesthetic of the watercolours in the poetry. In particular the image-poem page "Ich lebe durch das Anderssein" (I Live Through Otherness), in which the watercolour depicts a blue that grasps for the sky and the ocean, in whose emptied centre a dancing figure appears, presents the delightful freedom as well as the dangerous emptiness of modern artistry: "Nie sein zu dürfen wie man ist / … // Stumm sein umschlossen schwarz gemacht / wo Eigentum? durch uns es geht / und lacht und lacht und weint und weint"[38] (Never allowed to be who you are / … // Being mute enclosed made black / Where property? it passes through us / And laughs and laughs and cries and cries).

At a literary evening in spring 1960, to which Gerhard Altenbourg had invited his friends to his house in the Braugartenweg, the artist read some of his poems. The effect of this reading on Eva Schwalbe is reflected in her letter to her friend of 12 April 1960, in which motifs from *Salutation* such as the "labyrinth"[39] and thoughts like "otherness"[40] appear. Evidently, his friend's experiences of art were important creative stimuli for Altenbourg. Even though *Salutation*'s

breitet entspricht: Eine depressive Verstimmung kommt hier zum Ausdruck **(Kat. 29 d)**.[34] Zwar zeigt sich Altenbourgs Lyrik anders als René Chars moderne Prosagedichte eher an konventionellen lyrischen Formen orientiert – oftmals in strophisch gebauten Gedichten mit meist alternierenden Hebungen und Senkungen, einmal sogar gereimt.[35] Doch ungewöhnliche, ans *Absurde* grenzende Komposita wie »Schneckenpein«[36] und auf existenzielle Kämpfe hinweisende Abstrakta wie »Anderssein«[37] tragen die avancierte, surreale Ästhetik der Aquarelle auch in die Lyrik hinein. Gerade die Bild-Gedicht-Seite *Ich lebe durch das Anderssein*, hier zeigt das Aquarell ein nach Himmel und Meer greifendes Blau, in dessen ausgesparter Mitte eine tanzende Figur erscheint, setzt sowohl die beglückende Freiheit als auch die gefährliche Leere moderner Künstlerschaft in Szene: »Nie sein zu dürfen wie man ist / (…) // Stumm sein umschlossen schwarz gemacht / wo Eigentum? durch uns es geht / und lacht und lacht und weint und weint«.[38]

Zum literarischen Abend, zu dem Gerhard Altenbourg im Frühjahr 1960 seinen Freundeskreis in sein Haus im Braugartenweg eingeladen hatte, las der Künstler auch eigene Gedichte. Die Wirkung dieses Vortrags auf Eva Schwalbe zeigt sich in ihrem Brief an den Freund vom 12. April 1960, in dem sich Motive aus *Salutation* wie das »Labyrinth«[39] und Gedanken wie das »Anders-sein«[40] wiederfinden. Offenbar waren die Kunsterlebnisse der Freundin wichtige Schaffensimpulse für Altenbourg. Auch wenn sich der konkrete Entstehungsprozess von *Salutation* im Sommer 1960 nicht mehr rekonstruieren lässt, ist das Künstlerbuch doch Resultat und Teil des Gesprächs mit der Freundin, das auch nach der Übermittlung von *Salutation* als Geschenk für Eva Schwalbe im September 1960 fortgesetzt wurde.[41] Auch das Künstlerbuch *O Janus oh Janus* (1959–1961), in dem einige Gedichte aus *Salutation* enthalten sind, zählt zu dieser Schaffensphase.[42] Eva Schwalbes Kommentar strahlt aus dem bereits erwähnten Brief an Altenbourg zu einigen seiner Zeichnungen, die ihr Mann vom Künstler angekauft hatte,[43] unmittelbar auf die ästhetische Gestalt von *Salutation* aus: »Ich wußte nicht, daß Sie ein erotischer Surrealist sind.«[44]

specific process of creation in the summer of 1960 can no longer be reconstructed in detail, the artist's book is nevertheless the result of, and a part of, the dialogue with the friend, which continued after *Salutation* was given as a gift to Schwalbe in September 1960.[41] The artist's book *O Janus oh Janus* (1959–61), in which several poems from *Salutation* are included, likewise belongs to this creative phase.[42] Schwalbe's commentary in the letter to Altenbourg mentioned above radiates over some of the drawings, which her husband had purchased from the artist,[43] to directly touch on the aesthetic design of *Salutation*: "I didn't know that you were an erotic Surrealist".[44]

1 Altenbourg, Gerhard: Erlebnis 1959. Autograph A 1043, in: Janda, Annegret: Gerhard Altenbourg. Monographie und Werkverzeichnis, 3 Bde., Bd. 2, 1959–1976, Köln 2007, S. 95.
2 Ebd.
3 Vgl. Altenbourg, Gerhard: *Salutation* (W 60/27), in: Janda 2007 (wie Anm. 1), S. 287. Julia M. Nauhaus beschreibt das Künstlerbuch *Salutation* kenntnisreich. Vgl. Nauhaus, Julia M.: Gerhard Altenbourgs Künstlerbuch Salutation, in: Sparkassen-Kulturstiftung Hessen-Thüringen (Hrsg.): Salutation. Ein Künstlerbuch von Gerhard Altenbourg. Texte von Julia M. Nauhaus, Leipzig 2016, S. 5–15. Über Altenbourgs Künstlerbücher hat Christin Barbarino publiziert, »Salutation« wird hier knapp erwähnt. Vgl. Barbarino, Christin: Das Buchkunstwerk von Gerhard Altenbourg, Berlin 2018, S. 42, 336.
4 Abb. 1, in: Sparkassen-Kulturstiftung Hessen-Thüringen (Hrsg.): Salutation. Ein Künstlerbuch von Gerhard Altenbourg. Texte von Julia M. Nauhaus, Leipzig 2016, S. 26 (= Altenbourg 2016).
5 Vgl. Nauhaus 2016 (wie Anm. 3), S. 9.
6 Vgl. ebd.
7 Vgl. Eva Schwalbe an Gerhard Altenbourg, 22. Oktober 1959.
8 Zum Beispiel: *Neue Malerei, Form, Struktur, Bedeutung*, eine Schau informeller Malerei in der Münchener Städtischen Galerie 1960. Vgl. Eva Schwalbe an Gerhard Altenbourg, 12. September 1960.
9 Vgl. Eva Schwalbe an Gerhard Altenbourg, 27. September 1959.
10 Vgl. Eva Schwalbe an Gerhard Altenbourg, 12. April 1960.
11 Vgl. Eva Schwalbe an Gerhard Altenbourg, 18. Februar 1960.
12 Vgl. Eva Schwalbe an Gerhard Altenbourg, 4. April 1960.
13 Vgl. Eva Schwalbe an Gerhard Altenbourg, 19./22. September 1960.
14 Vgl. Eva Schwalbe an Gerhard Altenbourg, 12. April 1960.
15 Vgl. Eva Schwalbe an Gerhard Altenbourg, 22. Oktober 1959.
16 Vgl. Eva Schwalbe an Gerhard Altenbourg, 8. März 1960.
17 Zum »linkischen Gestus«, ein Begriff, der auf Roland Barthes und Henri Focillon zurückgeht, vgl. Heuß, Marit: Peter Handkes Bildpoetik. Notieren, Zeichnen, Erzählen, Göttingen 2022, S. 152.
18 Barthes, Roland: Cy Twombly oder Non multa sed multum, in: ders.: Der entgegenkommende und der stumpfe Sinn, 8. Aufl., Frankfurt a. M. 1990, S. 165–183, hier S. 170.
19 Altenbourg 2016 (wie Anm. 4), S.2, Abb. 2.
20 Ebd., S. 27, Abb. 3.
21 Char, René: Lettera amorosa. Zit. nach: ebd., S. 16.
22 Char, René: Lettera amorosa, in: ders.: Poésies. Dichtungen, hrsg. v. Jean-Pierre Wilhelm unter Mitarbeit von Christoph Schwerin, ins Deutsche übersetzt von Paul Celan, Johannes Hübner, Lothar Klünner, Jean-Pierre Wilhelm, Frankfurt a. M. 1959, S. 319.
23 Ebd. S. 315. Das im Künstlerbuch enthaltene Motto ist in Altenbourgs Exemplar der *Poésies* angestrichen. Vgl. Char 1959 (wie Anm. 22).
24 Bulucz, Alexandru: »Es drängt dich zu schreiben, als ob du mit dem Leben im Rückstand wärst«. Annäherung an René Char, Heidelberg 2025, S. 7.
25 Es sind vier Lesezeichen in die Abteilung »Hypnos« eingelegt. Vgl. Char 1959 (wie Anm. 22).
26 Vgl. Altenbourg, Gerhard: Narbenrisse beim Durchstreifen jener Hügellandschaft, in: Brusberg, Dieter (Hrsg.): Gerhard Altenbourg. Werk-Verzeichnis 1947–1969, unter Mitarbeit von Annegret Janda, zugl. Ausst.-Kat. Berlin / Baden-Baden / Hannover / Düsseldorf, Hannover 1969, S. 34 f., hier S. 34.
27 Vgl. Bulucz 2025 (wie Anm. 24), S. 9 f.
28 Vgl. Foucault, Michel: Dies ist keine Pfeife, aus dem Französischen von Walter Seitter, München 1974, S. 25.
29 Abb. 5. Altenbourg 2016 (wie Anm. 4), S. 18.
30 Zum Begriff »Textsubjekt« vgl. Burdorf, Dieter: Einführung in die Gedichtanalyse, Stuttgart 2015, S. 195.
31 Altenbourg 2016 (wie Anm. 4), S.16, Abb. 4.
32 Ebd., S. 17, Abb. 6.
33 Ebd., S. 19, Abb. 7.
34 Ebd., S. 23, Abb. 8.
35 Einen Beitrag zur Analyse der Lyrik Altenbourgs bietet eine Sammlung ausgewählter Lyrik des Künstlers, die erstmals isoliert vom Bildwerk rezipiert werden kann. Die Lyrik aus *Salutation* ist hier nicht enthalten, dafür aber ausgewählte Gedichte aus *O Janus oh Janus*. Vgl. Altenbourg, Gerhard: Wald minotaurisch. Gedichte, hrsg. v. Thorsten Ahrend/Stiftung Gerhard Altenbourg, mit einem Nachwort von Wulf Kirsten, Göttingen 2019, S. 37–48.

1 Gerhard Altenbourg, "Erlebnis 1959", Autograph A 1043, in Annegret Janda, *Gerhard Altenbourg. Monographie und Werkverzeichnis*, 3 vols. (Cologne: Wienand, 2004–10), vol. 2, 1959–1976, p. 95.
2 Ibid.
3 Gerhard Altenbourg, *Salutation* (W 60/27), in Janda, *Monographie und Werkverzeichnis* (n. 1 above), p. 287. Julia M. Nauhaus describes the artist's book *Salutation* knowledgeably; see Julia M. Nauhaus, "Gerhard Altenbourgs Künstlerbuch *Salutation*", in Sparkassen-Kulturstiftung Hessen-Thüringen (eds.), *Salutation. Ein Künstlerbuch von Gerhard Altenbourg. Texte von Julia M. Nauhaus* (Leipzig, 2016), pp. 5–15. Christin Barbarino discusses Altenbourg's artist's books and briefly mentions *Salutation*; see Christin Barbarino, *Das Buchkunstwerk von Gerhard Altenbourg* (Berlin: Bachmann, 2018), pp. 42, 336.
4 Sparkassen-Kulturstiftung Hessen-Thüringen (n. 3 above), p. 26.
5 Nauhaus (n. 3 above), p. 9.
6 Ibid.
7 Eva Schwalbe to Gerhard Altenbourg, 22 October 1959.
8 For example, *Neue Malerei, Form, Struktur, Bedeutung*, an exhibition on Art Informel painting in the Städtische Galerie in Munich in 1960. See Eva Schwalbe to Gerhard Altenbourg, 12 September 1960.
9 Eva Schwalbe to Gerhard Altenbourg, 27 September 1959.
10 Eva Schwalbe to Gerhard Altenbourg, 12 April 1960.
11 Eva Schwalbe to Gerhard Altenbourg, 18 February 1960.
12 Eva Schwalbe to Gerhard Altenbourg, 4 April 1960.
13 Eva Schwalbe to Gerhard Altenbourg, 19/22 September 1960.
14 Eva Schwalbe to Gerhard Altenbourg, 12 April 1960.
15 Eva Schwalbe to Gerhard Altenbourg, 22 October 1959.
16 Eva Schwalbe to Gerhard Altenbourg, 8 March 1960.
17 On the "awkward gesture", a term derived from Roland Barthes and Henri Focillon, see Marit Heuß, *Peter Handkes Bildpoetik. Notieren, Zeichnen, Erzählen* (Göttingen: Wallstein, 2022), p. 152.
18 Roland Barthes, "Cy Twombly oder Non multa sed multum", in idem, *Der entgegenkommende und der stumpfe Sinn*, 8th edn. (Frankfurt am Main: Suhrkamp, 1990), pp. 165–83, here p. 170.
19 Altenbourg (n. 4 above), p. 2, fig. 2.
20 Ibid., p. 27, fig. 3.
21 René Char, "Lettera amorosa", quoted in Altenbourg (n. 4 above), p. 16.
22 René Char, "Lettera amorosa", in idem, *Poésies. Dichtungen*, ed. Jean-Pierre Wilhelm with Christoph Schwerin, trans. into German by Paul Celan, Johannes Hübner, Lothar Klünner, Jean-Pierre Wilhelm (Frankfurt am Main 1959), p. 319.
23 Ibid., p. 315. The motto appearing in Altenbourg's artist's book is underlined in his copy of *Poésies*.
24 Alexandru Bulucz, *"Es drängt dich zu schreiben, als ob du mit dem Leben im Rückstand wärst". Annäherung an René Char* (Heidelberg: Verlag das Wunderhorn, 2025), p. 7.
25 There are four bookmarks in the section "Hypnos"; see Char (n. 22 above).
26 See Gerhard Altenbourg, "Narbenrisse beim Durchstreifen jener Hügellandschaft", in Dieter Brusberg (ed.), *Gerhard Altenbourg. Werk-Verzeichnis*

36 Altenbourg 2016 (wie Anm. 4), S.22, Abb. 9.
37 Ebd.
38 Ebd.
39 Eva Schwalbe an Gerhard Altenbourg, 12. April 1960.
40 Ebd.
41 So äußerte sich Eva Schwalbe in Briefen zu *Salutation*. Vgl. Nauhaus 2016 (wie Anm. 3), S. 12 f.
42 *O Janus oh Janus* (W 60/29) enthält folgende Gedichte aus *Salutation*: »Im Mai. Zärtlich ist das Blau der Stunden«, »O diese Dunkelheiten«, »Schlangenhaft umwunden«, »Heil mich Frau« (variiert in *Salutation*). Vgl. Janda 2007 (wie Anm. 1), S. 288.
43 Im Brief werden die Werktitel *Es grüßt die Heimat*, *Kommt zu uns* und *Anruf* erwähnt. *Anruf* (56/87) vgl. Janda, Annegret: Gerhard Altenbourg. Monographie und Werkverzeichnis, 3 Bde., Bd. 1, 1937–1958, Köln 2004, S. 175. *Es grüßt die Heimat* (54/4) vgl. ebd., S. 280. Vgl. Eva Schwalbe an Gerhard Altenbourg, 12. April 1960.
44 Eva Schwalbe an Gerhard Altenbourg, 12. April 1960.

1947–1969, unter Mitarbeit von Annegret Janda, exh. cat. Berlin / Baden-Baden / Hanover / Düsseldorf (Hanover: Verlag der Galerie Brusberg, 1969), pp. 34ff., here p. 34.
27 See Bulucz (n. 24 above), pp. 9ff.
28 See Michel Foucault, *Dies ist keine Pfeife*, trans. Walter Seitter (Munich: Carl Hanser, 1974), p. 25.
29 Fig. 5, Altenbourg (n. 3 above), p. 18.
30 On the term "Textsubjekt" (text subject), see Dieter Burdorf, *Einführung in die Gedichtanalyse* (Stuttgart: Metzler, 2015), p. 195.
31 Fig. 4, Altenbourg (n. 3 above), p. 16.
32 Fig. 6, Altenbourg (n. 3 above), p. 17.
33 Fig. 7, Altenbourg (n. 3 above), p. 19.
34 Fig. 8, Altenbourg (n. 3 above), p. 23.
35 A contribution to the analysis of Altenbourg's poetry is found in a collection of selected poems that separates them from the images for the first time. The poems from *Salutation* are not included here, but several poems from *O Janus oh Janus* are. See Gerhard Altenbourg, *Wald minotaurisch. Gedichte*, ed. Thorsten Ahrend/Stiftung Gerhard Altenbourg, with an epilogue by Wulf Kirsten (Göttingen: Wallstein, 2019), pp. 37–48.
36 Fig. 9, Altenbourg (n. 3 above), p. 22.
37 Ibid.
38 Ibid.
39 Eva Schwalbe to Gerhard Altenbourg, 12 April 1960.
40 Ibid.
41 According to Eva Schwalbe in letters referring to *Salutation*; see Nauhaus (n. 3 above), pp. 12ff.
42 *O Janus oh Janus* (W 60/29) includes the following poems from *Salutation*: "Im Mai. Zärtlich ist das Blau der Stunden" (In May. Tender is the blue of the hours), "O diese Dunkelheiten" (Oh these darknesses), "Schlangenhaft umwunden", "Heil mich Frau" (Heal me woman) (varied in *Salutation*). See Janda (n. 1 above), vol. 2, p. 288.
43 The letter mentions the works *Es grüßt die Heimat* (Greetings from the Homeland), *Kommt zu uns* (Come to Us) and *Anruf* (Call). On *Anruf* (56/87) see Janda (n. 1 above), vol. 1, p. 175. On *Es grüßt die Heimat* (54/4) see ibid., p. 280. See the letter from Eva Schwalbe to Gerhard Altenbourg, 12 April 1960.
44 Eva Schwalbe to Gerhard Altenbourg, 12 April 1960.

J'ai hâte de tenir dans mes mains la joie des tiennes.

René Char

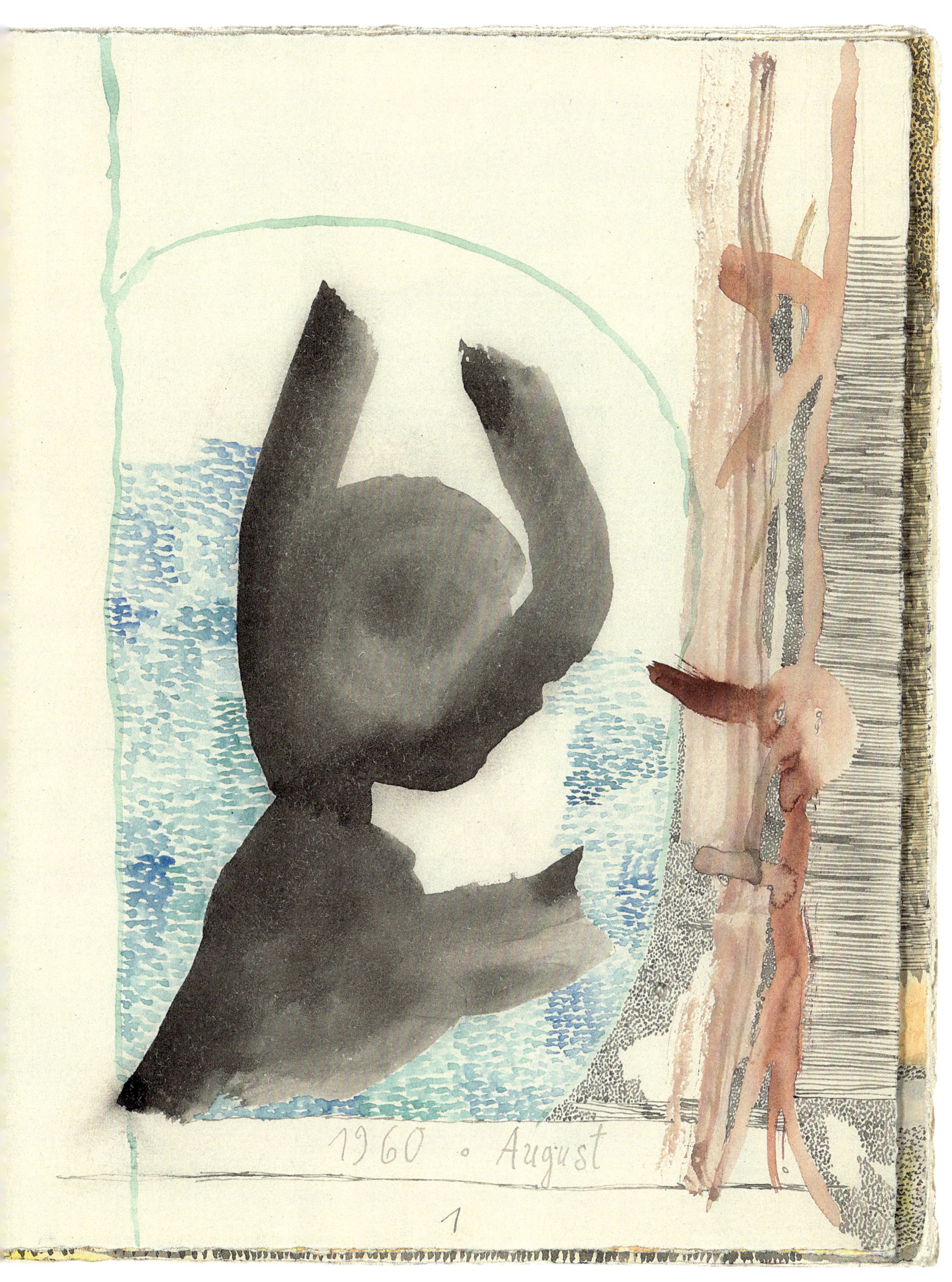

29 a Künstlerbuch *Salutation*, 1960, S. 0 f. |
Artist's book *Salutation*, 1960, pp. 0–1

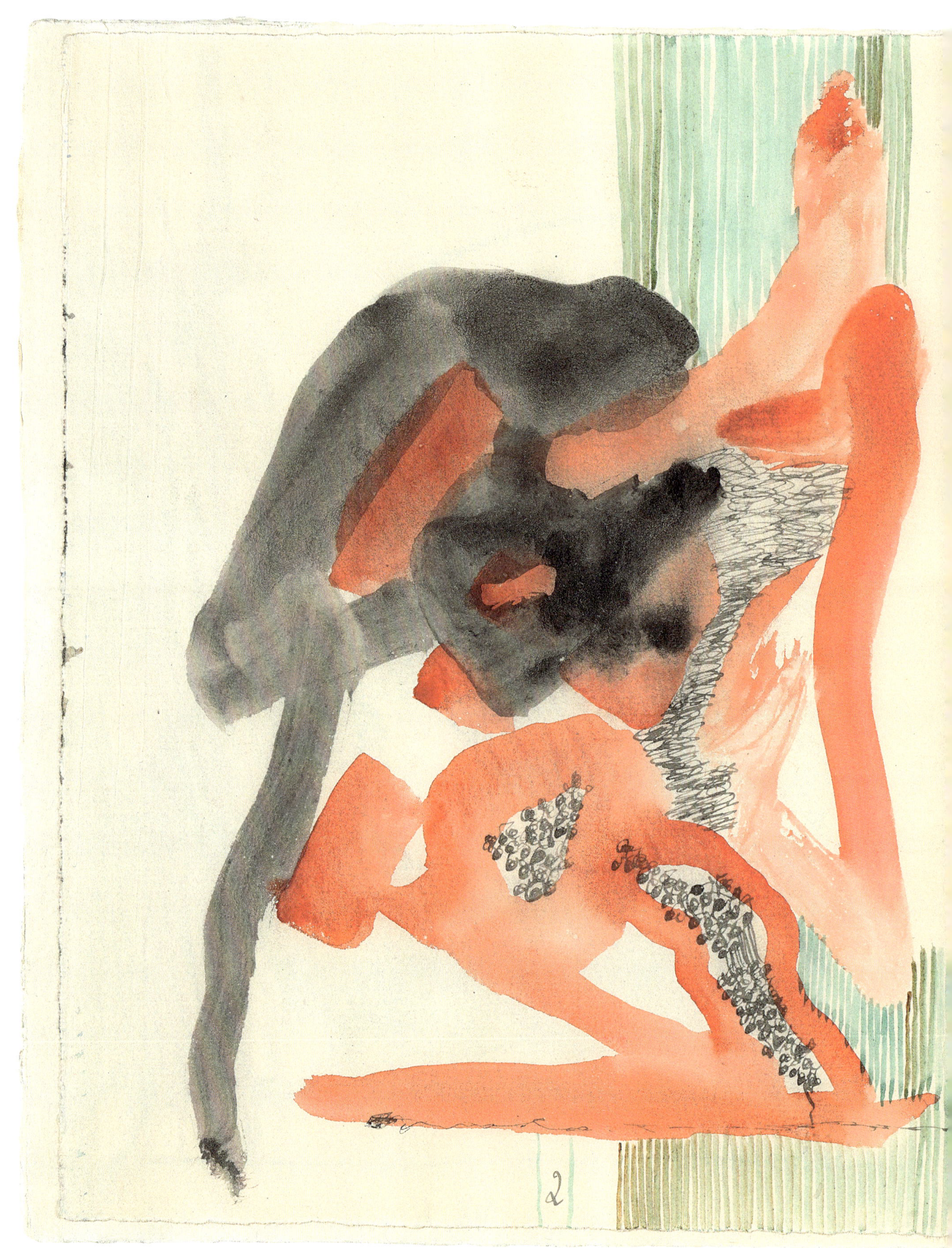

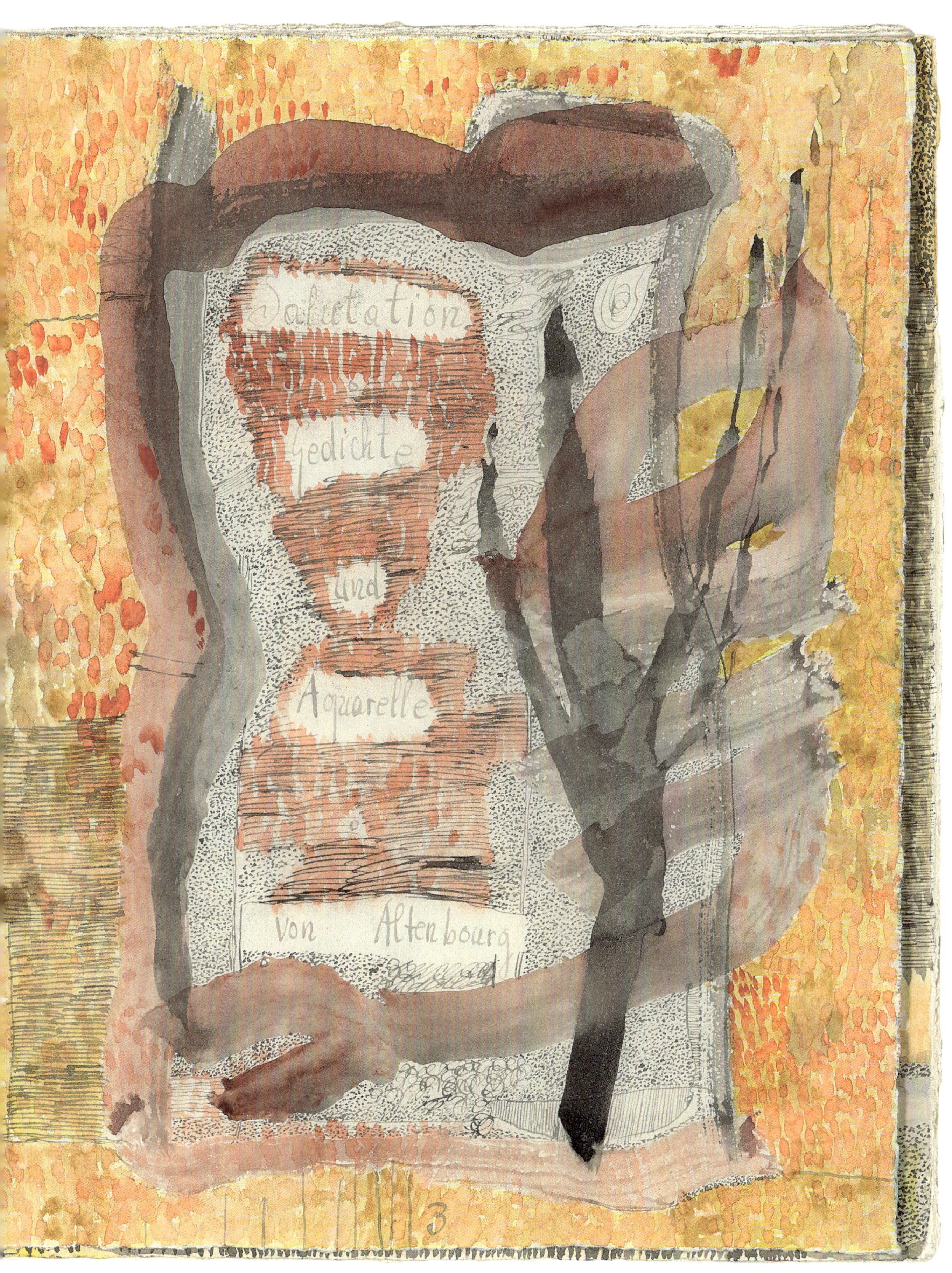

29 b Künstlerbuch *Salutation*, 1960, S. 2 f. |
Artist's book *Salutation*, 1960, pp. 2–3

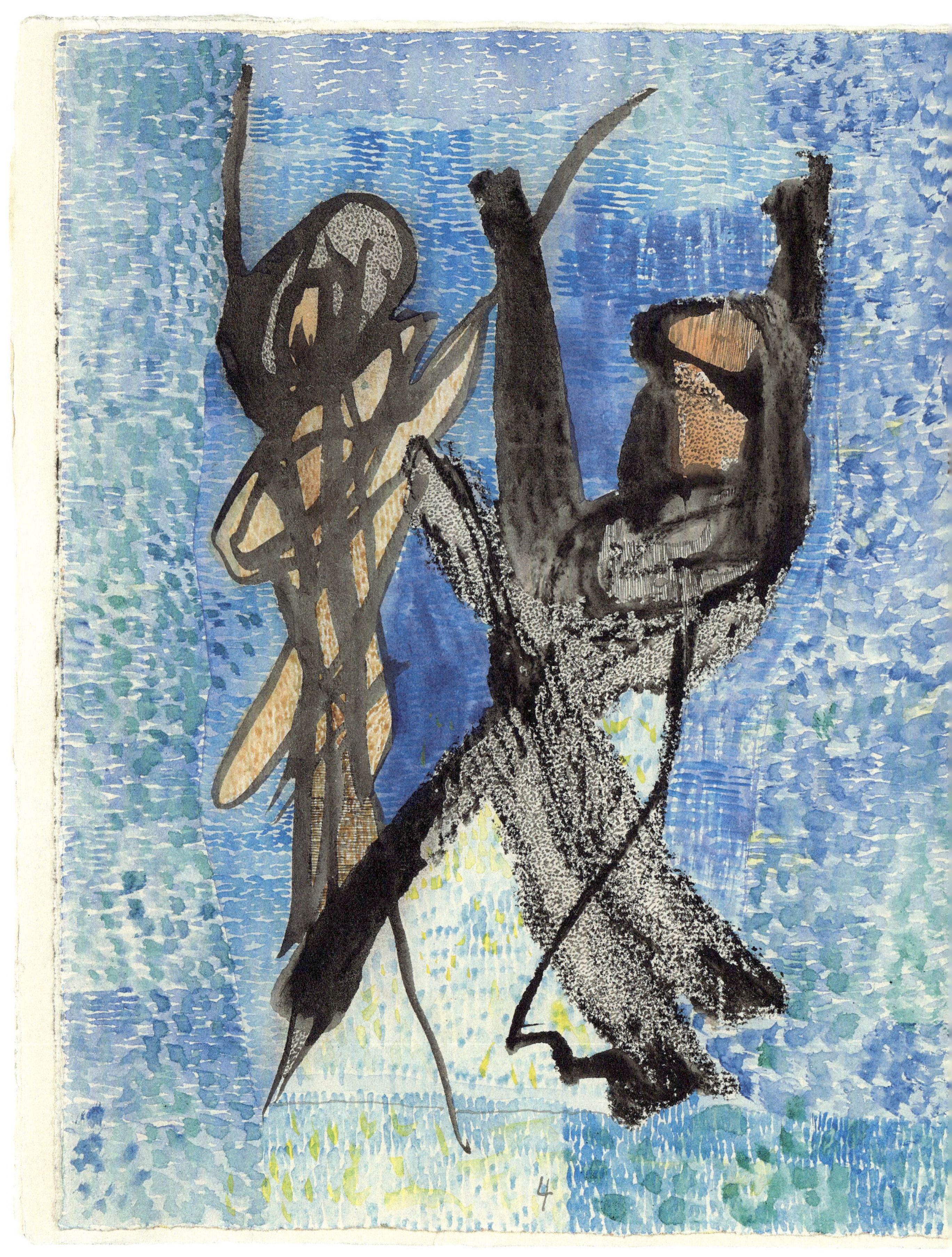
4

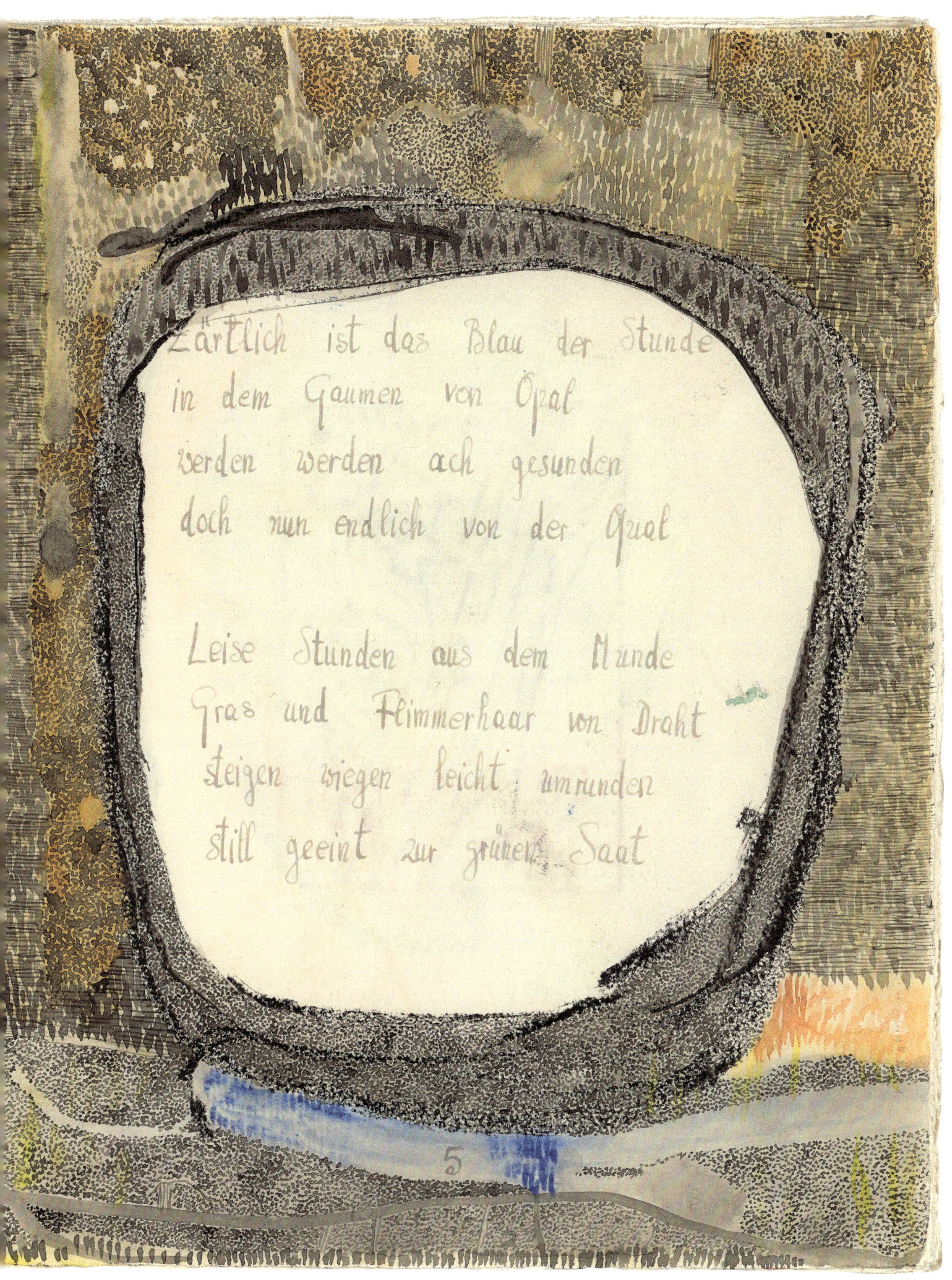

29 c Künstlerbuch *Salutation*, 1960, S. 4 f. |
Artist's book *Salutation*, 1960, pp. 4–5

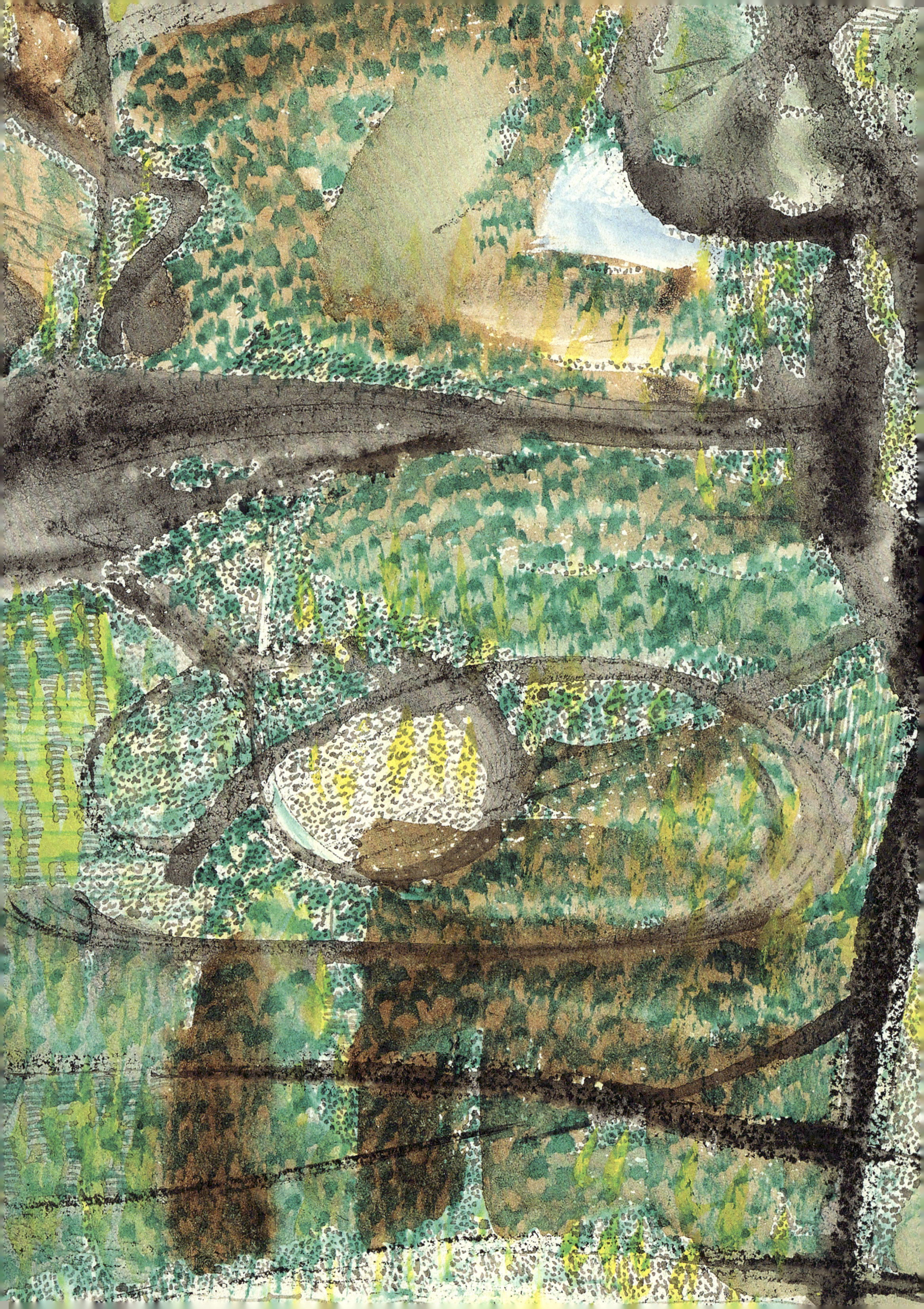

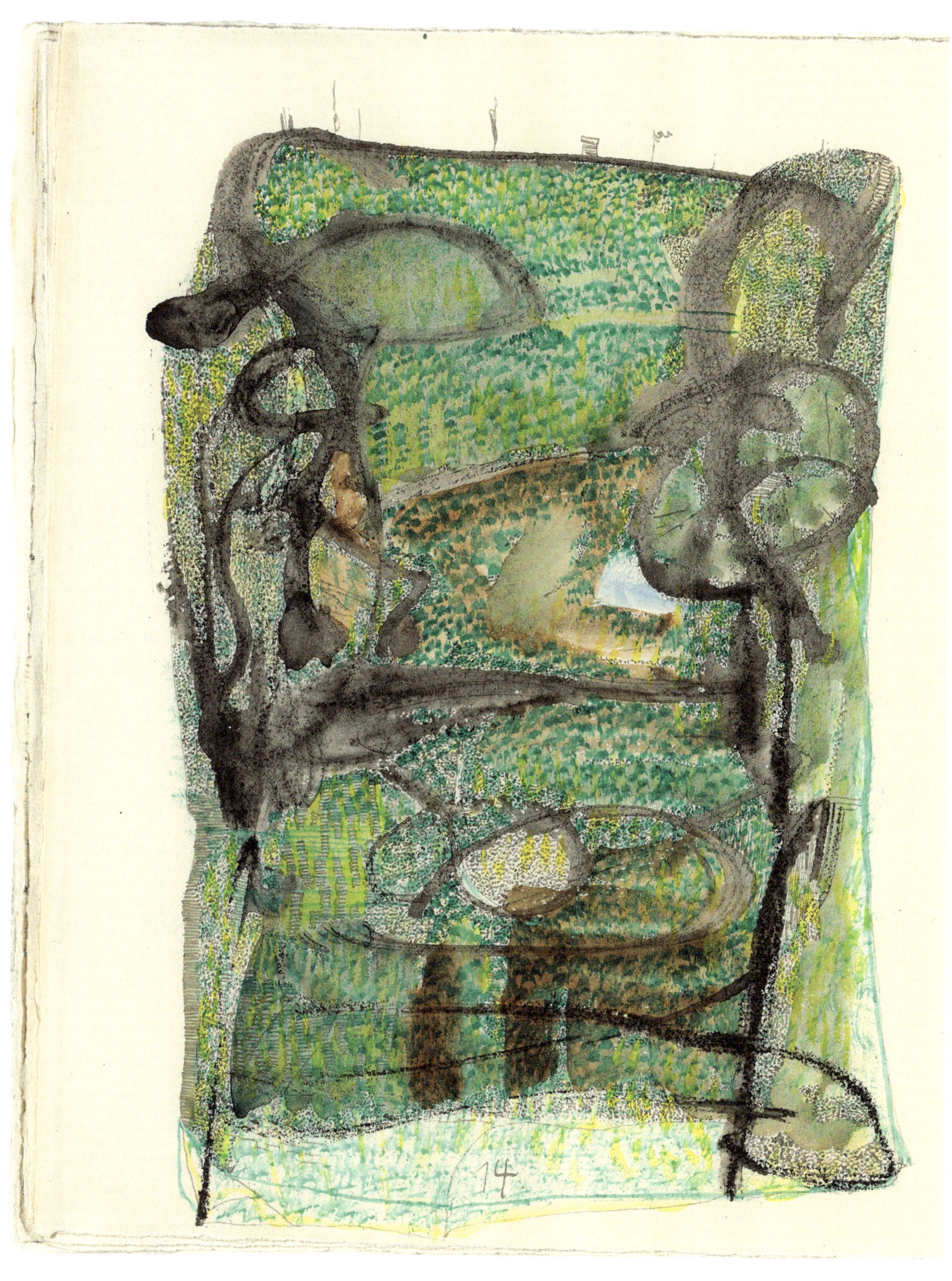

29 d Künstlerbuch *Salutation*, 1960, S. 14 |
Artist's book *Salutation*, 1960, p. 14

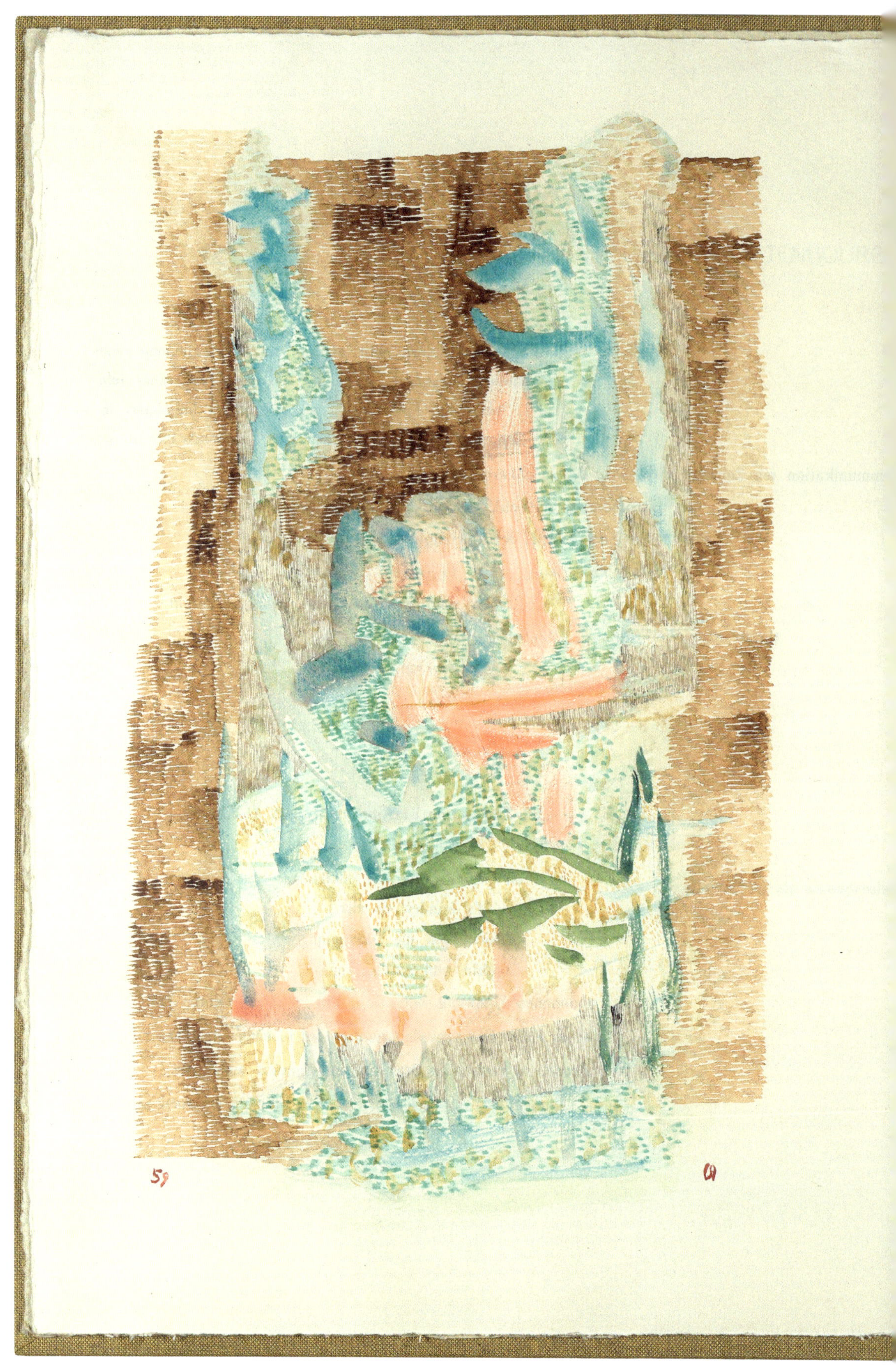

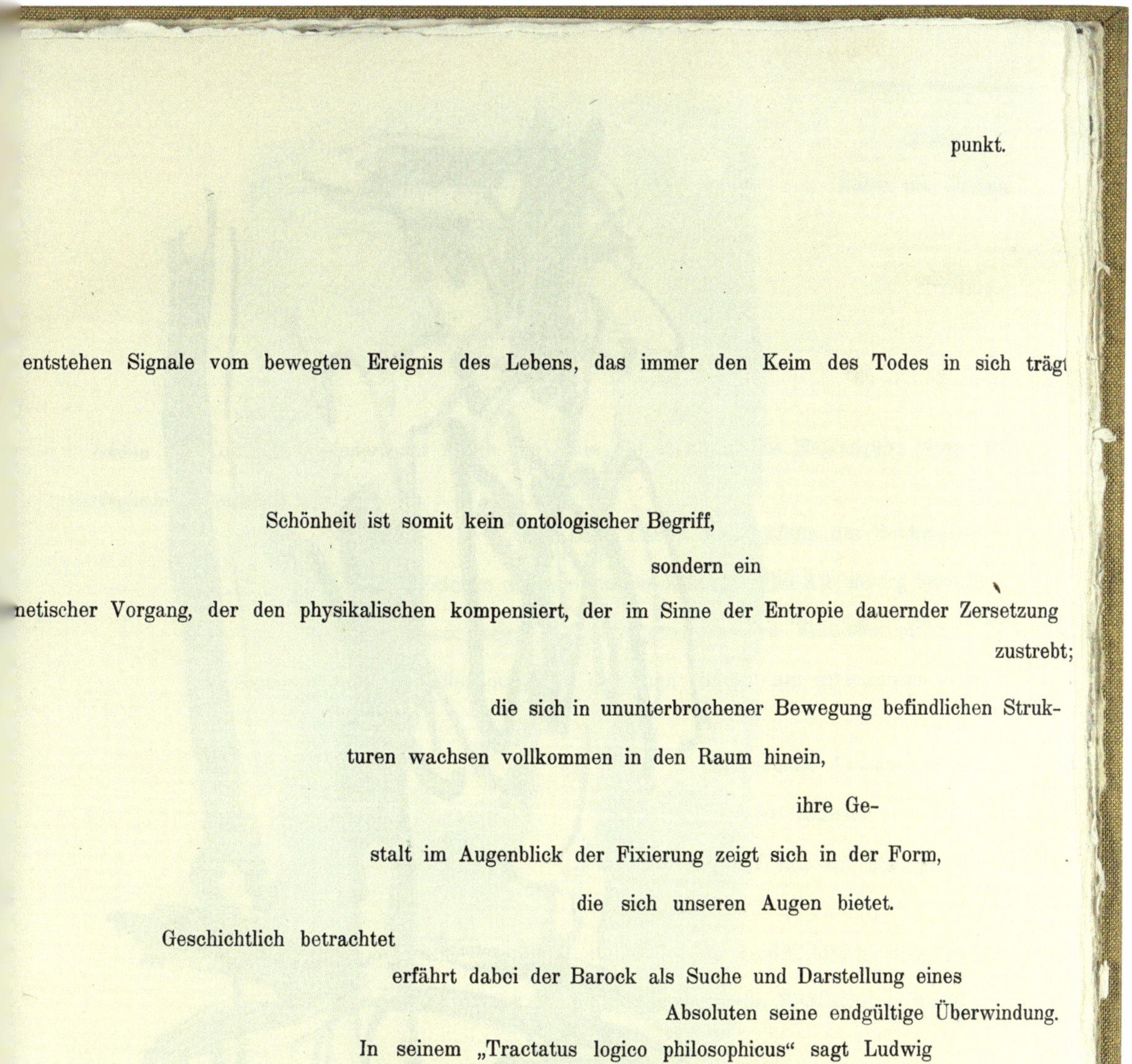

punkt.

entstehen Signale vom bewegten Ereignis des Lebens, das immer den Keim des Todes in sich trägt

Schönheit ist somit kein ontologischer Begriff,
sondern ein
netischer Vorgang, der den physikalischen kompensiert, der im Sinne der Entropie dauernder Zersetzung
zustrebt;
die sich in ununterbrochener Bewegung befindlichen Strukturen wachsen vollkommen in den Raum hinein,
ihre Ge-
stalt im Augenblick der Fixierung zeigt sich in der Form,
die sich unseren Augen bietet.
Geschichtlich betrachtet
erfährt dabei der Barock als Suche und Darstellung eines
Absoluten seine endgültige Überwindung.
In seinem „Tractatus logico philosophicus" sagt Ludwig
Wittgenstein: Die Form ist die Möglichkeit der Struktur.
Die Struktur der Tatsache besteht aus den Strukturen der
Sachverhalte. Die Gesamtheit der bestehenden Sachverhalte
ist die Welt.
Diese Gesamtheit der bestehenden Sachverhalte ist auch die Welt des Malers Gerhard Altenbourg,
sie wird bildlich
in einer Raumprojektion,
in der die Strukturen als ästheti-
sche Möglichkeiten erscheinen.

7

Spezielle Mittel sind dazu
erforderlich.

30 Künstlerbuch *Altenbourg Zehn Reproduktionen und zwei Originalzeichnungen*, 1958/59, S. 6 f. | Artist's book *Altenbourg Ten Reproductions and Two Original Drawings*, 1958–59, pp. 6–7

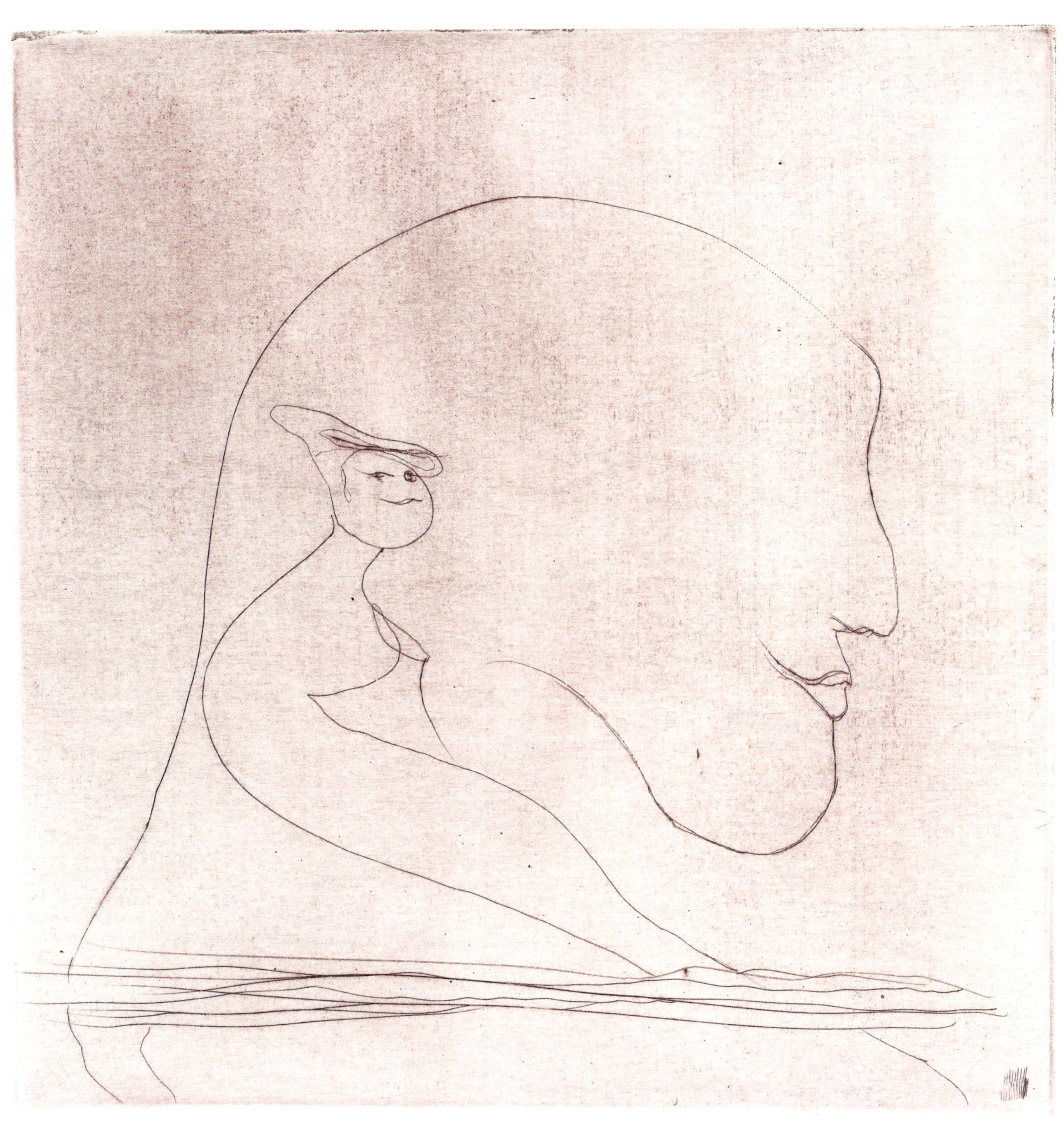

31 *Im Kopf ein pfiffiges Luder; schau, schau*, 1988 |
In the Head a Clever Hussy; Look, Look, 1988

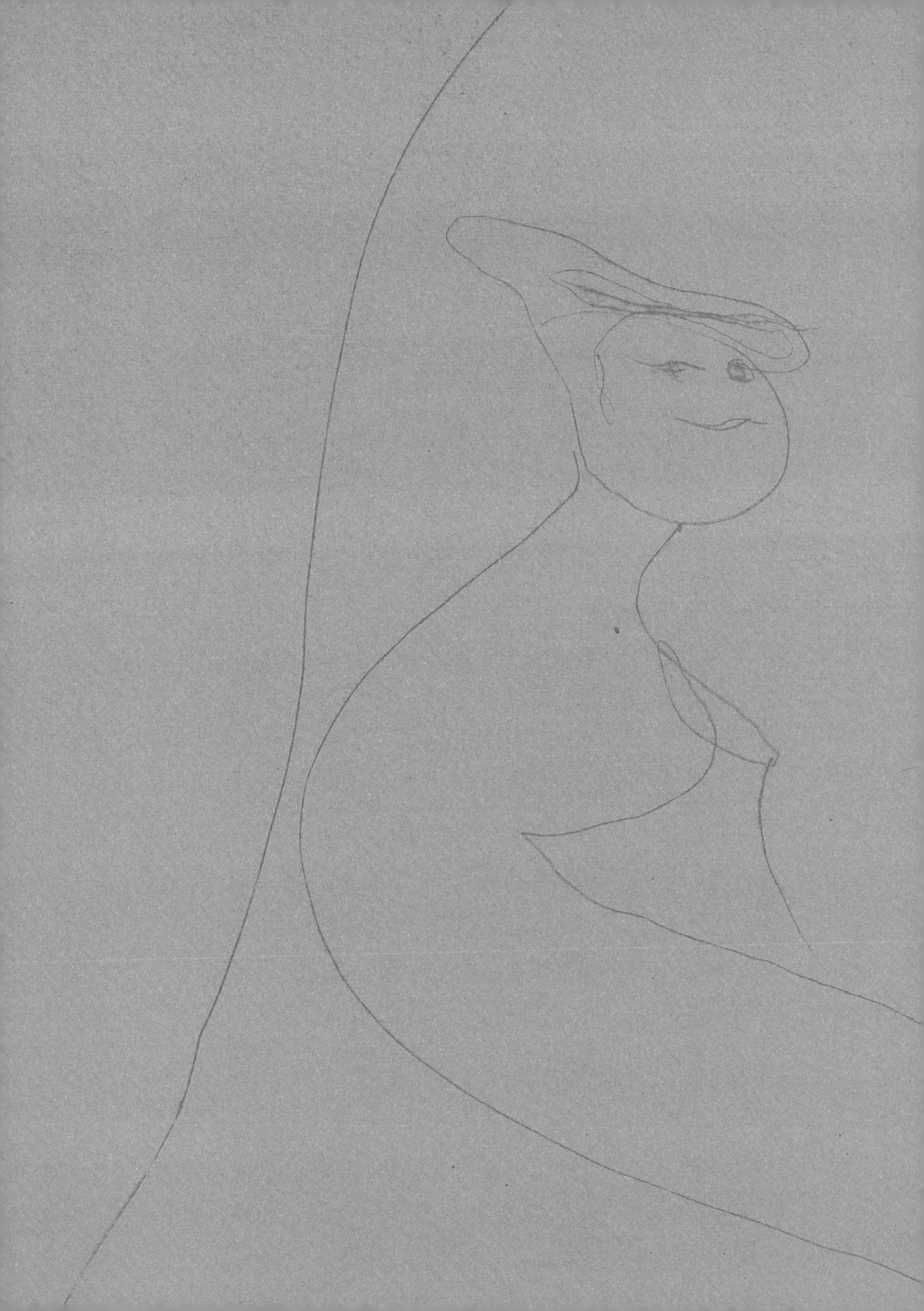

BIZZARE LANDSCHAFTEN & MIKROKOSMEN

BIZARRE LANDSCAPES & MICROCOSMS

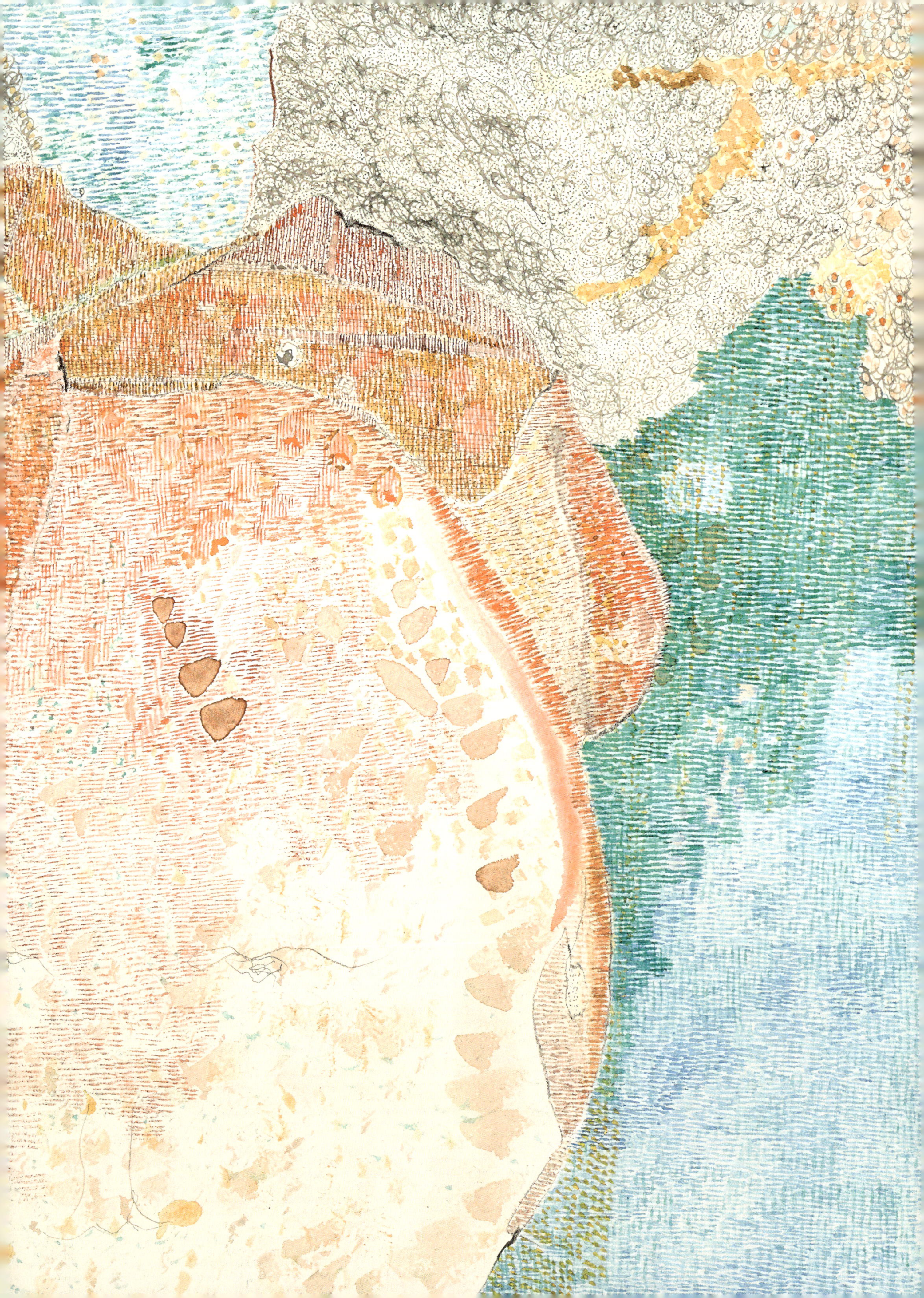

Sören Fischer

Mikroskopische Figurationen

Gerhard Altenbourg in Dialogen mit Egbert Kasper, Gabriela Oberkofler, Sebastian Rug, Ursula und Unica Zürn

Zeichnung und Welterschließung durch den mikroskopischen Blick

1972 vollendete Gerhard Altenbourg die großformatige Zeichnung *Unverwehet* (Abb. 1a). Es muss ein besonderer Moment für den »literarischen Maler«[1] gewesen sein, als er den Arbeitsprozess für beendet erklärte. Ahnte er, dass vor ihm eines seiner Hauptwerke lag? Das Werk reiht sich in eine Serie von Kopfbildern ein, die zum Kernsujet seines Schaffens zählen. Weit mehr als nur die abstrahierte Darstellung eines Kopfes, der aus landschaftlichen Formen erwächst, präsentiert sich das Bild als ein vibrierendes Feld aus abertausenden Zeichnungsoperationen: Da wurde gepunktet, gestrichelt, mit der Linie gehäkelt und gestrickt, da wurde nebeneinandergesetzt oder fadenartig verknäult, getupft, behutsam laviert. Altenbourg begegnet uns hier als Miniaturist. »Seine Striche, seine Farben, bilden einen Mikrokosmos«,[2] so Hermann Wiesler.

In *Unverwehet* gestaltete der Künstler einen nahansichtigen Ereignisraum, der mit seiner spannungsreichen Collage unterschiedlicher zeichnerischer »Feldstärken« für eine Dynamik verantwortlich ist, die das Bild auch aus der Distanz charakterisiert (Abb. 1b). Altenbourg wird als fantastischer »Handwerker im buchstäblichen Sinne des Wortes«[3] spürbar. Tausende feinste Bleistiftstriche sind aufs höchste verdichtet, erschaffen einen bildnerischen Mikrokosmos im Unschärfebereich zwischen Abstraktion und Naturassoziation.

Altenbourgs Zeichnungen sind mikroskopische Figurationen, sind Spuren rituellen Schaffens und prozessualen Denkens, sind Zeiteinschlüsse, eingeschrieben in den Flächenraum der verschiedenartigen Papiere, die Altenbourg so sehr liebte.[4] Insbesondere die Sichtbarmachung des prozesshaften Arbeitens offenbart Altenbourg als weit über seinen Einflussbereich hinausreichenden Zeichner des 20. Jahrhunderts, denn viele Zeichnerinnen und Zeichner der Gegenwart wenden sich der prozessualen Dimension von Zeichnung als einem Medium zu, das sich selbst befragt und das nicht steuerbare Ereignisse zulässt.

Microscopic Figurations

Gerhard Altenbourg in Dialogue with Egbert Kasper, Gabriela Oberkofler, Sebastian Rug, Ursula and Unica Zürn

Drawing and Discovering the World through the Microscopic Gaze

In 1972, Gerhard Altenbourg finished his large-format drawing *Unverwehet* (Unwavering; fig. 1a). It must have been a special moment for the "literary painter"[1] when he decided that the creative process for this work was complete. Did he sense that one of his greatest works stood before him? The drawing belongs to a series of pictures of heads, a frequent subject in his work. Much more than just an abstracted representation of a head that grows from landscape-like shapes, the image appears as a pulsating field created out of thousands of drawing gestures: dots, dashes, lines seemingly hooked and knitted, placed right next to each other or entangled like threads, dabs and finally careful applications of wash. Altenbourg operates here like a miniaturist: "His lines, his colours form a microcosmos", as Hermann Wiesler has observed.[2]

In *Unverwehet*, the artist created a close-up event space, whose charged collage of varied graphic "field densities" generates a dynamic that characterises the picture when seen from a distance (fig. 1b). Altenbourg assumes the role of the fantastical *Handwerker* "in the literal sense of working by hand".[3] Thousands of the thinnest pencil lines are set tightly together, creating a visual microcosmos in the fuzzy area between abstraction and association with nature.

Altenbourg's drawings are microscopic figurations, the traces of ritual making and

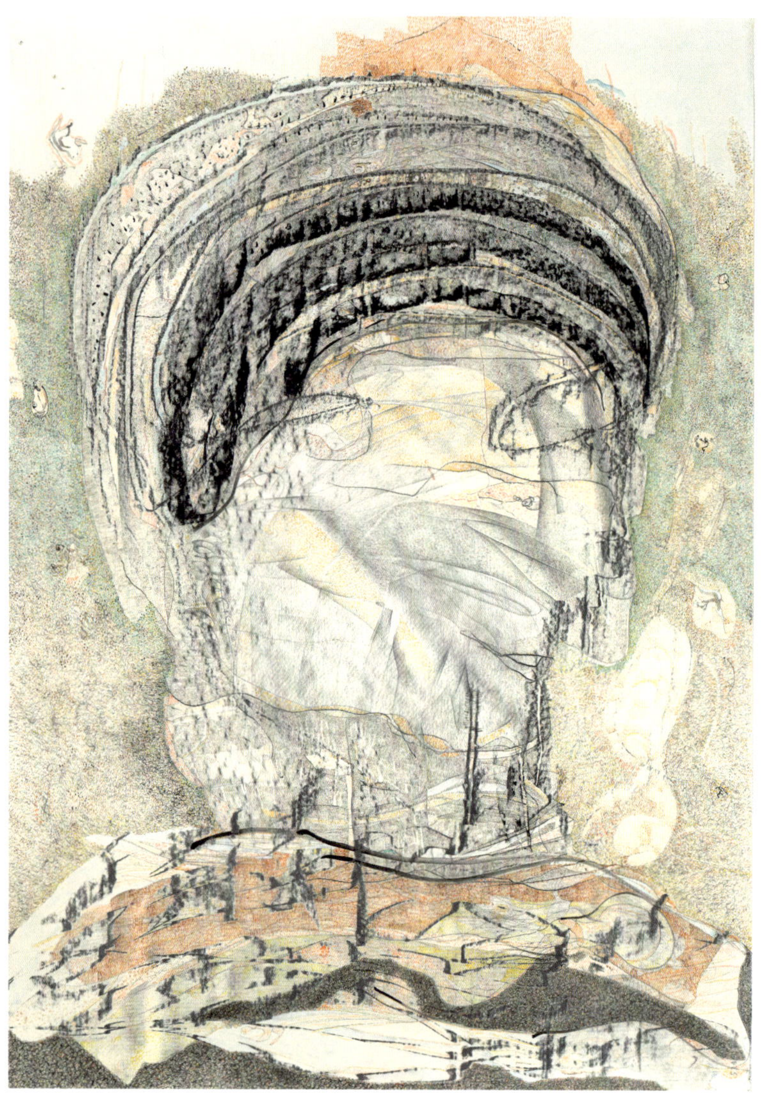

Abb. 1a Gerhard Altenbourg, *Unverwehet*, 1972, Grafit, Bleistift, Pastell, Kreide, Pinsel auf Schoellers Parole-Bütten, 1020 × 725 mm, Staatliche Kunstsammlungen Dresden, Kupferstich-Kabinett, Inv.-Nr. C 2012-68
Fig. 1a Gerhard Altenbourg, *Unverwehet* (Unwavering), 1972, graphite, pencil, pastel, chalk, brush on Schoeller Parole laid paper, 1020 × 725 mm, Staatliche Kunstsammlungen Dresden, Kupferstich-Kabinett, inv. no. C 2012-68

Eine sehr ähnliche Richtung verfolgte Unica Zürn. 1916 in Berlin geboren, erlebte Zürn die Diktatur des nationalsozialistischen Regimes und begann nach dem Krieg zu schreiben; auch Altenbourg besaß seit den 1980er-Jahren ein Bändchen von ihr.[5] Zürns bildnerisches Schaffen setzte 1953 ein, angeregt durch eine Reise nach Paris. Zürn arbeitete fast ausnahmslos zeichnerisch. In diesem Medium schuf sie eine Bildwelt, in der sie eine der wesentlichen Kunstströmungen der Französischen Moderne umkreiste: den Surrealismus, mit einem großen Gespür für die Ausdruckskraft winziger, akribisch gesetzter Linien, Punkte und Strukturen. Wie Altenbourg war auch Zürn dem Allerkleinsten auf der Spur – stets

processual thinking, inclusions of time inscribed in the two-dimensional space of the various types of paper he loved so much.[4] The visualisation of processual work in particular reveals Altenbourg as a twentieth-century draughtsman who influenced others far beyond his own sphere of activity, for many contemporary artists have turned to the process-oriented aspect of drawing as a medium that questions itself and produces aleatoric results.

A similar path was followed by Unica Zürn. Born in Berlin in 1916, Zürn lived through the dictatorship of the Nazi regime and began to write after the war. Altenbourg acquired a small book by her in the 1980s.[5] Zürn's visual art production began in 1953, inspired by a trip to Paris. She worked almost exclusively in drawing. In this medium, Zürn created a visual world that orbited around one of the most important art movements of French modernism, Surrealism, with great sensitivity for the expressive power of tiny, meticulously placed lines, dots and structures. Like Altenbourg, Zürn pursued the minuscule – always linked with a tendency towards the fantastic. Zürn worked, like the Surrealists, "with the effects of surprise and defamiliarisation".[6] In her universe of motifs, a clear distinction between human, animal or vegetal forms seems impossible. *La Serpenta* illustrates this in an exemplary manner (fig. 2). With her typical meticulousness, the artist, who like Altenbourg was represented by the Galerie Rudolf Springer, depicts an amorphous bundle of animal-like beings. Tentacles snake through the picture. The finest hairs shimmer, cellular structures pervade the composition as ornamentally depicted blobs, from which eyes seem to stare out. A fantastic visual world arises before us, recalling Altenbourg's formulation of "structural connections within mad encounters".[7]

For Zürn, drawing was something akin to a second alphabet, a "'seconde écriture', a writing freed from words".[8] This statement situates Zürn noticeably close to automatism, the technique that the Surrealists in France experimented with in the 1920s and introduced into art history.[9] For Zürn, however, the label of automatism can only be applied to a limited extent – just as with Altenbourg, whose large areas of dashes and dots suggest "dreamy" work processes only at first glance. Despite all their love of storytelling, Zürn and Altenbourg never questioned their roles as authors.

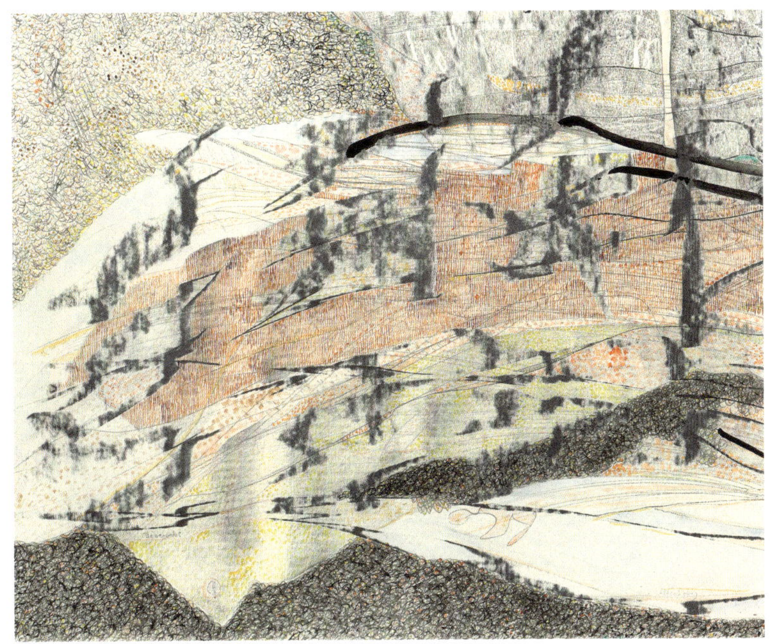

Abb. 1b Gerhard Altenbourg, *Unverwehet, Detail*, 1972, Grafit, Bleistift, Pastell, Kreide, Pinsel auf Schoellers Parole-Bütten, 1020 × 725 mm, Staatliche Kunstsammlungen Dresden, Kupferstich-Kabinett, Inv.-Nr. C 2012-68
Fig. 1b Gerhard Altenbourg, *Unverwehet* (Unwavering), detail, 1972, graphite, pencil, pastel, chalk, brush on Schoeller Parole laid paper, 1020 × 725 mm, Staatliche Kunstsammlungen Dresden, Kupferstich-Kabinett, inv. no. C 2012-68

Abb. 2 Unica Zürn, *O. T. [La Serpenta (The Serpent)]*, 1957, Öl auf Holz, 49,8 × 49,8 cm, Ubu Gallery, New York
Fig. 2 Unica Zürn, *O. T. [La Serpenta (The Serpent)]*, 1957, oil on panel, 49.8 × 49.8 cm, Ubu Gallery, New York

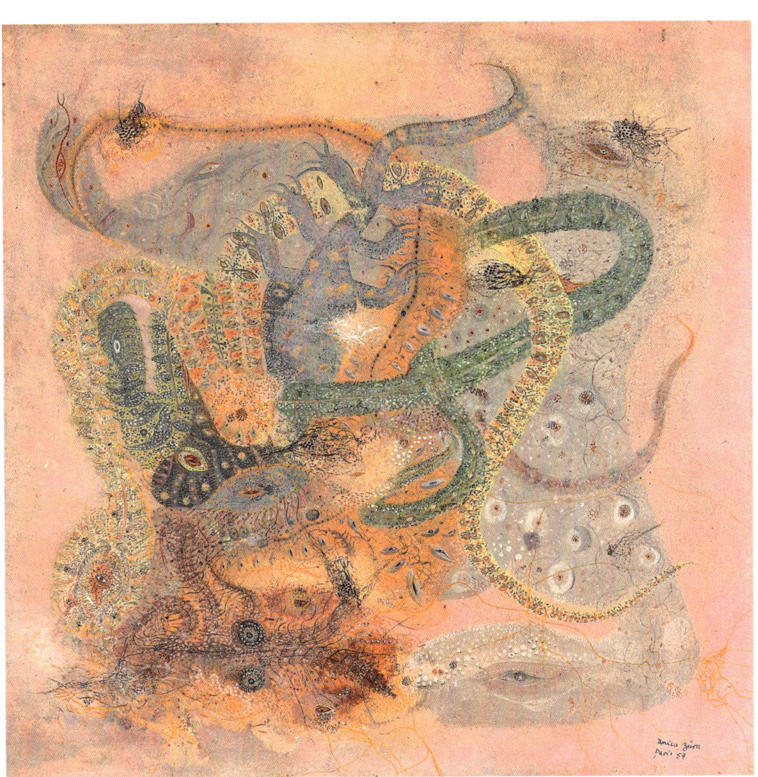

Point for Point in the Process: Minimalism, Ritual, Repetition

Sebastian Rug, a graduate of the Hochschule für Grafik und Buchkunst (Academy of Fine Arts) in Leipzig, is a contemporary artist who achieves the monumental through infinitesimal graphic arts. His work employs a strategy of an almost microscopic-analytic drawing technique, like that taken to masterful heights by Altenbourg.

Rug insists on making small-format drawings in which he takes the pencil to the very limits of its capabilities (fig. 3). From a distance his constructions appear like shimmering, delicate, dark grey cloths, like the finest textiles spreading out over portrait-format A4 sheets. The artist remarks that "I am interested in the smallest possible distances between the threads that can still be seen, which are microscopic".[10] The proximity of his former home in Leipzig to Altenburg has allowed the artist to visit the Lindenau-Museum regularly since the late 1990s. "Altenbourg," says Rug, "could almost be sensed in the building as a ghost.… When seeing Altenbourg's works for the first time, most people are probably astonished to realise how these very big, opulent pictures – you could almost call them watercolours – are constructed from the tiniest lines. This was for me, too, a fascinating discovery."[11]

Rug shares with Altenbourg a fascination for the microscopic. "My sheets explore the smallest possible distances. That's why assuming a microscopic perspective is so important."[12] Rug's drawing practice opens up a stimulating discourse on perception, since, as Altenbourg stated, a picture "is made for close-up and distant viewing at the same time".[13]

Consequently, Rug has hooked up and knotted together his lines like threads in a process of ritualised action (fig. 3). At its edges, the textile frays, revealing its fragility and marking it as *non finito*, implying that the process of drawing was perhaps merely interrupted. Rug follows an autopoietic working process, in which the picture is generated from itself, that is, from the repetition of similar actions, thus "growing" thread for thread.

Smallness and Timelessness

Gerhard Altenbourg's path to the essence of time was an extremely reflective one. He knew that lines are signs of time. "In psychology, in psychosomatics, in medicine, there is an appeal", said the artist, "for people to not

verbunden mit einem Hang zum Fantastischen. Zürn arbeitete, ähnlich wie die Surrealisten, »mit Überraschungs- und Verfremdungseffekten«.[6] In ihrer Motivwelt scheint eine klare Abgrenzung zwischen menschlichen, tierischen oder pflanzlichen Formen unmöglich. *La Serpenta* führt das exemplarisch vor Augen **(Abb. 2)**: Mit der für sie typischen Akribie zeichnete die Künstlerin, die, wie Altenbourg, von der Galerie Rudolf Springer vertreten wurde, ein amorphes Knäuel tierisch wirkender Wesen. Tentakeln schlängeln sich. Feinste Haare flimmern, zellenartige Strukturen durchziehen als ornamental gestaltete Flächen die Komposition, aus welcher Augen herauszuschauen scheinen. Eine fantastische Bildwelt tut sich auf, die an Altenbourgs Formulierung der »strukturellen Verknüpfungen innerhalb wahnwitziger Begegnungen«[7] erinnert.

Für Unica Zürn war Zeichnen so etwas wie eine zweite Schrift, eine »›seconde écriture‹, ein von Wörtern befreites Schreiben«.[8] Diese Formulierung rückt Zürn deutlich in die Nähe des Automatismus, also jener Technik, die seit den 1920er-Jahren von den Surrealisten in Frankreich erprobt und in die Kunstgeschichte eingeführt wurde.[9] Für Zürn gilt die Zuordnung zum Automatismus jedoch nur sehr eingeschränkt – wie auch für Altenbourg, dessen große Strich- und Punktefelder lediglich auf den ersten Blick »träumerische« Arbeitsprozesse suggerieren. Bei all der Fabulierfreude stellten sich Zürn und Altenbourg als Autorin bzw. Autor nie infrage.

Punkt für Punkt im Prozess. Minimalismus, Ritual, Wiederholung

Einer jener Künstler der Gegenwart, der im grafischen Reich des Allerkleinsten Großes schafft, ist Sebastian Rug. Der Absolvent der Leipziger Hochschule für Grafik und Buchkunst steht mit seinem Werk beispielhaft für die Strategie einer gleichsam mikroskopisch-analytischen Zeichentechnik, wie sie von Gerhard Altenbourg zur Meisterschaft gesteigert werden konnte.

Rug hat sich auf kleinformatige Zeichnungen kapriziert, mit denen er das technische Leistungsvermögen des Bleistifts an die Grenzen führt **(Abb. 3)**. Von Weitem erscheinen seine Gebilde wie zarte in Dunkelgrau schimmernde Tücher, wie feinste Textilien, die sich auf hochformatigen DIN-A4-Blättern ausbreiten. Dazu der Künstler: »Mich interessieren die kleinstmöglichen, noch darstellbaren Abstände zwischen den Fäden, die ins Mikroskopische gehen.«[10] Die Nähe seines früheren Lebensortes Leipzig zu Altenburg erlaubte dem Zeichner seit den späten 1990er-Jahren regelmäßige Besuche des Lindenau-Museums. »Altenbourg«, so Rug, »war dort gleichsam als Hausgeist präsent (…). Wenn man die Werke von Altenbourg zum ersten Mal wahrnimmt, ist es wohl für die Meisten eine große Verblüffung, zu sehen, wie sich diese zum Teil sehr großen, opulenten Bilder – man möchte fast sagen Aquarellgemälde – aus dem Allerkleinsten aufbauen. Das war auch für mich eine faszinierende Entdeckung.«[11]

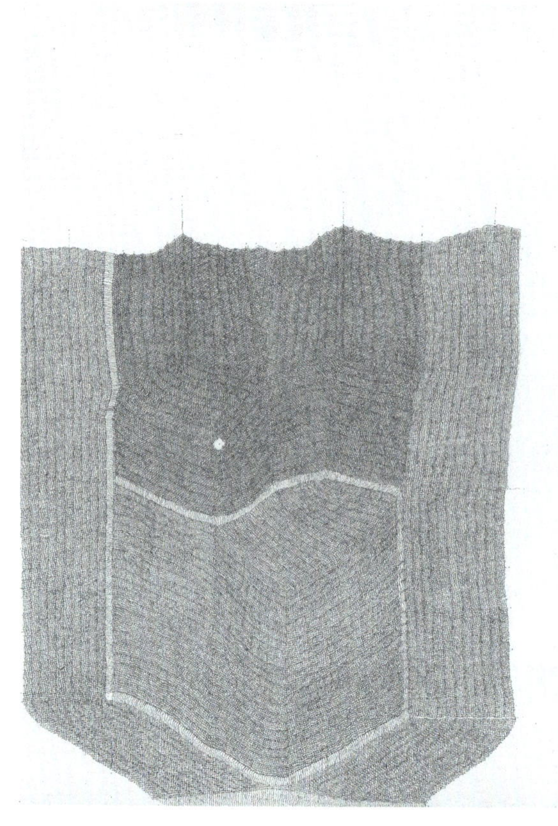

Abb. 3 Sebastian Rug, *Ohne Titel*, 2018, Bleistift, Papier, 295 × 210 mm, Museum Pfalzgalerie Kaiserslautern (mpk), Graphische Sammlung, Inv.-Nr. 21/3036
Fig. 3 Sebastian Rug, *Untitled*, 2018, pencil on paper, 295 × 210 mm, Museum Pfalzgalerie Kaiserslautern (mpk), Graphische Sammlung, inv. no. 21/3036

focus so strongly on themselves. They should forget, should be able to forget, 'be outside themselves'. One could call this 'stepping outside of time'. When I am drawing, I step outside of time".[14]

By means of working in phases, Altenbourg sought a state of expanded time: "There are drawings that are first laid out with the pencil, then a second layer is added over it, then a third, colourful things as well, up to eight, nine layers of drawing.… Yes, you need – to express it quantitatively – around twenty-four hours for such a small area.… In this work I need an injection of time to arrive at this timelessness."[15] This prolonged manner of working was the key to his creative quality: "I keep my works for so long because I am waiting for entry. I live for this moment, I always have thirty to fifty works lying around.… Only in this way can you enter the

Mit Altenbourg verbindet Rug die Faszination für das Mikroskopische: »Meine Blätter ergründen kleinstmögliche Abstände. Daher ist das Einnehmen der mikroskopischen Perspektive so wichtig.«[12] Rugs Zeichnung öffnet einen anregenden Diskurs über Wahrnehmung, da mit Altenbourg gesprochen, das Bild »für die Nah- und die Fernbetrachtung zugleich gemacht (ist).«[13]

So hat Rug die Fäden im Prozess einer ritualisierten Handlung additiv miteinander verknüpft und verknotet **(Abb. 3)**. An den Rändern franst das Gewebe aus, offenbart seine Fragilität und markiert als Non-finito, dass der Prozess des Zeichnens vielleicht nur unterbrochen wurde. Rug verfolgt eine autopoetische Arbeitsweise, in der das Bild gleichsam aus sich selbst, das heißt aus der Wiederholung ähnlicher Handlungen, entsteht, also Faden für Faden »wächst«.

Kleinteiligkeit und Zeitlosigkeit

Gerhard Altenbourgs Zugang zum Wesen der Zeit war ein äußerst reflektierter. Er wusste: Linien sind Zeitzeichen. »Es gibt in der Psychologie, in der Psychosomatik, in der Medizin den Aufruf«, so der Künstler, »daß der Mensch sich nicht so stark auf sich konzentrieren soll. Er soll vergessen, vergessen können, ›außer sich sein‹. Man könnte das ein ›Aus-der-Zeit-heraustreten‹ nennen. Wenn ich zeichne, trete ich aus der Zeit heraus.«[14]

Über seine in Phasen operierende Arbeitsweise suchte Gerhard Altenbourg den Zustand der gedehnten Zeit: »Es gibt Zeichnungen, die erst mit Bleistift angelegt worden sind, dann kommt eine zweite Schicht darüber, dann eine dritte, auch farbige Dinge, bis zu acht, neun Überzeichnungen. (…) Ja, man braucht eben, um das quantitativ auszudrücken, für so ein kleines Feld an die 24 Stunden Arbeit, (…) Ich brauche bei dieser Arbeit einen Einfluß von Zeit, um zu dieser Zeitlosigkeit zu kommen.«[15] In dieser gedehnten Arbeitsweise lag der Schlüssel für seine schöpferische Qualität: »Ich sitze bei meiner Arbeit deswegen so lange, weil ich auf den Zugang warte. Auf diesen Zeitpunkt lebe ich hin, immer habe ich 30 bis 50 Arbeiten liegen, (…) Nur so gelingt der Einstieg in das Wesen der Dinge, denn die Geduld spielt eine große, große Rolle.«[16] Wie das in Blau- und Rosatönen schimmernde Werk *Flügel der Morgenröte* vor Augen führt **(Kat. 40, vgl. Detail S. 90)**, erreichte Altenbourg das Festhalten der Zeit durch die Punkt-für-Punkt- und Strich-für Strich-Protokollierung der Langsamkeit – auch in Reminiszenz an die über die Zeit gedehnten Wachstumsvorgänge der Natur allgemein.

Ein Künstler, der sich bis heute von der zeitentschleunigten »Setzkunst« Altenbourgs inspirieren lässt, ist Egbert Kasper. Der Künstler arbeitet seit Anfang der 1990er-Jahre freischaffend in der Oberlausitz. Zu einer ersten Begegnung mit dem Werk Altenbourgs kam es Ende der 1980er-Jahre, als Kasper im Dresdener Kupferstich-Kabinett die Sonderausstellung *Gerhard Altenbourg. Zeichnungen und Graphik* (1986/87) besuchte. Für Kasper war dies eine Ausstellung, »die mein Staunen förmlich überrollte. Damals noch expressiv malend, wurde ich mit einer inneren Welt konfrontiert, die ich nur aus Paul Klees Buch

essence of things, for patience plays a big, big role".[16] As is clear in the drawing *Flügel der Morgenröte* (Wings of Dawn; **cats. 40**), which shimmers in blue and pink tones, Altenbourg achieved the halting of time by recording slowness point-for-point and dash-for-dash – recalling as well the universal cycles of growth in nature stretching over time.

An artist who continues to be inspired by Altenbourg's temporally decelerated "art of setting" is Egbert Kasper, who has been working independently since the early 1990s in the Oberlausitz region of eastern Germany. He first encountered Altenbourg's works at the end of the 1980s, when Kasper visited the exhibition *Gerhard Altenbourg. Zeichnungen und Graphik* (Gerhard Altenbourg: Drawings and Graphic Works; 1986–87) at the Kupferstich-Kabinett (Collection of Drawings and Prints) in Dresden. For Kasper this was a show that "literally overwhelmed me with astonishment. At that time I still painted in an expressive style, but here I was confronted with an inner world that I had only known from Paul Klee's book *Die Zwitschermaschine* (The Twittering Machine; 1981).[17] His engagement with Altenbourg led, albeit independently, to the 1994 drawing *Hinaus – Hinauf* (Outward – Upward; **fig. 4**).

Out of innumerable tiny scribblings, minuscule hooks and interweaving lines, Kasper has imagined a world that rejects a clear-cut spatiality, spreading out primarily across two dimensions, generated from (cell) fragments and internal structures. As the artist has noted, "graphic openness and density have become fundamental principles for me, thanks to Gerhard Altenbourg. To this day I am fascinated by the overwhelming pictorial surface of his drawings and the connection to poetry, what one could call 'line-language forms'."[18] Similar to Altenbourg, Zürn and Rug, Kasper's drawings "grow" directly while drawing amid the charged fields of automatism, intuition and experience, evolving out of themselves in autopoiesis.

Delicate and Tiny: The Poetification of Nature. Mindfulness and Ecological Sensitisation

Together with Altenbourg, Ursula Bluhm-Schultze, known as Ursula, was a key representative of the imaginative and surrealistic assimilation of nature. Similar to the other artists discussed in this essay, her works explore the interstices between abstraction, figuration and a

Die Zwitscher-Maschine (1981) kannte.«[17] In Auseinandersetzung mit Altenbourg, aber dennoch eigenständig, entstand 1994 die Zeichnung *Hinaus – Hinauf* **(Abb. 4)**.

Aus unzähligen kleinsten Kritzeleien, Häkchen und Linienverwebungen hat Kasper eine Welt imaginiert, die auf eine dezidierte Räumlichkeit verzichtet, sich primär in der Fläche ausdehnt, und die aus (Zell-)Fragmenten und Binnenstrukturen aufgebaut ist. Dazu der Künstler: »Die grafische Offenheit und die Verdichtung wurden dank Gerhard Altenbourg zu Grundprinzipien. Bis heute fasziniert mich die überbordende Bildfläche seiner Zeichnungen und die Verbindung zur Poesie, die man ›Strichsprachgebilde‹ nennen könnte.«[18] Ähnlich wie bei Altenbourg, Zürn und Rug »wachsen« die Zeichnungen von Kasper im Spannungsfeld zwischen Automatismus, Intuition und Erfahrung unmittelbar beim Zeichnen, entspinnen sich autopoetisch aus sich selbst heraus.

Zart und klein: die Poetisierung der Natur. Achtsamkeit und ökologische Sensibilisierungen

Eine wichtige Vertreterin der fantasievoll-surrealistischen Anverwandlung an die Natur war neben Altenbourg Ursula Bluhm-Schultze. Ähnlich wie die anderen in diesem Aufsatz besprochenen Künstler umkreisen ihre Werke den Grenzbereich zwischen Abstraktion, Figuration und Naturnähe. Mit Altenbourg verbindet sie nicht nur die dezidierte kleinteilige Bilderschließung, auch die Lust am Fabulieren findet sich bei ihr in einer ebensolchen Intensität. Ursula, die mit Altenbourg auch die gemeinsame Arbeit mit der Galerie von Dieter Brusberg (Hannover) verband, beschrieb ihre Werke als »Gegenwelt zur Außenwelt«,[19] die aus »Augen-Erlebnissen und Traum-Situationen«[20] geboren seien. Ihr zumeist farbenreicher, sehr ornamentaler Zugriff auf die Zeichnung verdeutlicht ein Blick auf das Blatt *Eine weihnachtliche Reise für meinen lieben Bär* **(Abb. 5)**. Aus neben- und übereinanderliegenden, jeweils unterschiedlich strukturierten Flächen hat die Künstlerin eine Traumlandschaft gewoben, durch die das Auge wandern kann: »Rhythmus und Musterung verändern, heben und senken sich, neigen mal hierhin und mal dorthin, doch ist die Darstellung im Ganzen ein Gewebe, wirkt fast wie gehäkelt.«[21] Sehr vergleichbar mit Altenbourg hob Ursula die Kategorien zwischen Pflanzen, Menschen, Architektur und Landschaft auf, provozierte ein anregendes Vexierspiel.[22]

Durch seine kleinteilige Arbeitsweise kennzeichnete auch Altenbourg Natur und Welt als zerbrechlich und kostbar. Seine Bilder sagen: Da war jemand mit Behutsamkeit unterwegs, öffnete einen erweiterten Blick auf die Schöpfung. Altenbourg umschrieb dies wie folgt: »In diesen Schichtungen sind viele Erfahrungen eingewebt, eingeschlossen, die sich erfahren lassen im Winde dessen, was sich im Wort Zeit ausspricht und als solches erdgeschichtliche und individuelle Zeit auf eine Fläche bringt. (…) Eine solche Fläche wächst; ihr Wachstum ist ein Sich-öffnen und ein aus der obersten Fläche in die untergelagerten Tiefen Hinabschauen, bis zu den Rändern hin (…).«[23]

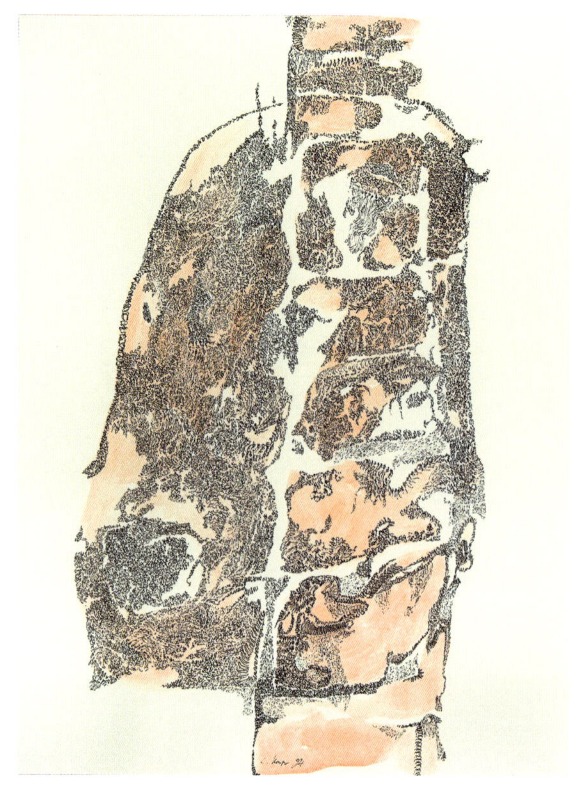

Abb. 4 Egbert Kasper, *Hinaus – Hinauf*, 1994, Feder in Tusche, Aquarell auf Papier, 478 × 359 mm, Privatbesitz
Fig. 4 Egbert Kasper, *Hinaus – Hinauf* (Outward – Upward), 1994, pen with India ink and aquarelle on paper, 478 × 359 mm, private collection

proximity to nature. She resembles Altenbourg artistically, not only in her decidedly microscopic pictorial composition, but in a similarly intensive pleasure in inventing stories. Moreover, like Altenbourg she was also represented by Dieter Brusberg's gallery in Hanover. Ursula described her work as the "counterworld to the external world",[19] born from "eye experiences and dream situations".[20] Her frequently colourful, emphatically ornamental approach to drawing is immediately apparent in a work like *Eine weihnachtliche Reise für meinen lieben Bär* (A Christmas Journey for My Dear Bear; **fig. 5**). Here the artist has woven together a dream landscape out of areas lying next to and overlapping each other, each structured in a different manner, generating a landscape through which the eye can wander: "Rhythm and pattern vary, rise and fall, lean sometimes in one direction and sometimes in the other, yet on the whole the representation is a weaving that almost seems crocheted".[21] Like Altenbourg, Ursula dissolved the boundaries

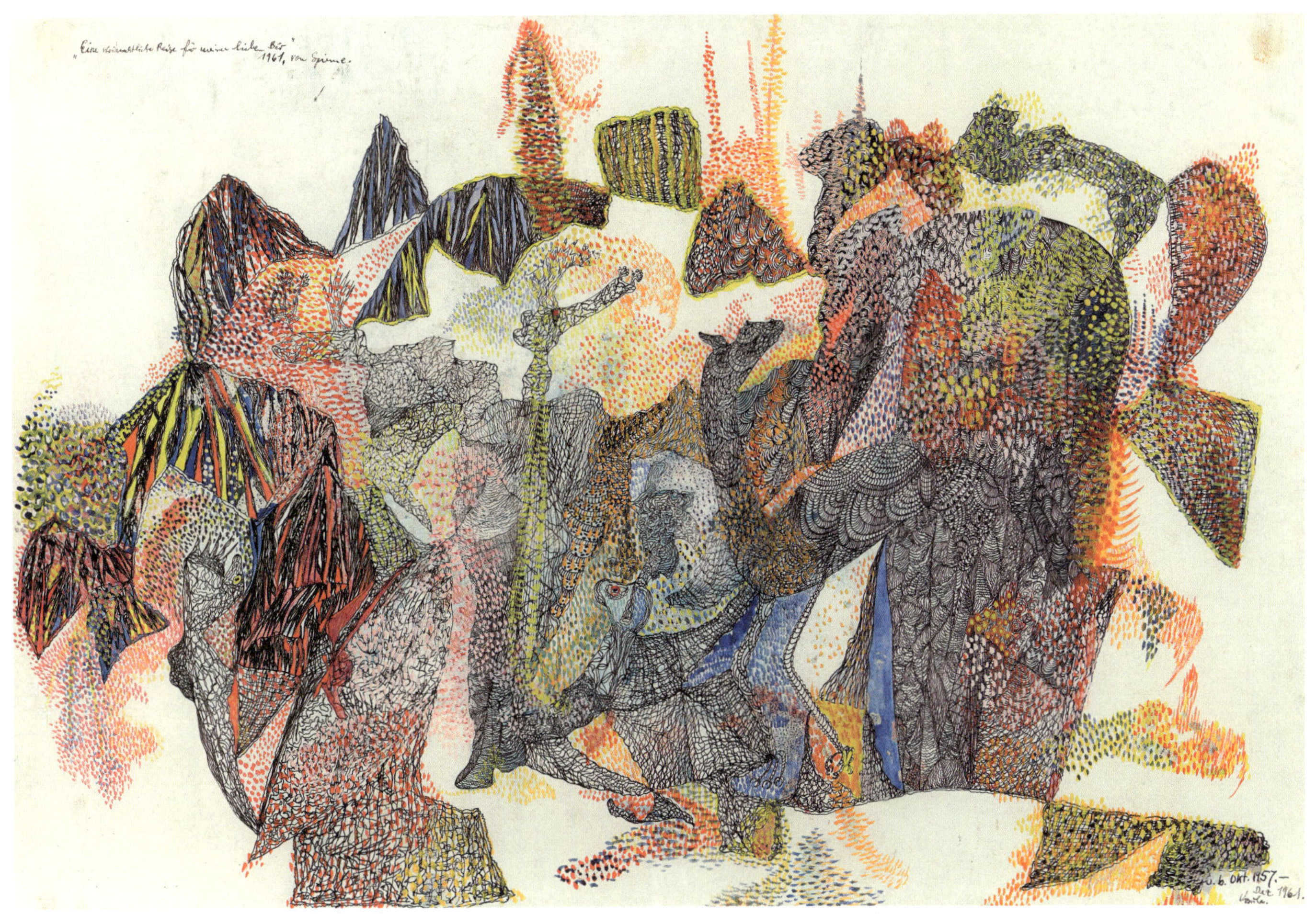

Abb. 5 Ursula (Ursula Bluhm), *Eine weihnachtliche Reise für meinen lieben Bär*, 1957/1961, Tusche und Aquarell auf Papier, 38 × 57,5 cm, Museum Ludwig, Köln, Nachlass Bernard Schultze und Ursula Schultze-Bluhm, Inv.-Nr. NaBS0834
Fig. 5 Ursula (Ursula Bluhm), *Eine weihnachtliche Reise für meinen lieben Bär* (A Christmas Trip for My Dear Bear), 1957/1961, India ink and watercolour on paper, 38 × 57.5 cm, Museum Ludwig, Cologne, estate of Bernard Schultze and Ursula Schultze-Bluhm, inv. no. NaBS0834

Altenbourg war kein aktivistischer Künstler. Aber er hat eine Kunst geschaffen, die die Betrachterinnen und Betrachter aktivieren kann, über die Fragilität der Natur nachzudenken. Hier offenbart sich die bis in die aktuelle Gegenwart hineinwirkende ökologisch-gesellschaftliche Dimension seines Werks. Seine Bilder, in denen wir »Gnomen und Chimären, Mänaden und Sylphen, beunruhigenden Fabelwesen und amüsanten Plagegeistern, zusammengesetzt aus zoomorphen und biomorphen Elementen«[24] begegnen, sind zeitlose Mahnungen, diese Welt und ihre ebenso fabelhafte wie träumerische Schönheit dauerhaft zu bewahren.

between plant, people, architecture and landscape, provoking an exhilarating game of deceptions.[22]

By means of his minuscular working method, Altenbourg too denoted nature and the world as fragile and precious. His pictures declare: here was someone who moved with care, opening up an expanded gaze on creation. Altenbourg described this himself: "many experiences are woven, are embedded, into these layers, experiences that can be lived in the wind of what is spoken in the word 'time', and as such fusing geological and individual time within a single surface.... Such a surface grows; its growth is the opening up of itself and the looking downwards from the uppermost surface into the underlying depths, all the way to the edges."[23]

Altenbourg was not an activist artist. Yet he created a body of work that can activate the observer to reflect on the fragility of nature. It is this aspect that manifests the ecological and social dimension of his work, which continues to have a strong impact today. His pictures, in

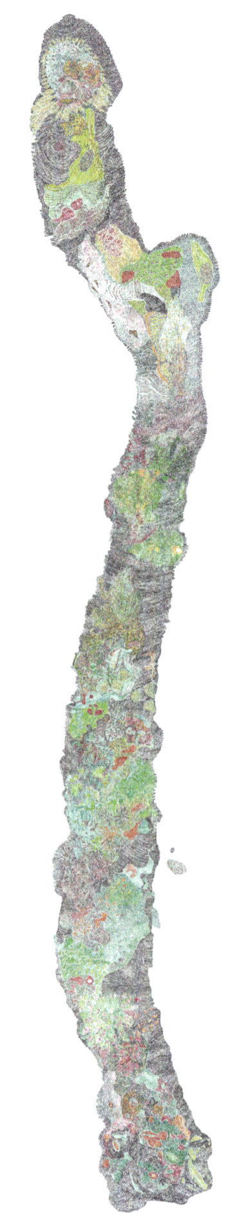

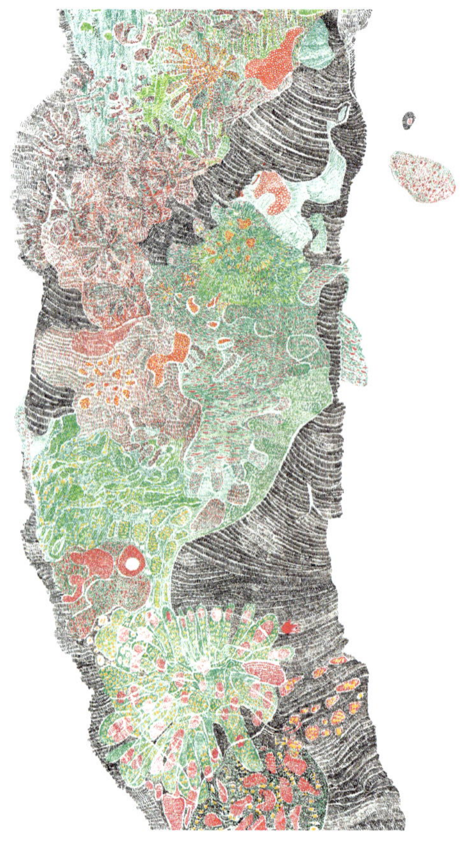

Abb. 6a Gabriela Oberkofler, *Ein halbes Jahr später (Stöckchen)*, 2019, Aquarell auf Papier, 2000 × 1150 mm, Villa Merkel, Esslingen, Graphische Sammlung, Inv.-Nr. 3661
Fig. 6a Gabriela Oberkofler, *Ein halbes Jahr später (Stöckchen)* (Half a Year Later (Little Stick)), 2019, watercolour on paper, 2000 × 1150 mm, Villa Merkel, Esslingen, Graphische Sammlung, inv. no. 3661

Abb. 6b Gabriela Oberkofler, *Ein halbes Jahr später (Stöckchen)* (Detail), 2019, Aquarell auf Papier, 2000 × 1150 cm, Villa Merkel, Esslingen, Graphische Sammlung, Inv.-Nr. 3661
Fig. 6b Gabriela Oberkofler, *Ein halbes Jahr später (Stöckchen)* (Half a Year Later (Little Stick)), detail, 2019, watercolour on paper, 2000 × 1150 mm, Villa Merkel, Esslingen, Graphische Sammlung, inv. no. 3661

Altenbourgs Bilder leisten weiterhin wichtige Beiträge zu aktuellen Diskursen der jüngeren Gegenwartskunst. Dialogische Bezüge lassen sich beispielsweise zu Gabriela Oberkofler ausmachen. Die Konzeptkünstlerin verbindet in ihrem Werk zeichnerische, bildhauerische und installative Ansätze; stets die Themen Natur, Landschaft und Mensch umkreisend, oftmals unter Einbeziehung lebender Pflanzen oder konservierter Proben. Sie beschreibt in ihren Arbeiten unter anderem die Entfremdung des Menschen von der Natur, auch die Gewalt, die der Mensch seiner Umwelt antut. In diesem Sinne bezieht ihre Kunst kritisch

which we encounter "gnomes and chimeras, maenads and sylphs, disquieting mythical creatures and disturbing ghost-like beings, composed out of zoomorphic and biomorphic elements", are timeless admonitions to preserve this world and its marvellous, dreamlike beauty forever.[24]

Altenbourg's pictures continue to be a vital point of reference in discussions of contemporary art today. Dialogic correspondences can be detected with the art of Gabriela

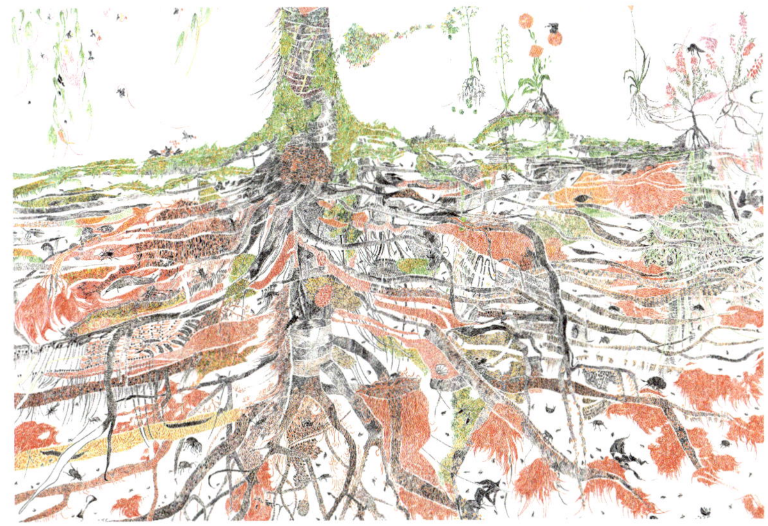

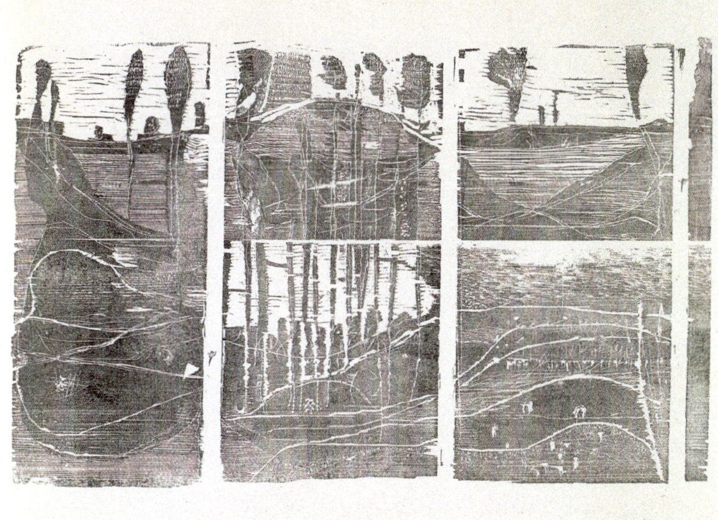

Abb. 7 Gabriela Oberkofler, *Ein Stück kritische Zone (ohne Wasser)* (Detail), 2021, dreiteilig, Tusche auf Papier, je 2200 × 1140 cm, im Besitz der Künstlerin
Fig. 7 Gabriela Oberkofler, *Ein Stück kritische Zone (ohne Wasser)* (A Piece of Critical Zone [Without Water]), detail, 2021, three parts, India ink on paper, each 2200 × 1140 mm, collection of the artist

Abb. 8 Gerhard Altenbourg, *Das sind die Wege wurzelentlang*, 1974, Holzschnitt in Grau, auf Hosho-Papier, 438 × 697 mm (Darstellung), 582 × 978 mm (Blatt), Lindenau-Museum Altenburg, Inv-Nr. G 1983-263
Fig. 8 Gerhard Altenbourg, *Das sind die Wege wurzelentlang* (Those Are the Paths Along the Root), 1974, woodcut in grey on Hosho paper, 438 × 697 mm (image), 582 × 978 mm (sheet), Lindenau-Museum Altenburg, inv. no. G 1983-263

Stellung. Sie selbst deutet ihr Werk weniger als »technische Bildsprache denn als Gesellschaftsbild«.[25]

Oberkofler verfolgt bei der Darstellung der Natur einen stark analytischen Weg. Sie sammelt im Sinne eines Naturarchivs Tierpräparate und Samenkörner. Oberkofler präpariert und seziert zeichnerisch. Wie in der großformatigen Zeichnung *Ein halbes Jahr später (Stöckchen)* zu sehen ist

Oberkofler. This conceptual artist combines drawing, sculpture and installation in her approach, her work persistently addressing the issues of nature, landscape and humans and often incorporating living plants or conserved samples. In her works, she describes, among other subjects, the alienation of humans from nature and the violence that humans inflict on their environment. In this sense, her art takes a critical stance. She herself interprets her work less as a "technical pictorial language than an image of society".[25]

Oberkofler pursues an intensely analytical method in her representation of nature. She collects prepared animals and seed samples as though for a nature archive. She taxidermies and dissects by drawing. As can be seen in the large-format drawing *Ein halbes Jahr später (Stöckchen)* (Half a Year Later (Little Stick), figs. 6a–b), her depictions appear like preserved microscopic specimens between glass slides. A seething mass of cells and organic microstructures extends across the surface. The category of space is deliberately reduced, allowing the flat, objective presentation of the traces of life to come to the fore. The artist has almost completely eschewed outlines. Instead, the individual structures and cellular islands are grouped together without membranes and left unprotected. Everything appears porous, vulnerable, fragile. Oberkofler counters the exiguousness of the depiction by the monumental dimensions of the image: the minuscule has been enlarged into the gigantic.

The potential extending under the earth in Oberkofler's drawings is potently visible in the three-part work *Ein Stück kritische Zone (ohne Wasser)* (A Piece of Critical Zone (Without Water)). Here the artist experimented with thousands of dots, dashes and lines to make a deep cut through the forest ground (fig. 7). Layers are charted that fuse "geological and individual time within a single surface"[26] in the spirit of Altenbourg, presenting the astonishing ecosystem of a tree rich in roots.

One is strongly reminded of Altenbourg's woodcut *Das sind die Wege wurzelentlang* (Those Are the Paths Along the Root; fig. 8). "It is perhaps the first time in modern landscape painting", notes Florian Illies about Altenbourg, "that an artist bestows as much attention on what is hidden underneath the ground as to what is visible above".[27] Altenbourg laid bare the structures below ground, stripped the landscape of its protective crust, made us aware of

(Abb. 6a, 6b), wirken ihre Darstellungen wie mikroskopierte Präparate zwischen Glasplättchen. Ein Gewusel aus Zellen und organischen Kleinstrukturen dehnt sich in der Fläche aus. Die Kategorie des Raums tritt bewusst zurück und lässt die flächig-sachliche Präsentation von Lebensspuren in den Vordergrund treten. Fast vollständig verzichtete die Künstlerin auf Konturen. Vielmehr präsentieren sich die einzelnen Strukturen und Zellinseln als hüllen- und schutzlos. Alles wirkt offenporig, verletzbar, fragil. Die Winzigkeit des Dargestellten konterkariert Oberkofler durch das monumentale Bildmaß: Das Allerkleinste ist ins Riesenhafte vergrößert.

Das unter die Erde reichende Potenzial von Oberkoflers Zeichnungen tritt kraftvoll in der dreiteiligen Arbeit *Ein Stück kritische Zone (ohne Wasser)* zutage. Die Künstlerin erprobte in tausenden Punkten, Strichen und Linien einen tiefen Schnitt durch den Waldboden (Abb. 7). Schichtungen werden markiert, die auch im Sinne Altenbourgs »erdgeschichtliche und individuelle Zeit auf eine Fläche«[26] bringen, die das Ökosystem eines wurzelreichen Baums staunend vor Augen führen.

Stark fühlt man sich erinnert an Altenbourgs Holzschnitt *Das sind die Wege wurzelentlang* (Abb. 8). »Es ist vielleicht das erste Mal in der modernen Landschaftsmalerei«, so Florian Illies über Altenbourg, »daß ein Künstler dem Verborgenen unterhalb des Erdbodens ebensoviel Aufmerksamkeit angedeihen läßt wie dem Offensichtlichen oberhalb.«[27] Altenbourg legte die Strukturen des Untergrunds offen, nahm der Landschaft ihre schützende Kruste, machte uns aufmerksam auf das, was dem Auge ansonsten verborgen bliebe. Seine Werke beschreiben Innenwelten, sie öffnen Vorstellungsräume zwischen Naturabbildung und Fabulierkunst, sie lassen staunen, und sie inspirieren nachfolgende Künstlergenerationen bis zum heutigen Tag.

Der Autor dankt Roland Krischke und Silvia Schmitt-Maaß für die freundliche Einladung an diesem Katalog mitarbeiten zu dürfen. Ferner ergeht Dank an Eva Busch, Viera Karpiakova, Egbert Kasper, Werner Klein, Ada Komppa, Gabriela Oberkofler, Angela Rietschel, Sebastian Rug, Gabi Schulte-Lünzum und Ulrike Weippert.

1 Vgl. Dieckmann, Friedrich: Ausflug zu Altenbourg. Ein Reisebericht, in: Brusberg, Dieter/Ströch, Anneliese: Gerhard Altenbourg. Der Gärtner. Eine Monografie in Bildern, Frankfurt a. M. 1996, S. 12–29, hier S. 15.
2 Vgl. Wiesler, Hermann: Zeichenkunst als Kritzel-Erkenntnis, in: Schmierer, Elisabeth/Fontaine, Susanne/Grünzweig, Werner/Brzoska, Matthias (Hrsg.): Töne – Farben – Formen: Über Musik und die bildenden Künste, Lilienthal 1995, S. 275–285, hier S. 284.
3 Vgl. ebd., S. 278.
4 Vgl. Fischer, Sören: Bütten, Japanpapier, Karton. Zum Papier als Objekt und Ort bei Gerhard Altenbourg, in: Maaz, Bernhard/Günther, Daniela/Fischer, Sören (Hrsg.): terra Altenbourg. Die Welt des Zeichners, Ausst.-Kat. Kupferstich-Kabinett, Staatliche Kunstsammlungen Dresden, Berlin/München 2014, S. 150–162.
5 In Altenbourgs Bibliothek hat sich das Buch von Unica Zürn *Der Mann im Jasmin. Dunkler Frühling* (Frankfurt a. M./Berlin/Wien 1982) erhalten.
6 Vgl. Lutz, Helga: Schriftbilder und Bilderschriften. Zum Verhältnis von Text, Zeichnung und Schrift bei Unica Zürn, Stuttgart 2003, S. 79.
7 Vgl. Altenbourg, Gerhard: Betrachtungen vom Arbeitstisch aus, 1966 in: Lang, Lothar (Hrsg.): Die Handzeichnung. Kunstkabinett am Institut für Lehrerweiterbildung, Berlin-Pankow 1967, S. 2 f. Zit. nach: (Altenbourg,

what otherwise remains hidden to the eye. His works describe interior worlds, they open up spaces of imagination between the depiction of nature and storytelling, they astonish us, and they inspire succeeding generations of artists to the present day.

The author wishes to thank Roland Krischke and Silvia Schmitt-Maaß for the invitation to contribute to this catalogue. My thanks also go to Eva Busch, Viera Karpiakova, Egbert Kasper, Werner Klein, Ada Komppa, Gabriela Oberkofler, Angela Rietschel, Sebastian Rug, Gabi Schulte-Lünzum and Ulrike Weippert.

1 Friedrich Dieckmann, "Ausflug zu Altenbourg. Ein Reisebericht", in Dieter Brusberg and Anneliese Ströch, *Gerhard Altenbourg. Der Gärtner. Eine Monografie in Bildern* (Frankfurt am Main: Insel, 1996), pp. 12–29, here p. 15.
2 Hermann Wiesler, "Zeichenkunst als Kritzel-Erkenntnis", in Elisabeth Schmierer, Susanne Fontaine, Werner Grünzweig and Matthias Brzoska (eds.), *Töne – Farben – Formen: Über Musik und die bildenden Künste* (Lilienthal: Laaber, 1995), pp. 275–85, here p. 284.
3 See ibid., p. 278. The German word *Handwerker*, which means tradesman, craftsman, artisan or manual worker, translates literally as "hand worker".
4 See Sören Fischer, "Bütten, Japanpapier, Karton. Zum Papier als Objekt und Ort bei Gerhard Altenbourg", in Bernhard Maaz, Daniela Günther and Sören Fischer (eds.), *terra Altenbourg. Die Welt des Zeichners*, exh. cat. Kupferstich-Kabinett, Staatliche Kunstsammlungen Dresden (Berlin/Munich: Deutscher Kunstverlag, 2014), pp. 150–62.
5 A book by Unica Zürn, *Der Mann im Jasmin. Dunkler Frühling* (Frankfurt am Main/Berlin/Vienna: Ullstein, 1982), is preserved in Altenbourg's library.
6 See Helga Lutz, *Schriftbilder und Bilderschriften. Zum Verhältnis von Text, Zeichnung und Schrift bei Unica Zürn* (Stuttgart: J.B. Metzler, 2003), p. 79.
7 See Gerhard Altenbourg, "Betrachtungen vom Arbeitstisch aus, 1966", in Lothar Lang (ed.), *Die Handzeichnung. Kunstkabinett am Institut für Lehrerweiterbildung* (Berlin: Institut für Lehrerweiterbildung, 1967), pp. 2ff. Quoted in Gerhard Altenbourg and Lothar Lang, *Gerhard Altenbourg / Lothar Lang – Briefwechsel 1965–1988*, transcribed with commentary by Katrin Roth, ed. Christa Grimm (Leipzig: Lehmstedt, 2008), p. 41.
8 Wolfgang Knapp, "Surrealistischer Kontext und Rezeption", in Erich Brinkmann et al. (eds.), *Unica Zürn. Bilder 1953–1970*, exh. cat. Neue Gesellschaft für Bildende Kunst, Berlin / Museum Bochum / Gerhard-Marcks-Haus, Bremen (Berlin: Brinkman und Bose, 1998), pp. 208–11, here p. 211.
9 See Uwe M. Schneede, *Die Kunst des Surrealismus. Malerei, Skulptur. Dichtung, Fotografie, Film* (Munich: Beck, 2006), pp. 23–32.
10 In conversation with the author, October 2025.
11 Ibid.
12 Ibid.
13 See Gerhard Altenbourg, "Klar dem Nächtlichen

Gerhard/Lang, Lothar:) Gerhard Altenbourg / Lothar Lang – Briefwechsel 1965–1988, bearb. u. komm. v. Katrin Roth, hrsg. von Christa Grimm, Leipzig 2008, S. 41.
8 Knapp, Wolfgang: Surrealistischer Kontext und Rezeption, in: Brinkmann, Erich et al.: Unica Zürn. Bilder 1953–1970, Ausst.-Kat. Neue Gesellschaft für Bildende Kunst, Berlin / Museum Bochum / Gerhard-Marcks-Haus, Bremen, Berlin 1998, S. 208–211, hier S. 211.
9 Vgl. Schneede, Uwe M.: Die Kunst des Surrealismus. Malerei, Skulptur. Dichtung, Fotografie, Film, München 2006, S. 23–32.
10 Im Gespräch mit dem Autor, Oktober 2025.
11 Ebd.
12 Ebd.
13 Vgl. Altenbourg, Gerhard: Klar dem Nächtlichen verschwistert, in: Altenbourg, Gerhard: Ich-Gestein: Arbeiten aus zwei Jahrzehnten, Berlin/Frankfurt a. M./Wien 1971, (Anhang:) handschriftlicher, paginierter und als Faksimile gedruckter Text von Gerhard Altenbourg, S. 1–6, hier S. 5.
14 (Altenbourg, Gerhard/Mennekes, Friedhelm:) Im Gespräch (Interview mit Friedhelm Mennekes), in: Grinten, Franz Joseph von der/Mennekes, Friedhelm: Abstraktion und Kontemplation. Auseinandersetzung mit einem Thema der Gegenwartskunst, Stuttgart 1987, S. 234–241, hier S. 236.
15 Ebd., S. 237.
16 Ebd., S. 238.
17 Mitteilung an den Autor, Oktober 2025.
18 Ebd.
19 Zit. nach: Diederich, Stephan: »Auf den Stufen zum Inneren des Kopfes«. Ein Blick in Ursulas Bild-Welten, in: Diederich, Stephan/Kuhlmann, Helena: Ursula. Das bin ich. Na und? That's me. So what? Ausst.-Kat. Museum Ludwig, Köln, Köln 2023, S. 10–25, hier S. 15.
20 Ebd.
21 Vgl. Kuhlmann, Helena: »fast wie eine innere Uhr«. Die Metamorphose als ontologisches Prinzip in der Kunst Ursulas, in: Diederich/Kuhlmann 2023 (wie Anm. 19), S. 26–39, hier S. 29.
22 Vgl. Diederich, Stephan/Kuhlmann, Helena: Werke. Alles fließt, in: Diederich/Kuhlmann 2023 (wie Anm. 19), S. 135.
23 Altenbourg, Gerhard: Findungen, 1966. Zit. nach: Altenbourg/Lang 2008 (wie Anm. 7), S. 38 f., hier S. 38.
24 Zweite, Armin: »Im Erinnern ist die Wirklichkeit, im Ungreifbaren das Hiersein«. Altenbourgs Verhältnis zur Tradition – eine Anmerkung, in: ders. (Hrsg.): Gerhard Altenbourg. Im Fluß der Zeit, Ausst.-Kat. K20-Kunstsammlung am Grabbeplatz, Düsseldorf / Kupferstich-Kabinett, Staatliche Kunstsammlungen Dresden / Staatliche Graphische Sammlung, München, München 2003, S. 17–28, hier S. 25 f.
25 Vgl. Baumann, Günter: »Glokale Welten« – Heimat als Lebensform, in: Gerlinde-Beck-Stiftung (Hrsg.): Gabriela Oberkofler, Gerlinde-Beck Preis für Skulptur der Gerlinde-Beck-Stiftung, Ausst.-Kat. Grafenau, Grafenau 2018, S. 9 f., hier S. 9.
26 Vgl. Altenbourg 1966 (wie Anm. 23), hier S. 38.
27 Illies, Florian: Anmerkungen zur Geschichte der Linie im Werk Gerhard Altenbourg, in: Brusberg/Ströch 1996 (wie Anm. 1), S. 33–58, hier S. 46.

verschwistert", in Gerhard Altenbourg, *Ich-Gestein. Arbeiten aus zwei Jahrzehnten* (Berlin/Frankfurt am Main/Vienna: Propyläen, 1971), (appendix) handwritten, paginated text by Gerhard Altenbourg, printed as a facsimile pp. 1–6, here p. 5.
14 Gerhard Altenbourg and Friedhelm Mennekes, "Im Gespräch (Interview mit Friedhelm Mennekes)", in Franz Joseph von der Grinten and Friedhelm Mennekes, *Abstraktion und Kontemplation. Auseinandersetzung mit einem Thema der Gegenwartskunst* (Stuttgart: Verlag Katholisches Bibelwerk, 1987), pp. 234–41, here p. 236.
15 Ibid., p. 237.
16 Ibid., p. 238.
17 Communication to the author, October 2025.
18 Ibid.
19 Quoted in Stephan Diederich, "'Auf den Stufen zum Inneren des Kopfes'. Ein Blick in Ursulas Bild-Welten", in Stephan Diederich and Helena Kuhlmann, *Ursula. Das bin ich. Na und? (That's Me. So What?)* exh. cat. Museum Ludwig, Cologne (Cologne: Walther König, 2023), pp. 10–25, here p. 15.
20 Ibid.
21 See Helena Kuhlmann, "'fast wie eine innere Uhr'. Die Metamorphose als ontologisches Prinzip in der Kunst Ursulas", in Diederich and Kuhlmann (n. 19 above), pp. 26–39, here p. 29.
22 See Stephan Diederich and Helena Kuhlmann, "Werke. Alles fließt", in Diederich and Kuhlmann, *Ursula* (n. 19 above), p. 135.
23 Gerhard Altenbourg, "Findungen, 1966". Quoted in Altenbourg and Lang (n. 7 above), pp. 38ff., here p. 38.
24 Armin Zweite, "'Im Erinnern ist die Wirklichkeit, im Ungreifbaren das Hiersein'. Altenbourgs Verhältnis zur Tradition – eine Anmerkung", in Armin Zweite (ed.), *Gerhard Altenbourg. Im Fluß der Zeit*, exh. cat. K20-Kunstsammlung am Grabbeplatz, Düsseldorf / Kupferstich-Kabinett, Staatliche Kunstsammlungen Dresden / Staatliche Graphische Sammlung München (Munich: Prestel, 2003), pp. 17–28, here pp. 25ff.
25 See Günter Baumann, "'Glokale Welten' – Heimat als Lebensform", in Gerlinde-Beck-Stiftung (eds.), *Gabriela Oberkofler, Gerlinde-Beck Preis für Skulptur der Gerlinde-Beck-Stiftung*, exh. cat. Grafenau (Grafenau: Gerlinde-Beck-Stiftung, 2018), pp. 9ff., here p. 9.
26 See Altenbourg (n. 23 above), p. 38.
27 Florian Illies, "Anmerkungen zur Geschichte der Linie im Werk Gerhard Altenbourg", in Brusberg and Ströch (n. 1 above), pp. 33–58, here p. 46.

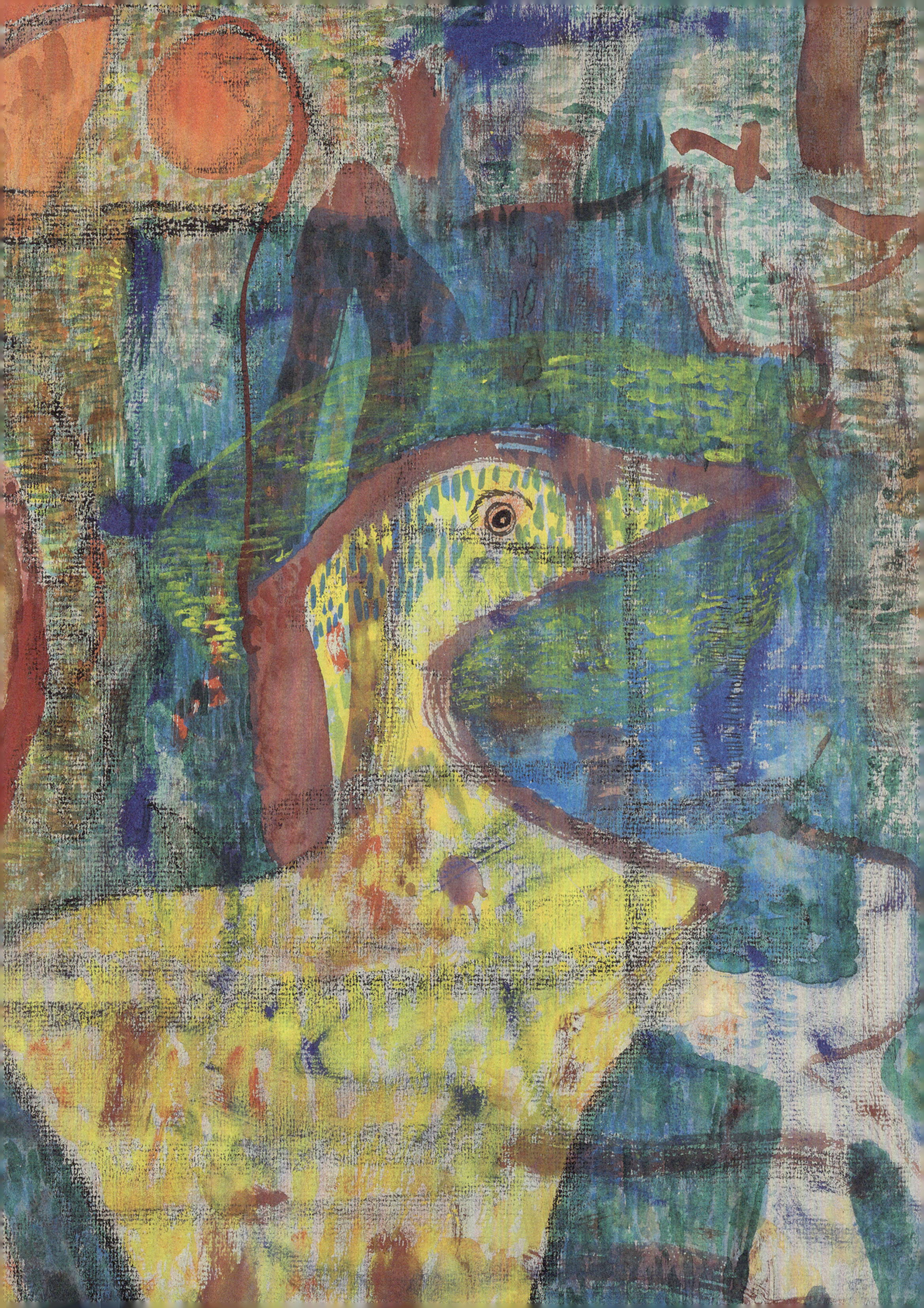

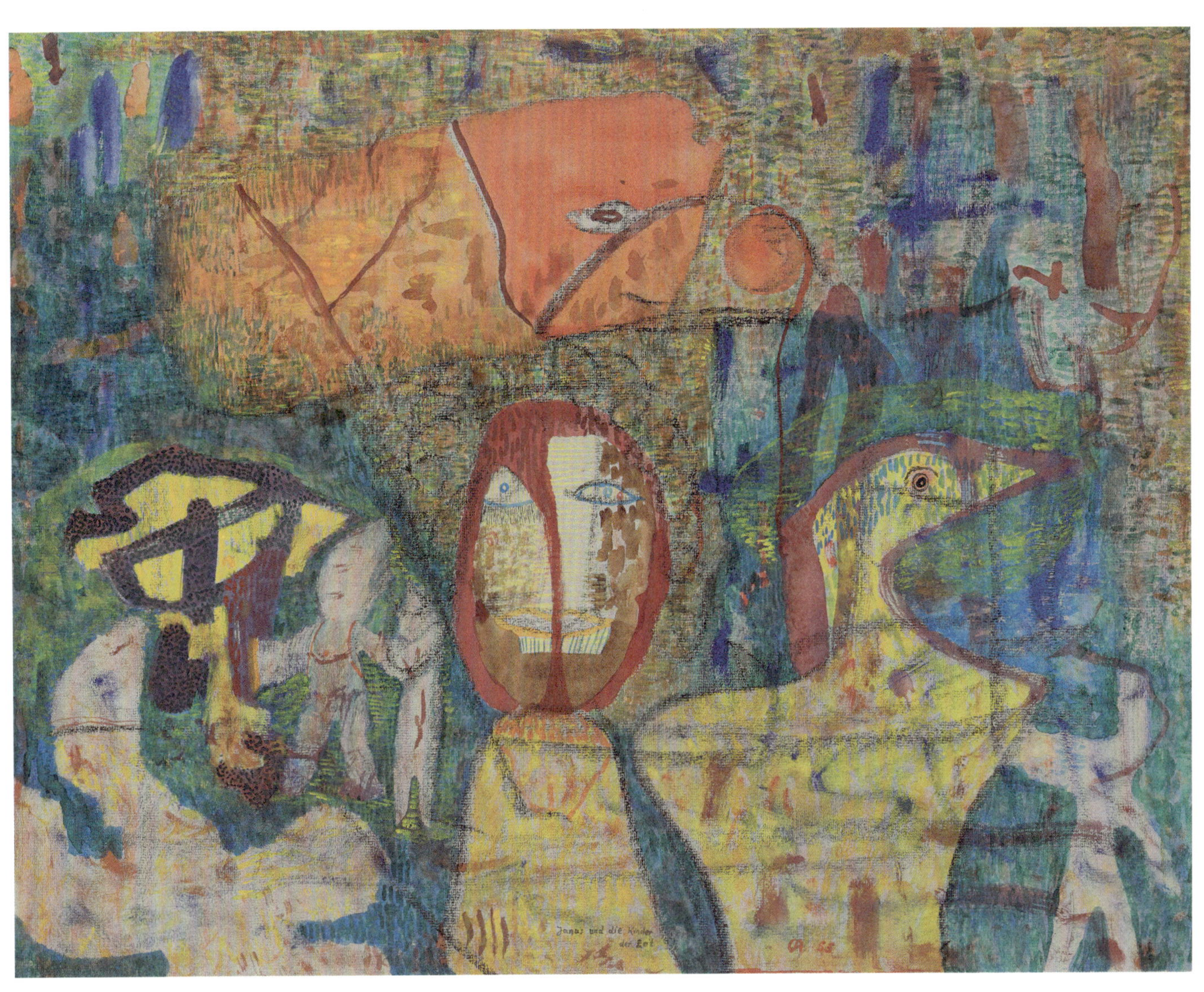

32 *Janus und die Kinder der Zeit*, 1955 |
Janus and the Children of Time, 1955

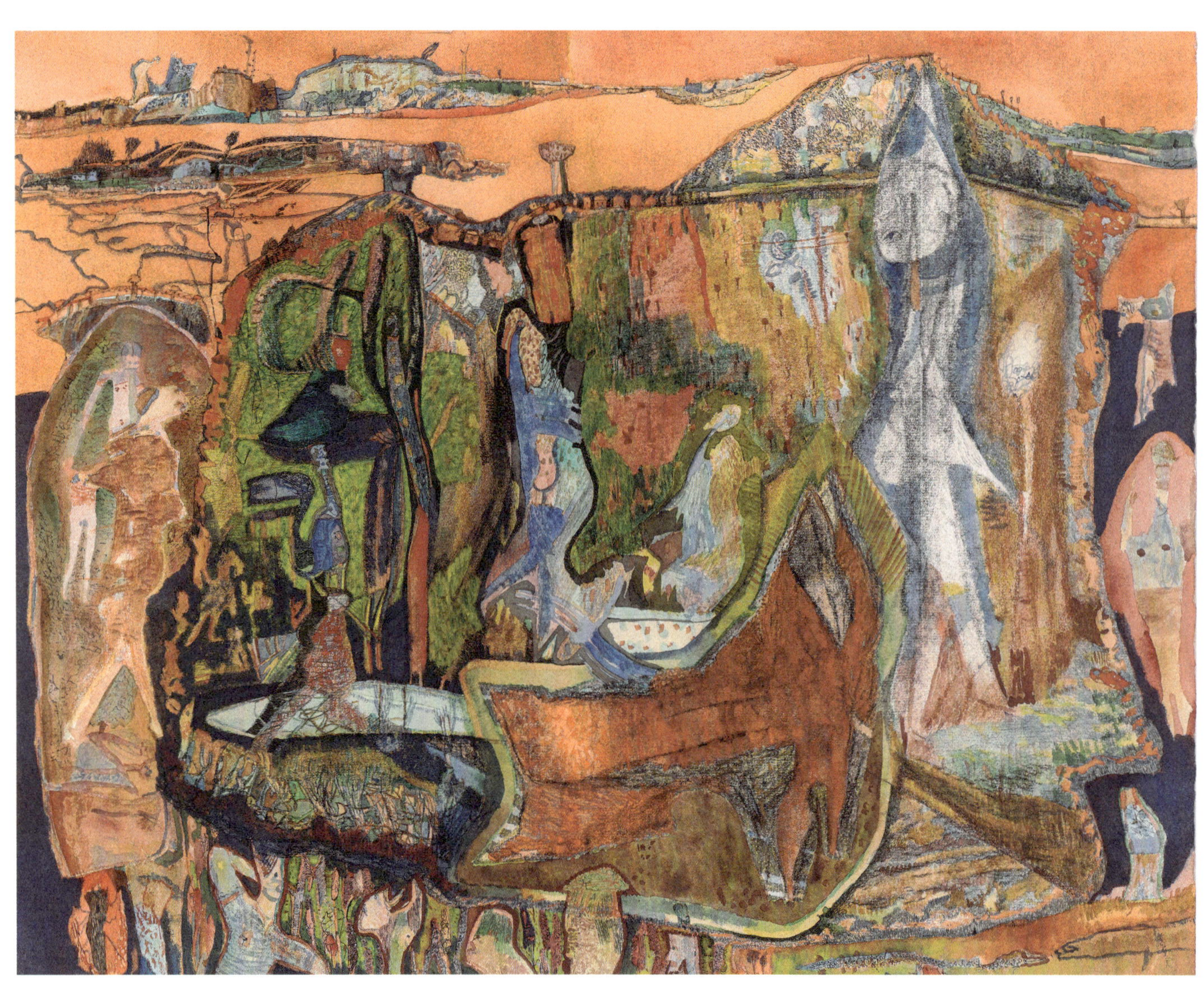

33 *Spiel auf zweierlei Ebenen*, 1956 |
Game on Two Levels, 1956

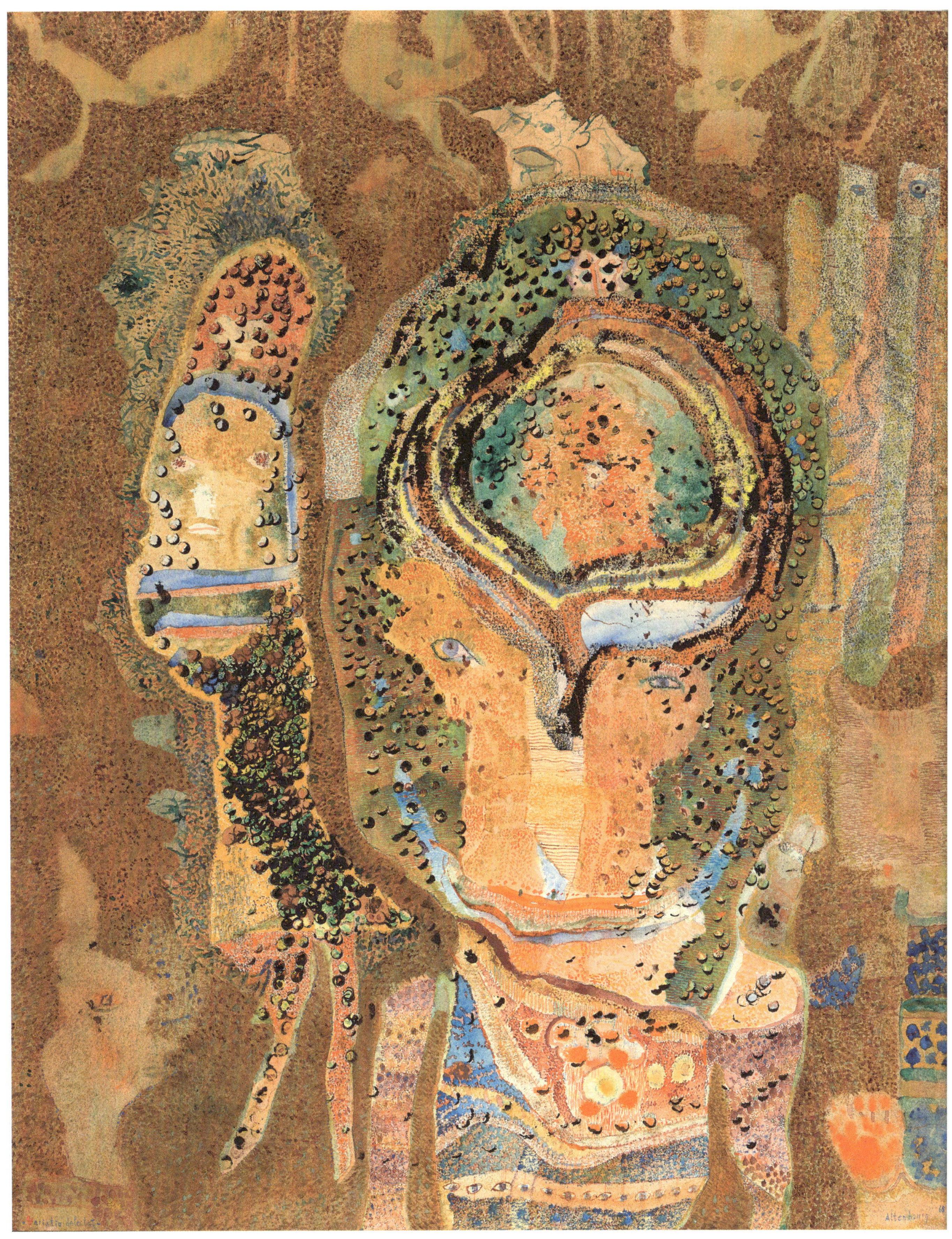

34 *Variatio delectat*, 1968

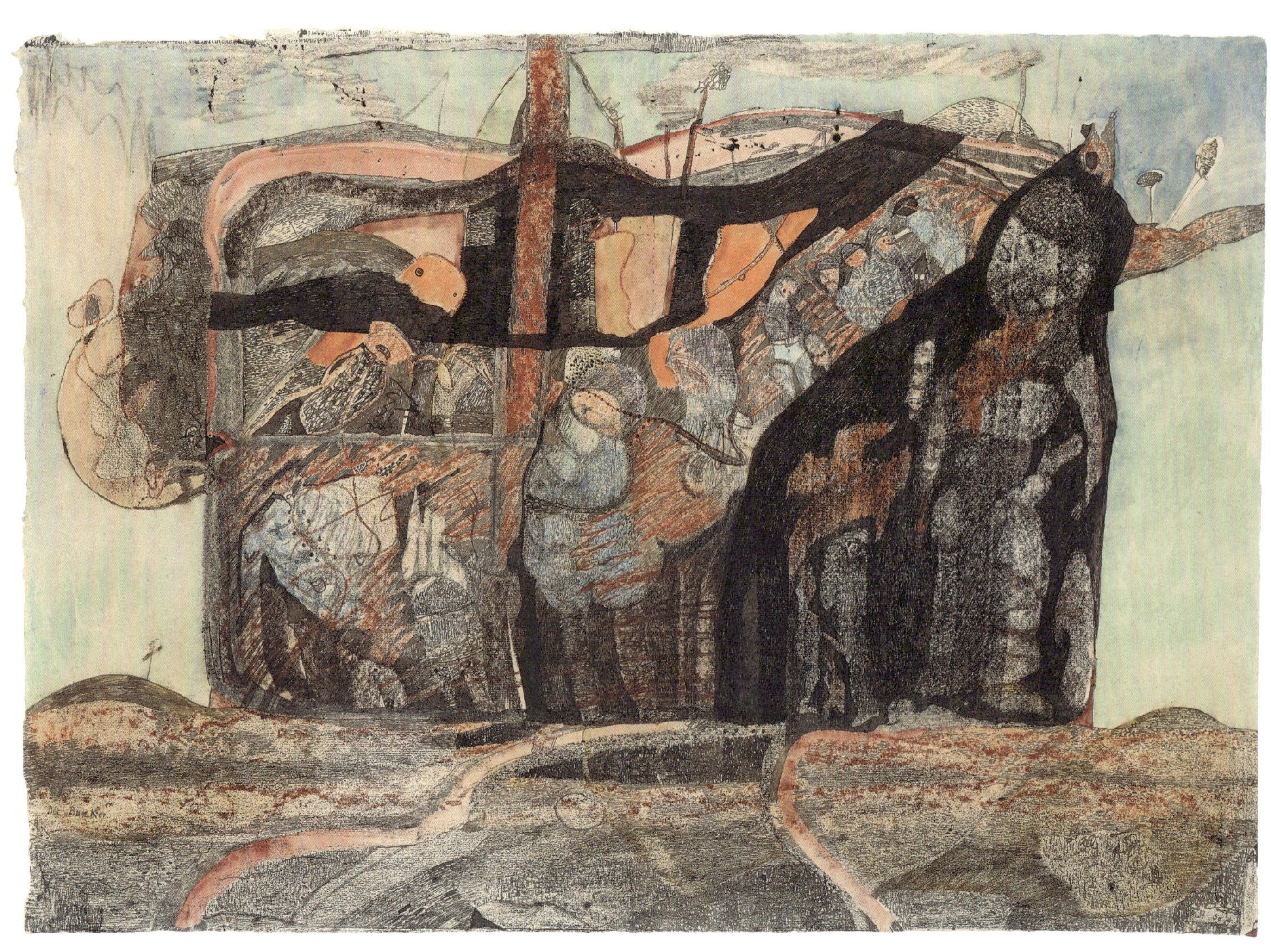

35 *Der Bunker*, 1956 | *The Bunker*, 1956

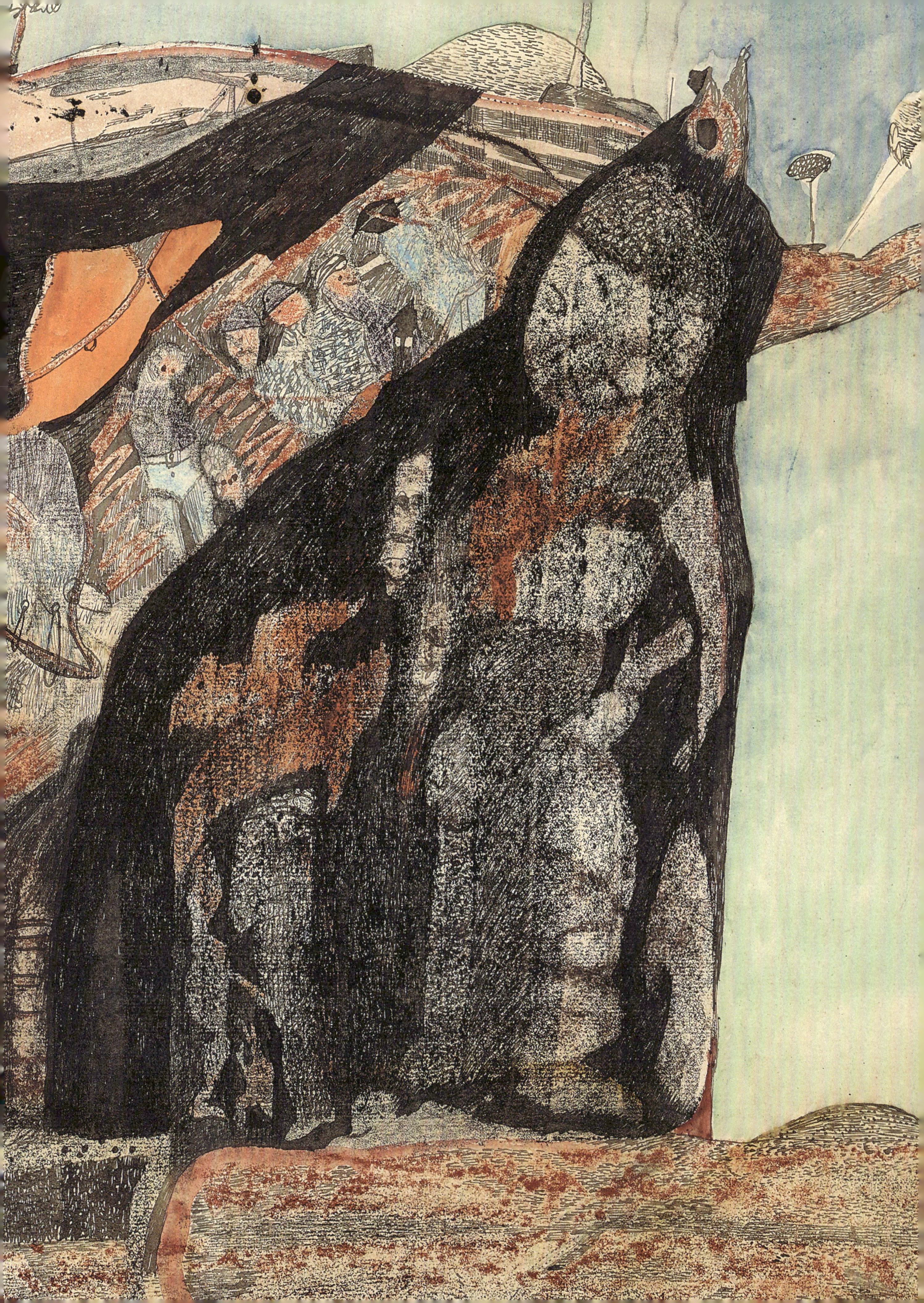

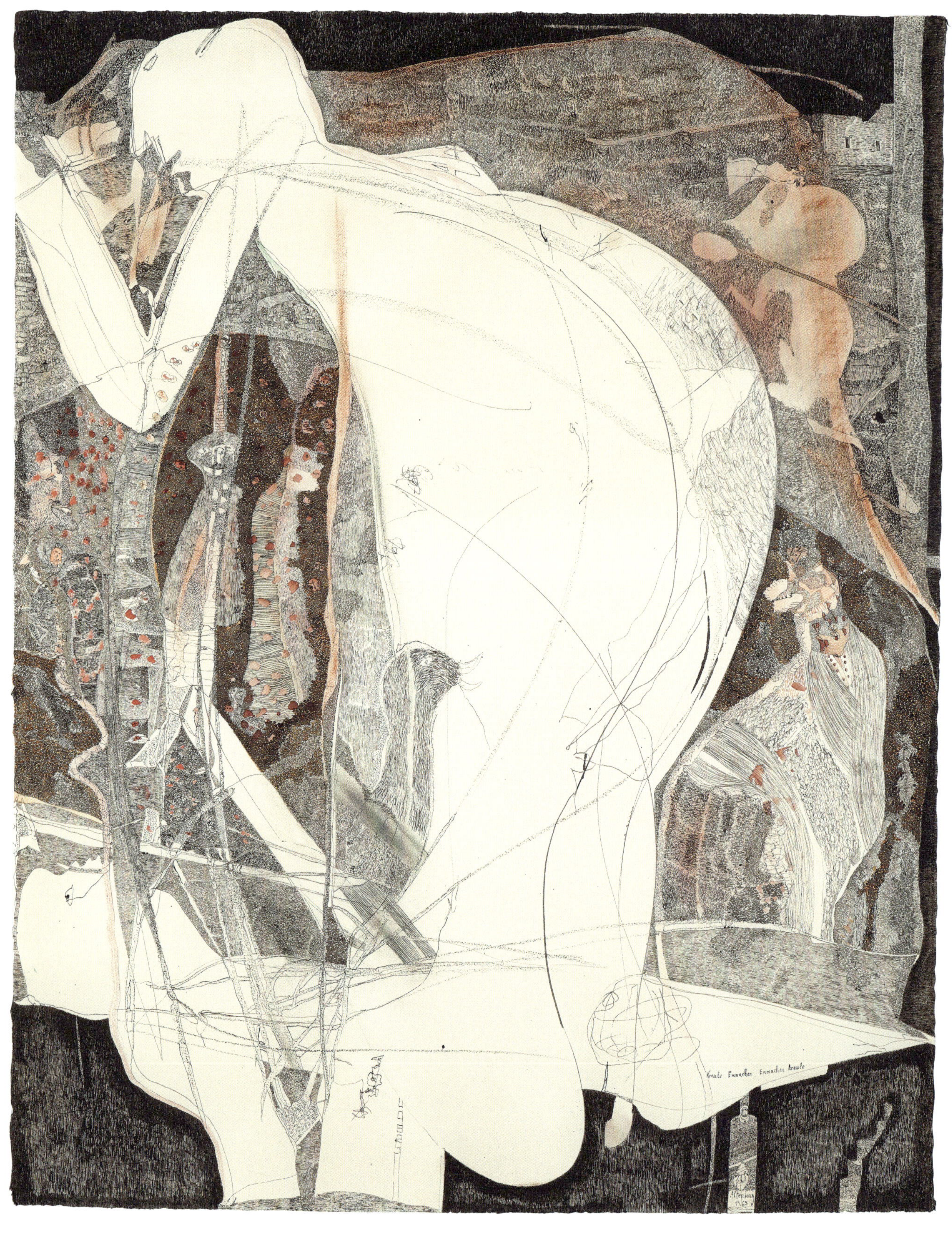

36 *Kraule Emmachen, Emmachen Kraule*, 1967 | *Crawl Emmachen, Emmachen Crawl*, 1967

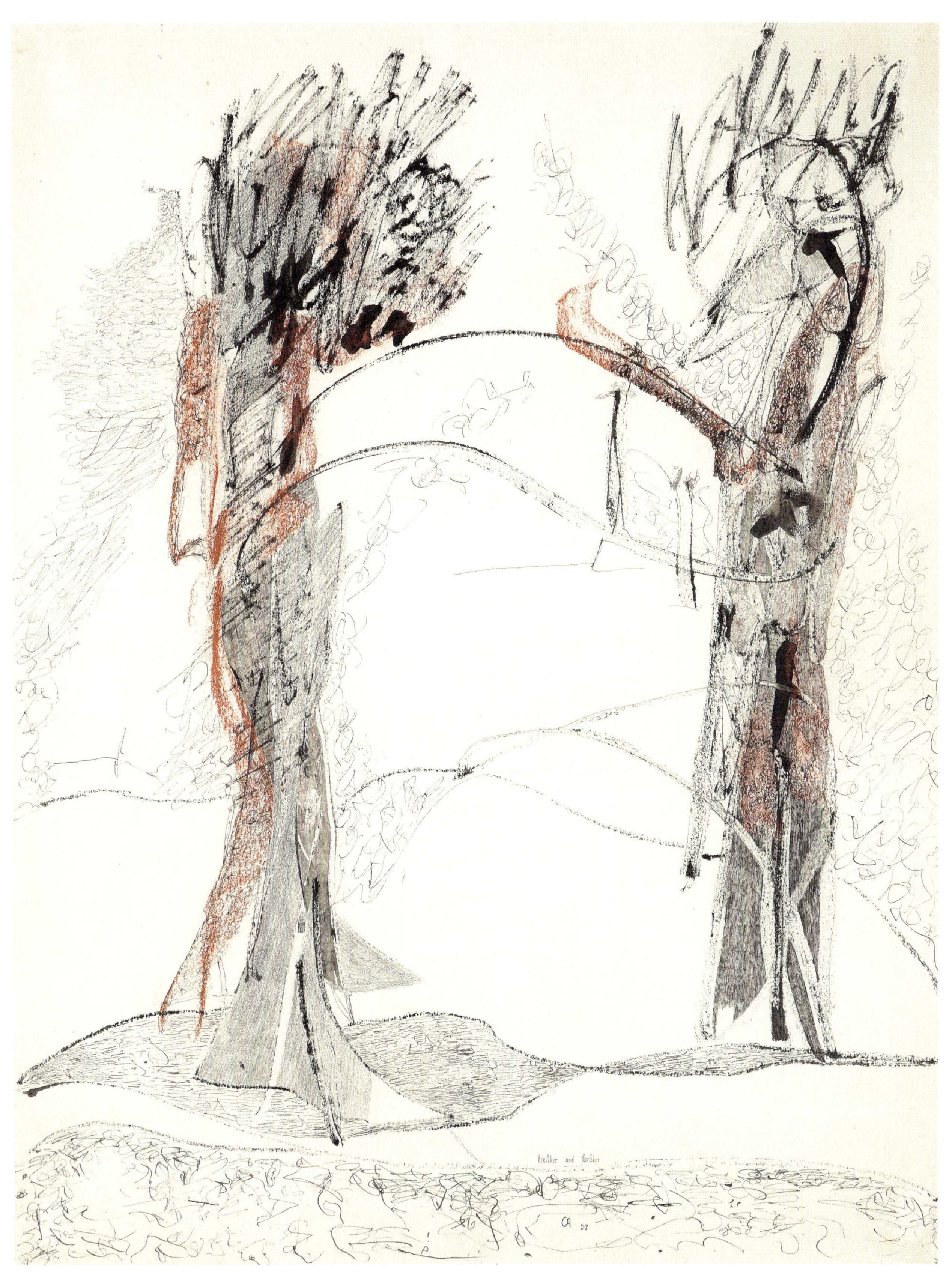

37 *Hinüber und Herüber*, 1958 |
Back and Forth, 1958

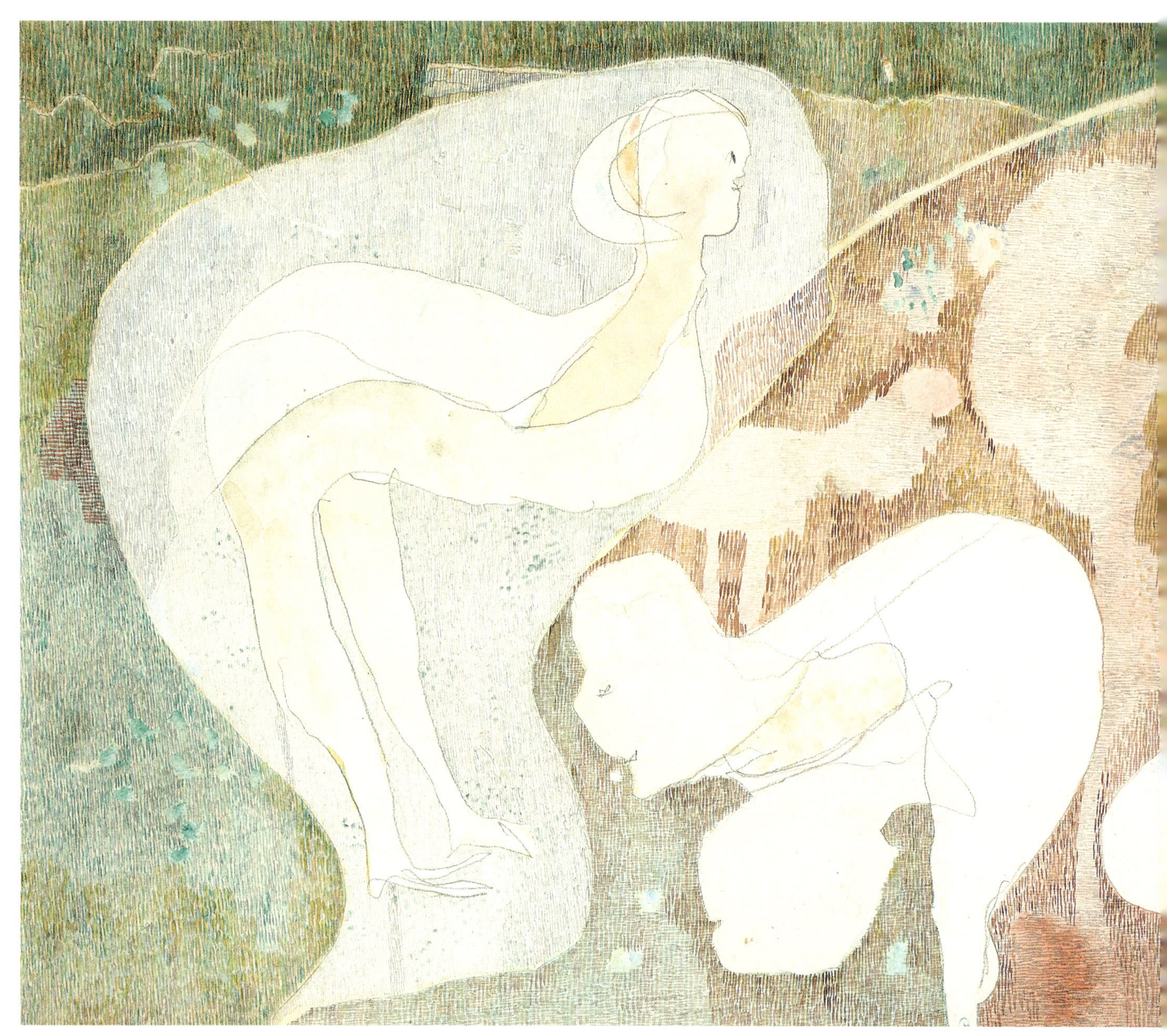

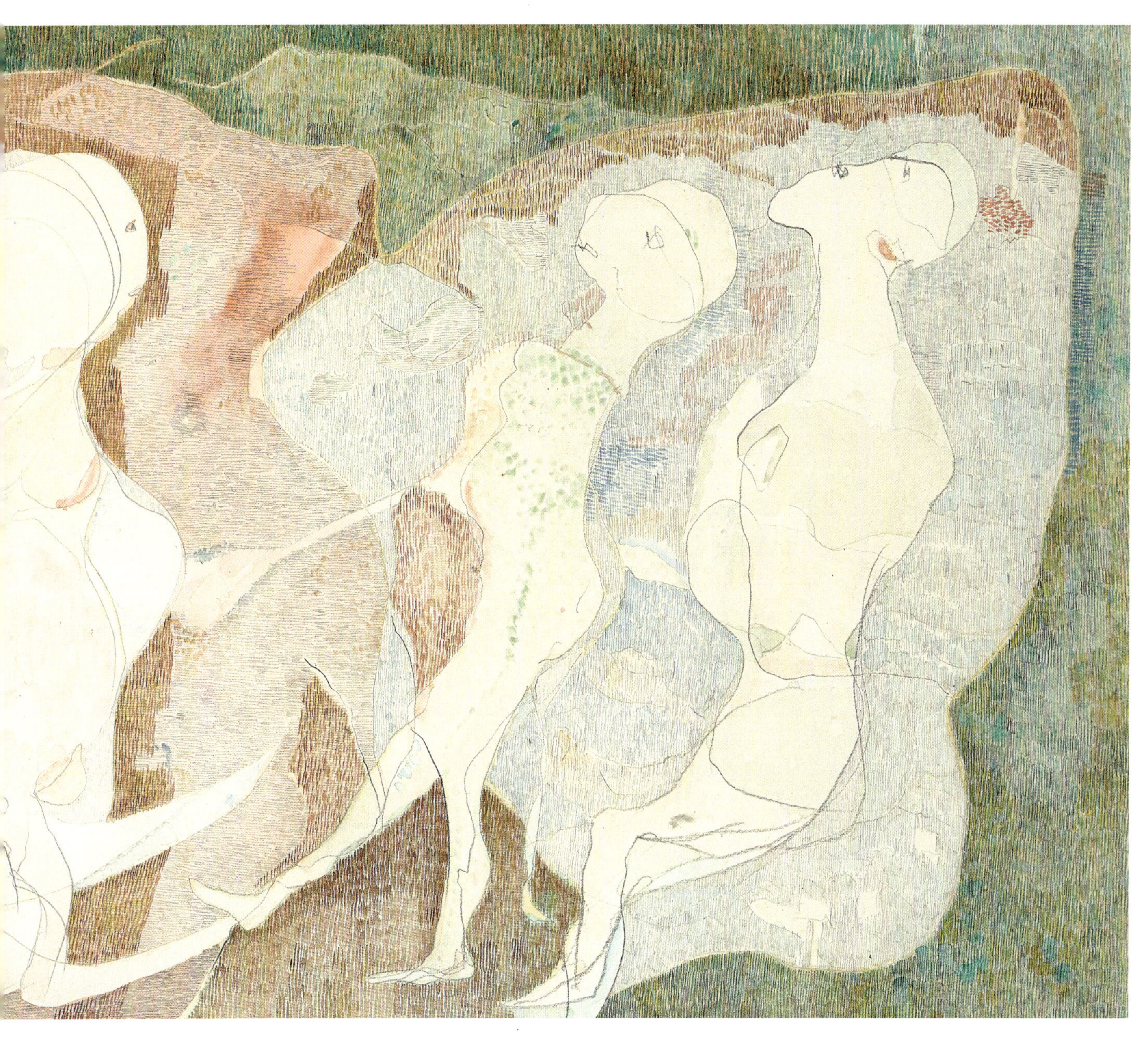

38 *in Honigmondtracht*, 1970 |
In Honeyed Moon Costume, 1970

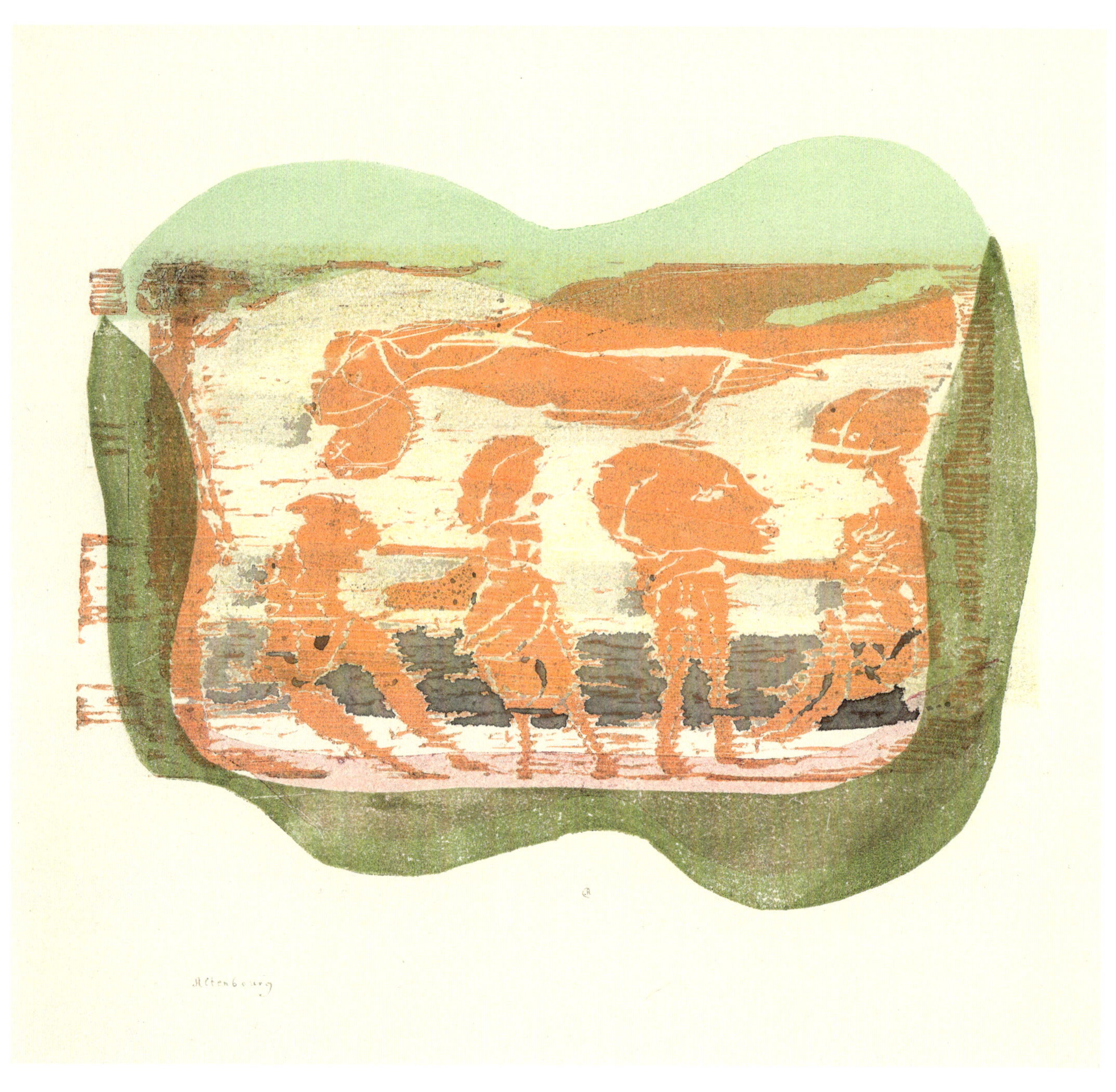

39 *Wenn der januskörfige nachtbeheimatete Vogel in den wahnwitzigen Mittag gleitet in das Waldnest unter den Tälerschwingen, in Leidensglück, getigert und fessellos*, 1980 | *When the Two-Faced Nocturnal Bird Glides into the Mad Midday in the Forest Nest Beneath the Valley-Wings, in Blissful Suffering, Striped and Unbound*, 1980

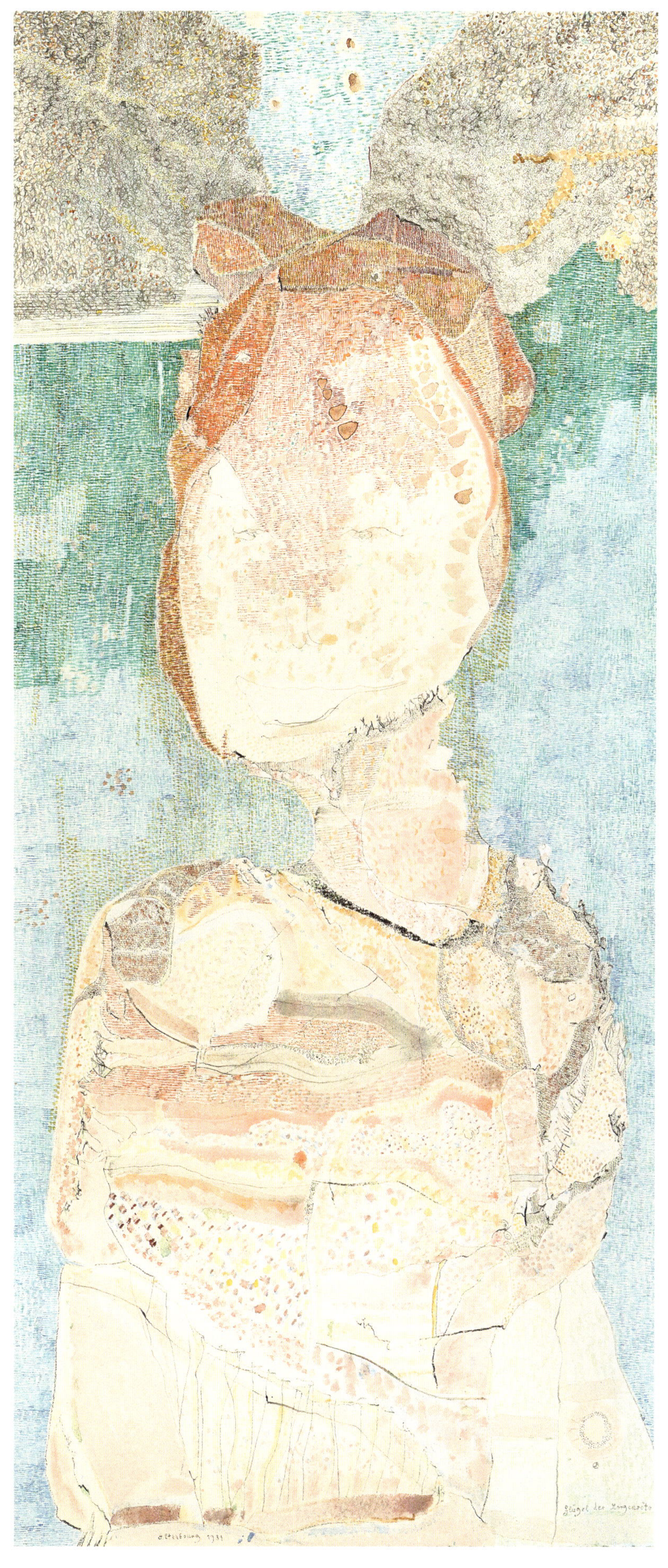

40 *Flügel der Morgenröte*, 1981 |
Wings of Dawn, 1981

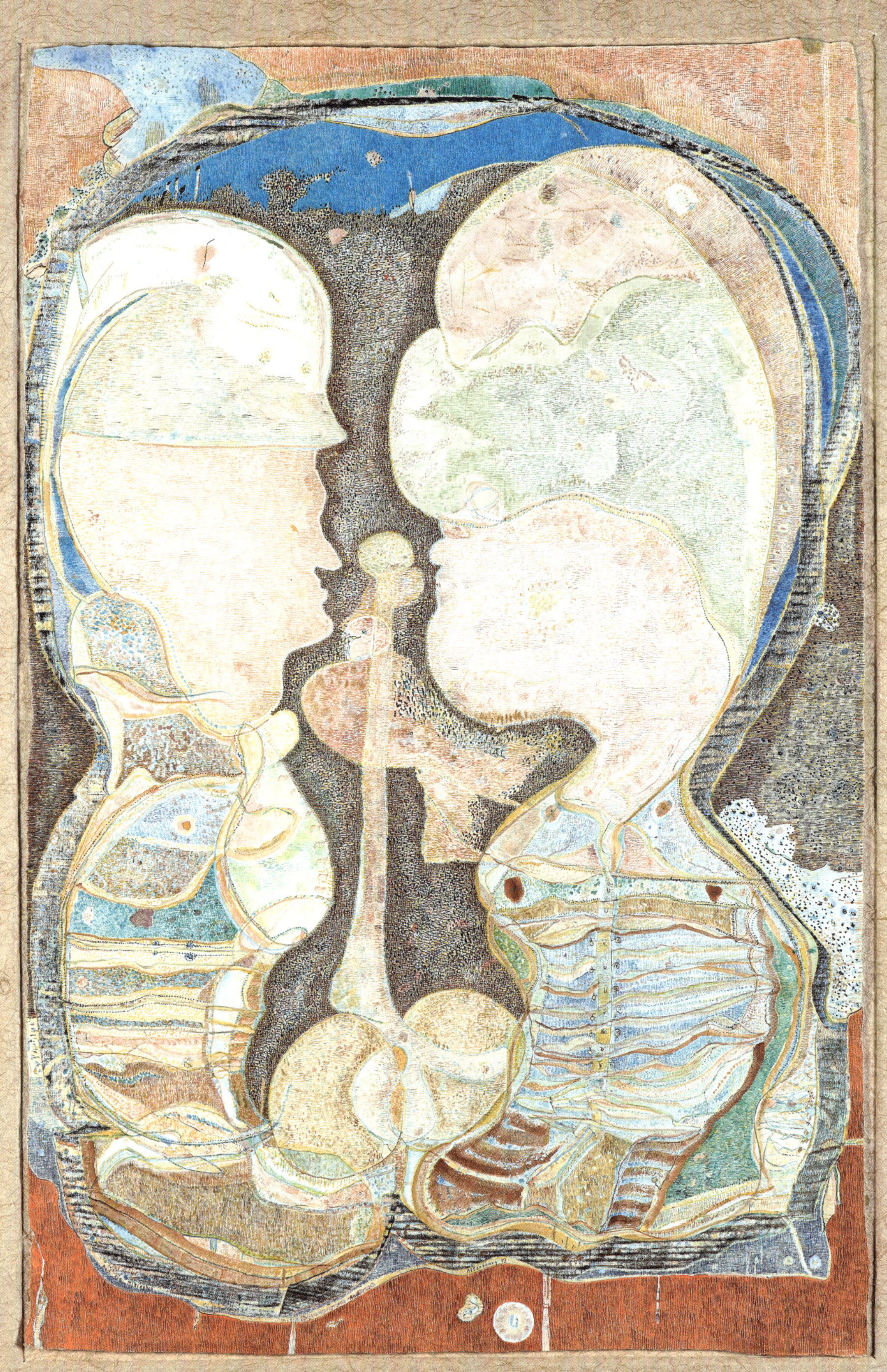

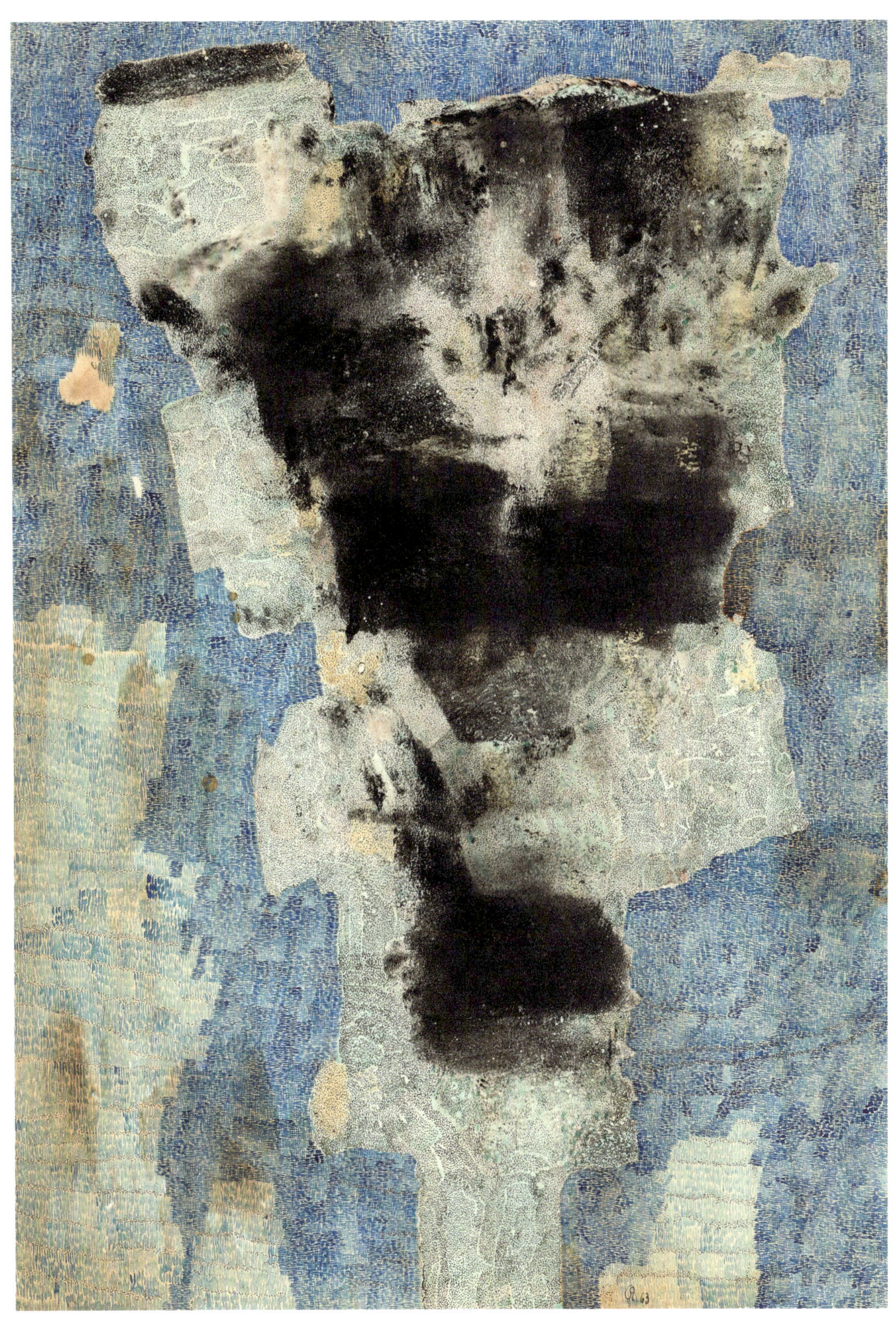

41 *Auch ein Mikrophon*, 1973 |
Also a Microphone, 1973

42 *Huldigung für Quirinius Kuhlmann*, 1963 |
Homage for Quirinius Kuhlmann, 1963

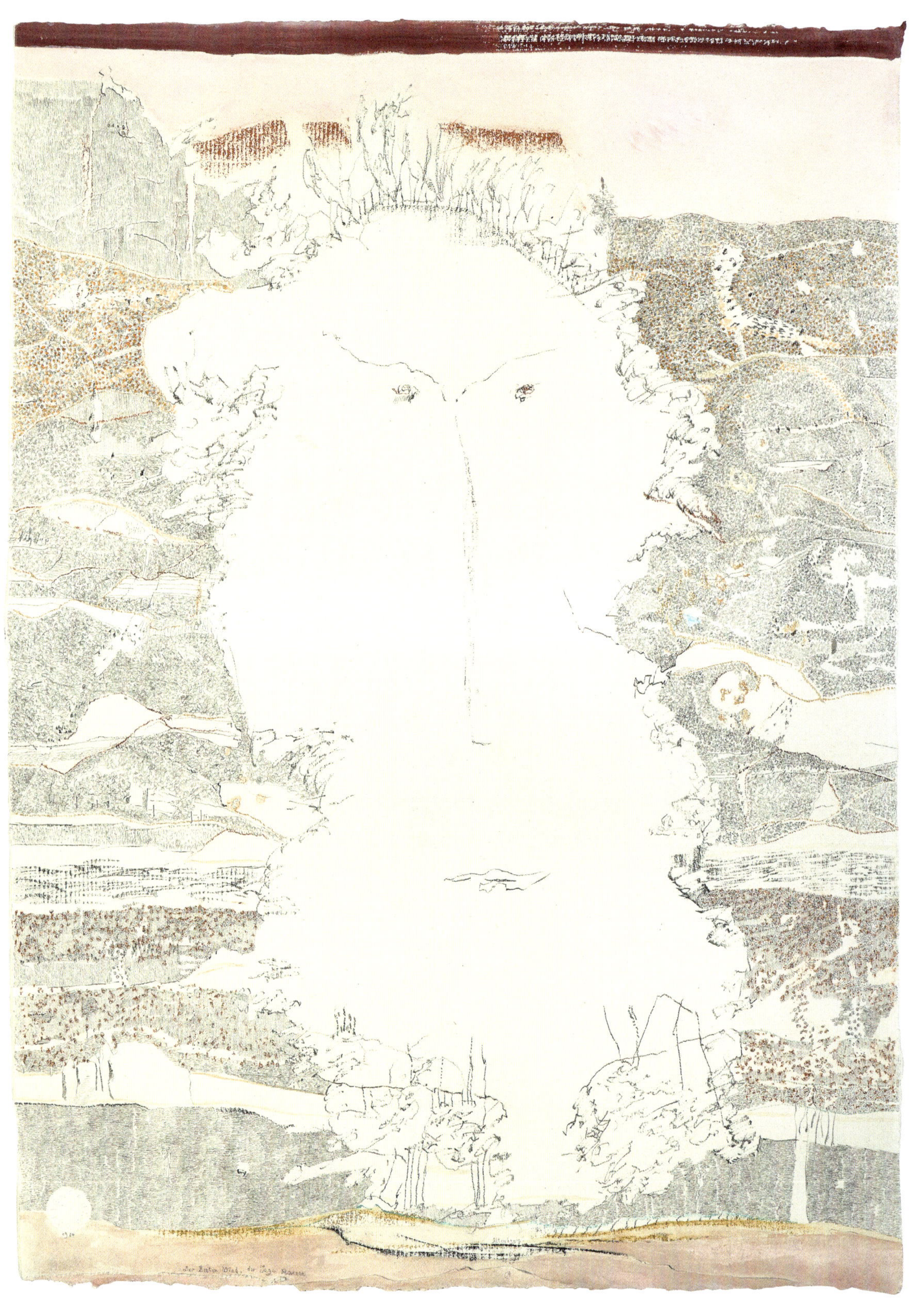

43 *Der Zeiten Wind, der Tage Raunen*, 1984 | *The Wind of the Times, the Murmuring of the Days*, 1984

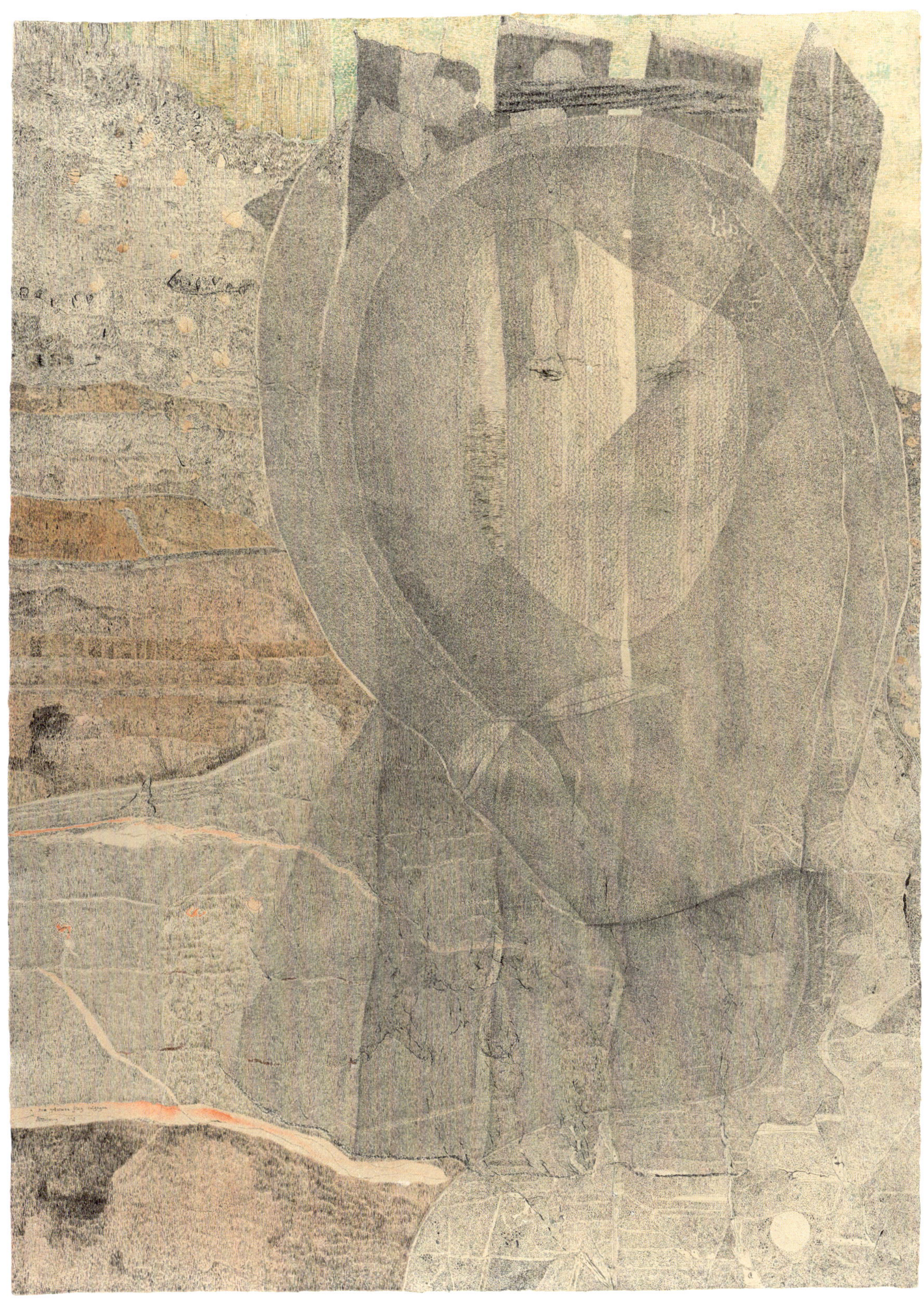

44 *Dem geheimen Flug entgegen*, 1978 |
Towards the Secret Flight, 1978

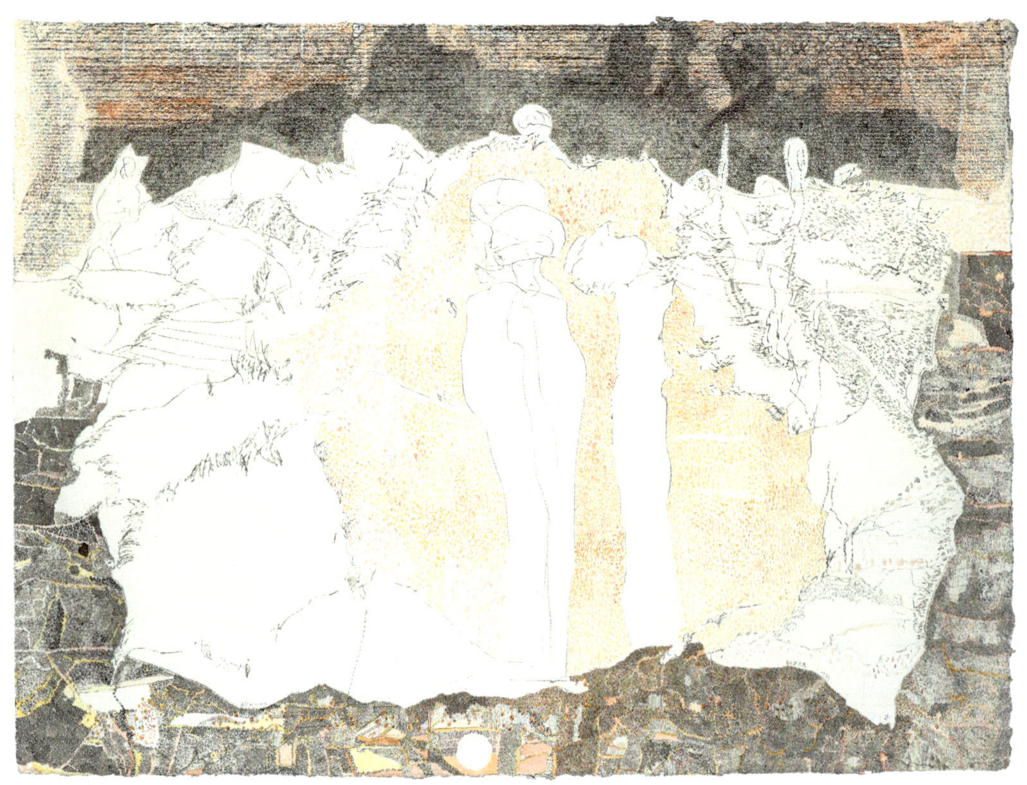

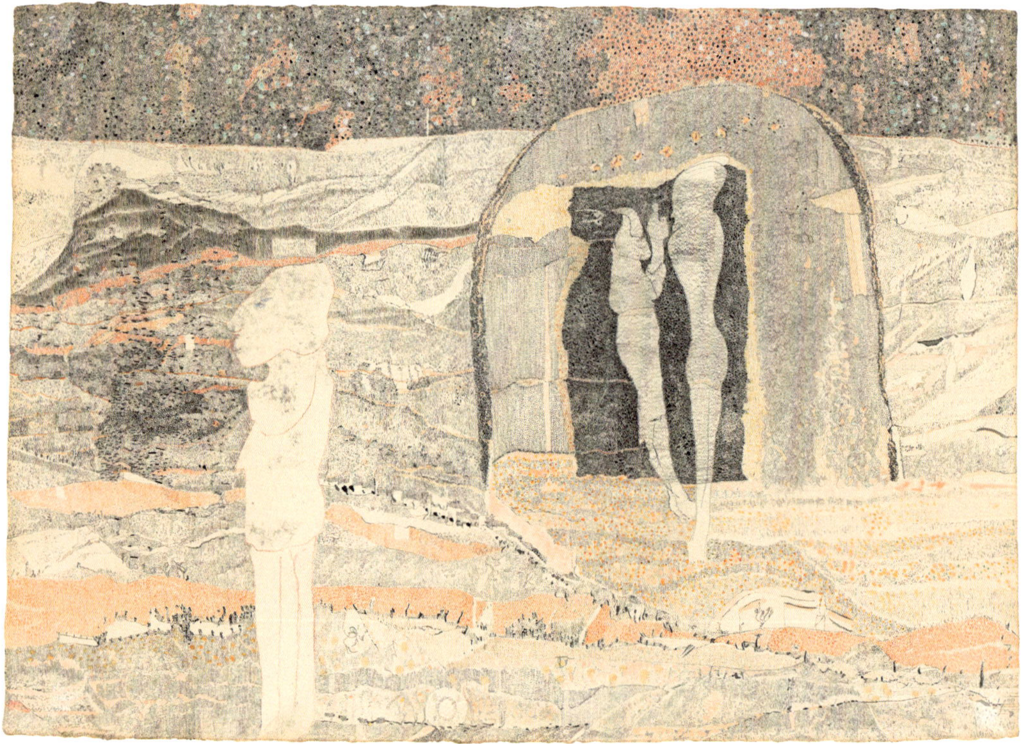

45 *Sunem*, 1984

46 *Knurrbarts brüchiges Schweigen im Wind*, 1989 | *Knurrbart's Fragile Silence in the Wind*, 1989

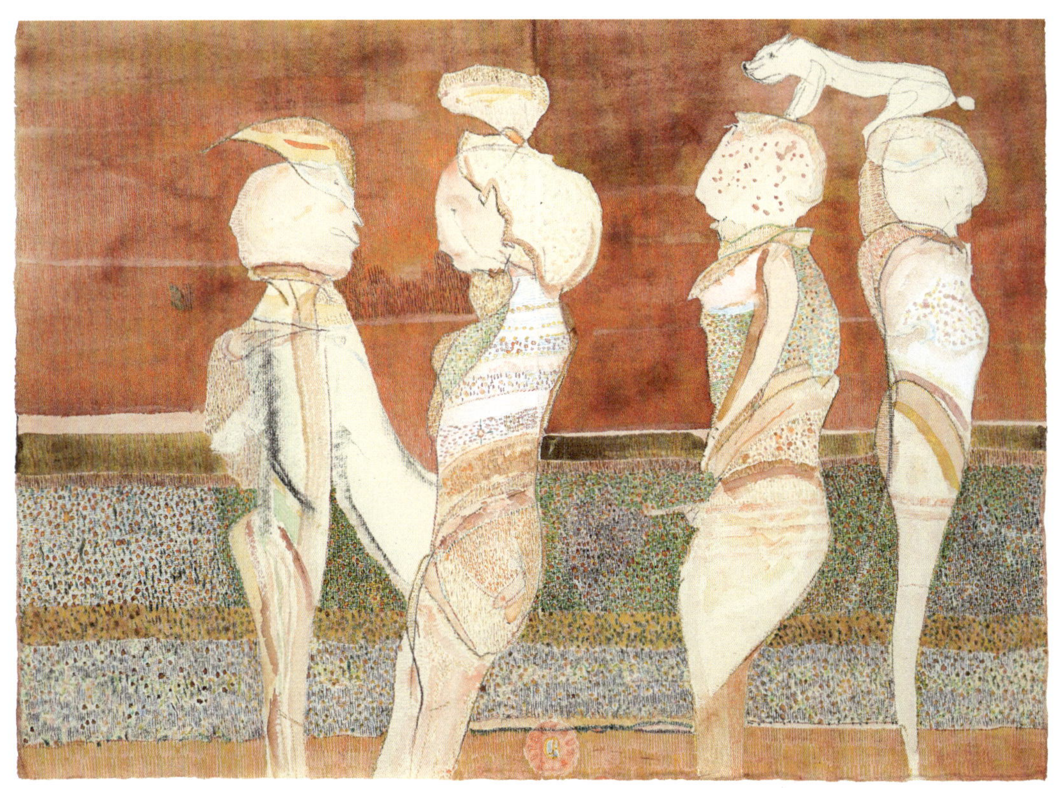

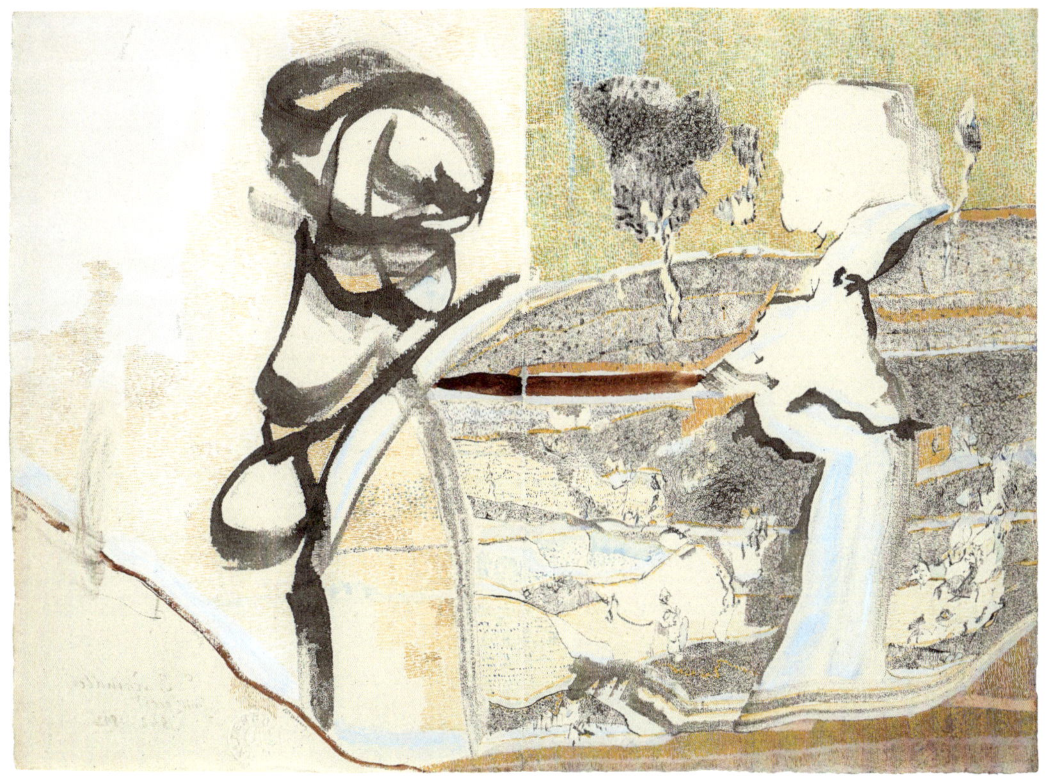

47 O. T. [Wie ägyptische Gottheiten bekrönt], undatiert | Untitled [Crowned Like Egyptian Gods], no date

48 O. T. [Zwei alte Schachteln], undatiert | Untitled [Two Old Biddies], no date

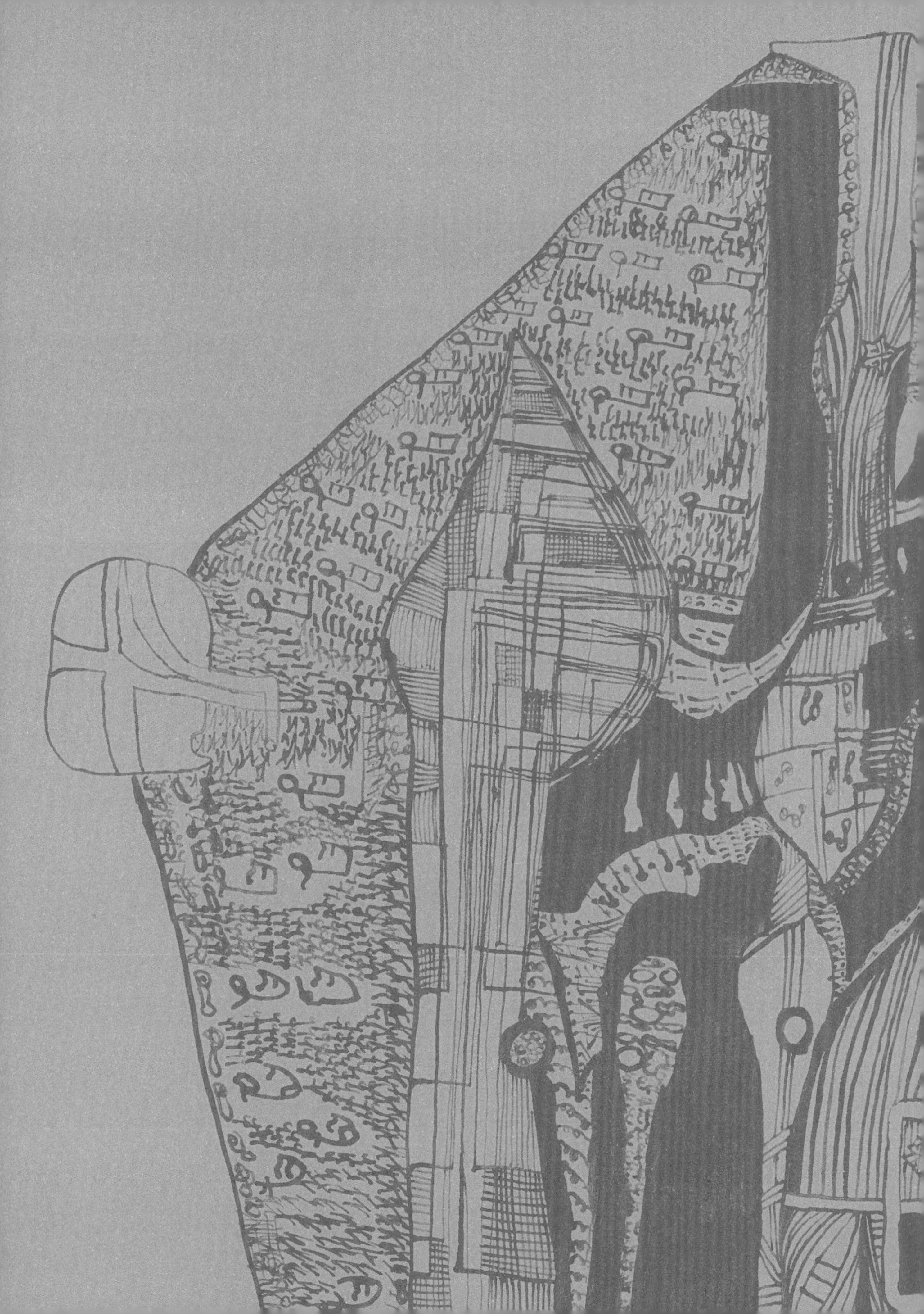

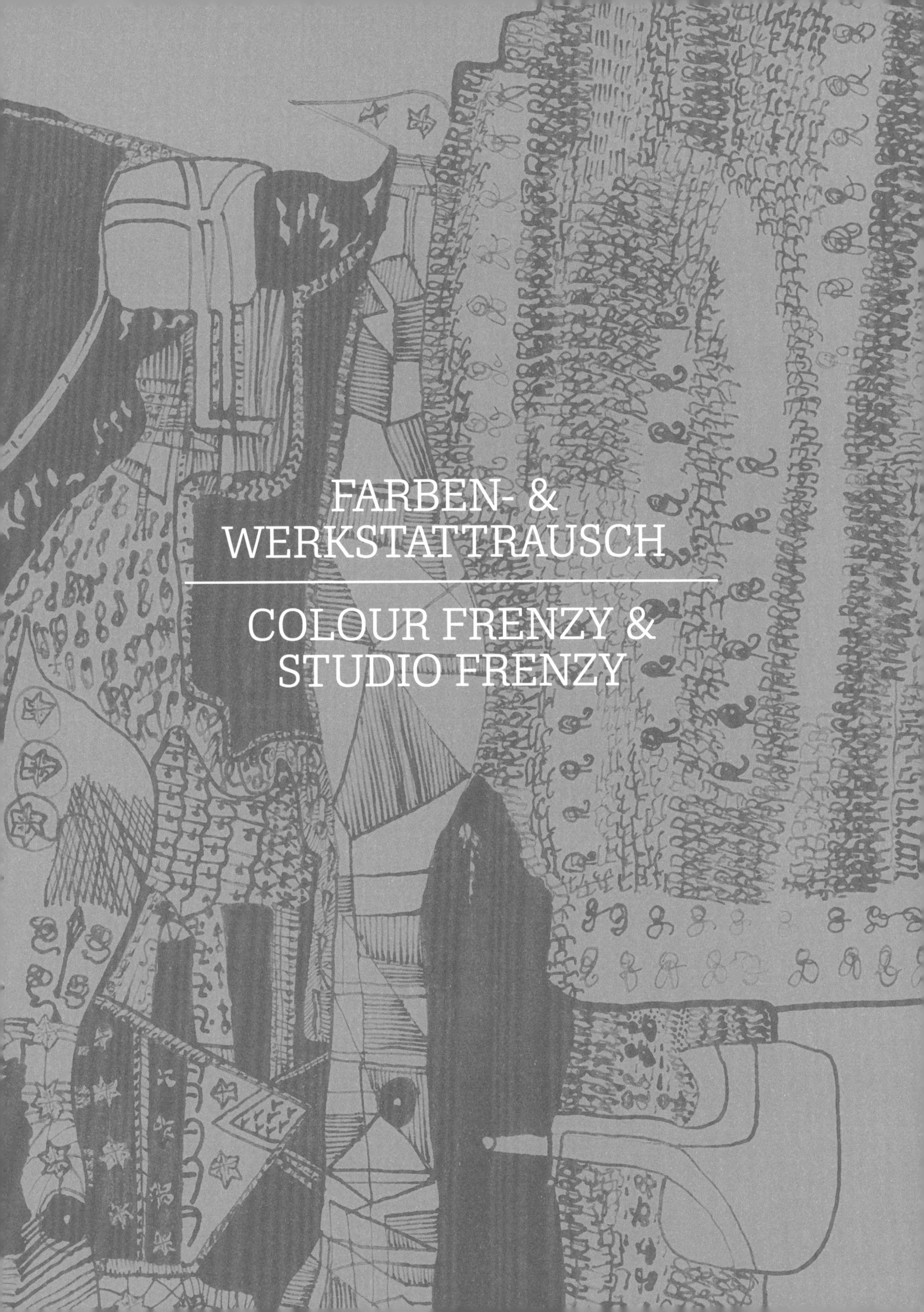

FARBEN- & WERKSTATTRAUSCH

COLOUR FRENZY & STUDIO FRENZY

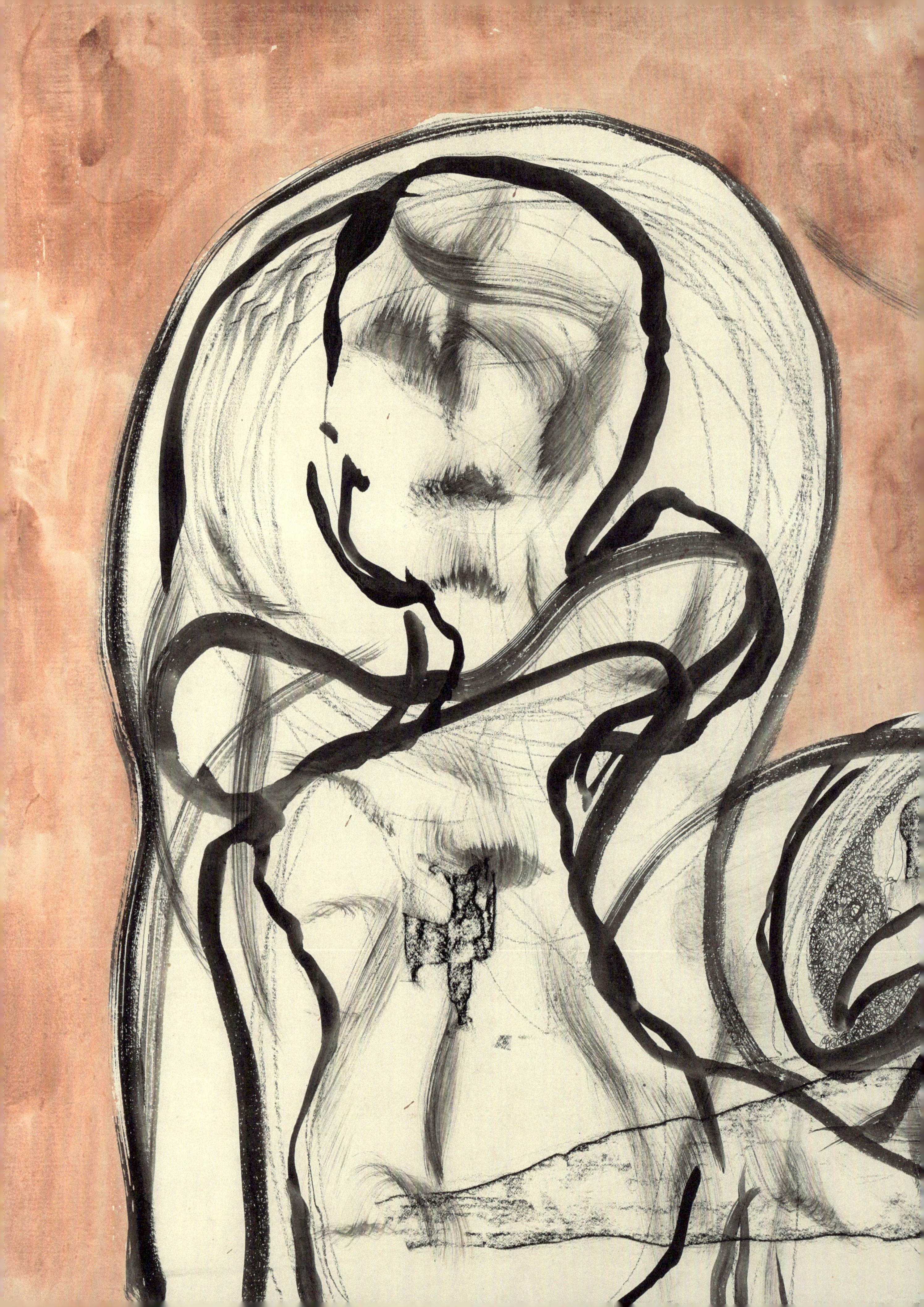

Steffen Krautzig

»Man fühlt sich dann als Medium«

Zufall und Automatismus bei Gerhard Altenbourg

Im *Manifeste du Surréalisme* (1924), dem Gründungsdokument der gleichnamigen Kunstbewegung, beschrieb André Breton die Verbindung zwischen Surrealität und Realität als Radikalmetapher: Je weiter zwei vom Künstler unbewusst in Beziehung gesetzte Bildbereiche voneinander entfernt seien, desto schöner der metaphorische Blitz oder Funke.[1] Max Ernst wandte diesen Kerngedanken des Surrealismus direkt auf die Bildende Kunst an: Durch die Technik der Frottage (frz. *frotter*, ab-/reiben) entstandene Bildelemente arrangierte und kombinierte er im Frontispiz für die 1929 erschiene *Nouvelle édition* des Manifests so, dass sie individuellste Metaphernblitze, ergo Deutungen ermöglichen. Gerhard Altenbourg studierte Max Ernst in zahlreichen Publikationen seiner Privatbibliothek und sah einige originale Arbeiten vermutlich 1954 in einer Ausstellung des Galeristen Rudolf Springer in Berlin.[2]

Zwar »verschließen« sich Altenbourgs Arbeiten absichtlich »Kategorisierungen« und »verweigern Gefolgschaft«,[3] dennoch wird hier der Versuch unternommen, anhand einiger auf Zufall und Automatismus basierender Techniken in Altenbourgs Werk Parallelen zum Surrealismus aufzuzeigen, einer Kunstrichtung, in der Mehr- und Uneindeutigkeiten ebenfalls zentral sind.

Die große, von Annegret Janda im Nachlass Altenbourgs aufgefundene und betitelte, undatierte und unsignierte, mit dem Prägestempel versehene Zeichnung *Zwei verbunden durch die kleine Eva* (Kat. 49, vgl. Details S. 122, 130) erschließt sich nicht auf den ersten Blick. Eine allgemeine Aussage des Künstlers über die langwierigen Entstehungsprozesse seiner Werke hilft bei der Spurensuche: »Es gibt Zeichnungen, die erst mit Bleistift angelegt worden sind, dann kommt eine zweite Schicht darüber, dann eine dritte, auch farbige Dinge, bis zu acht, neun Überzeichnungen.«[4] Beim Nachvollzug der Werkgenese lässt sich ablesen, dass Altenbourg die Fläche rund um die amorphe Figuration mit rotbrauner Farbe zuletzt ausgefüllt hat. Davor kamen die Umrisse mit breiten schwarzen Pinselstrichen, davor wiederum dünne Feder- oder Bleistiftstriche, sodass ganz am

"Then You Feel Like a Medium"

Chance and Automatism in Gerhard Altenbourg's Practice

In the *Manifeste du Surréalisme* (1924), the constitutive document of the Surrealist movement, André Breton described the link between surreality and reality as a radical metaphor: the greater the distance between the two pictorial areas that the artist has unconsciously brought into relation, the more beautiful the metaphorical bolts of lightning or the spark between them.[1] Max Ernst applied this central idea of Surrealism directly to the visual arts: he arranged and combined visual elements formed through frottage (from the French *frotter*, "to rub") in the frontispiece of the *Nouvelle édition* of the manifesto (1929) to generate the most individual flashes of lightning – and thus meaning. Gerhard Altenbourg studied Ernst through numerous publications in his private library and presumably saw several original works in 1954 at an exhibition in the Galerie Rudolf Springer in Berlin.[2]

Although Altenbourg's works deliberately "reject categorisation" and "refuse to obey", [3] his use of chance and automatism reveals similarities with Surrealism, an art movement in which ambiguity and inconclusiveness were key concepts.

The large-format drawing *Zwei verbunden durch die kleine Eva* (Two Linked by Little Eve, cat. 49, see details pp. 122, 130) is undated and unsigned, but marked with a blind stamp; it was discovered in the artist's estate by Annegret Janda, who also gave it its title. At

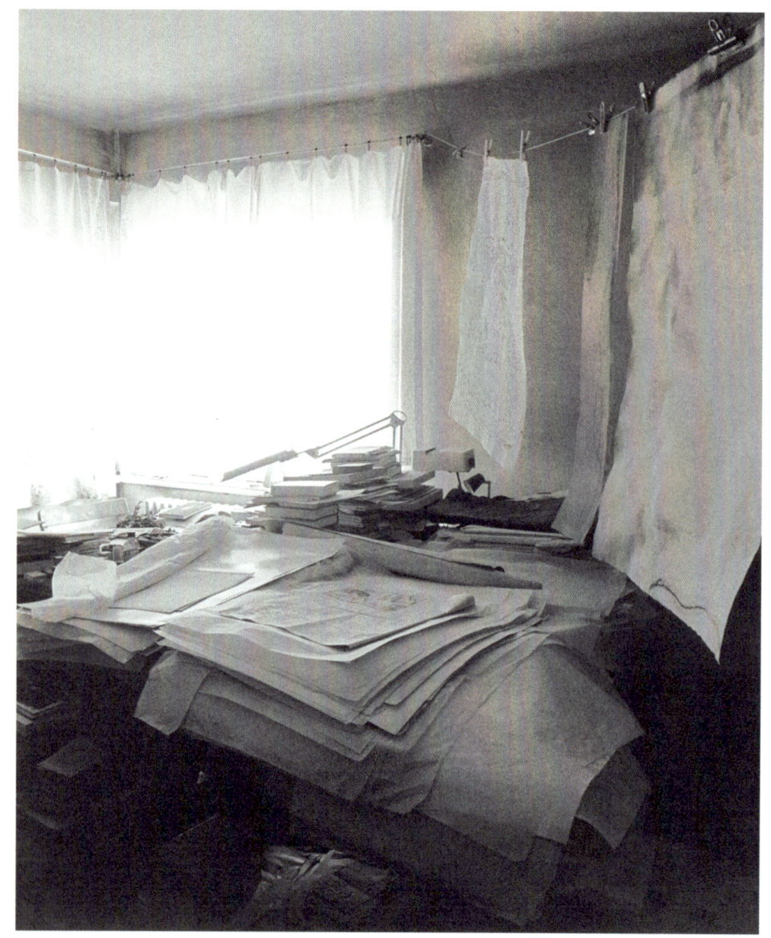

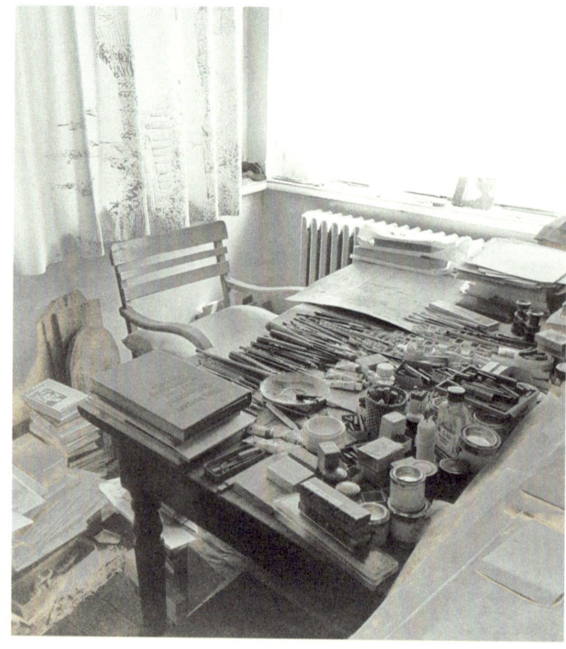

Abb. 1, 2 Ulrich Lindner, *Arbeitszimmer und Arbeitsplatz von Gerhard Altenbourg*, 1990, zwei Schwarz-Weiß-Fotografien, aus: Ulrich Lindners Mappe *Gerhard Altenbourg. »Dies Haus als Aufgabe«*, 1991, Stiftung Gerhard Altenbourg, Inv.-Nrn. SGA 6095-17-Ks, SGA 6095-19-Ks
Figs. 1–2 Ulrich Lindner, *Gerhard Altenbourg's Study and Workplace*, 1990, two black-and-white photographs, from Ulrich Lindner's portfolio *Gerhard Altenbourg. "Dies Haus als Aufgabe"* (This House as Purpose, 1991), Gerhard Altenbourg Foundation, inv. nos. SGA 6095-17-Ks, SGA 6095-19-Ks

Beginn insgesamt sieben kleine und mittelgroße Durchriebe entstanden, zufällig verteilt und angeordnet auf dem ursprünglich noch leeren Blatt. Erst die nach vermutlich langen Pausen getätigten Arbeitsschritte stellten Zusammenhänge zwischen allen Bildteilen her. Ulrich Lindners Fotografien aus Altenbourgs Arbeitszimmer zeigen Zeichenmaterialien und Stapel großformatiger Papierbögen sowie Zeichnungen, die offen auf dem Schreibtisch liegen, um jederzeit an ihnen weiterarbeiten zu können **(Abb. 1, 2).** Wenn wir Jandas Titelvorschlag folgen, befinden sich die durchgeriebenen Formen an wichtigen Positionen von zwei menschlichen Halbfiguren, jeweils in Herz- oder Brusthöhe und bei der rechten Figur im Gesicht. Das größte durch Frottage entstandene Element liegt mittig im unteren Bildviertel und verbindet die beiden Unterkörper. Janda gibt in ihrem Titelvorschlag den Hinweis auf *Kleine Eva*, ein nach Altenbourgs Zeichnungen entstandener, 32,5 × 6,5 cm großer Kupferbeschlag, der sich seit 1964 als Intarsie an der Außenseite der Tür (Standbild *Gib Acht*) im oberen Flur seines Künstlerhauses befindet **(Abb. 3).**[5] Auch wenn die genaue Datierung der Zeichnung unklar ist, kann sie durch Identifizierung der anderen Durchriebe weiter eingegrenzt werden: Die Frottage der Metallarbeit *Kleine Eva* muss

first glance, the drawing resists interpretation, but a statement by the artist on the protracted processes of creation of his works might aid us in searching for clues to its meaning: "There are drawings that are first laid out with the pencil, then a second layer is added over it, then a third, colourful things as well, up to eight, nine layers of drawing."[4] The reconstruction of the drawing's genesis shows that Altenbourg filled in the space around the amorphous figures with a red-brown colour as a last step. Previously, he had drawn the outlines with broad black brushstrokes, and before that had applied thin pen or pencil lines, so that at the very beginning he made a total of seven small and mid-sized frottages, distributed and arranged aleatorically on the empty sheet. It was thus only the individual working phases, presumably executed after long interruptions, that established the connections between the individual components of the picture. Ulrich Lindner's photographs of Altenbourg's studio show drawing materials

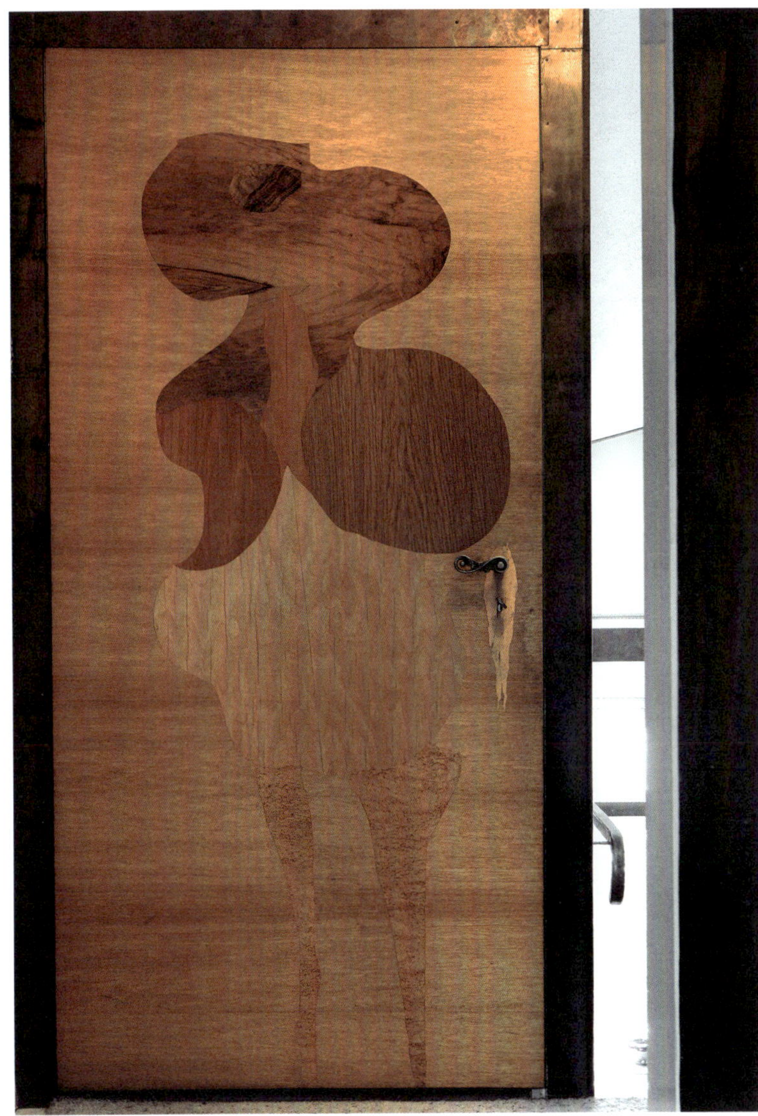

Abb. 3 Gerhard Altenbourg, *Standbild Gib acht* mit *Kleine Eva*, 1964, Tür mit Holzintarsien und Metallapplikationen zum Treppenhaus ins Dachgeschoss, Stiftung Gerhard Altenbourg, Inv.-Nr. SGA 5998-A
Fig. 3 Gerhard Altenbourg, *Standbild Gib acht* (Still Image Be Careful) with *Kleine Eva* (Little Eve), 1964, door with wood inlay and metal applications for the stairs to the attic floor, Gerhard Altenbourg Foundation, inv. no. SGA 5998-A

1964 oder davor entstanden sein.[6] Auf der Rückseite der Tür befindet sich mit dem Beschlag *Kleiner Adam* das Gegenstück. Betätigen der Türklinke, Einführen oder Abziehen des Türschlüssels werden sexuell aufgeladen. Körper und Sexualität sind – wie auch bei Max Ernst und im Surrealismus allgemein – Themen, auf die Altenbourg sowohl bei der Tür, bei dem Durchrieb, als auch im gesamten Blatt anspielt.

Die »Entdeckung« der Frottage durch Max Ernst ist eine der legendären Anekdoten der Kunstgeschichte.[7] Er habe die Technik im Jahr 1925 angesichts zerkratzter Fußbodendielen eines Hotelzimmers erfunden.[8] Das Durchreiben von grobflächigen Strukturen mit Grafitstift oder Zeichenkohle auf Papier unterliegt zwar den Regeln des Zufalls, »doch die

and piles of large-format sheets of paper, as well as drawings lying openly on the table, so that Altenbourg could work on them at any moment (figs. 1–2). If one accepts Janda's title, then the forms caused by the frottages are situated in key positions within the two half-figures, each at the height of the heart or breast, and, in the figure on the right, in the face as well. The largest frottage shape lies in the centre of the lower quarter of the image, linking the two figures' lower halves. In her suggestion for the title, Janda refers to *Kleine Eva*, a 32.5 × 6.5 cm copper fitting made after Altenbourg's drawings, which since 1964 has been an inlay decorating the external side of the door (*Standbild Gib Acht* (Still-Image Pay Attention)) on the upper landing of his house (fig. 3).[5] Although the exact date of the drawing is unknown, its approximate period of creation can be further delimited by identifying the other rubbings. The frottage of the metalwork *Kleine Eva* (Little Eve) had to be made no later than 1964.[6] On the other side of the door is its counterpart, the relief *Kleiner Adam* (Little Adam). Turning the doorknob, inserting or withdrawing the key, are sexually charged in this door. The body and sexuality are subjects – like in Ernst and in Surrealism in general – that Altenbourg alludes to in the door, in the frottages and in the entire drawing.

The "discovery" of frottage by Max Ernst is a legendary tale in art history.[7] He supposedly invented the technique in 1925 when encountering the grooves in the scratched wooden floor of a hotel room.[8] The rubbing of rough structures with pencil or charcoal on paper is subject to chance, "but the elaboration of the picture itself is made by the artist's hand"[9] – in Ernst and Altenbourg, however, at different moments and to varying degrees. Both artists employed frottage in new contexts, combining it frequently with other techniques. While Ernst integrated his rubbings into his work process very early on, as for example in the series *Histoire naturelle* (1925), and single-mindedly incorporated them into the immanent pictorial logic of his works (fig. 4), Altenbourg left them open-ended as long as possible. As Annegret Janda describes it:

"For St. (Ströch) too does not begin with a specific subject, rather he covers the paper with lines and drawings out of which a subject gradually coalesces. Only from a certain point in the creation of work does he know what it will become and then pursues this goal consistently.... It is not so that he first sees a picture

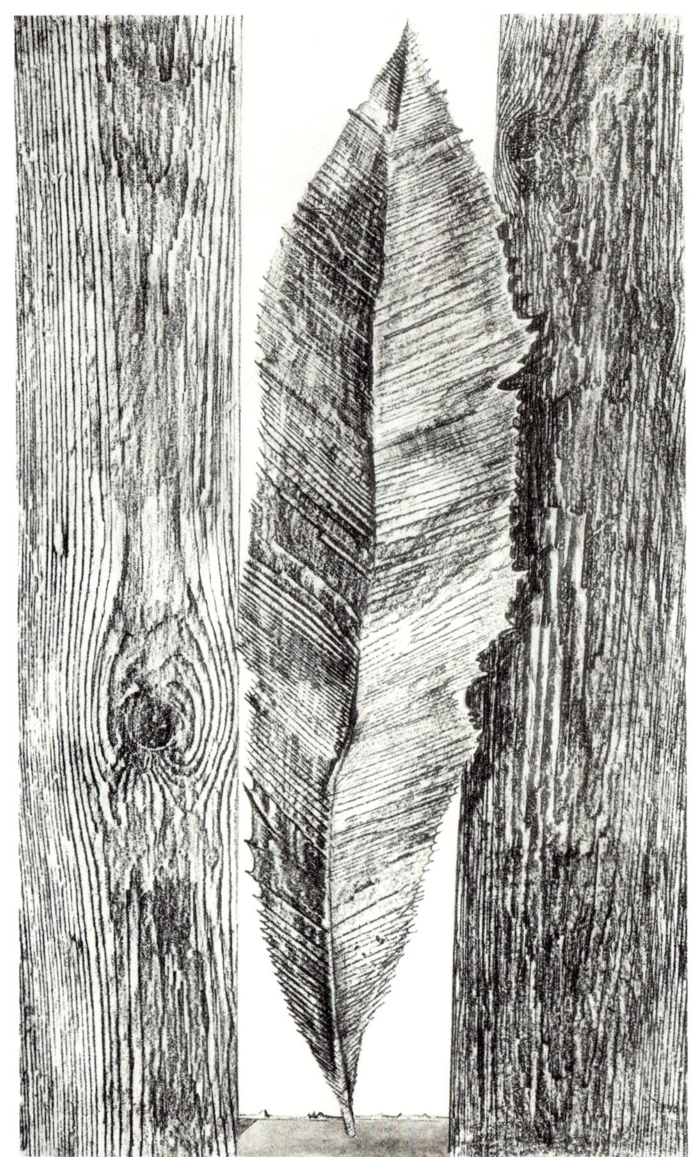

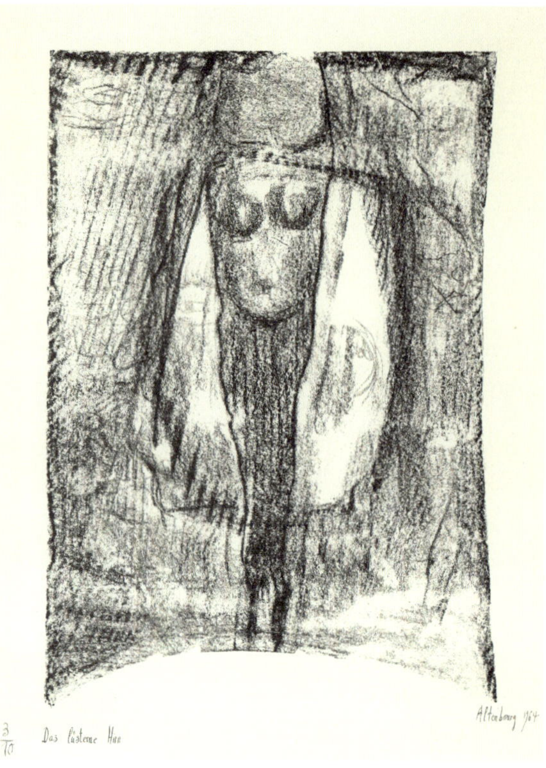

Abb. 4 Max Ernst, *Les mœurs des feuilles* (Blatt 18 der Mappe *Histoire naturelle*), 1926, Lichtdruck, 50 × 32 cm, Sprengel Museum Hannover, Inv.-Nr. F-B-S 21.B 18
Fig. 4 Max Ernst, *Les mœurs des feuilles* (The Habit of Leaves, sheet 18 from the portfolio *Histoire naturelle*), 1926, collotype, 50 × 32 cm, Sprengel Museum Hannover, inv. no. F-B-S 21.B 18.

Abb. 5 Gerhard Altenbourg, *Das lüsterne Hirn*, 1964, Lithografie, 3/10, 384 × 288 mm (Blatt), 325 × 225 mm (Darstellung), Stiftung Gerhard Altenbourg, Inv.-Nr. SGA 1847-L
Fig. 5 Gerhard Altenbourg, *Das lüsterne Hirn* (The Lustful Brain), 1964, lithograph, 3/10, 384 × 288 mm (sheet), 325 × 225 mm (image), Gerhard Altenbourg Foundation, inv. no. SGA 1847-L

Ausgestaltung des Bildes selbst erfolgt durch die Hand des Künstlers« – bei Ernst und Altenbourg allerdings zu unterschiedlichen Zeitpunkten und ungleich stark ausgeprägt.[9] Beide setzten ihre Frottagen in neue Kontexte, sie kombinierten sie zudem häufig mit anderen Techniken. Während Ernst seine Durchreibungen, zum Beispiel in der Serie *Histoire naturelle* (1925), sehr früh im Werkprozess und zielgerichtet in eine immanente Bildlogik einband **(Abb. 4)**, ließ Altenbourg alles so lange wie möglich offen. Annegret Janda beschreibt dies so: »Denn auch St. (Ströch, Anm. SK) beginnt nicht ein bestimmtes Thema, sondern er bedeckt das Papier mit Linien und Zeichen, aus denen erst allmählich ein Thema wird. Erst von einem bestimmten Punkt der Arbeit an weiß er, was es werden soll und verfolgt dann diesen Weg konsequent. (…) Es ist also nicht so, daß ihm ein Bild vor Augen

mentally and then he visualises it, rather he begins freely until the laws of the forms already visible force him in a specific direction. Only at the very end does he give it a title, after long observation and meditation, as an aid for the observer to enter its pictorial world. That's why the titles leave so much unsettled."[10]

Since Altenbourg did not give the work a title and did not sign, monogram or date it as he usually did, this drawing may be viewed as incomplete. Whether and which further work phases could have been carried out can only be speculated. Moreover, he would probably not have revealed – in a Surrealist sense – the connection with the copper relief *Kleine Eva*, in

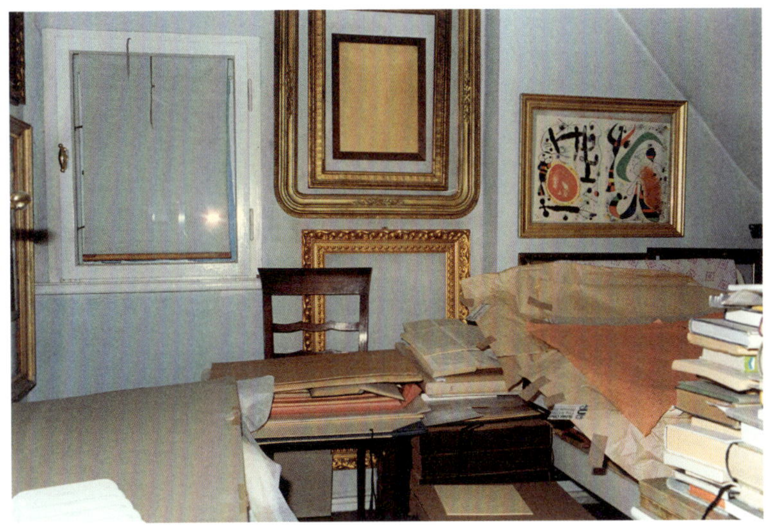

Abb. 6 *Blick in die Dach- und Schlafkammer von Gerhard Altenbourg*, 1990, Farbfotografie, Privatbesitz, 101 × 149 mm, Stiftung Gerhard Altenbourg, Inv.-Nr. SGA F2006
Fig. 6 *View of Gerhard Altenbourg's Attic and Bedroom*, 1990, coloured lithograph, private collection, 101 × 149 mm, Gerhard Altenbourg Foundation, inv. no. SGA F2006

steht und er es nur sichtbar macht, sondern er fängt ungebunden an, bis ihn die Gesetze der bereits sichtbaren Formen in eine bestimmte Richtung zwingen. Erst ganz zum Schluss entsteht nach eingehender Betrachtung und Meditation der Titel als Hilfe für den Betrachter, in die Bildwelt einzutreten. Deshalb lassen die Titel so viel offen.«[10]

Da Altenbourg den Titel nicht selbst vergeben und das Blatt nicht wie üblich signiert, monogrammiert oder datiert hat, ist diese Zeichnung im Grunde genommen unvollendet. Ob und welche weiteren Arbeitsschritte gefolgt wären, kann nur Vermutung bleiben. Auch hätte er – im Sinne des Surrealismus – den Zusammenhang zum Kupferblech *Kleine Eva* wahrscheinlich nicht verraten, um neue, ungeplante Deutungsspielräume zu öffnen. Sicher ist jedoch, dass er viele unterschiedliche Verbindungsfäden zwischen seinen Papierarbeiten und den im Haus installierten Objekten, zum Beispiel eigenen Druckstöcken, geknüpft hat. Auch *Kleine Eva* taucht in anderen Zusammenhängen wieder auf, unter anderem in der Lithografie *Das lüsterne Hirn* (1964, Abb. 5).

Die kleine Zeichnung *Luftgeist, lächelnd* trägt Altenbourgs Prägestempel und ist von ihm in der rechten unteren Ecke auf 1984 datiert und signiert – sicher mit demselben Bleistift, mit dem der Künstler millimetergroße Punkte und Striche als Gesicht und Hals auf den größten Farbklecks des Blattes gesetzt hat **(Kat. 50)**. Aus einem Neben- bzw. Abfallprodukt – Papier, auf dem zu nasse Pinsel in kleinen Tupfen abgestrichen und unterschiedliche Farben ausprobiert wurden – entsteht durch einen metaphorischen Funkenschlag ein Kunstwerk. Der zufällige Farbverlauf des Kleckses lässt sich nun als menschlicher Kopf mit Hut interpretieren. Wahrscheinlich erst danach beschnitt Altenbourg die linke Seite

order to open up a new, unplanned range of interpretations. It is known, however, that he spun many different threads of connections between his works on paper and the objects installed in his house, for example his printing blocks. The *Kleine Eva* reappears in other contexts as well, among them the lithograph *Das lüsterne Hirn* (The Lustful Brain, 1964, **fig. 5**).

The small drawing *Luftgeist, lächelnd* (Airy Spirit, Smiling) is marked with Altenbourg's blind stamp and is signed and dated by him in the lower right corner to 1984 – surely with the same pencil he used to set the millimetre-sized dots and dashes as face and neck on the largest of the stains of tempera and watercolour distributed around the sheet **(cat. 50)**. A metaphorical lightning bolt has created an artwork out of a waste or by-product: a sheet of paper on which a brush loaded with too much paint is wiped or on which different colours are tested. The chance shape of the stain of colour can now be interpreted as a human head wearing a hat. Only later did Altenbourg presumably cut the sheet down on the left side, so that the head is situated in the upper quarter, like in a traditional figure drawing, and there is enough space left for the observer to project associations, such as regards the body. The work's title was again formulated by Annegret Janda, and so this drawing, too, should be regarded as unfinished.

The history of art is full of chance stains, dabs and spots (or, in Leonardo's case, crumbling walls) inspiring the imagination of artists.[11] Altenbourg's drawings *Luftgeist, lächelnd* and *Flirt mit dem Steckenpferd* (Flirt with the Hobby Horse, **cats. 50, 51**) do not qualify as "klecksography" (aleatoric inkblots) as understood by the eighteenth and nineteenth centuries, since he does not place stains on the sheet as a starting point to work on them further, but instead utilises existing stains like ready-mades or *objets trouvés* in a Dadaist or Surrealist sense. In his method of working, he again took his own works as the starting point, weaving together an autonomous and self-contained oeuvre out of these interconnections. His work with fluid paints, which not only transformed their physical condition as stains during the process of drying on absorbent paper, but only materialised at all into an aleatoric shape on the paper, suited Altenbourg, who was a connoisseur and aficionado of paper.[12] This approach has parallels with Joan Miró – Altenbourg possessed an art print by Miró **(fig. 6)**[13] – and Henri Michaux, whose books he knew.[14]

des Blattes, damit sich der Kopf wie bei einer klassischen Figurenzeichnung mittig im oberen Viertel befindet und es ausreichend Projektionsfläche für die Assoziationen der Betrachter gibt, zum Beispiel für einen Körper. Der Titel der Arbeit stammt von Annegret Janda, insofern wäre auch diese Zeichnung als unvollendet zu betrachten.

In der Kunstgeschichte regten zufällige Kleckse, Tupfen, Flecken (oder im Falle Leonardo da Vincis verwitterte Mauern) häufig die Fantasie von Künstlerinnen und Künstlern an.[11] Altenbourgs Zeichnungen *Luftgeist, lächelnd* und *Flirt mit dem Steckenpferd* **(Kat. 50, 51)** sind aber keine Klecksographien im Sinne des 18. und 19. Jahrhunderts, da er die Flecken nicht zum Zwecke der Weiterverarbeitung auf das Blatt platziert, sondern er bereits vorhandene Kleckse wie Readymades oder *objets trouvés* im Dada- und Surrealismus weiterverwendet hat. Dabei nutzte er erneut eigene Arbeiten als Ausgangspunkt, erschuf mit diesen Querverbindungen ein autarkes und in sich geschlossenes Gesamtwerk. Die Arbeit mit flüssigen Farben, die als Kleckse auf saugfähigem Papier während des Trocknens nicht nur ihren Aggregatzustand änderten, sondern sich auf dem Papier überhaupt erst zu einer zufälligen Form materialisierten, passte gut zu dem Papierkenner und -liebhaber Altenbourg.[12] Formale Parallelen finden sich bei Joan Miró, von dem Altenbourg einen Kunstdruck besaß **(Abb. 6)**[13] und bei Henri Michaux, dessen Bücher er kannte.[14]

Die 1950 entstandene, signierte und datierte Tuschezeichnung *Ammonon Gillitige* **(Kat. 16)** gibt absichtlich Rätsel auf. Zwar scheint rechts eine sitzende, anthropomorphe Figur, jedoch ist eine eindeutige Interpretation unmöglich. Die Linien links und der kryptische Bildtitel bieten keine Hilfe. Stilistisch übereinstimmend mit anderen Zeichnungen aus dem gleichen Jahr sind hingegen die abwechslungsreichen Binnenstrukturen (Waben, Kringel, Punkte usw.), mit denen einige Flächen gefüllt sind. Auch hier kann ein Blick auf den Entstehungsprozess immerhin etwas Klarheit schaffen. Altenbourg selbst zog Parallelen zum bekanntesten automatischen Verfahren des Surrealismus: »Man muß den Kater kraulen, bis er schnurrt, bis die Linie vergeistigt wird. Es ist zu spüren, es ist wie ein inneres Leuchten. In diesem Zustand wird plötzlich das Papier zu einer anderen Bühne. Man fühlt sich dann als Medium.«[15] Oder mit den Worten Bretons, der im ersten Surrealistischen Manifest über die *Écriture automatique* schrieb: »Versetzen Sie sich in den passivsten oder den rezeptivsten Zustand, dessen sie fähig sind. (…) Schreiben Sie schnell, ohne vorgefaßtes Thema, schnell genug, um nichts zu behalten (…).«[16] Der Schreibende, hier der Zeichnende, weiß während der Tätigkeit also nicht, was er zu Papier bringt. Anders als bei ähnlichen Arbeiten der frühen Schaffensphase hilft der später hinzugefügte Werktitel nun aber nicht bei der Interpretation, denn er entstammt vollständig Altenbourgs Fantasie.

Beschreibungen übernatürlicher Inspirationen sind im 20. Jahrhundert indes keine Seltenheit. Die Surrealisten priesen vor allem die Kunst von Außenseitern, weil diese, ohne die Regeln anderer zu beachten, allein aus ihrer Vorstellungskraft schöpften.[17] Ein Beispiel sind die Zeichnungen von Madge Gill, in denen alle Binnenflächen mit kleinsten

The India ink drawing *Ammonon Gillitge* **(cat. 16)**, signed, dated and created in 1950, is purposefully puzzling. Despite the anthropomorphic figure sitting on the right, a definitive interpretation is impossible. The lines on the left and the cryptic title offer no clues. Stylistic similarities with other drawings from the same year, however, are evident in the varied internal structures (honeycombs, curls, dots, etc.) that occupy some of the areas. Here too a glance at the creative process can offer at least some indications. Altenbourg himself drew parallels to the best-known procedure used by Surrealists: "You have to stroke the cat until it starts to purr, until the line becomes spiritual. You can sense it, it is like an inner glow. In this state the paper suddenly becomes another kind of stage. Then you feel like a medium."[15] Or, to put it in Breton's words, who described *écriture automatique* in the first Surrealist Manifesto: "Put yourself in as passive, or receptive, a state of mind as you can.... Write quickly, without any preconceived subject, fast enough so that you will not remember what you're writing."[16] The person writing – in this case drawing – does not know what they are putting down on paper during the activity. In contrast to similar works from his early creative period, the artwork's title added later on does not aid interpretation, since it emanates entirely from Altenbourg's imagination.

Descriptions of supernatural sources of inspiration are not at all uncommon in the twentieth century. The Surrealists praised the works of outsider artists because they drew solely from their power of imagination, without heeding the rules of others.[17] An example is the drawings by Madge Gill, in which all the internal surfaces are filled in with the smallest structures.[18] Similarities between Altenbourg's ink works of the 1950s can also be found with the works of Surrealist artist Unica Zürn, who, like Altenbourg, participated in *documenta 2* in 1959 and was also represented by the Galerie Brusberg.[19]

Altenbourg knew the artists mentioned here at the very least from publications in his private library. He adapted the described aleatoric techniques and combined them with other procedures. One reason his works remain so fascinating today is because viewing them through the lens of Surrealist practices is only one of many possible perspectives.

Strukturen ausgefüllt sind.[18] Ähnlichkeiten zwischen Altenbourgs Tuschzeichnungen der 1950er-Jahre gibt es auch zu Werken der surrealistischen Künstlerin Unica Zürn, die genau wie Altenbourg 1959 an der documenta 2 teilnahm und ebenfalls von der Galerie Brusberg vertreten wurde.[19]

Altenbourg kannte die erwähnten Künstlerinnen und Künstler mindestens aus Publikationen seiner Bibliothek. Er adaptierte die beschriebenen Zufallstechniken und kombinierte sie mit anderen Verfahren. Sein Werk ist auch deswegen bis heute so faszinierend, weil der Zugang über den Surrealismus und dessen Theorien nur eine von vielen möglichen Perspektiven darstellt.

1 Vgl. Puff-Trojan, Andreas: Der Surrealismus. Kunst, Literatur, Leben, München 2024, S. 21, 67 f.
2 Vgl. Prinz, Ursula: Chronologie, in: Gachnang, Johannes (Hrsg.): Der gekrümmte Horizont: Kunst in Berlin 1945 – 1967. Ausst.-Kat. Akademie der Künste, Berlin, Berlin 1980, S. 11–30, hier S. 19 f.
3 Vgl. Flügge, Matthias: Getrennte Wege, einander berührend, in: Jenaer Kunstverein e.V. (Hrsg.): Souveräne Wege. 1949–1989. Sechs Künstler in der DDR, Ausst.-Kat. Stadtmuseum Jena, Jena 1997, S. 12–15, hier S. 14.
4 (Altenbourg, Gerhard/Mennekes, Friedhelm:) Im Gespräch (Interview mit Friedhelm Mennekes), in: Grinten, Franz Joseph von der/Mennekes, Friedhelm: Abstraktion – Kontemplation. Auseinandersetzung mit einem Thema der Gegenwartskunst, Stuttgart 1987, S. 237.
5 Vgl. Janda, Annegret (Hrsg.): – sah ichs wie Feuer glänzen um und um –. Werkverzeichnis der Metallarbeiten und zugehörigen Zeichnungen von Gerhard Altenbourg, Ausst.-Kat. Grassimuseum, Museum für Kunsthandwerk Leipzig, Berlin 1994, S. 212 f.
6 Genau wie die Lithografien *Das lüsterne Hirn* (Abb. 5) und *Es waren drei*, in denen Altenbourg ebenfalls Durchriebe der *Kleinen Eva* weiterbearbeitete; vgl. ebd. S. 213.
7 Zu Aussagekraft, Wahrheitsgehalt und Bedeutung von Künstleranekdoten vgl. Busch, Werner: Die Künstleranekdote 1760–1960, München 2020, S. 24 ff.
8 Vgl. Spies, Werner: Max Ernst. Frottagen, Stuttgart 1968, S. 5 f.
9 Vgl. Puff-Trojan 2024 (wie Anm. 1), S. 73.
10 Annegret Janda an Erhart Kästner, 23. März 1969, in: (Altenbourg, Gerhard/Kästner, Erhart:) Das dritte Auge. Ein Dialog der Freunde Gerhard Altenbourg und Erhart Kästner. Mit einem Geleitwort von Eduard Beaucamp und Texten von Dieter Brusberg, Dieter Hoffmann, Roland Jäger, Werner Schmidt und Bernard Schultze, Frankfurt a. M./Leipzig 1992, S. 36.
11 Vgl. Ketelsen, Thomas (Hrsg.): Die Klecksographie – Zwischen Fingerübung und Seelenschau, Ausst.-Kat. Graphisches Kabinett, Wallraf-Richartz-Museum & Fondation Corboud, Köln 2013.
12 Vgl. Klinke, Thomas: Der Klecks auf Papier – Ein kapillares Phänomen, in: ebd., S. 54–58.
13 Das heute nicht mehr im Künstlerhaus vorhandene Querformat ist eine Kombination der zwei hochformatigen Farblithografien Mirós *Le Jour* (links) und *La Nuit* (rechts), die 1953 mit anderen in der Mappe *Derrière le miroir* von der Pariser Galerie Maeght herausgegeben wurden. Vgl. Joan Miró. Der Lithograph II. 1953 – 1963, mit einem Vorwort von Raymond Queneau, Genf/Paris 1975. Wann der Druck entstand, wann Altenbourg ihn an die Wand hing und wo er ihn erwarb, ist nicht bekannt.
14 Zu Bestellungen Gerhard Altenbourgs von Büchern, Farben etc. über Solgärd und Rolf Walter vgl. Beloubek-Hammer, Anita: Gerhard Altenbourg. Das gezeichnete Ich. Neuerwerbung der Sammlung Solgärd und Rolf Walter und Bestand des Berliner Kupferstichkabinetts, Ausst.-Kat. Kupferstichkabinett, Staatliche Museen zu Berlin, Petersberg 2015, S. 24 ff.
15 Altenbourg/Mennekes 1987 (wie Anm. 4), S. 238.
16 Zit. nach: Schulze, Holger: Das aleatorische Spiel. Erkundung und Anwendung der nichtintentionalen Werkgenese im 20. Jahrhundert, München 2000, S. 78, Anm. 29.
17 Vgl. Presler, Gerd: L'Art Brut. Kunst zwischen Genialität und Wahnsinn, Köln 1981, S. 25. Eine Ausgabe dieses Buches befindet sich bis heute in Altenbourgs Privatbibliothek.
18 Ebd. S. 71 ff.
19 Vgl. den Beitrag von Sören Fischer im vorliegenden Band.

1 Andreas Puff-Trojan, *Der Surrealismus. Kunst, Literatur, Leben* (Munich: Beck, 2024), pp. 21, 67ff.
2 Ursula Prinz, "Chronologie", in Johannes Gachnang and Akademie der Künste (eds.), *Der gekrümmte Horizont. Kunst in Berlin 1945–1967*, exh. cat. Akademie der Künste, Berlin (Berlin: Interessengemeinschaft Berliner Kunsthändler, 1980), pp. 11–30, here pp. 19ff.
3 Matthias Flügge, "Getrennte Wege, einander berührend", in Jenaer Kunstverein e.V. (ed.), *Souveräne Wege. 1949–1989. Sechs Künstler in der DDR*, exh. cat. Stadtmuseum Jena (Jena: Jenaer Kunstverein, 1997), pp. 12–15, here p. 14.
4 Gerhard Altenbourg and Friedhelm Mennekes, "Im Gespräch (Interview mit Friedhelm Mennekes)", in Franz Joseph von der Grinten and Friedhelm Mennekes, *Abstraktion – Kontemplation. Auseinandersetzung mit einem Thema der Gegenwartskunst* (Stuttgart: Verlag Katholisches Bibelwerk, 1987), p. 237.
5 Annegret Janda (ed.), *– sah ichs wie Feuer glänzen um und um –. Werkverzeichnis der Metallarbeiten und zugehörigen Zeichnungen von Gerhard Altenbourg*, exh. cat. Grassimuseum, Museum für Kunsthandwerk Leipzig (Berlin: Faber & Faber, 1994), pp. 212ff.
6 Just like in the lithographs *Das lüsterne Hirn* (fig. 5) and *Es waren drei* (There were Three), in which Altenbourg also incorporated rubbings from *Kleine Eva;* see ibid., p. 213.
7 On the validity, truthfulness and meaning of artists' anecdotes, see Werner Busch, *Die Künstleranekdote 1760–1960* (Munich: Beck, 2020), pp. 24ff.
8 See Werner Spies, *Max Ernst. Frottagen* (Stuttgart: Hatje, 1968), pp. 5ff.
9 See Puff-Trojan (n. 1 above), p. 73.
10 Annegret Janda to Erhart Kästner, 23 March 1969, in Gerhard Altenbourg and Erhart Kästner, *Das dritte Auge. Ein Dialog der Freunde Gerhard Altenbourg und Erhart Kästner. Mit einem Geleitwort von Eduard Beaucamp und Texten von Dieter Brusberg, Dieter Hoffmann, Roland Jäger, Werner Schmidt und Bernard Schultze* (Frankfurt am Main/Leipzig: Insel, 1992), p. 36.
11 See Thomas Ketelsen (ed.), *Die Klecksographie – Zwischen Fingerübung und Seelenschau*, exh. cat. Graphisches Kabinett, Wallraf-Richartz-Museum & Fondation Corboud (Cologne: Wallraf-Richartz-Museum, 2013).
12 See Thomas Klinke, "Der Klecks auf Papier – Ein kapillares Phänomen", in ibid., pp. 54–58.
13 The landscape-format picture is no longer at the artist's house; it was made by combining two portrait-format colour lithographs by Miró, *Le Jour* (The Day, left) and *La Nuit* (The Night, right), which were published by the Paris gallery Maeght together with other lithographs in 1953 in the portfolio *Derrière le Miroir*. See *Joan Miró. Der Lithograph II. 1953–1963*, preface by Raymond Queneau (Geneva/Paris: Maeght Éditeur / Weber, 1975). When the lithograph was made, where Altenbourg acquired it and when he hung it on the wall is not known.
14 On Gerhard Altenbourg's orders of books, paints, etc. from Solgärd and Rolf Walter, see Anita Beloubek-Hammer, *Gerhard Altenbourg. Das gezeichnete Ich. Neuerwerbung der Sammlung Solgärd und Rolf Walter und Bestand des Berliner Kupferstichkabinetts*, exh. cat. Kupferstichkabinett, Staatliche Museen zu Berlin (Petersberg: Imhof, 2015), pp. 24ff.
15 See Altenbourg and Mennekes (n. 4 above), p. 238.
16 "Le Manifeste du Surréalisme" (1924), from André Breton, *Manifestoes of Surrealism*, trans. Richard Seaver and Helen R. Lane (Ann Arbor: University of Michigan Press, 1969), p. 29.
17 See Gerd Presler, *L'Art Brut. Kunst zwischen Genialität und Wahnsinn* (Cologne: DuMont, 1981), p. 25. An edition of this book is still present today in Altenbourg's library.
18 Ibid., pp. 71ff.
19 See the essay by Sören Fischer in this volume.

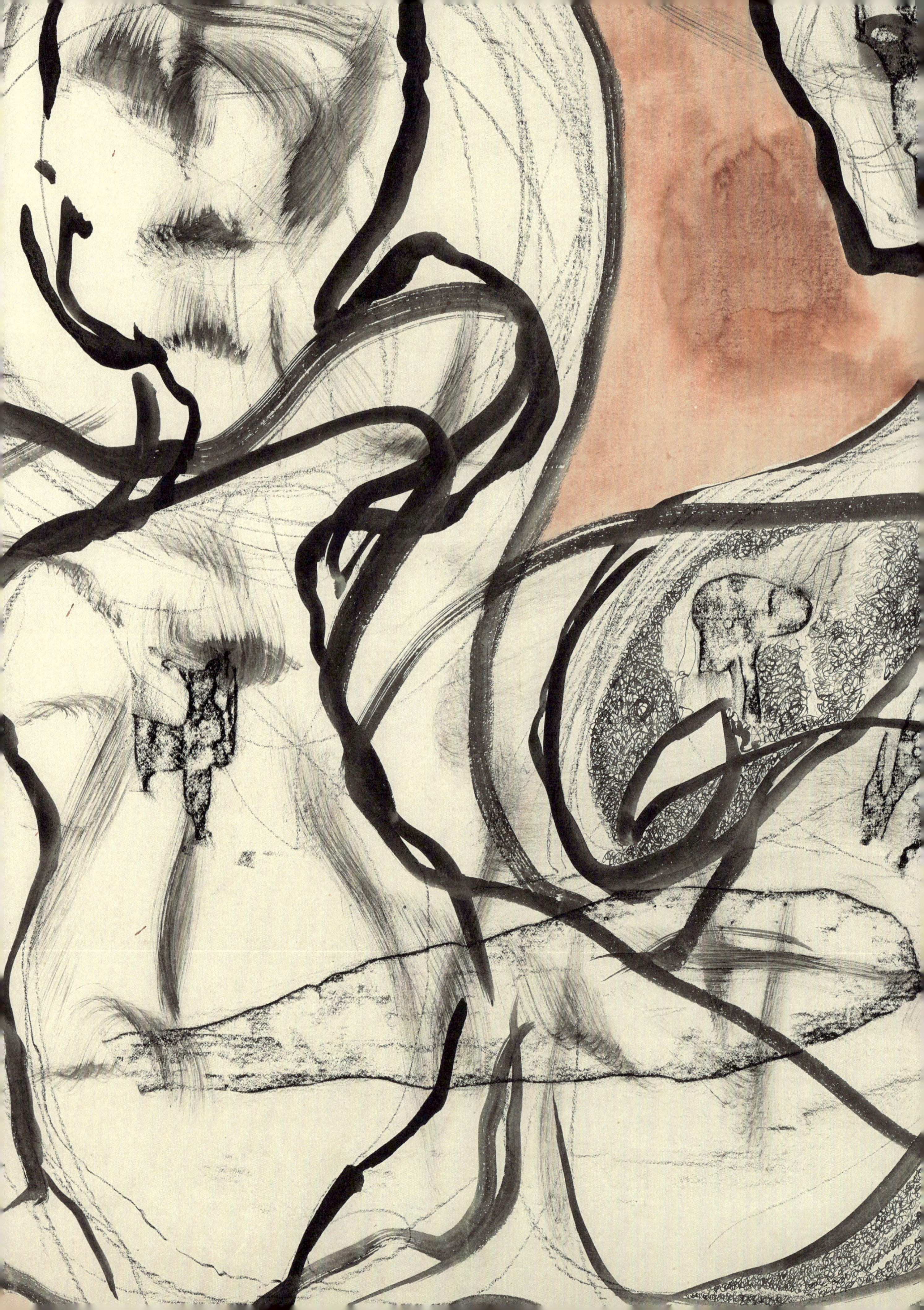

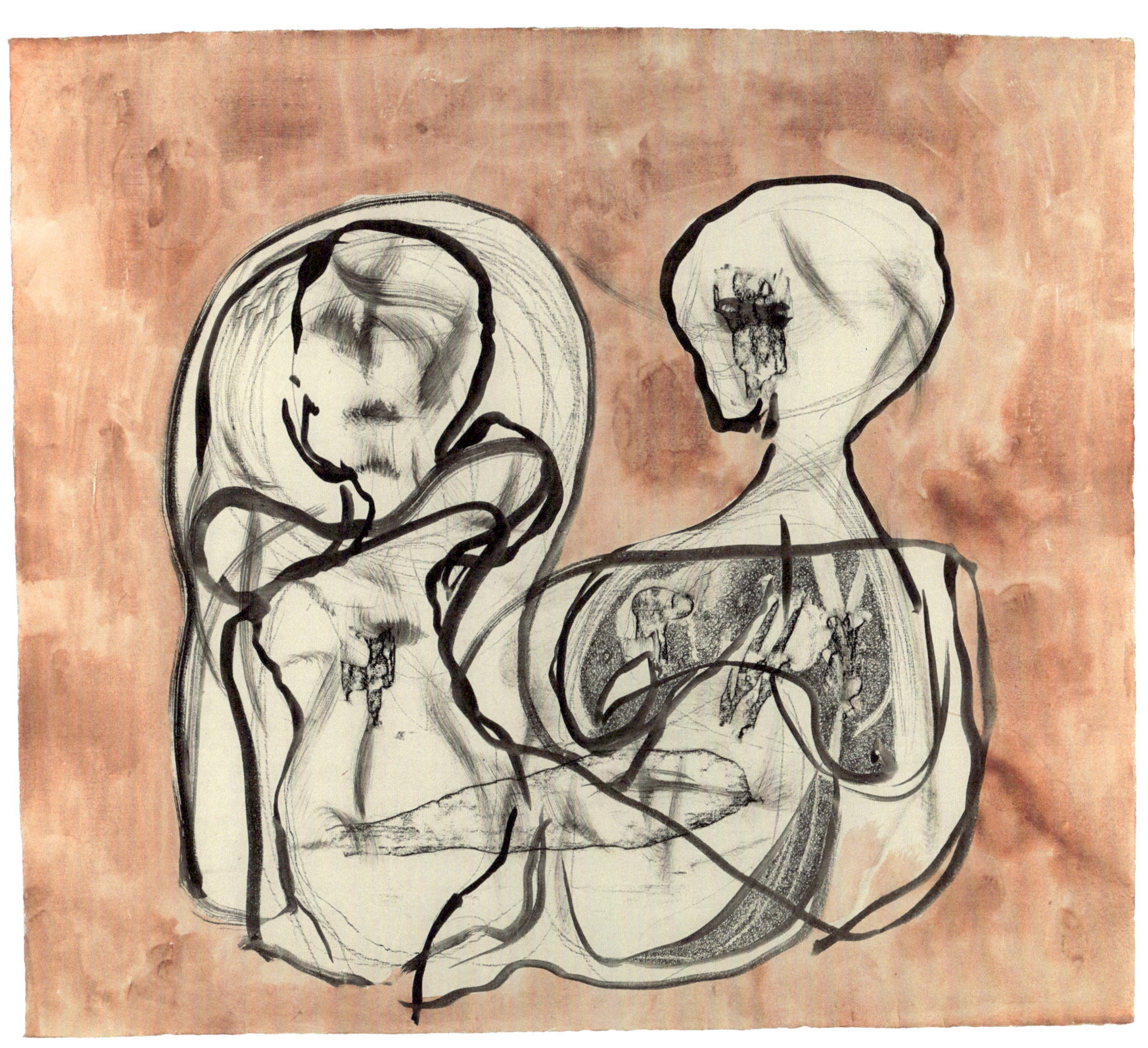

49 O. T. [Zwei verbunden durch die kleine Eva], undatiert | Untitled [Two Linked by Little Eve], no date

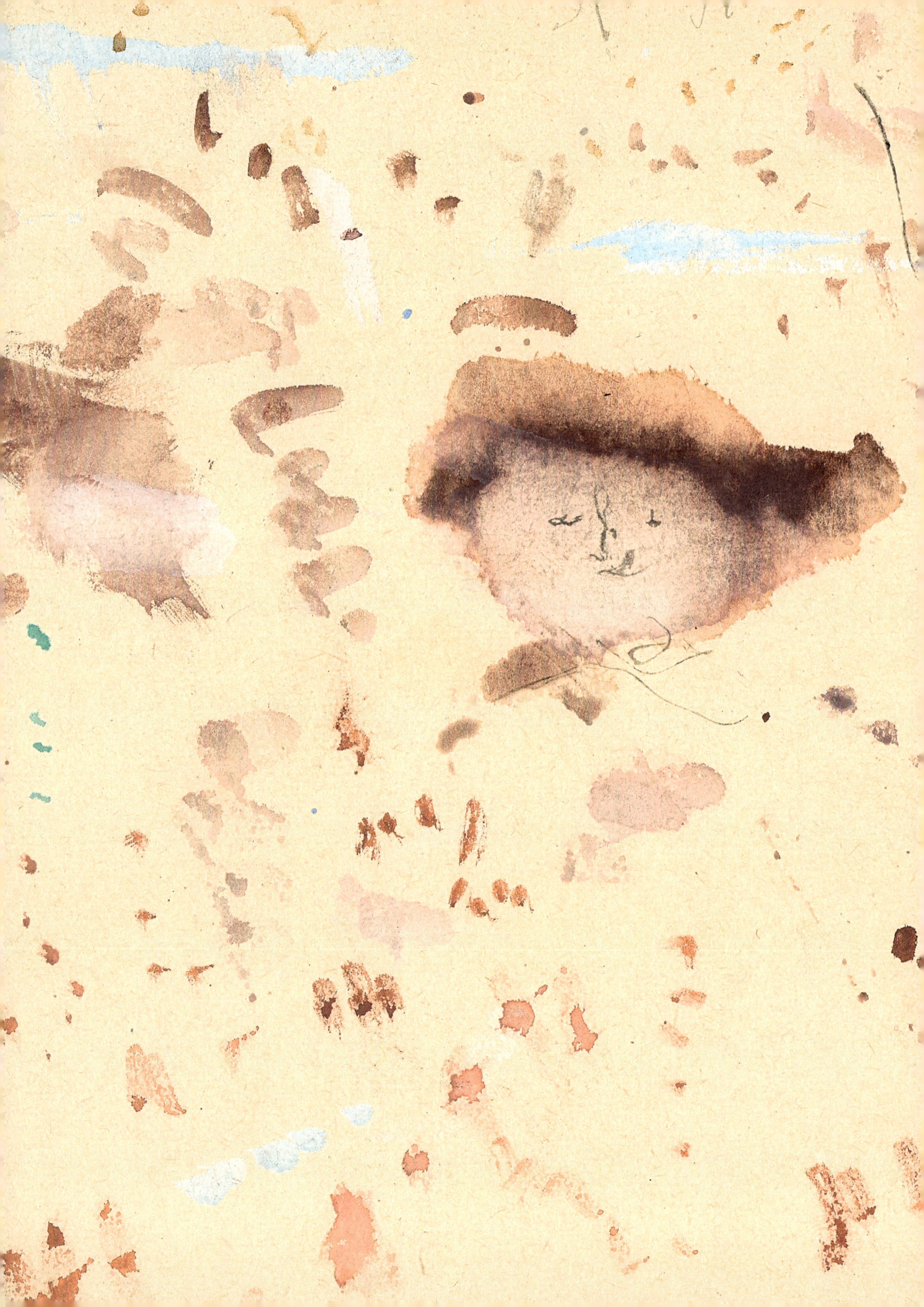

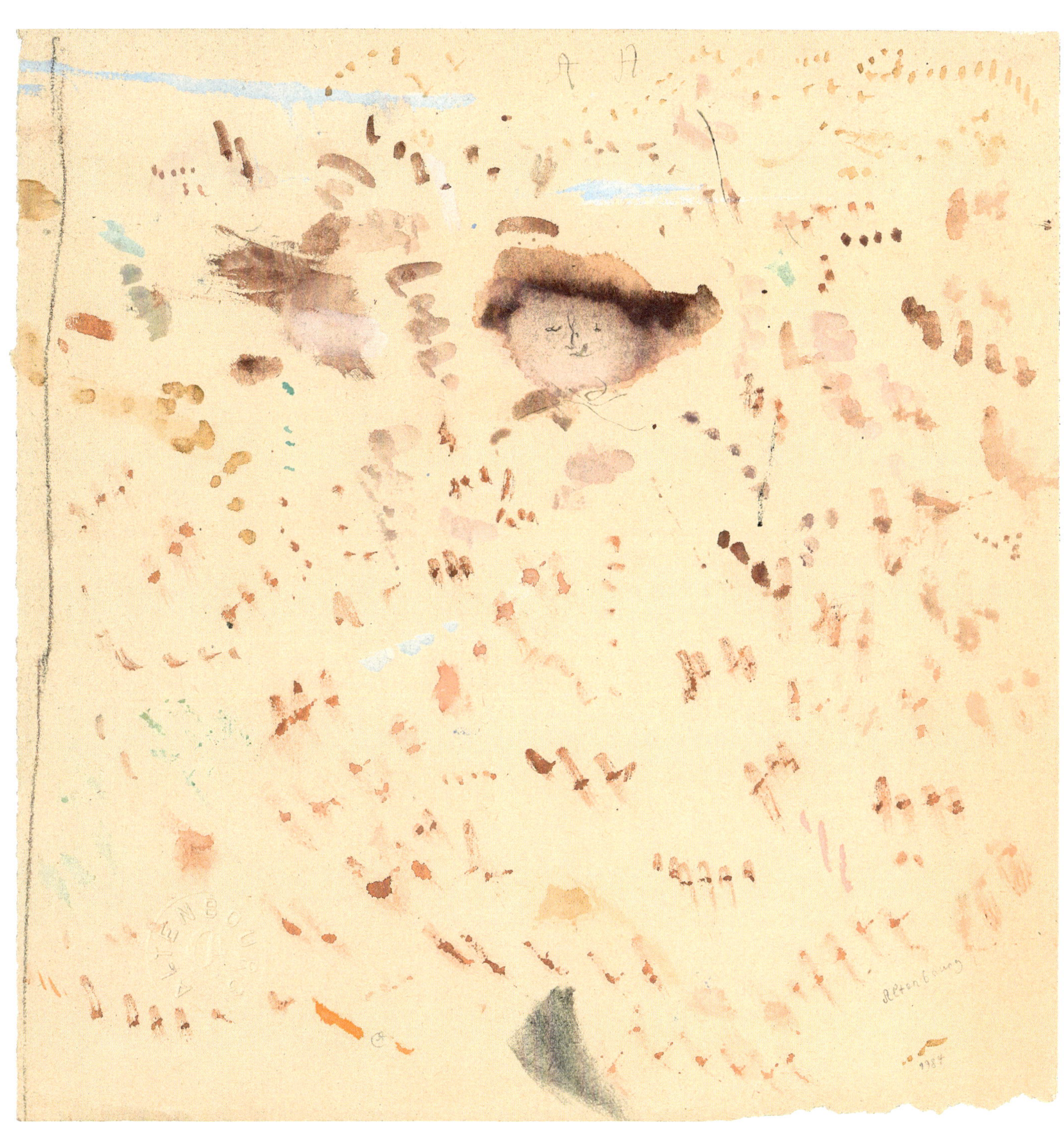

50 O. T. [Luftgeist, lächelnd], 1984 |
Untitled [Airy Spirit, Smiling], 1984

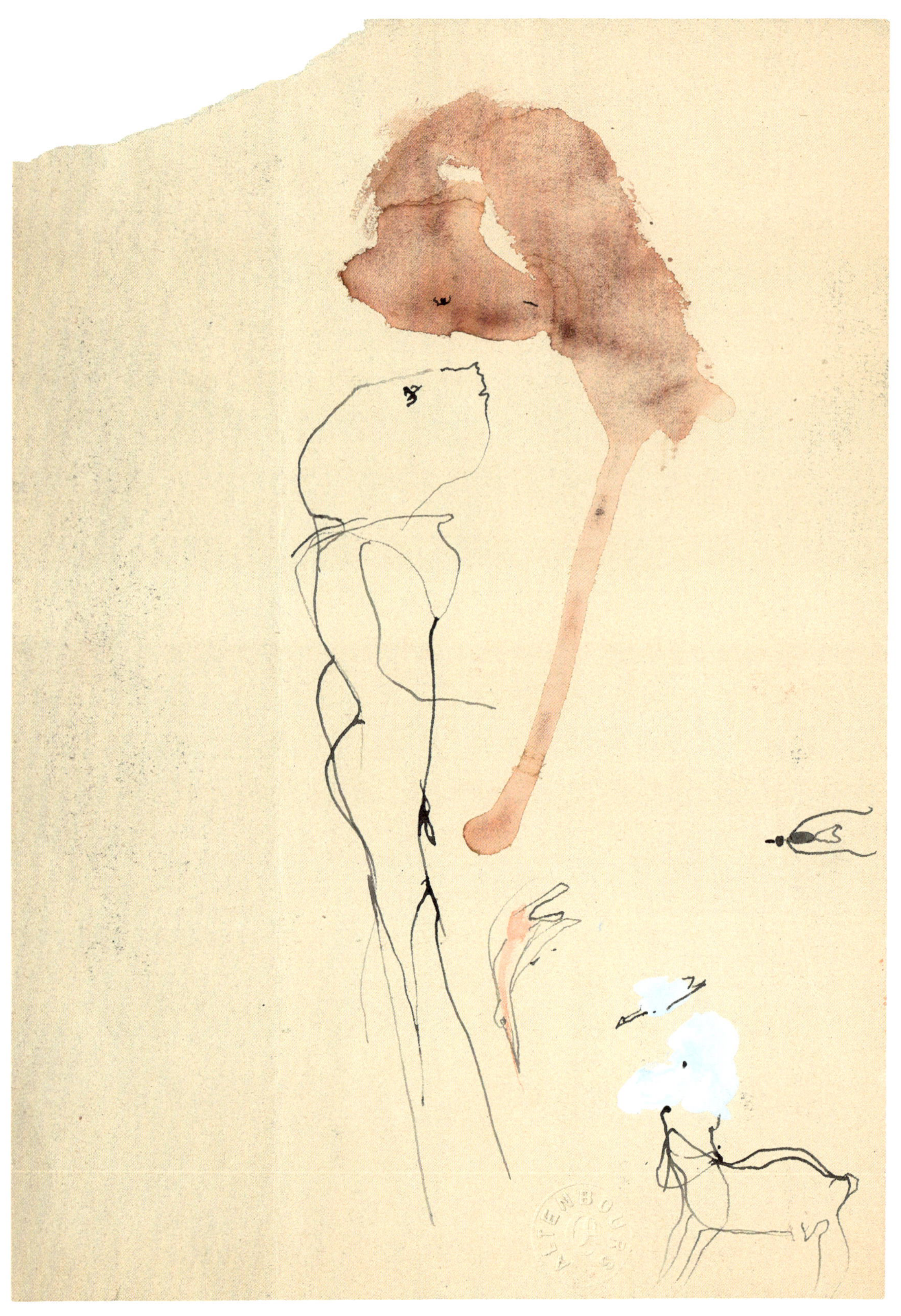

51 O. T. [Flirt mit dem Steckenpferd], undatiert | Untitled [Flirt with the Hobby Horse], no date

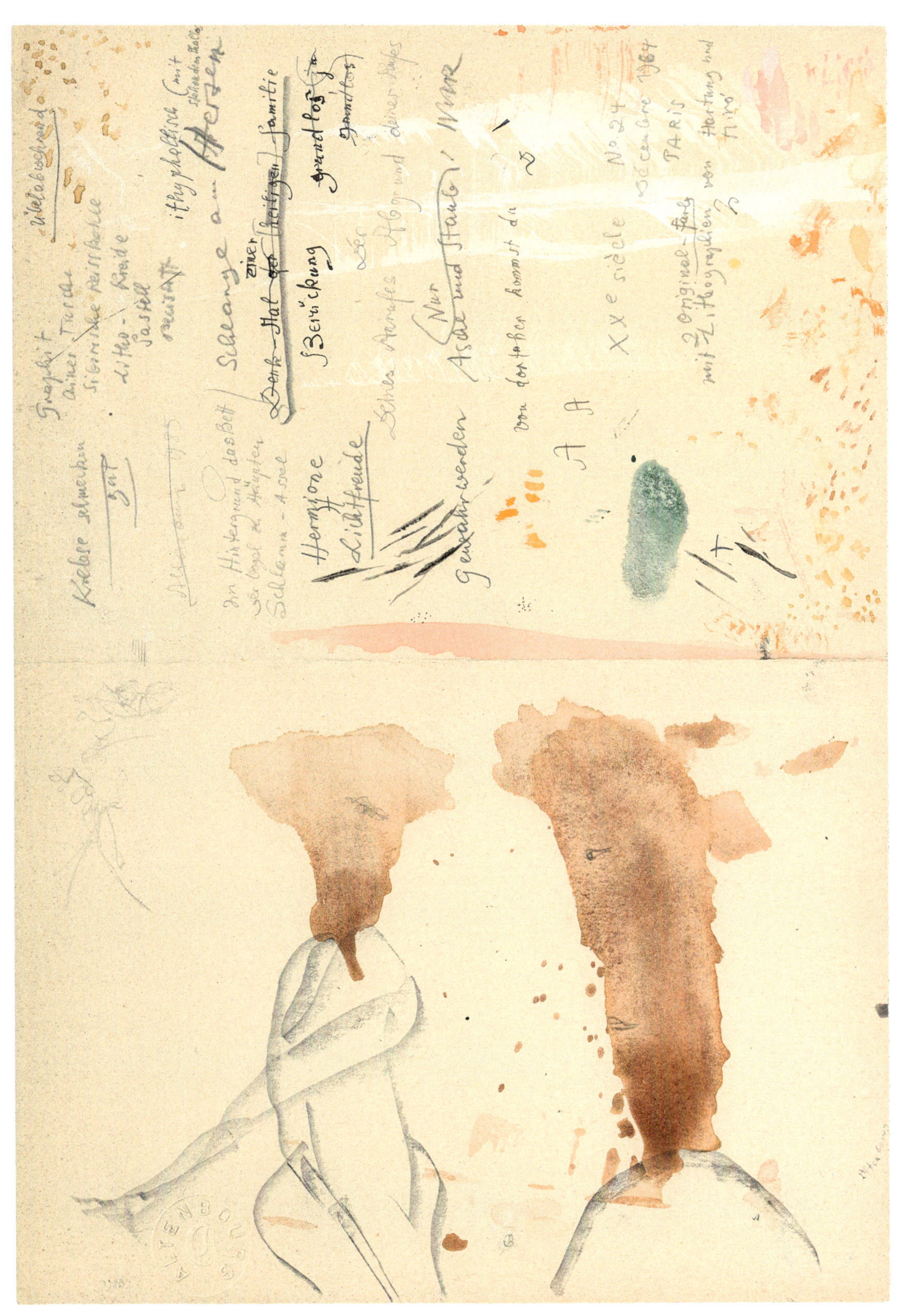

52 *Krebse schmecken gut*, 1985 |
Crabs Taste Good, 1985

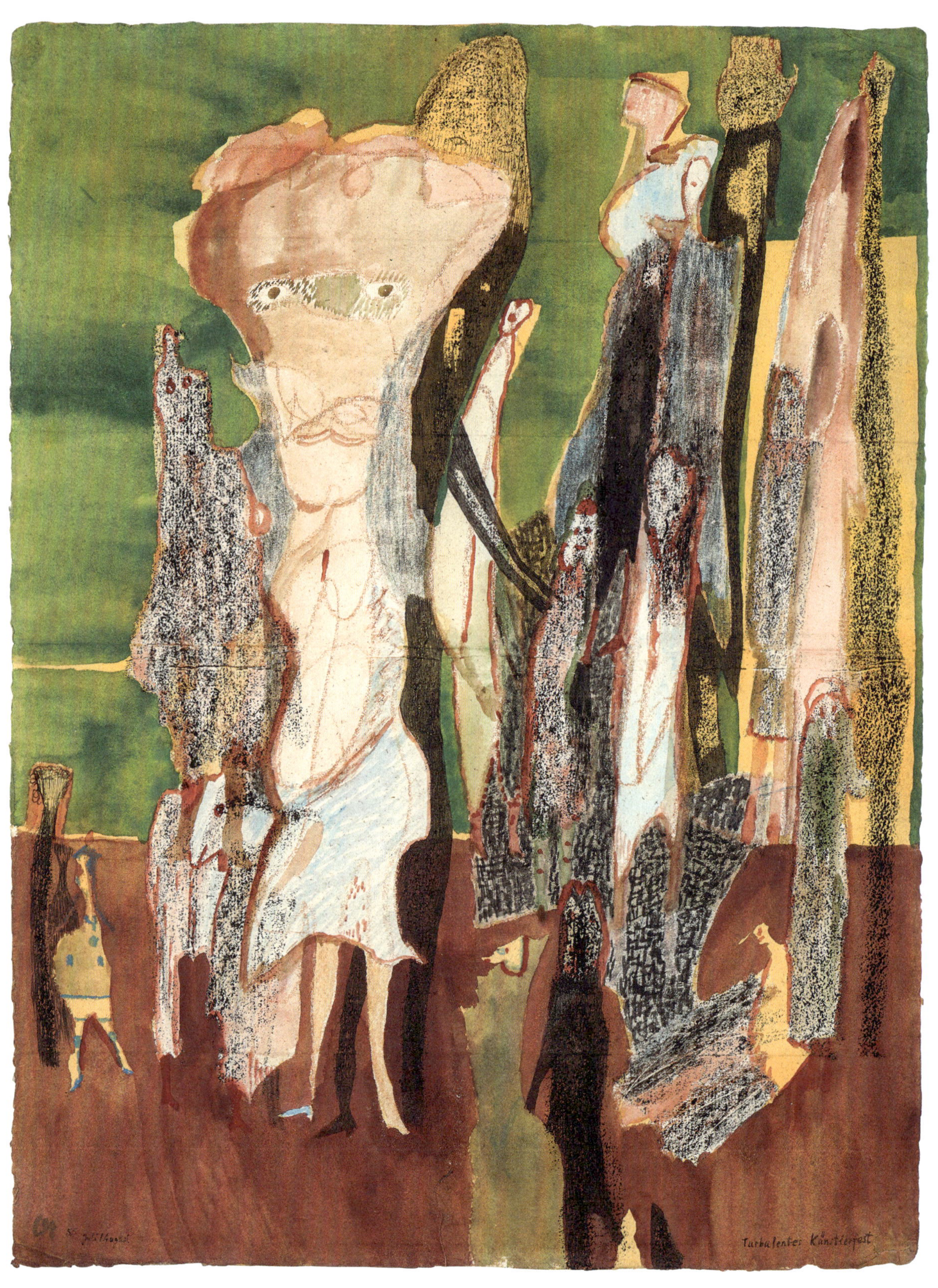

53 *Turbulentes Künstlerfest*, 1955 |
Turbulent Artists' Party, 1955

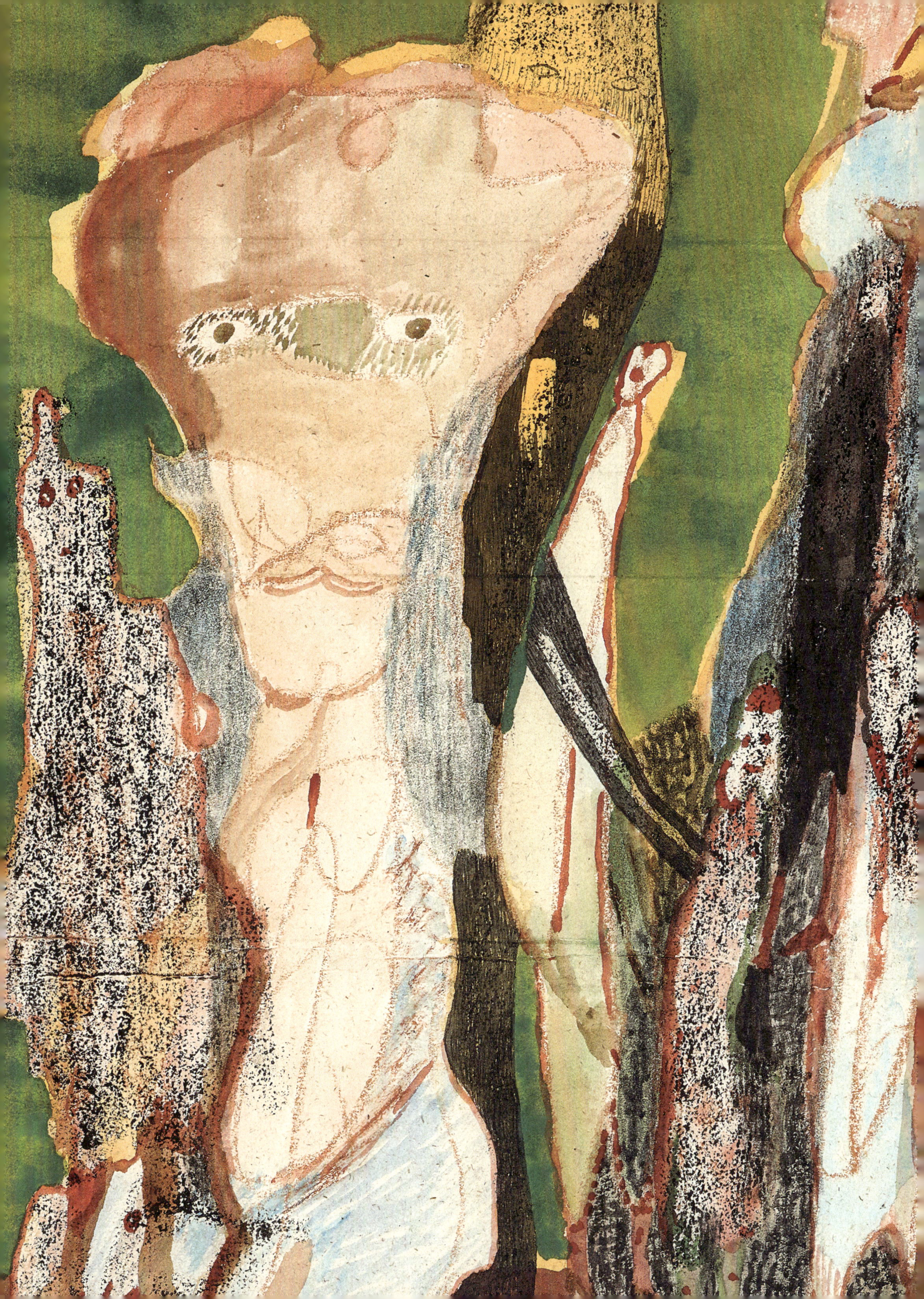

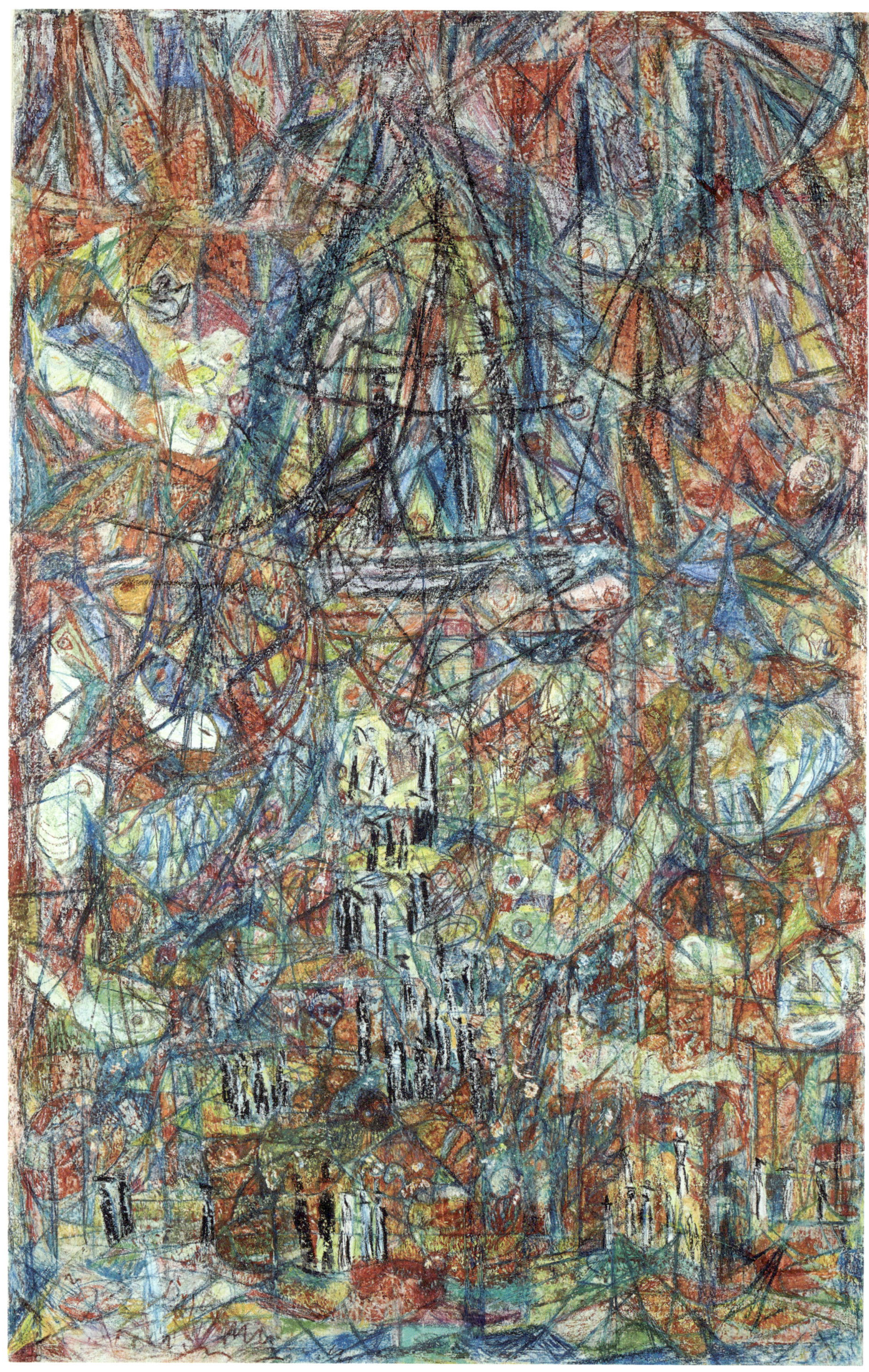

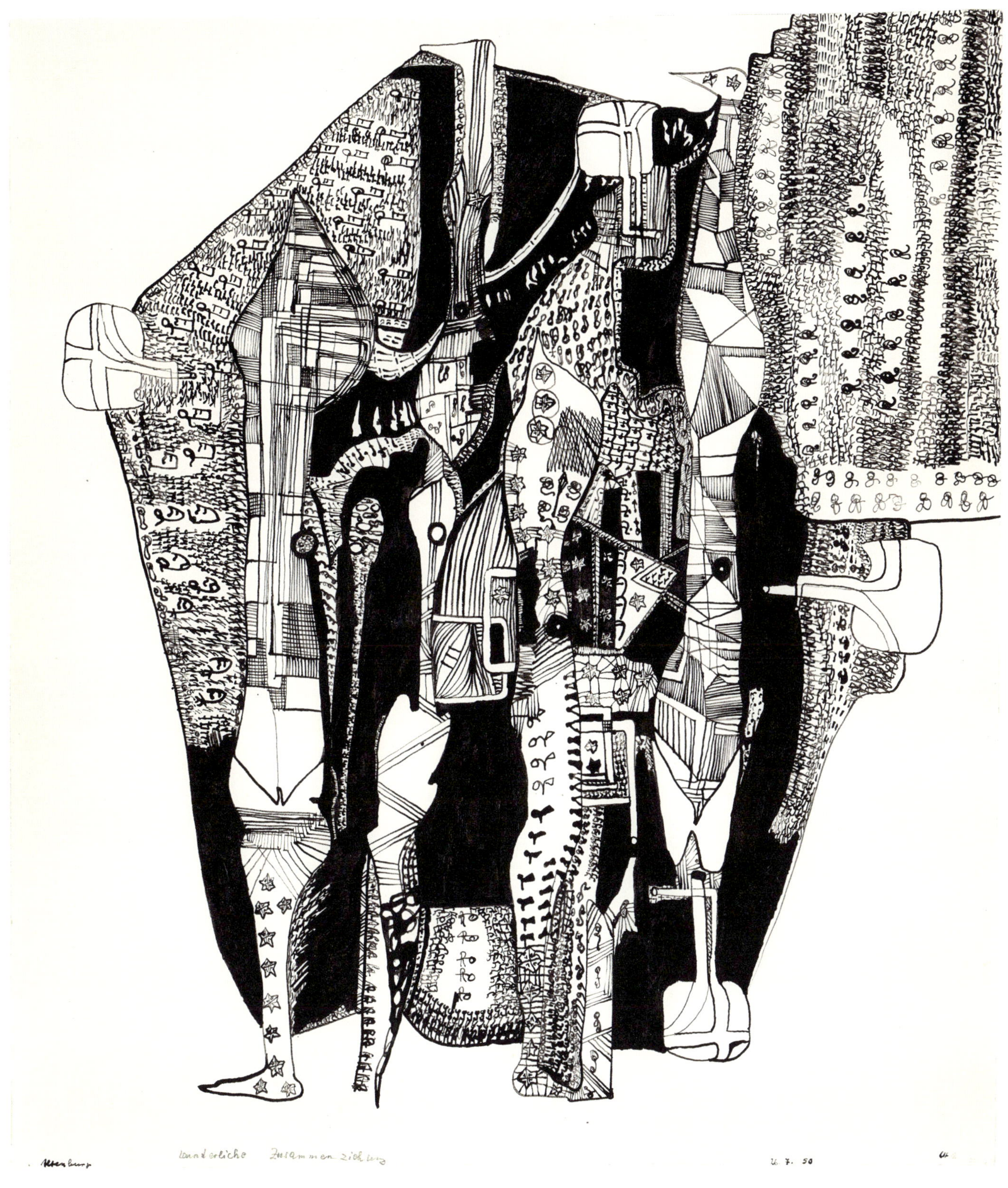

54 *Tiefsee-Jahrmarkt*, 1948 | *Deep Sea Fair*, 1948

55 *Wunderliche Zusammenziehung*, 1950 | *Miraculous Contraction*, 1950

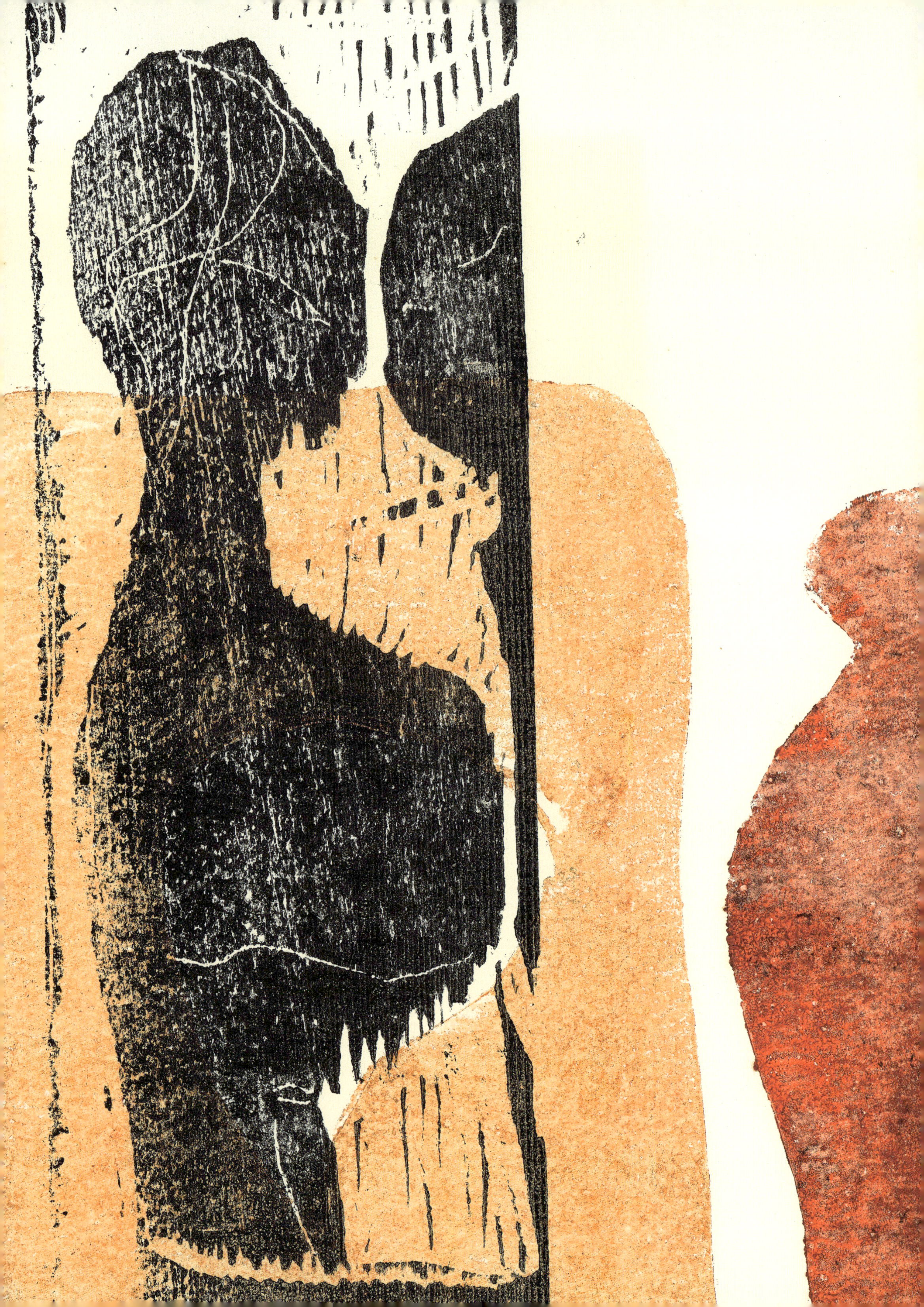

Manuela Büchting

Von Zufallsfunden und *Mekönkchen*

Ansätze der Kunstvermittlung zur Kunst von Gerhard Altenbourg

Gerhard Altenbourg ist als fantastischer Zeichner und Druckgrafiker für die Kunstvermittlung an den Altenburger Museen wertvoll und inspirierend. Wie können wir uns dem Künstler heute annähern? Auf welche Weise stellt sein umfangreiches Werk eine Inspiration dar? Und welche Impulse können wir in der Bildungsarbeit für Kinder und Erwachsene durch seine Kunst setzen?

Ein erster Zugang zu seiner Kunst gelingt, indem wir die Linien des Künstlers weiterdenken und versuchen, seine grafischen Details zu entschlüsseln. Gerhard Altenbourg selbst hat dazu notiert: »Linien ertrinken in Flächenseen, tauchen wieder auf und wachsen neu gestärkt und verstärkt weiter.«[1] In der Kunstvermittlung geschieht die Annäherung zunächst durch das gemeinsame Anschauen der Werke. Betrachtende entwickeln im Gespräch ihre eigenen Geschichten. Anschließend entstehen im *studio* im Lindenau-Museum Zeichnungen, Druckgrafiken und Plastiken, Hörstücke, Podcasts oder experimentelle Musikstücke **(Abb. 1, 2)**. Altenbourgs Figuren regen die Fantasie an. Wundersame Monster, Tiere und bewegte Landschaften werden in Geschichten lebendig, Gedanken und Träume sichtbar. Die Ideen der Betrachtenden verbinden sich mit den Motiven des Künstlers.

Beim Blick auf Altenbourgs skizzenhafte, teils unvollendete Zeichnungen fällt auf, dass der Künstler Farbkleckse durch zarte Bleistiftlinien ergänzt hat. Tusche- oder Wasserfarbenflecken hat er ungeordnet auf Papiere aufgetragen oder auch zufällige Arbeitsspuren durch den Pinsel hinterlassen, die er später weiterzeichnete. Aus den Spuren jeder Geste und Entscheidung des Künstlers entstanden zeichnerische Gedanken, die in Geschichten und Figuren mündeten.[2] Tatsächlich ist der Zufall auch ein wichtiges Element in der Kunstvermittlung. Kinder und Erwachsene werden in den Kursen zum Experimentieren angeregt: Aus Flecken, Sprenkeln und Tupfern entstehen wundersame Wesen, Tiere und

Of Serendipities and *Mekönkchen*

Approaches to Art Education and the Work of Gerhard Altenbourg

The work of the fantastic graphic artist and printer Gerhard Altenbourg is vital and inspiring for art education at the Altenburger Museen. How can we approach the artist today? In what ways is his extensive oeuvre an inspiration? What inspiration can we draw from his art for our education and outreach projects with children and adults?

One way to approach Altenbourg's work is to follow the artist's lines further and thus understand the graphic details. Gerhard Altenbourg himself noted: "Lines drown in lakes, reappear and grow, strengthened and intensified."[1] In art education, the first phase is to view the works together, and from there participants develop their own stories through discussion. This is followed by the creation of drawings, prints, sculptures, audio pieces, podcasts or experimental music pieces in the *studio* at the Lindenau-Museum **(figs. 1, 2)**. Altenbourg's figures stimulate the imagination. Wondrous monsters, animals and animated landscapes come to life in stories, while thoughts and dreams become visible. The observers' ideas fuse with the artist's motifs.

Looking at Altenbourg's sketch-like, partially unfinished drawings, it is striking how he complemented spots of colour with delicate pencil lines. He applied ink or watercolour stains randomly on paper or left chance traces with the brush, shapes that he later filled in with drawing. The traces of each gesture and each

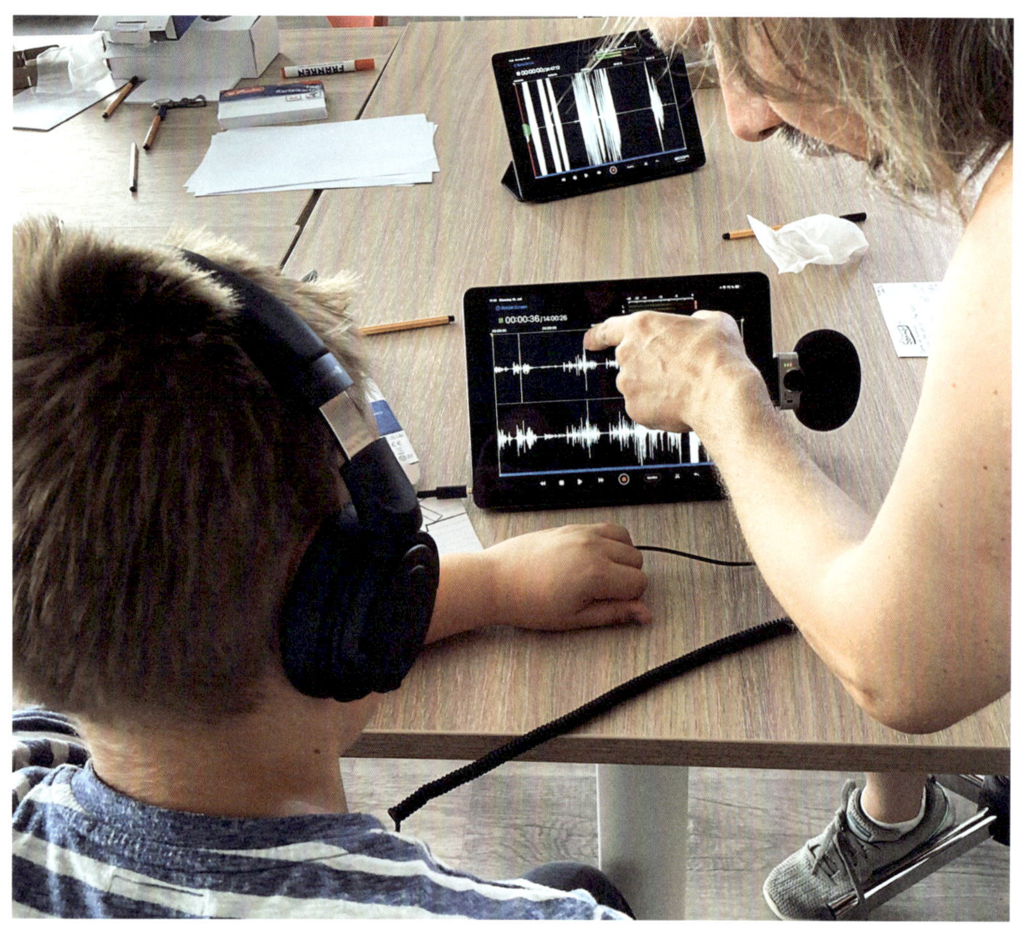

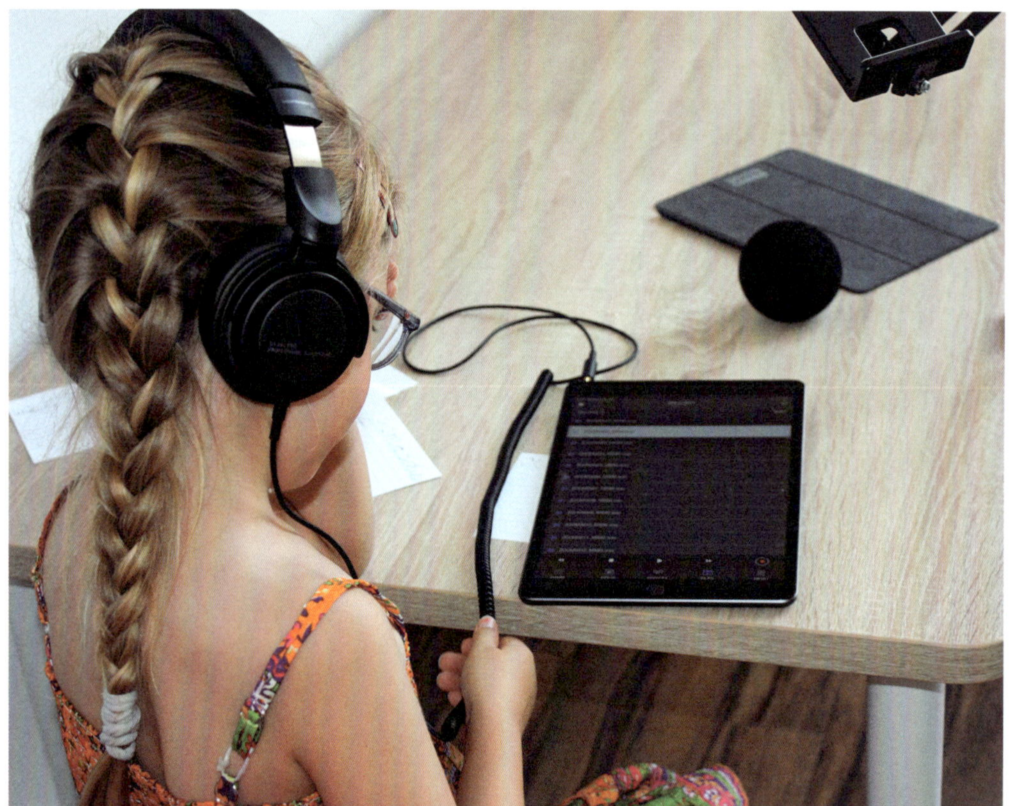

Abb. 1–2 Im studioDIGITAL werden Podcasts erstellt
Figs. 1–2 Podcasts are recorded in the studioDIGITAL

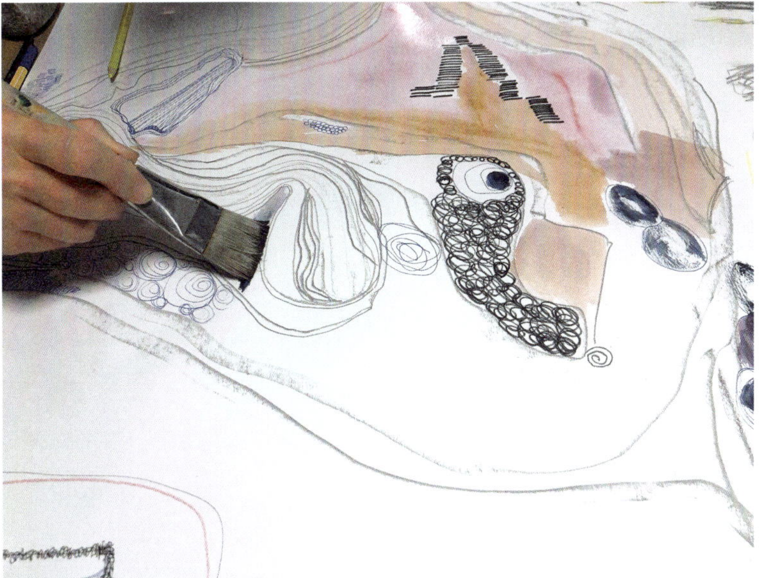

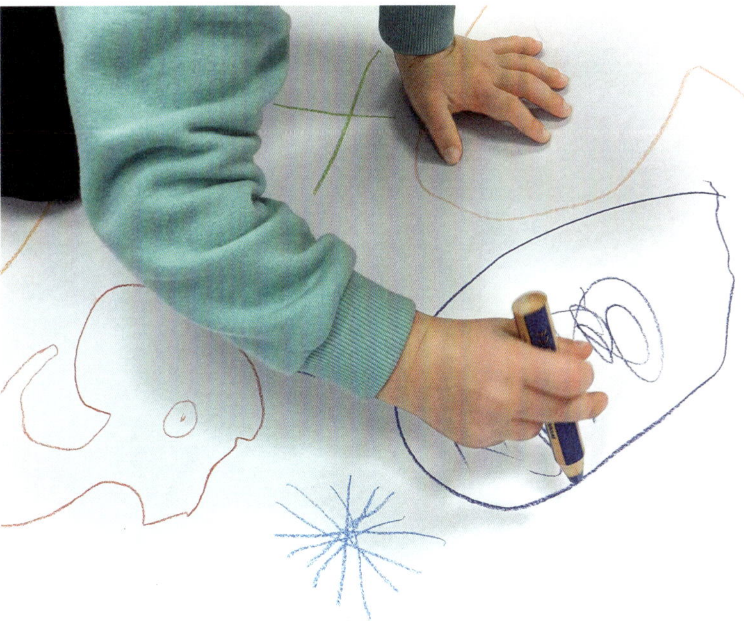

Abb. 3–4 Experimentelle Zeichnungen und Monotypie, Momentaufnahmen aus dem ATELIER im *studio* und im studioBAMBINI
Figs. 3–4 Experimental drawings and monotypes, snapshots from the ATELIER in the *studio* and in the studioBAMBINI

Mikrokosmen. Was sich daraus entwickelt, kann aus einem spontanen Impuls intuitiv hervorgebracht werden. Techniken wie Monotypie, eine Drucktechnik die einen einmaligen Abdruck erschafft, forcieren diese Zufallsexperimente. Auch Frottage[3] bietet sich an, verwunschene Landschaften oder wundersame Wesen zu gestalten. Der offene ästhetischen Prozess lädt dazu ein, Gewohntes anders zu denken und dabei Neues zu erschaffen **(Abb. 1, 2)**.

decision made by the artist give rise to graphic ideas that culminate in stories and figures.[2]

As a matter of fact, chance is an important component of art education as well. In our courses, children and adults are encouraged to experiment: stains, speckles and dabs give rise to wondrous creatures, animals and microcosms. How these inventions develop further might be entirely spontaneous and intuitive. Techniques such as monotype, a printing technique that creates a single impression, encourage such random experiments. Frottage[3] is also an exciting method for creating magical landscapes and wondrous creatures. The open aesthetic process invites us to think differently about the familiar and create something new in the process **(figs. 1–2)**.

Gerhard Altenbourg created figures that he carefully incised in woodcuts, calling them *Mekönkchen*. He printed these in countless variations on paper, from transparent paper to laid paper, which has haptic qualities that were particularly important to him. In this way he made woodcuts that he combined and printed in serial print runs. Similarly, the *studio* employs a variety of techniques and skills in making woodcuts: wood is worked on with different tools, colours are chosen and finally the images are printed and collaged. For participants, this offers innumerable opportunities for trying things out and developing ideas **(figs. 3–4)**.

Altenbourg's art inspires us through its freedom in how the line is used, whether in a drawing, in the overlapping of surfaces or in the combination of prints. His way of working was concentrated and meditative. He often needed several weeks or months for a drawing, working on multiple sheets at the same time until late at night. As the artist explained in an interview, "When I'm drawing, I step outside of time".[4] This creative peace allowed him to make drawings with stories of mythological figures and creatures, as well as to invent characters such as the faceless *Mekönkchen* from several printing blocks **(cats. 56–57)**. His work is characterised not only by its wealth of graphic detail, but also the way in which it stimulates the imagination of observers to develop their own images and stories. When they begin making art, participants enter an artistic process that can lead them to experience "flow".[5] Experimentation and intellectual connection with their own life-worlds allow participants to delve into the fantastic world of Gerhard Altenbourg and to become creatively active themselves.

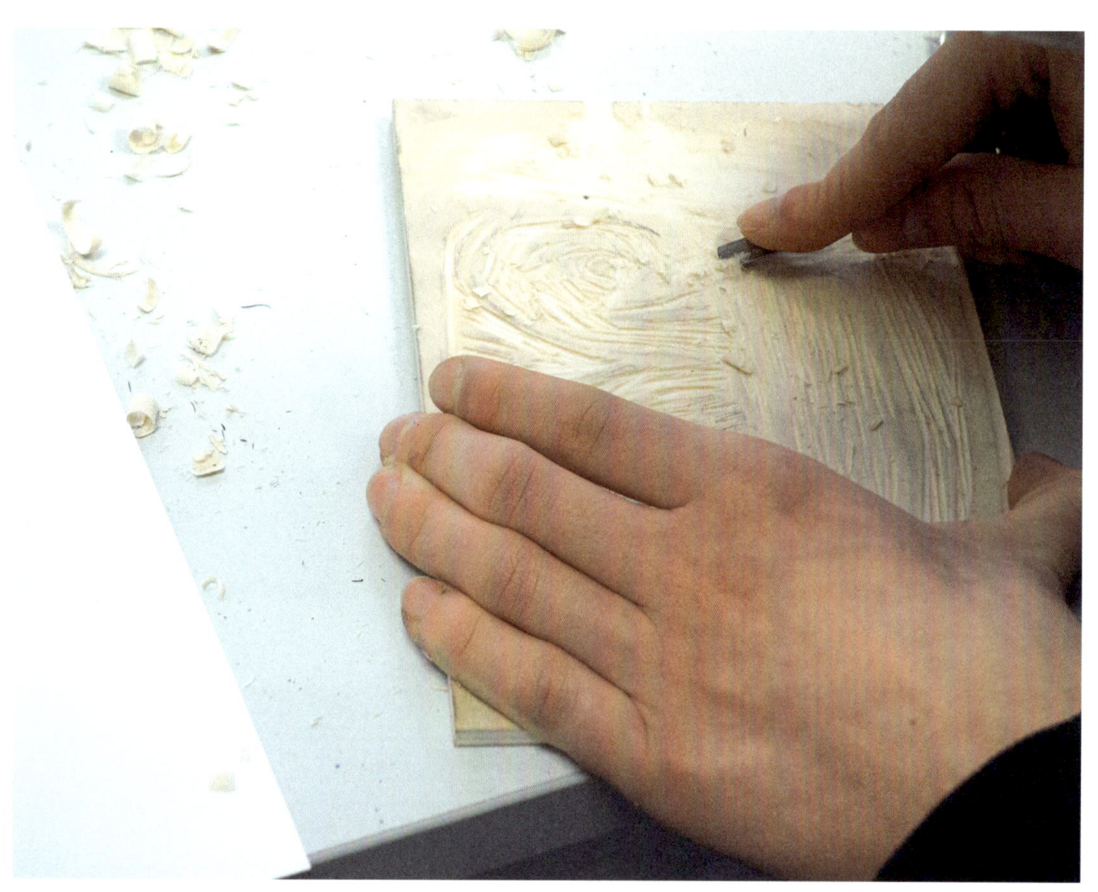

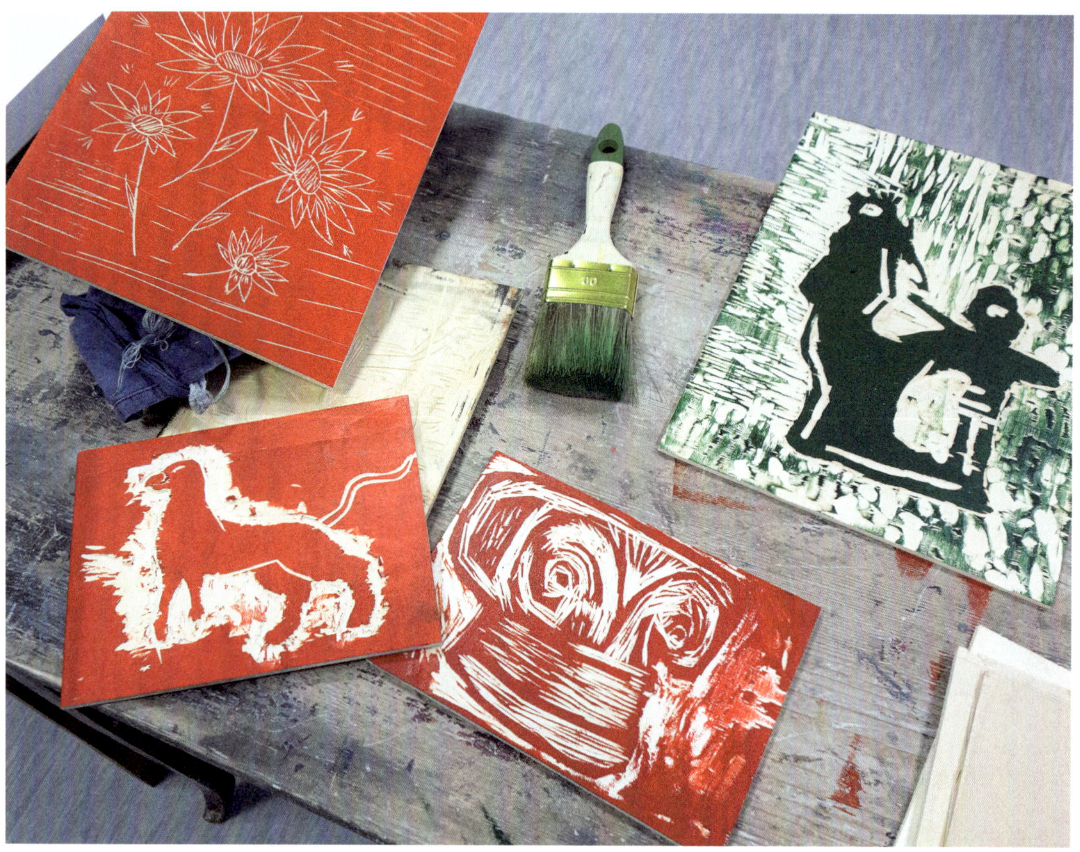

Abb. 5–6 Im GRAFIKstudio des Lindenau-Museums werden Holzschnitte und Abdrucke erstellt
Figs. 5–6 Woodcuts and prints are made in the GRAFIKstudio of the Lindenau-Museum

Gerhard Altenbourg erstellte sorgfältig in den Holzschnitt eingearbeitete Figuren, die er »Mekönkchen« nannte. Diese druckte er in unzähligen Variationen auf Papier. Von Transparentpapier bis zu Büttenpapier, deren Haptik für den Künstler besonders wichtig war. So erschuf er Holzschnitte, die er in seriellen Druckvorgängen kombinierte und abdruckte.

Gleichermaßen fließen auch im *studio* bei der Erstellung von Holzschnitten verschiedene Techniken und Fähigkeiten zusammen: Holz wird mit Werkzeugen bearbeitet, Farben werden ausgewählt, anschließend die Motive gedruckt und collagiert. Für Teilnehmende bietet dies dabei unzählige Möglichkeiten des Ausprobierens und der Entfaltung **(Abb. 3, 4)**.

Die Kunst Altenbourgs inspiriert durch ihre Freiheit mit dem Umgang mit der Linie bei einer Zeichnung, in der Überlagerung von Flächen oder in das Kombinieren von Druckgrafiken. Seine Arbeitsweise war konzentriert und meditativ. Oft benötigte er mehrere Wochen oder Monate für eine Zeichnung, arbeitete an mehreren Werken gleichzeitig bis tief in die Nacht. Dazu sagte der Künstler in einem Interview: »Wenn ich zeichne, trete ich aus der Zeit heraus.«[4] Diese schöpferische Ruhe erlaubt es, Zeichnungen mit Geschichten von mythologischen Gestalten und Fabelwesen anzufertigen, aber auch Erfindungen wie das gesichtslose »Mekönkchen« mit mehreren Druckstöcken **(Kat. 56, 57)** entstehen zu lassen. Sein Werk zeichnet sich nicht nur durch seinen grafischen Detailreichtum aus, sondern auch durch die Art und Weise, wie es die Fantasie anregt, sodass Betrachtende eigene Bilder und Geschichten entwickeln. Beim Selbergestalten erfahren sie einen künstlerischen Prozess, der bis zum »Flow«[5] führen kann. Das Experimentieren und die gedanklichen Verbindungen zur eigenen Lebenswelt ermöglichen es, in die fantastische Welt von Gerhard Altenbourg einzutauchen und selbst schöpferisch aktiv zu werden.

1 Vgl. Altenbourg, Gerhard: Versuch einer Merkmal-Fixierung, 1962, in: Altenbourg, Gerhard: Tatauierte Litaneien. Aufrisse und Weg-Spindeln, Berlin/Paris (Privatdruck) 1962, S. 5–17. Zit. nach: Janda, Annegret: Gerhard Altenbourg. Monographie und Werkverzeichnis, 3 Bde., Bd. 2, 1959–1976, Köln 2007, S. 50 f., hier S. 51.

2 »Im Prinzip liest man jedes Werk als eine Summe aus Gesten und Entscheidungen auf der sinnlich-materiellen Ebene wie auf der davon nicht zu trennenden Ebene des Bildes der Zeichen und Bildbegriffe in der Imagination des Mitbewegtseins.« Selle, Gert: Gebrauch der Sinne: eine kunstpädagogische Praxis, Reinbek bei Hamburg 1993, S. 233.

3 Das ist eine künstlerische Technik der Abreibung von Oberflächenstrukturen auf das Papier.

4 (Altenbourg, Gerhard/Mennekes, Friedhelm:) Im Gespräch (Interview mit Friedhelm Mennekes), in: Grinten, Franz Joseph van der/Mennekes, Friedhelm: Abstraktion und Kontemplation. Auseinandersetzung mit einem Thema der Gegenwartskunst, Stuttgart 1987, S. 234–241, hier S. 236.

5 »Flow« bezeichnet den Zustand völliger Vertiefung und Konzentration, in dem eine Person vollständig in eine Tätigkeit eintaucht. Der Psychologe Mihály Csíkszentmiályi prägte den Begriff in den 1970er-Jahren in seinem Buch *Flow: The Psychology of Optimal Experience*. Vgl. Nakamura, Jeanne/Csíkszentmihályi, Mihály: The Concept of Flow, in: Csíkszentmihályi, Mihály: Flow and the Foundations of Positive Psychology, Dordrecht/Heidelberg 2014, S. 239–263.

1 See Gerhard Altenbourg, "Versuch einer Merkmal-Fixierung, 1962", in Gerhard Altenbourg, *Tatauierte Litaneien. Aufrisse und Weg-Spindeln* (Berlin/Paris: private printing, 1962), pp. 5–17. Quoted in Annegret Janda, *Gerhard Altenbourg. Monographie und Werkverzeichnis*, 3 vols. (Cologne: Wienand, 2004–10), vol. 2, 1959–1976, pp. 50ff., here p. 51.

2 "In general, one reads every artwork as a sum of gestures and decisions at the sensorial-material level, as well as at another level of the picture - inseparable from the previous one - of signs and pictorial concepts in the imagination of being involved." Gert Selle, *Gebrauch der Sinne: eine kunstpädagogische Praxis* (Reinbek bei Hamburg: Rowohlt, 1993), p. 233.

3 In this technique, surface structures are rubbed and thus transferred onto paper.

4 Gerhard Altenbourg and Friedhelm Mennekes, "Im Gespräch (Interview mit Friedhelm Mennekes)", in Franz Joseph van der Grinten and Friedhelm Mennekes, *Abstraktion und Kontemplation. Auseinandersetzung mit einem Thema der Gegenwartskunst* (Stuttgart: Verlag Katholisches Bibelwerk, 1987), pp. 234–41, here p. 236.

5 "Flow" is the state of complete immersion and concentration arising when a person is entirely involved in an activity. The psychologist Mihály Csíkszentmihályi coined the term in the 1970s in his book *Flow: The Psychology of Optimal Experience*. See Jeanne Nakamura and Mihály Csíkszentmihályi, "The Concept of Flow", in Mihály Csíkszentmihályi, *Flow and the Foundations of Positive Psychology* (Dordrecht/Heidelberg: Springer Netherlands, 2014), pp. 239–63.

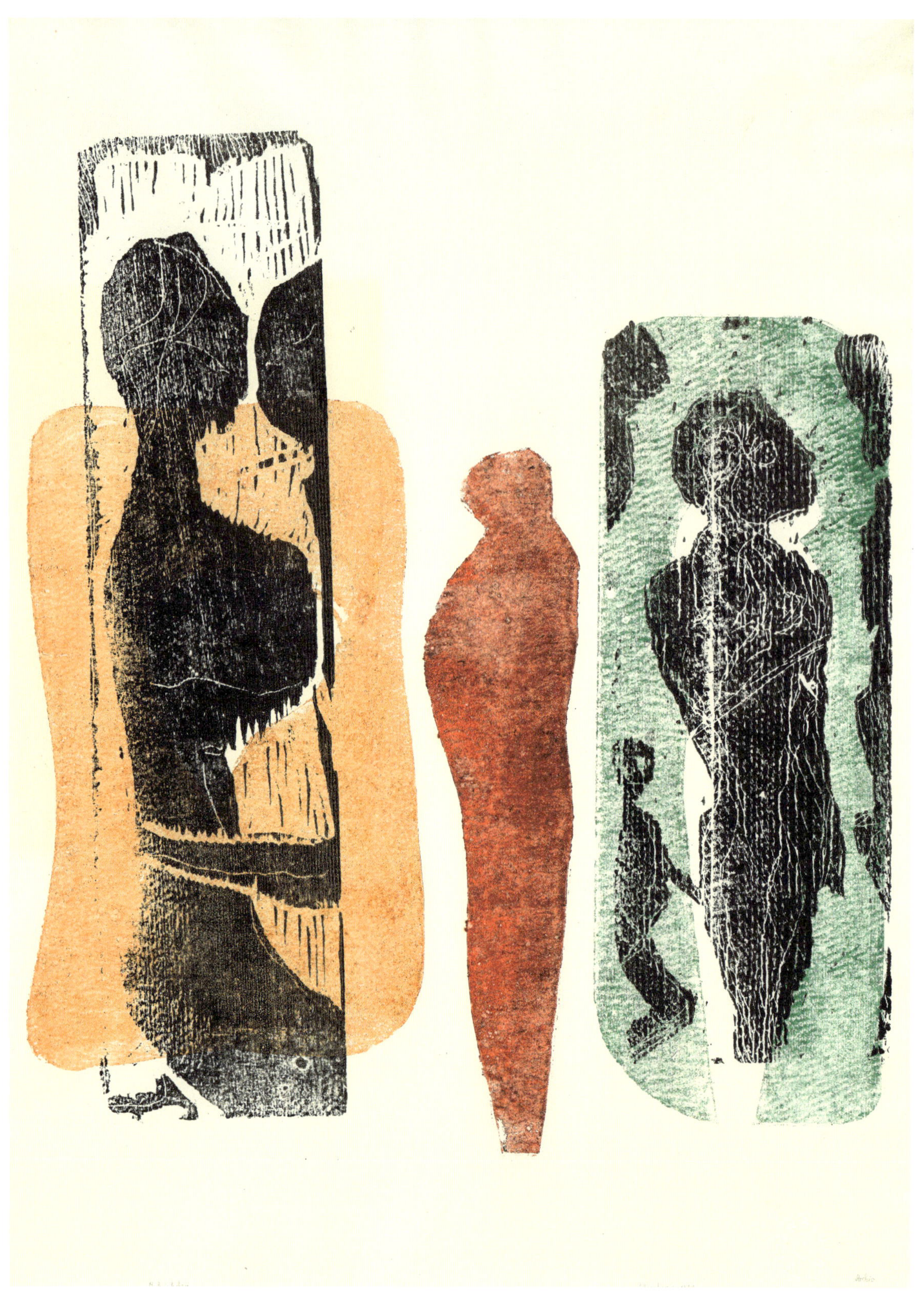

56 *Mekönkchen*, 1969

57 *Glossen um eine Figur, die ich das gesichtlose Mekönkchen nenne*, 1969 | *Glosses on a Figure I Call the Faceless Mekönkchen*, 1969

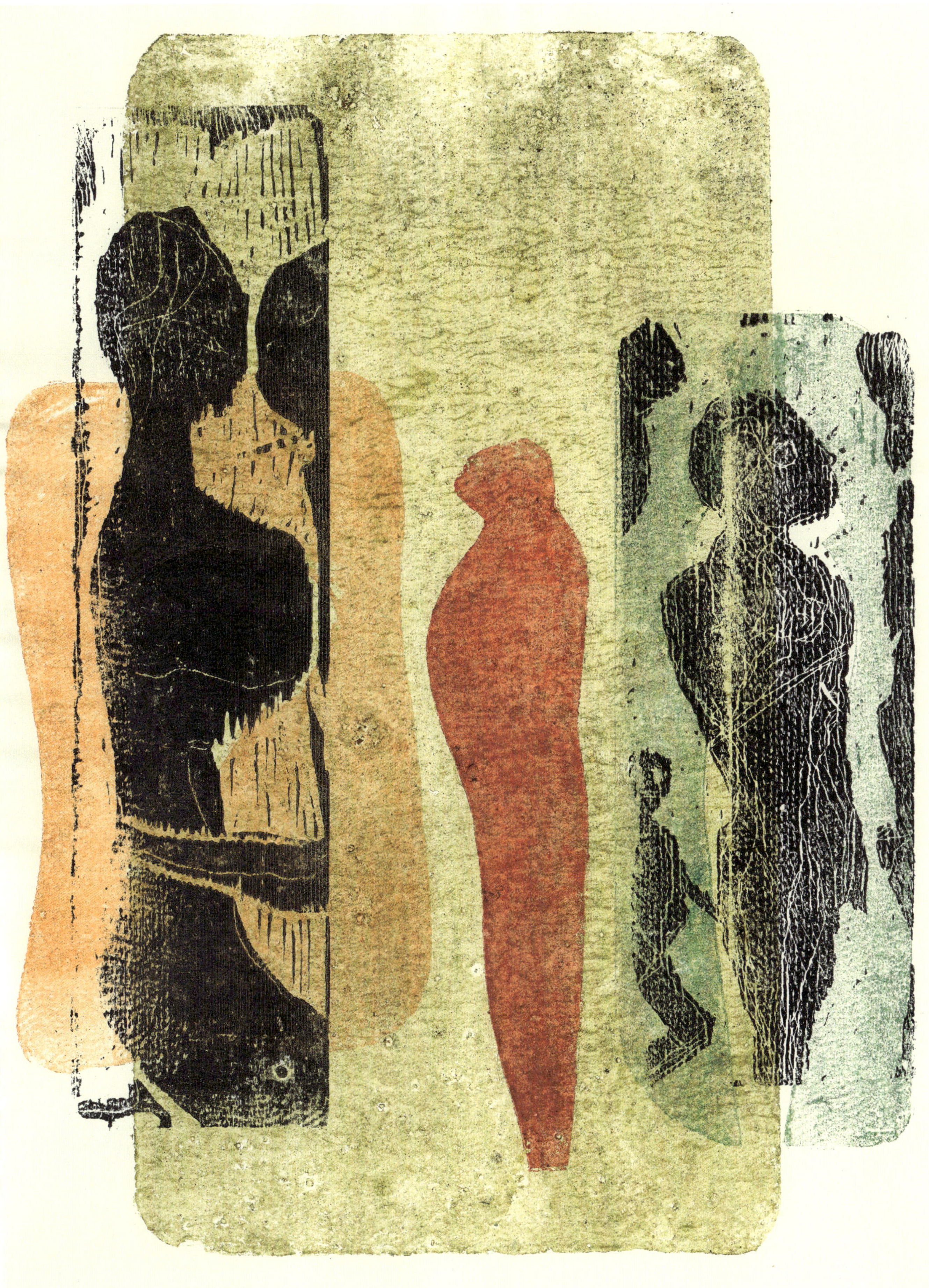

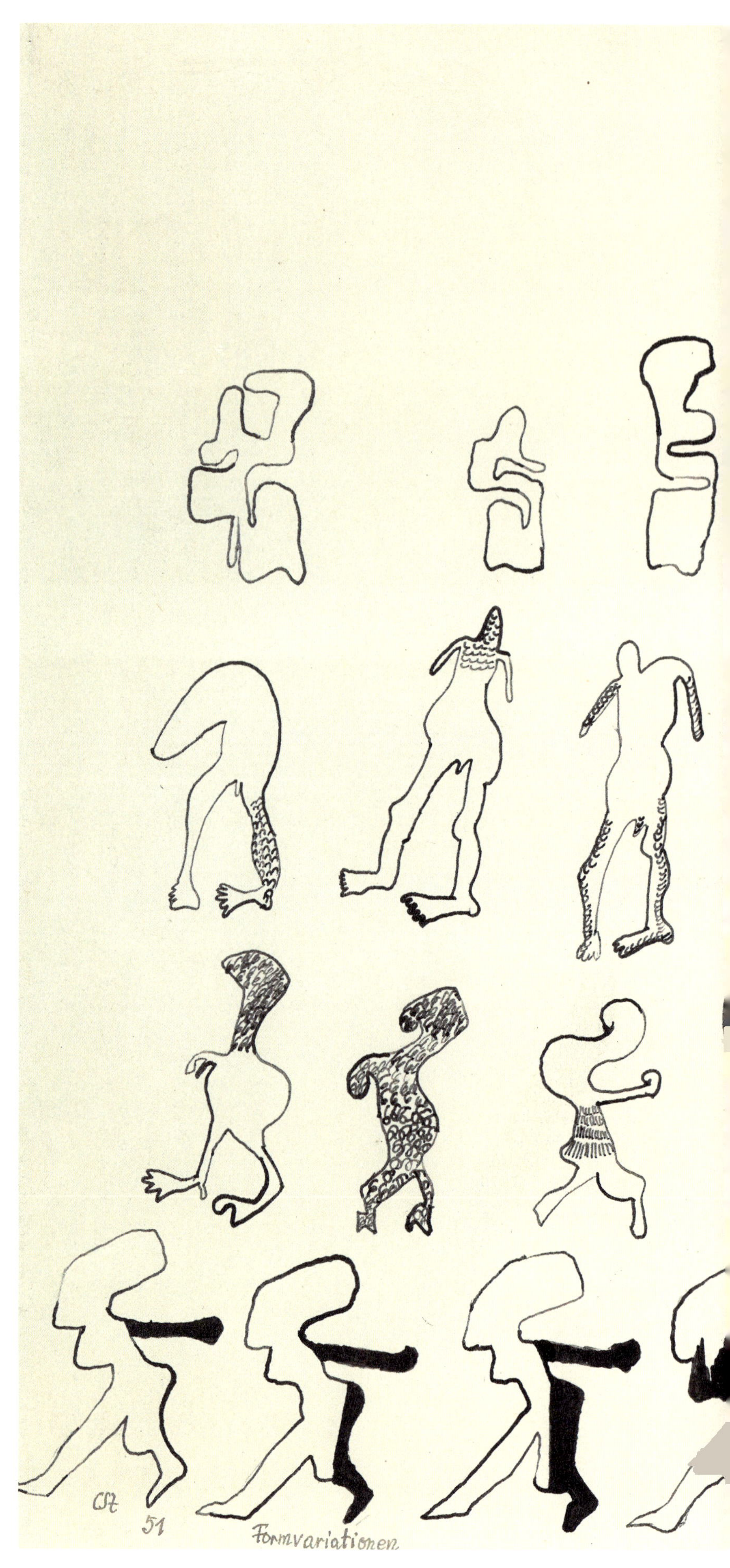

58 *Formvariationen*, 1951 | *Form Variations*, 1951

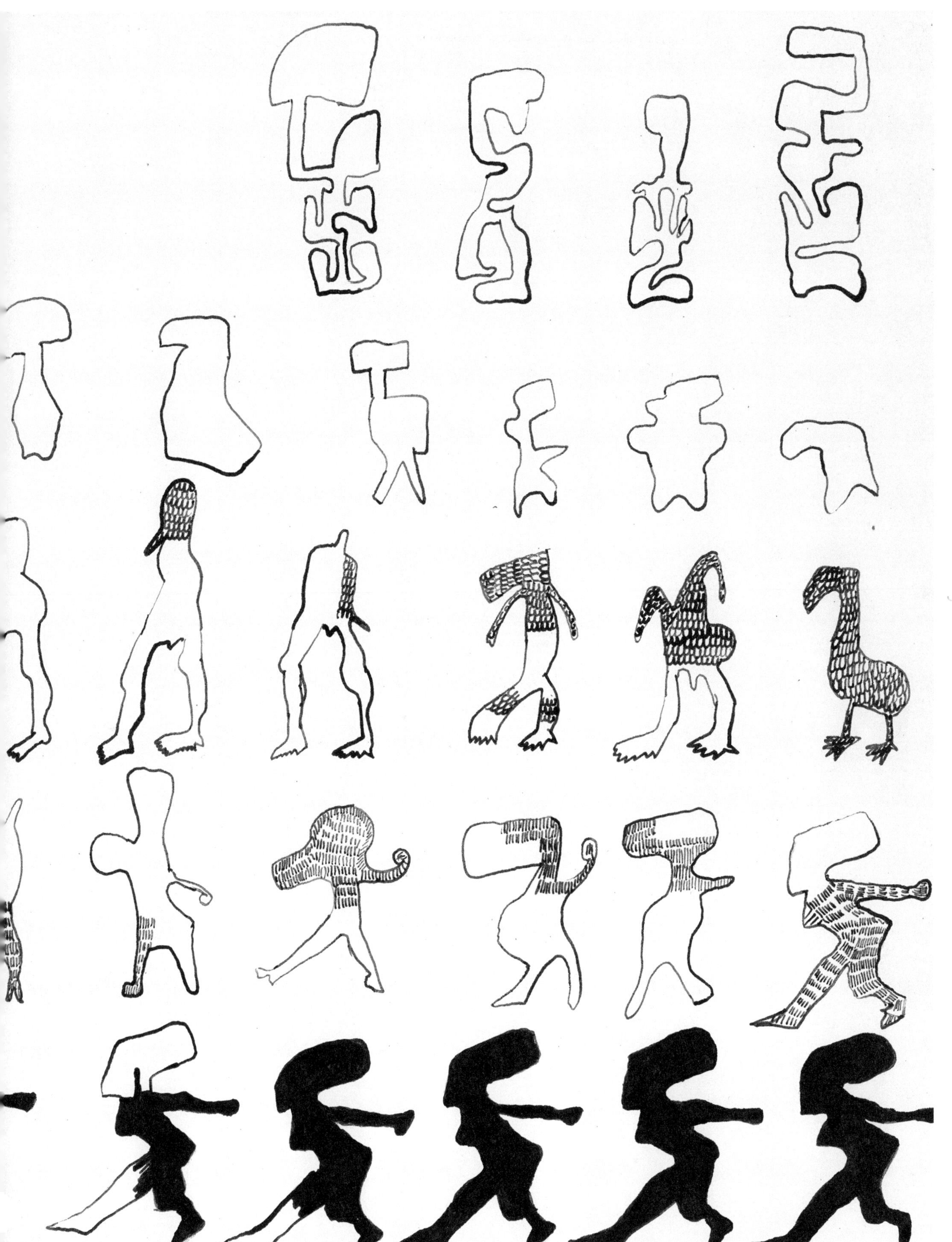

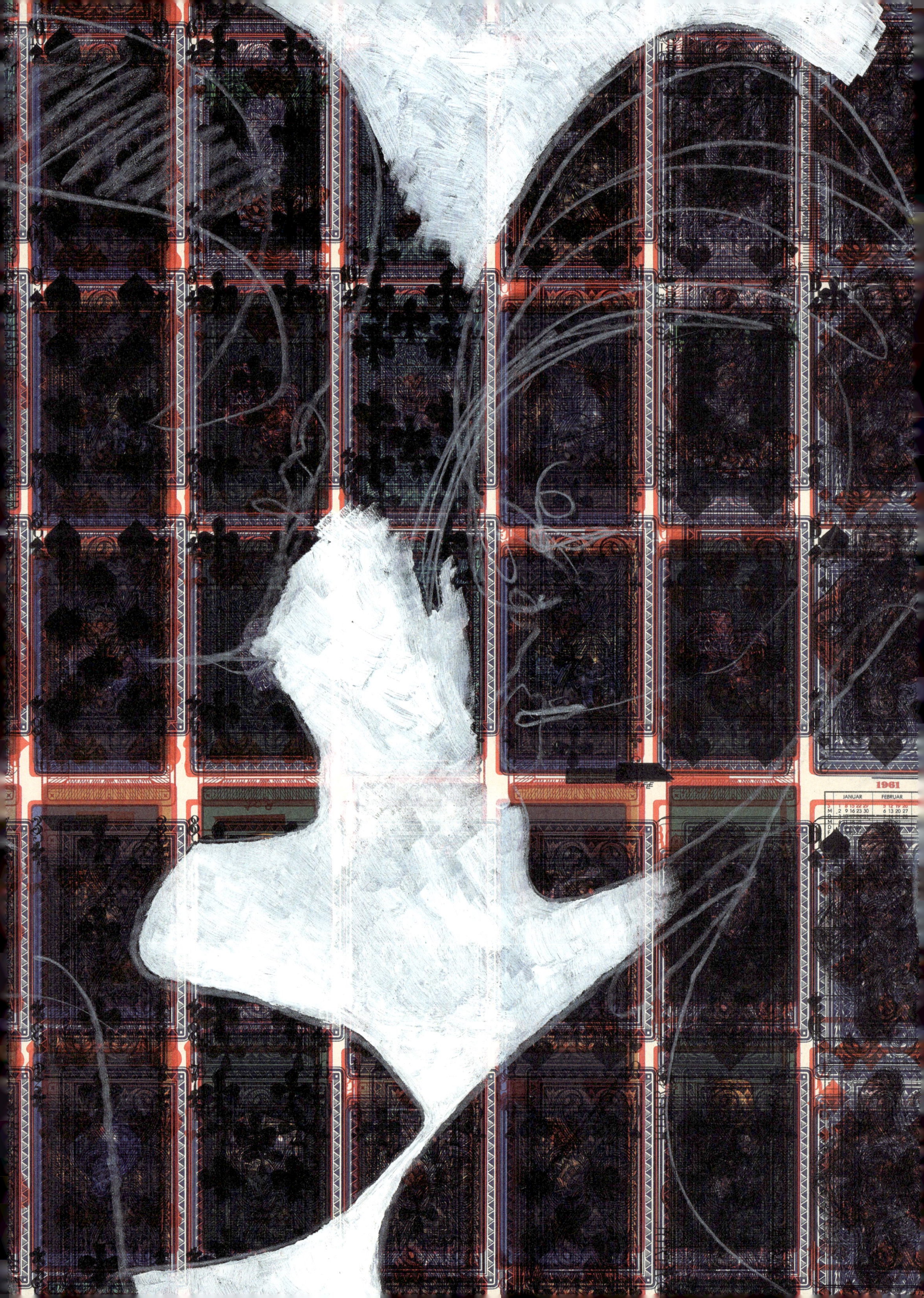
1961
JANUAR
FEBRUAR

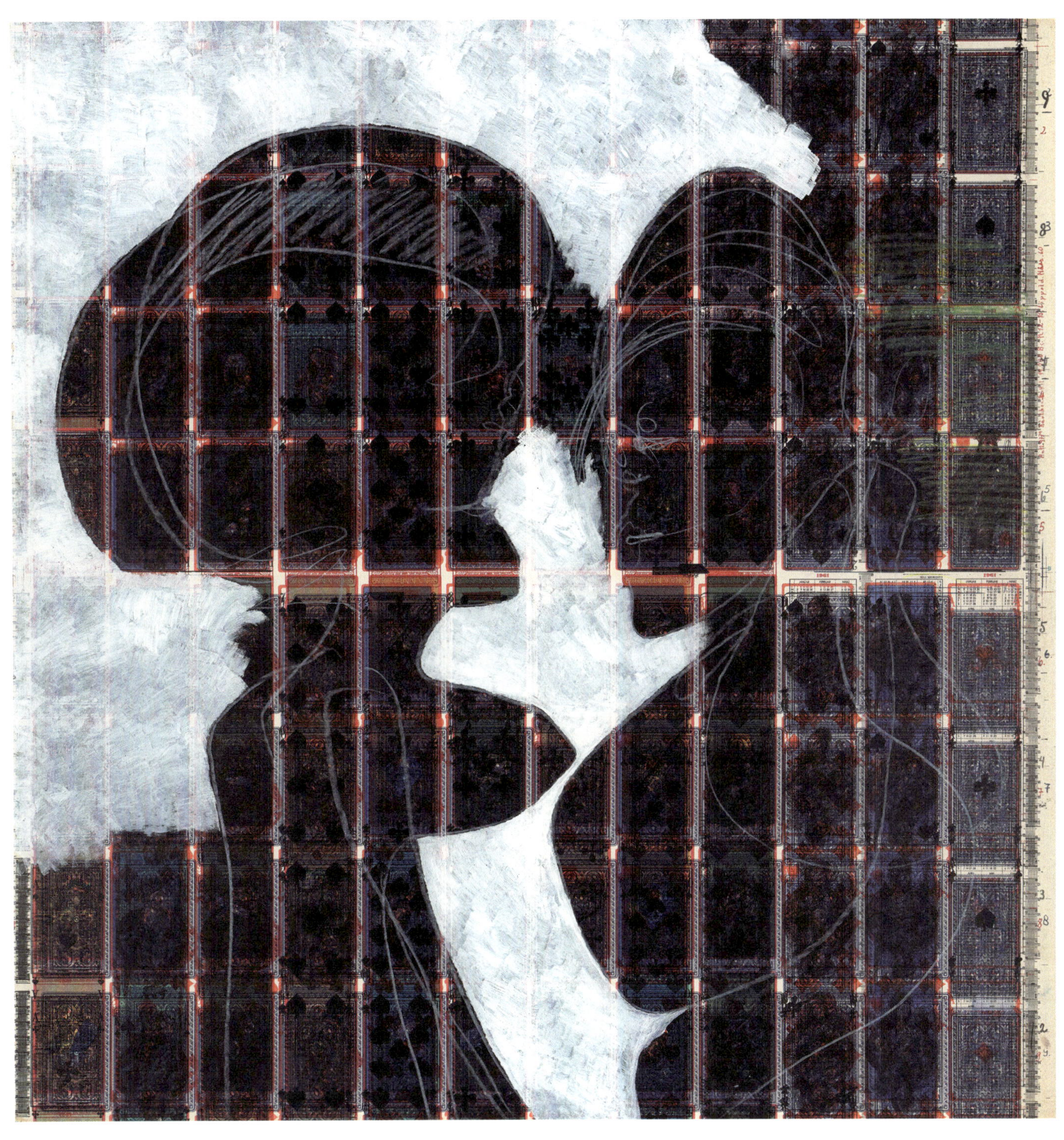

59 O. T. [Das groteske Schattenbild], undatiert |
Untitled [The Grotesque Shadow Picture], no date

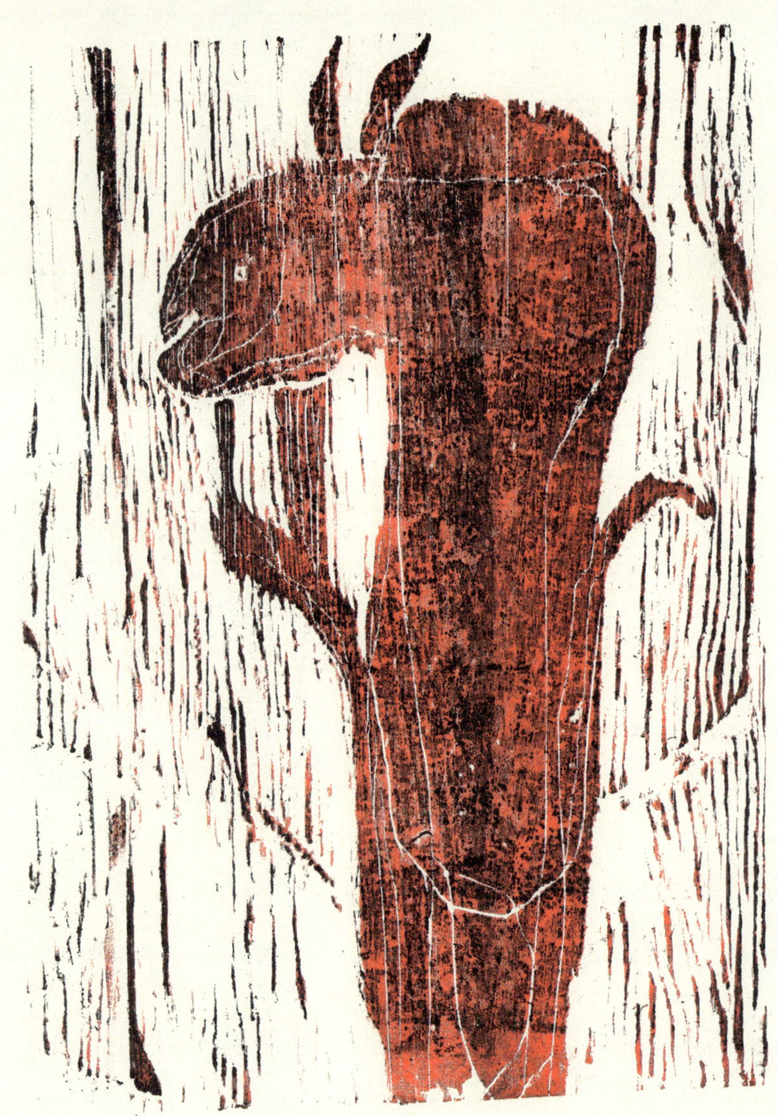

Gierig witternd die Trauben

6/10 d

Altenbourg
1973

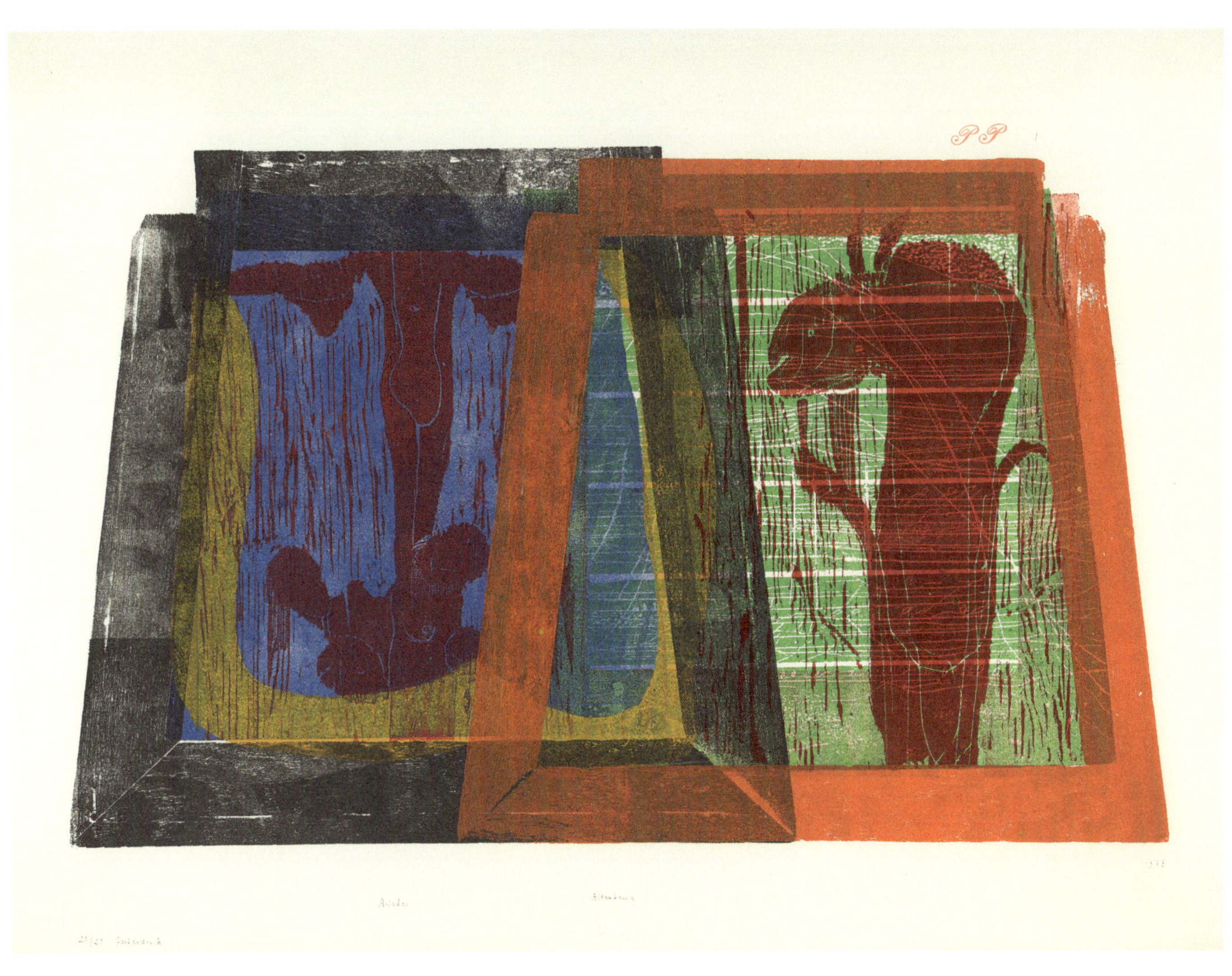

60 *Gierig witternd die Trauben*, 1973 |
Greedily Smelling the Grapes, 1973

61 *Ariadne*, 1973

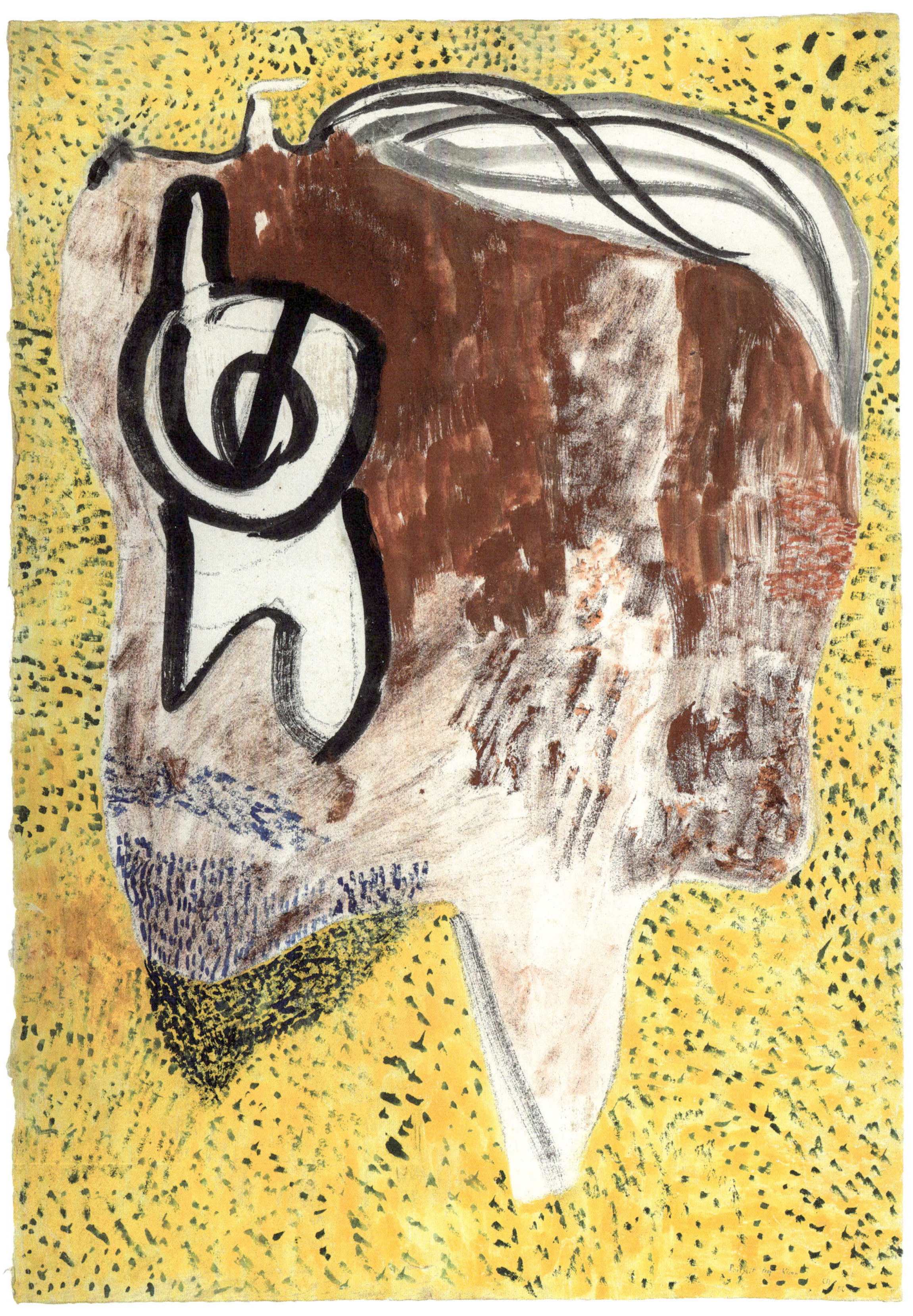

62 *Portrait Prof. Klemm*, 1956 |
Portrait of Prof. Klemm, 1956

63 O. T. [Roter Kopf], undatiert |
Untitled [Red Head], no date

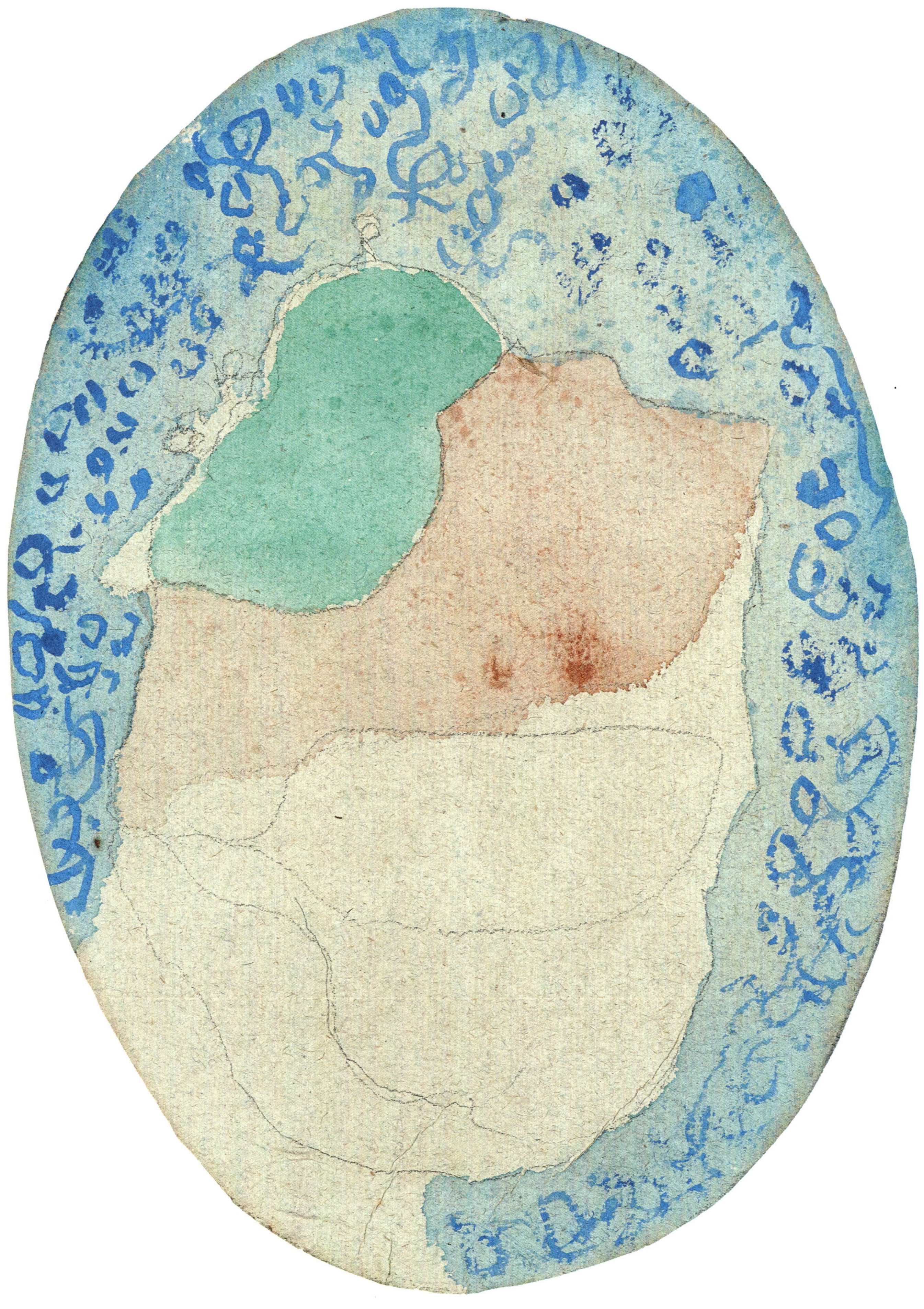

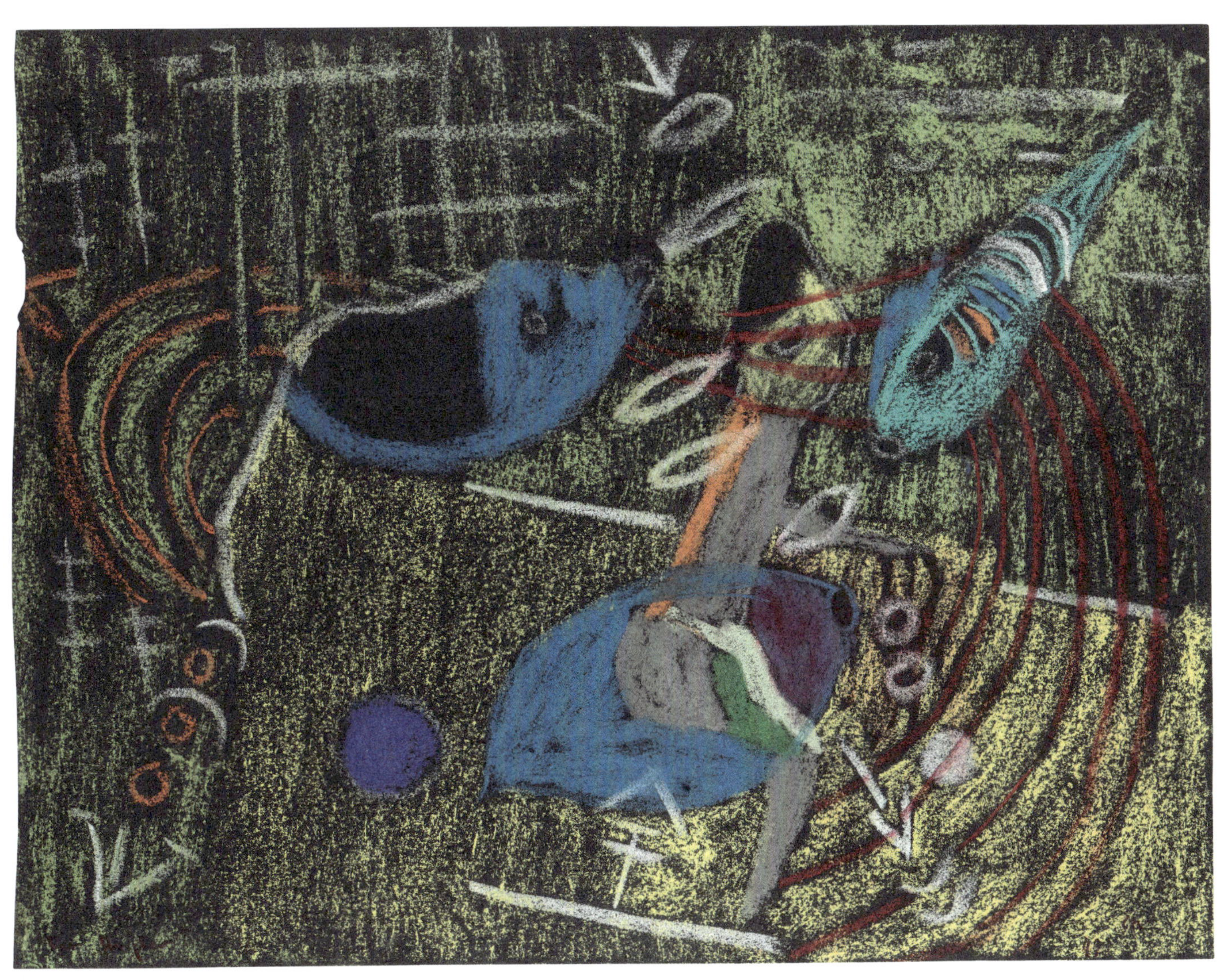

64 O. T. [Das Damenbildnis mit dem grünen Häubchen], undatiert | Untitled [The Portrait of a Woman with the Green Bonnet], no date

65 *Der Angler*, 1949 | *The Fisherman*, 1949

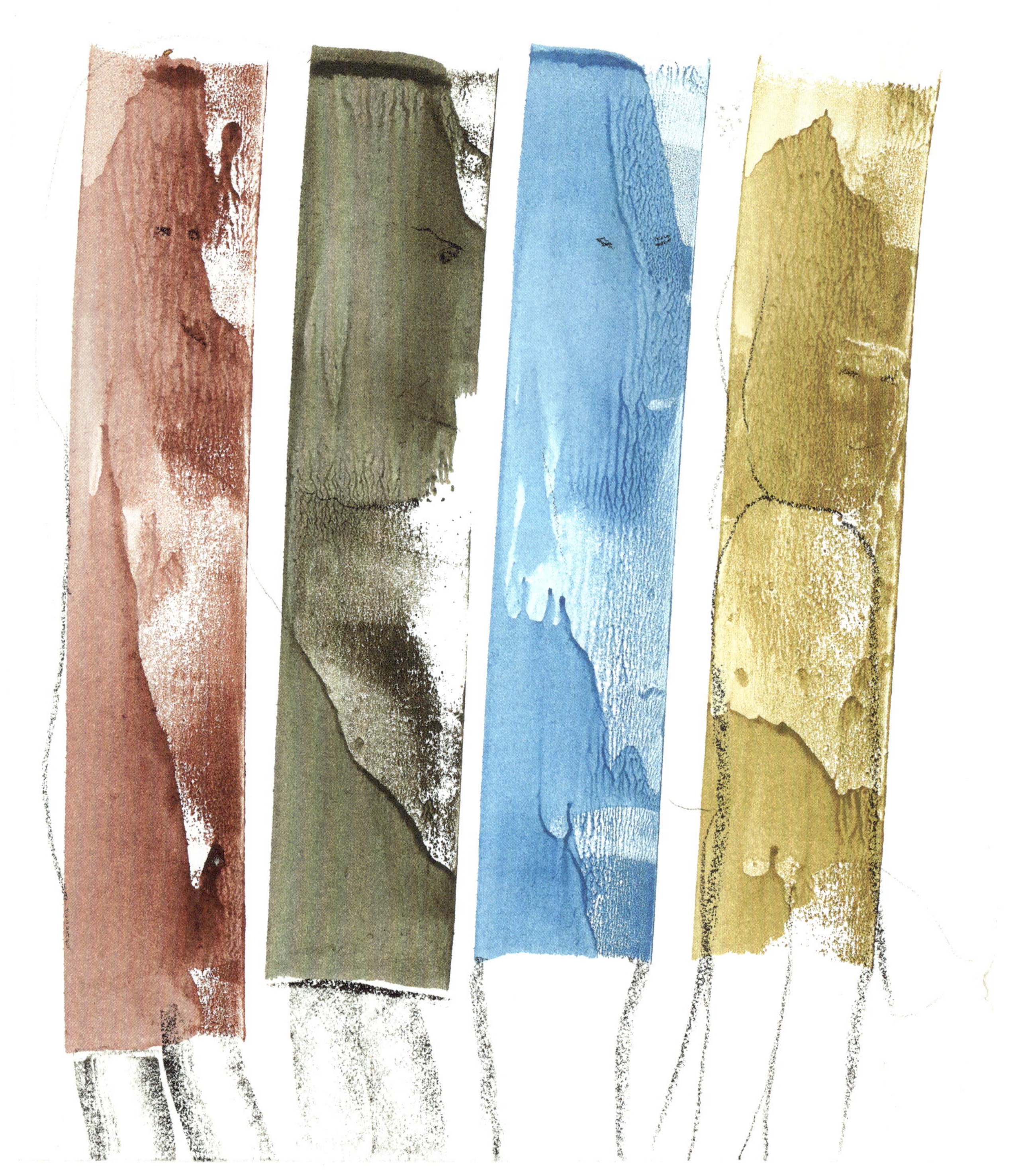

66 O. T. [Aufmarsch der vier Großkopfigen], undatiert | Untitled [March of the Four Big Heads], no date

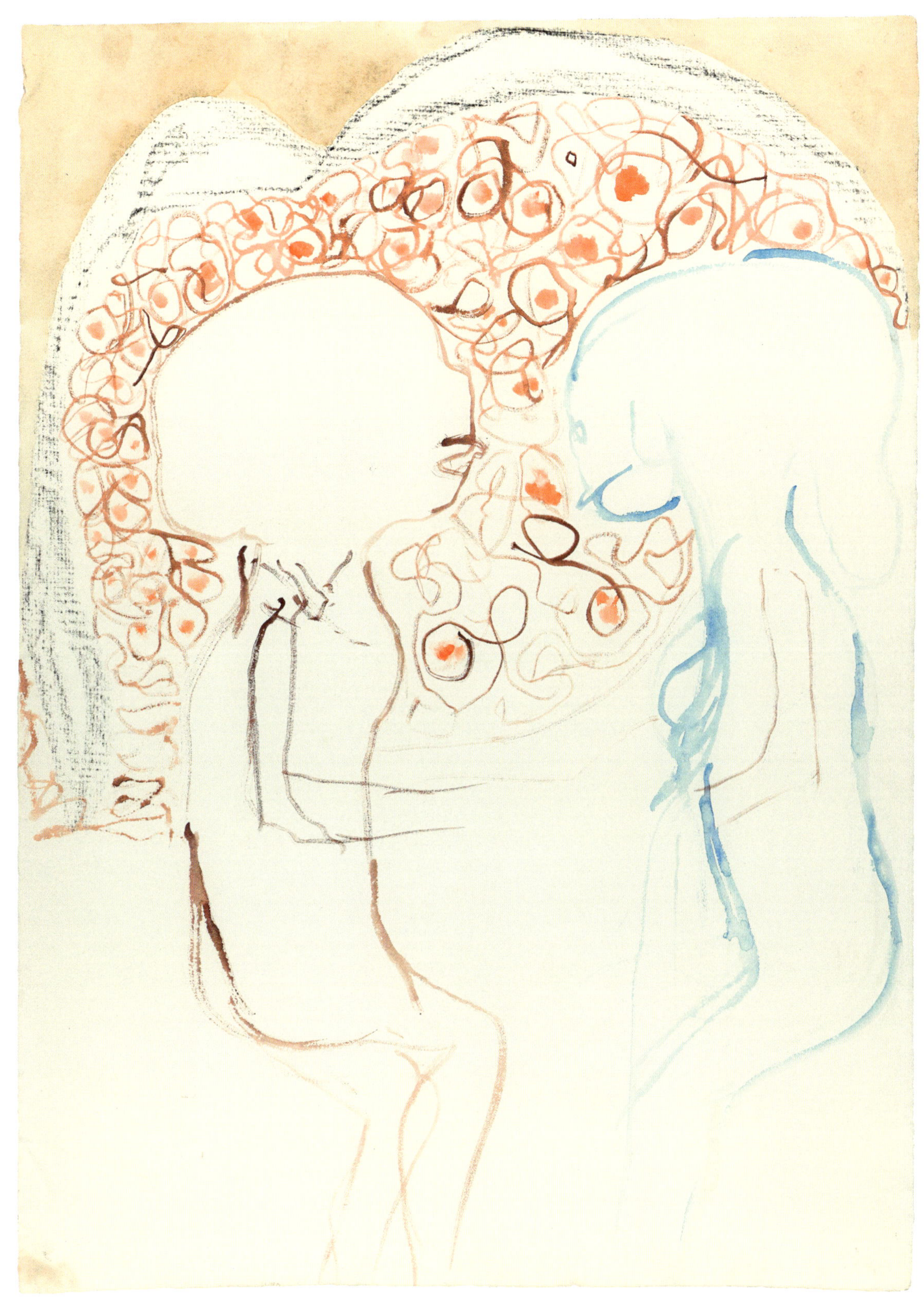

67 O. T. [Rötel und Bläuchen im Rosenhag], undatiert | Untitled [Rötel and Bläuchen in the Rose Arbour], no date

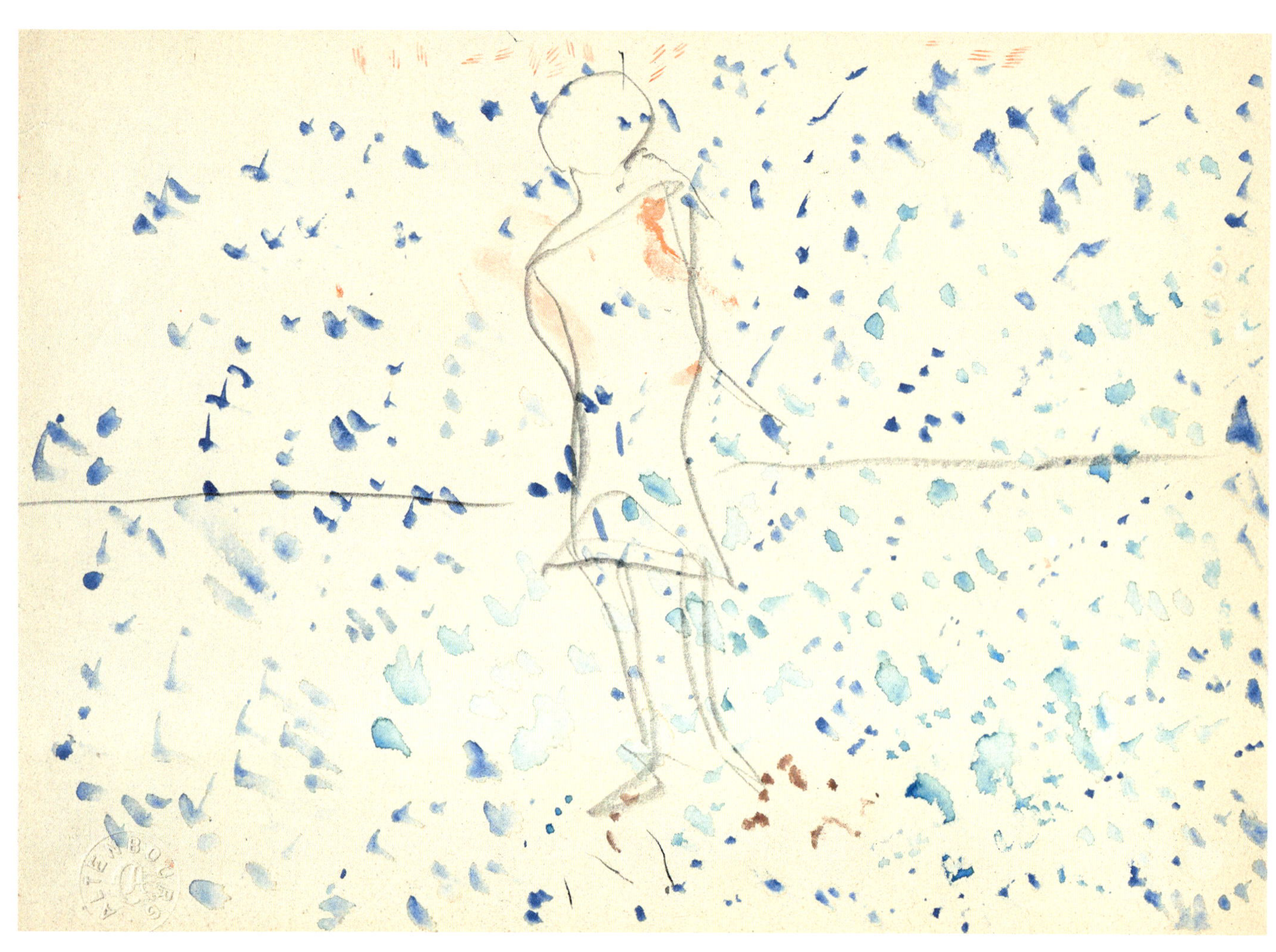

68 O. T. [Einsam im Gestöber], undatiert | Untitled [Alone in a Flurry], no date

69 O. T. [Nachdenken über das Rinnen der Zeit], undatiert | Untitled [Reflecting on the Passage of Time], no date

1.) graubraune Papiere für
Pergament + Leinwand 3x
3.) Tempera einpinseln!

× Altenbourg × Rimmer ×

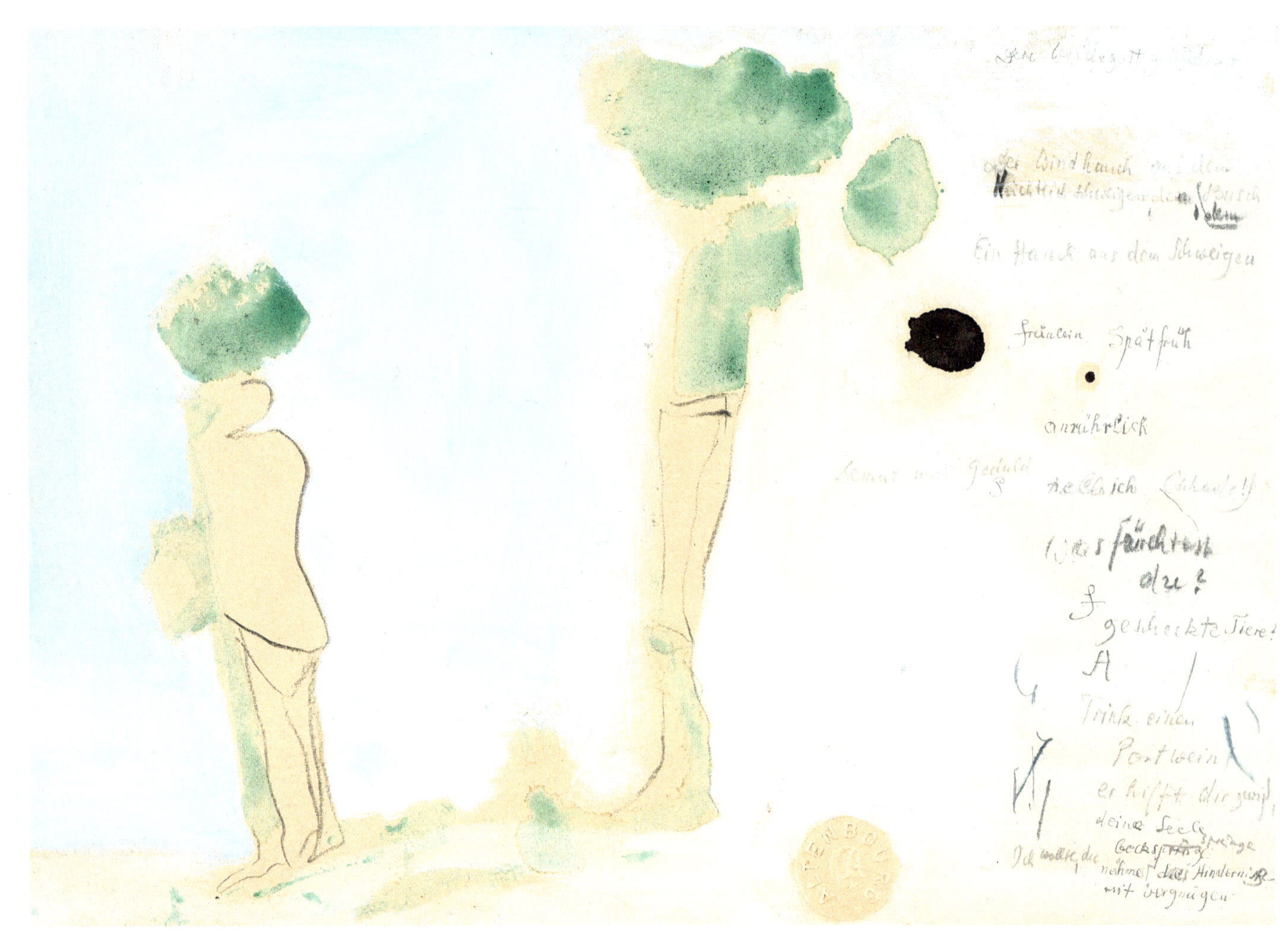

70 O. T. [Dem Weidegott gewidmet], undatiert | Untitled [Dedicated to the God of Pasture], no date

71 O. T. [Baumnymphen], undatiert | Untitled [Dryads], no date

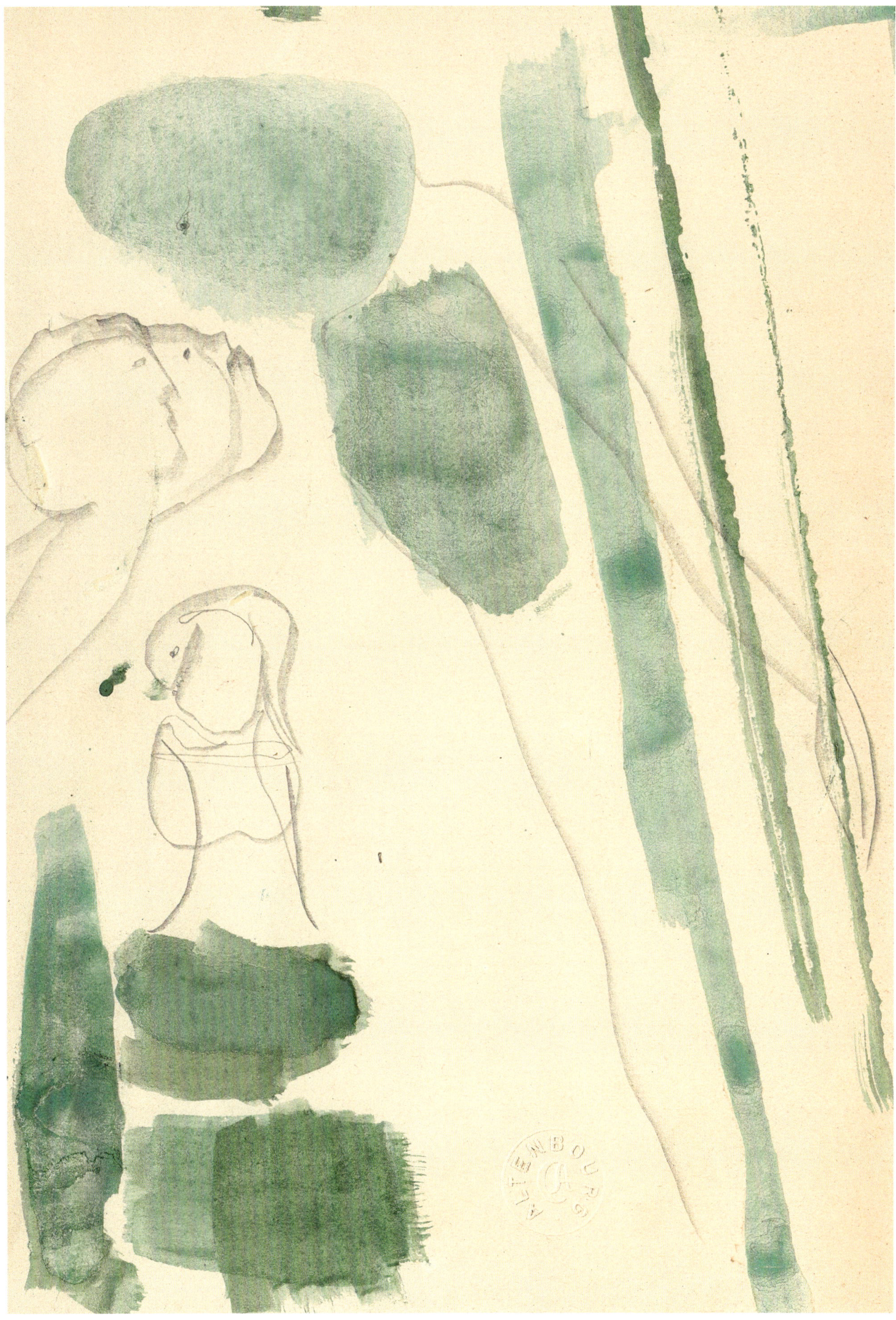
ALTENBOURG

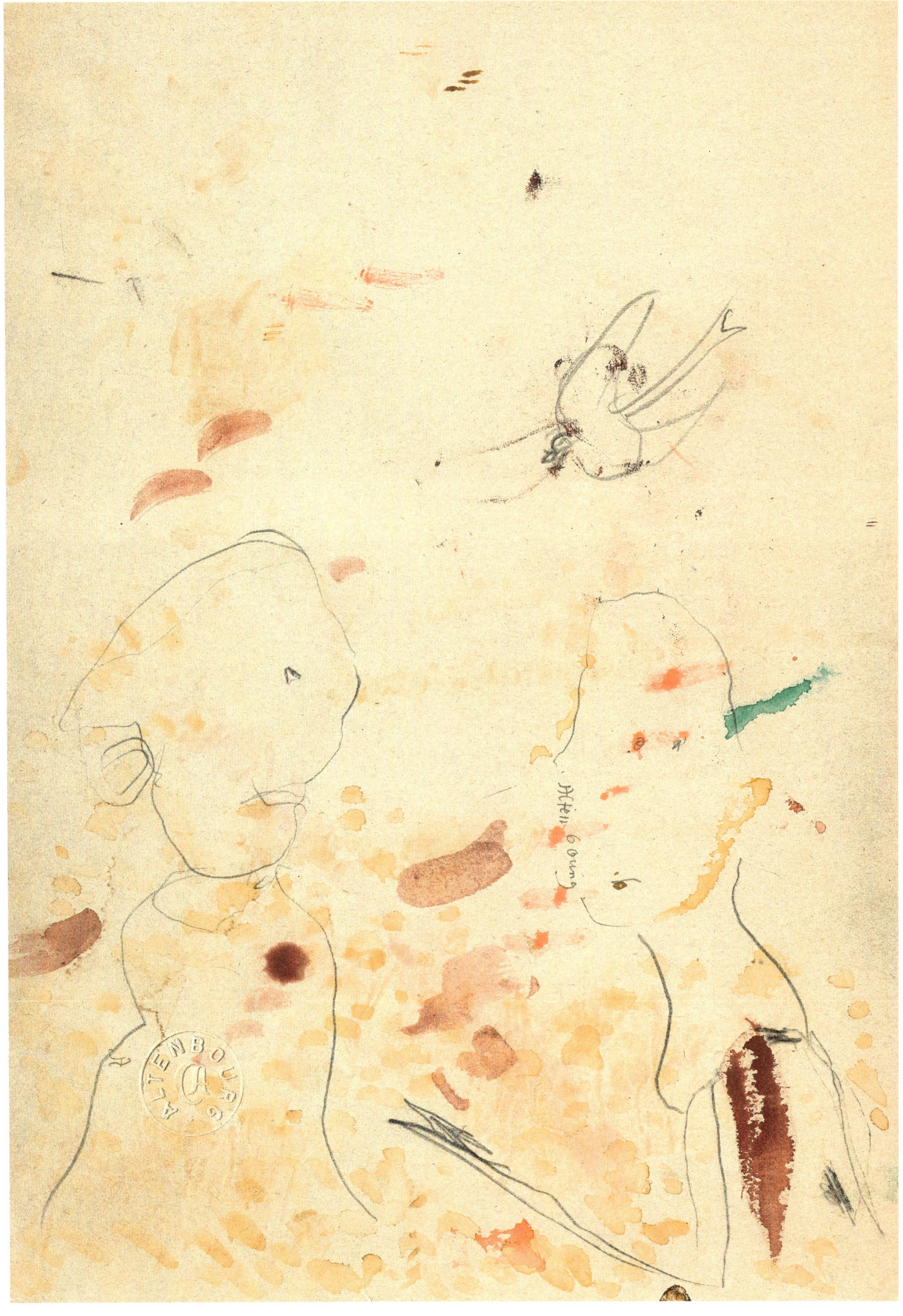
ALTEMBOURG

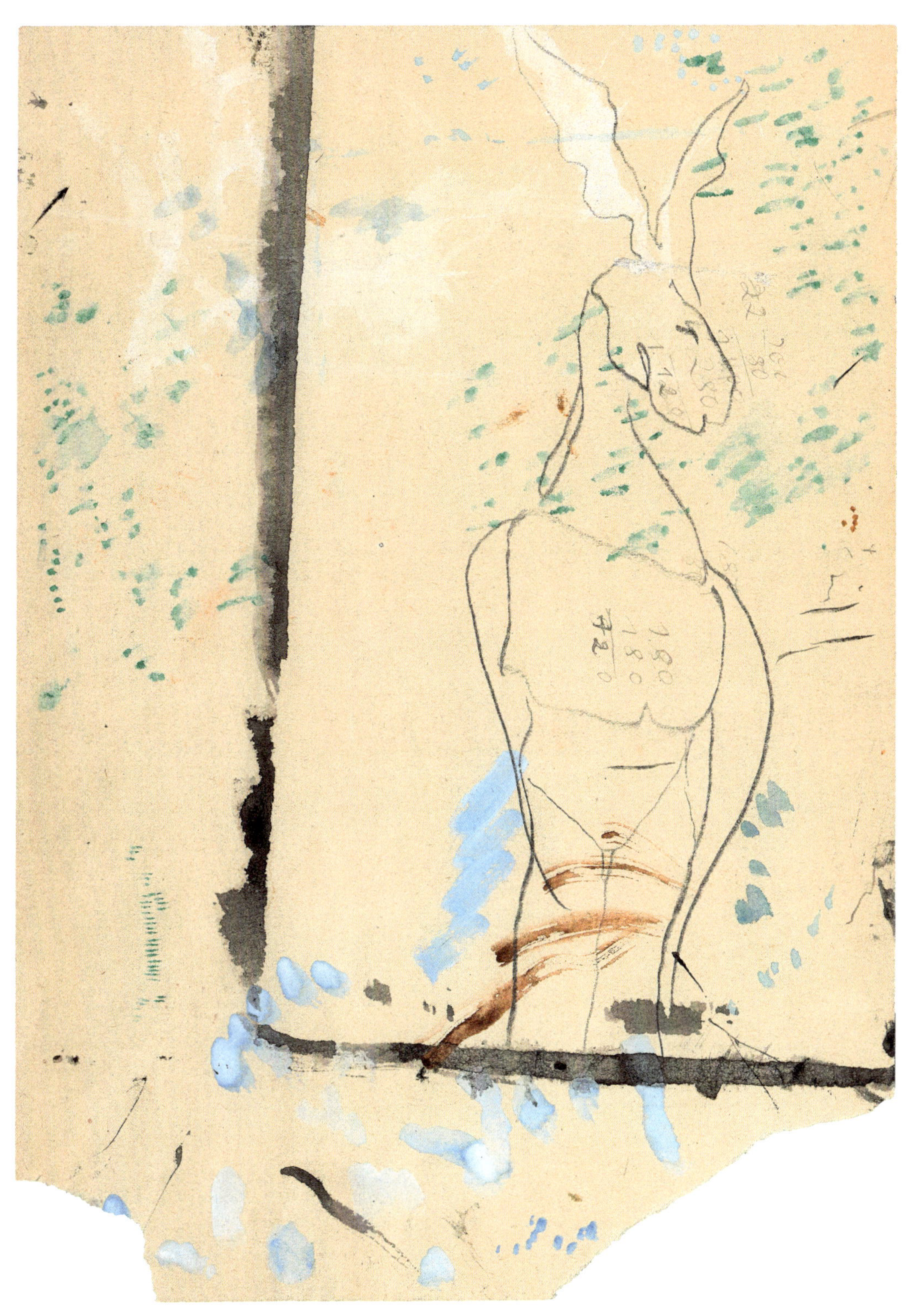

72 O. T. [Mit Altenbourg im Profil], undatiert | Untitled [With Altenbourg in Profile], no date

73 O. T. [Zettel, träumend], undatiert | Untitled [Zettel, Dreaming], no date

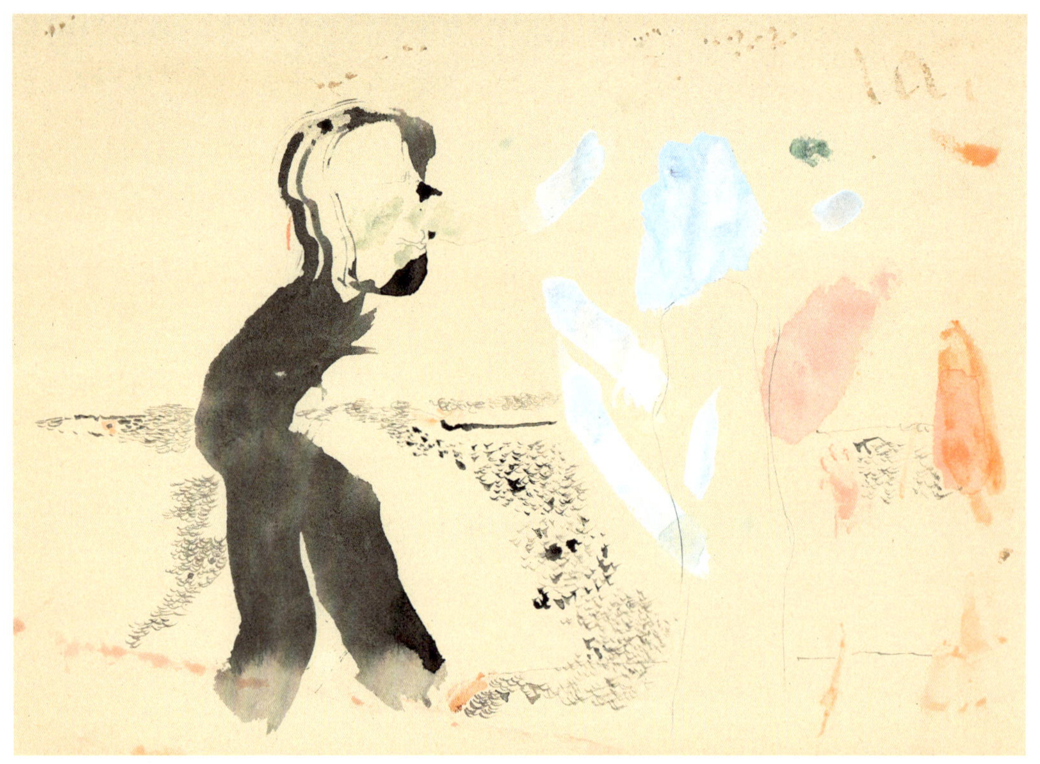

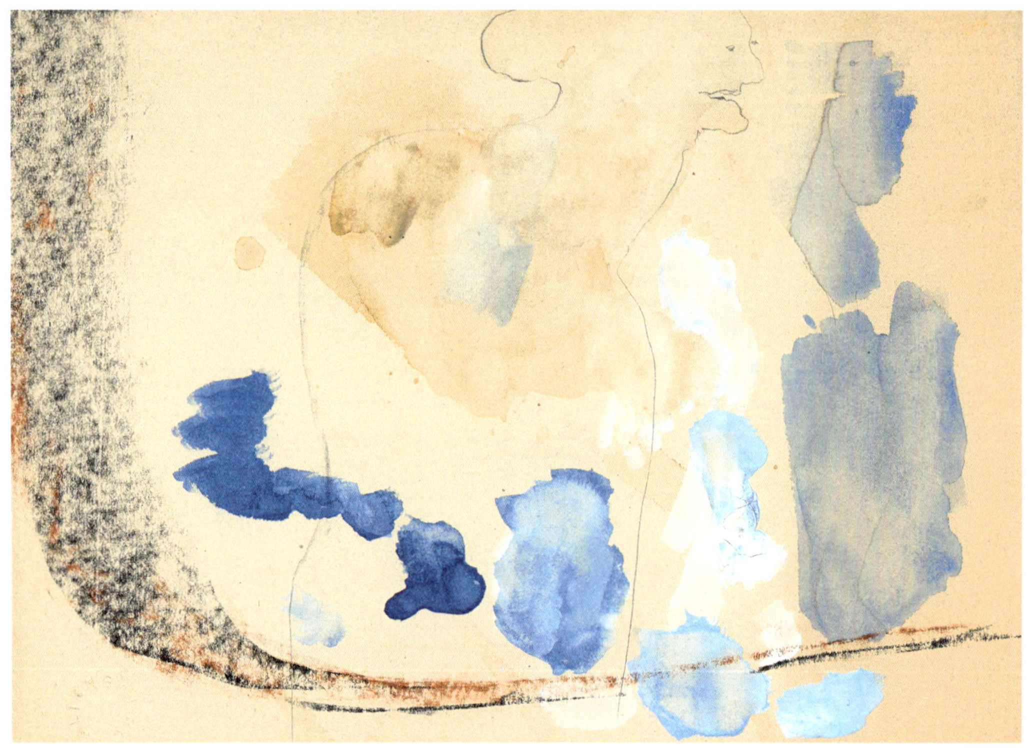

74 O. T. [Gespräch mit dem Moorgeist], undatiert | Untitled [Conversation with the Bog Spirit], no date

75 O. T. [Die bucklige Alte im Gespräch mit dem Luftgeist], undatiert | Untitled [The Hunchbacked Old Woman in Conversation with the Airy Spirit], no date

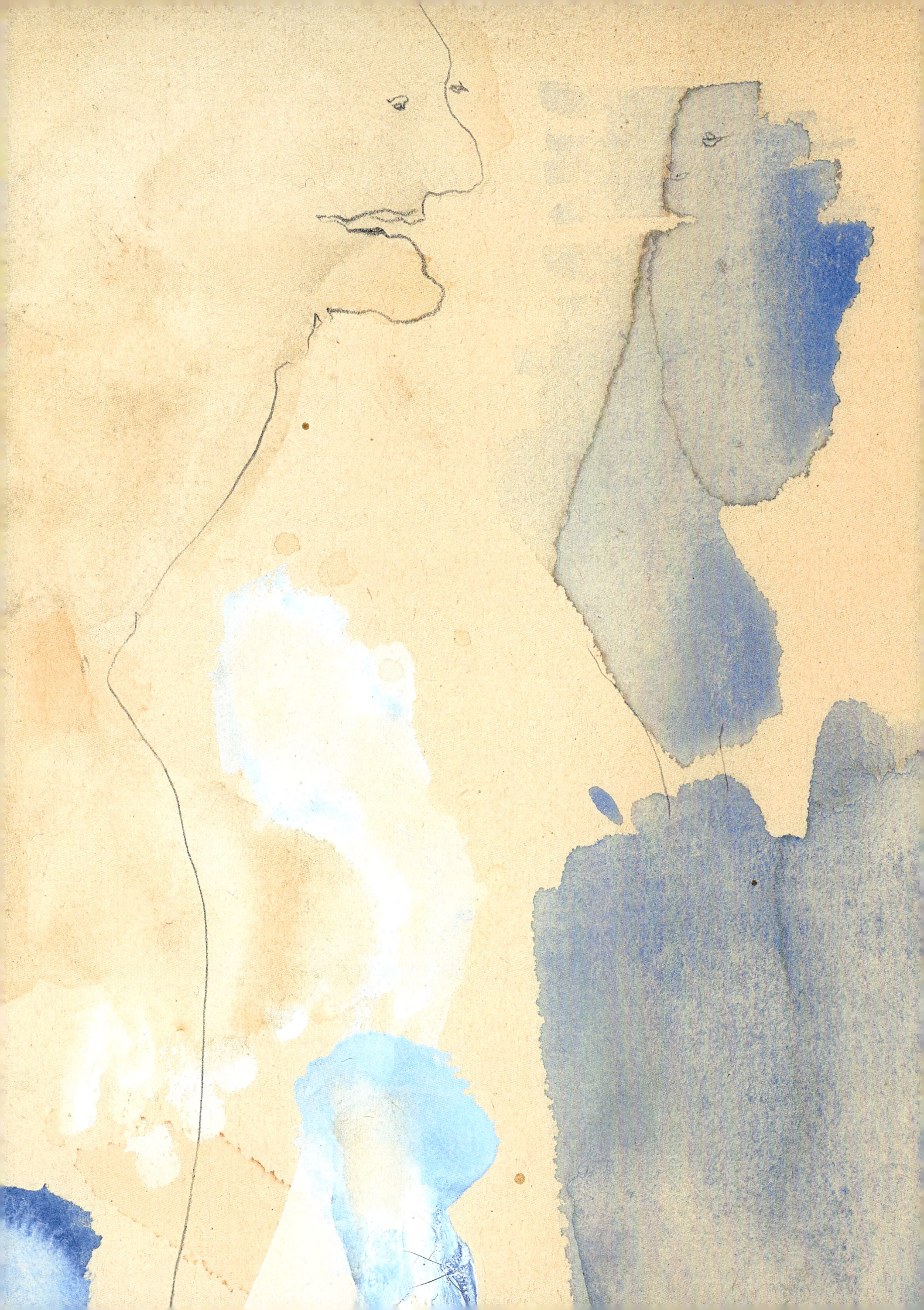

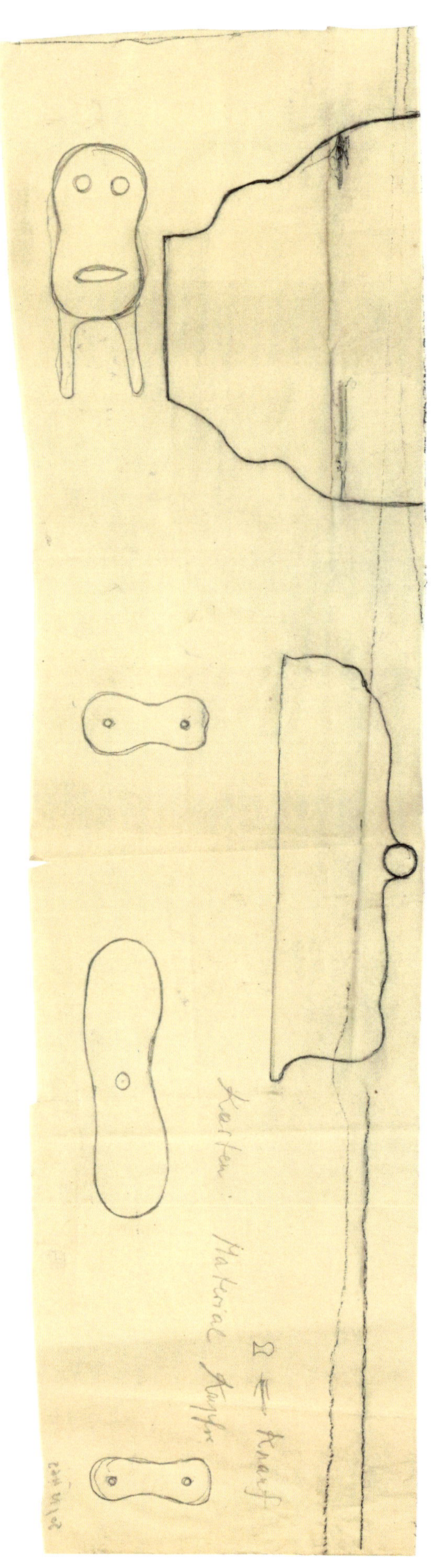

76 O. T., Werkzeichnung für Beschläge auf Fensterrahmen, undatiert | Untitled, technical drawing for fittings on window frames, no date

77 O. T., Schriftblatt mit mehreren Skizzen für Gitter am Künstlerhaus und im Garten von Gerhard Altenbourg, undatiert | Untitled, sheet with several sketches for fences at the artist's house and garden by Gerhard Altenbourg, no date

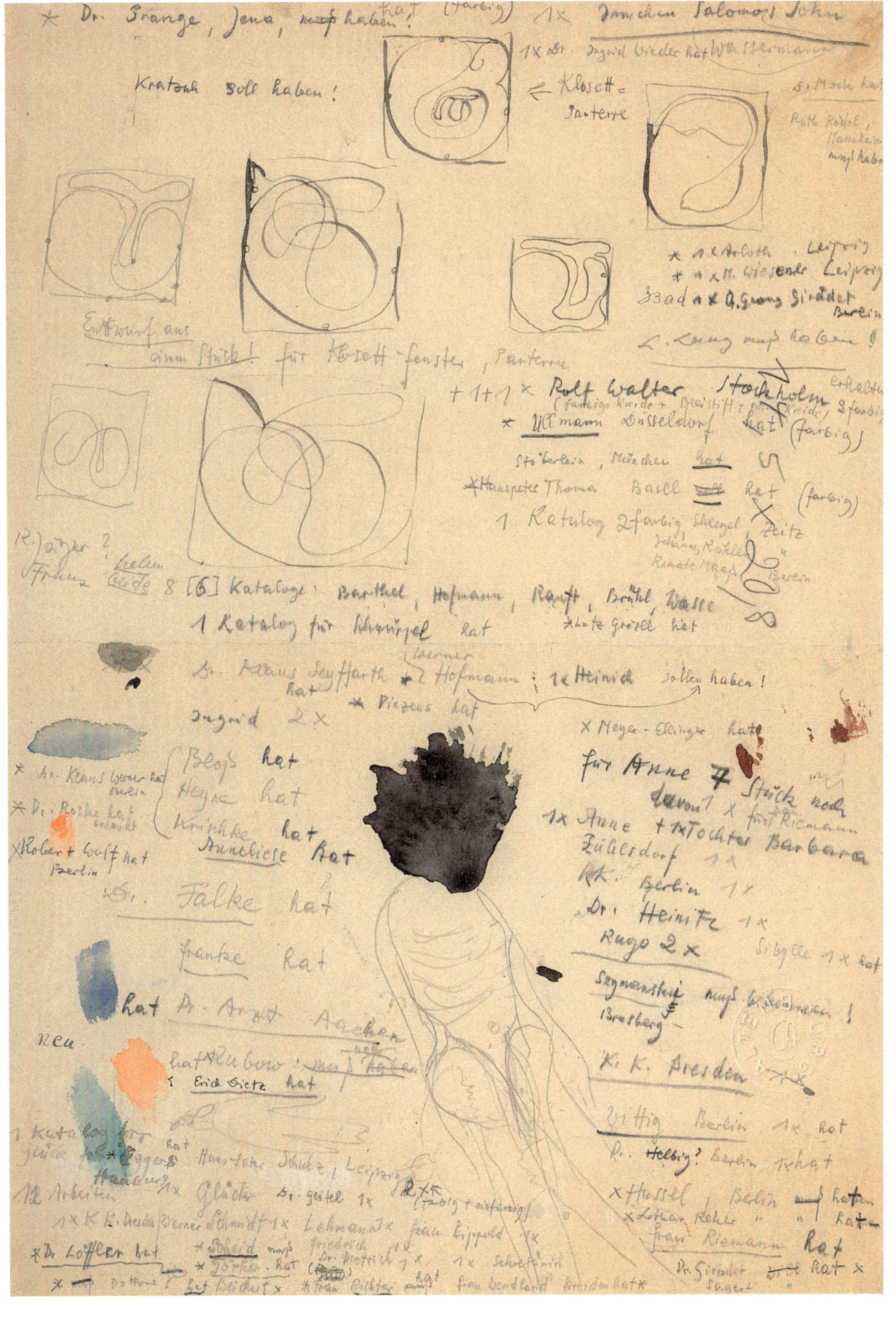

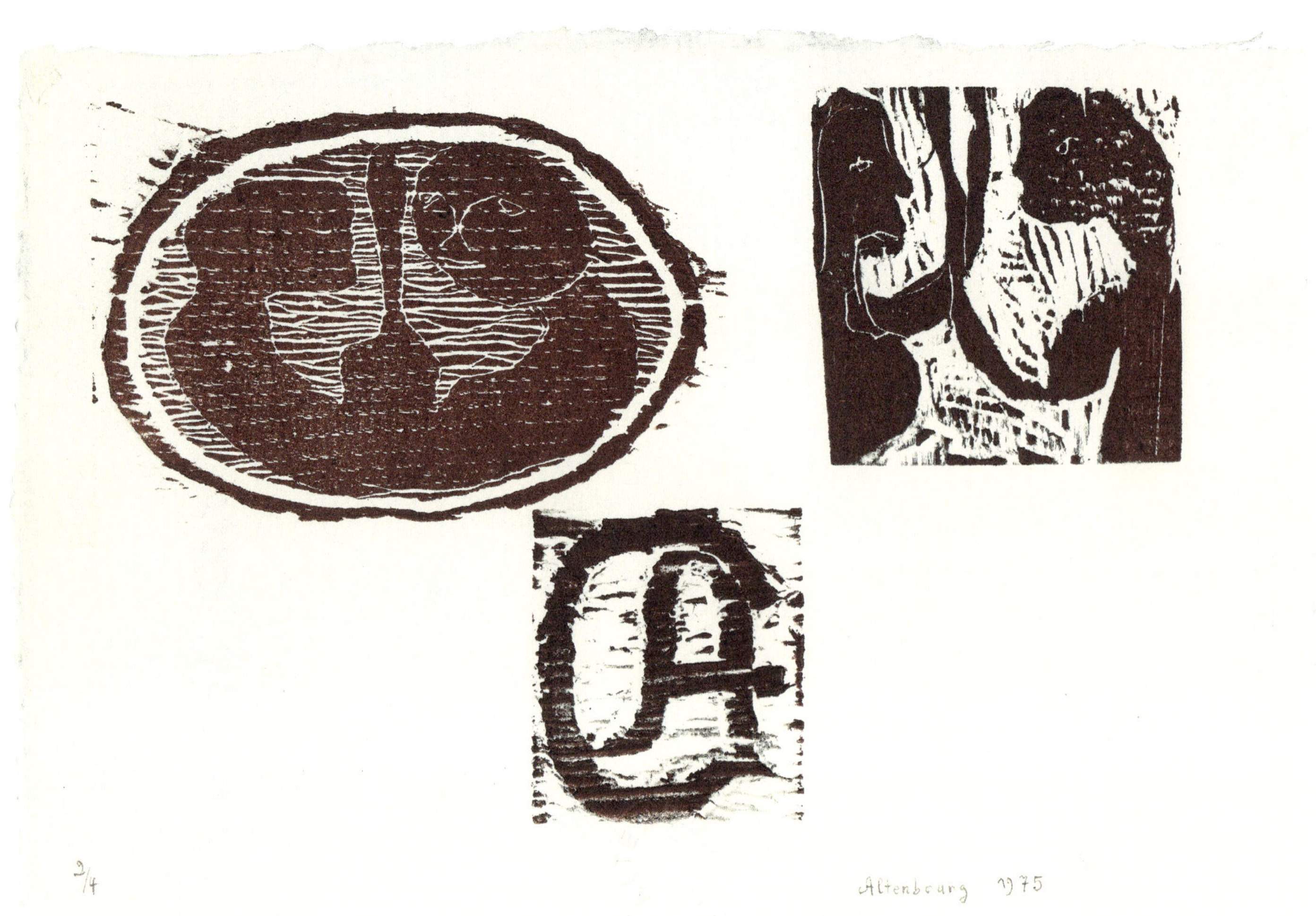

78 *über dem großen Monogramm: In den Wellen der Nacht*, 1975 | *Over the Large Monogram: In the Night's Waves*, 1975

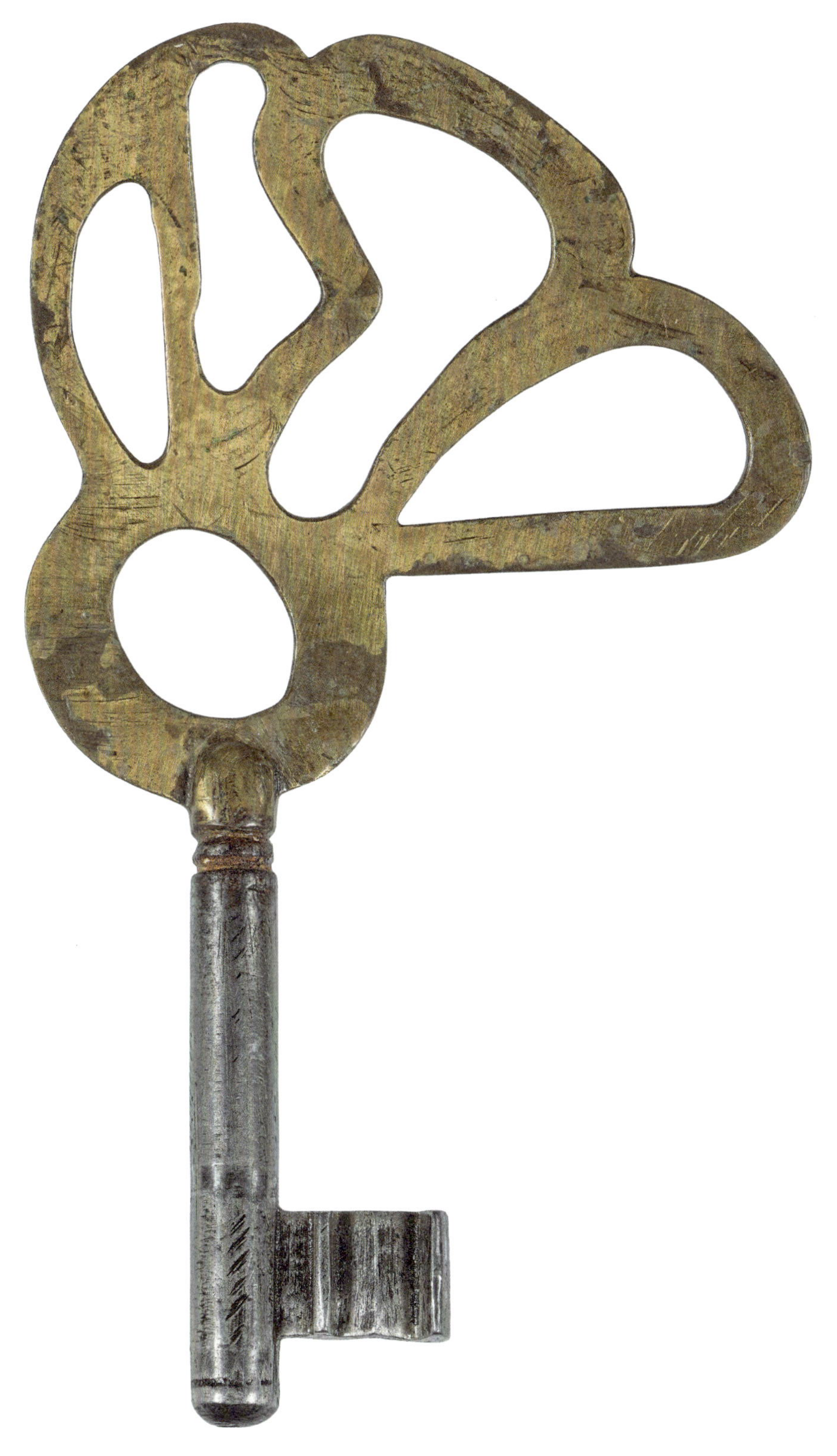

79 Gerhard Altenbourgs Schlüssel zum Arbeitszimmer im Künstlerhaus, 1960–1979 | Gerhard Altenbourg's Key to the Studio in His House, 1960–79

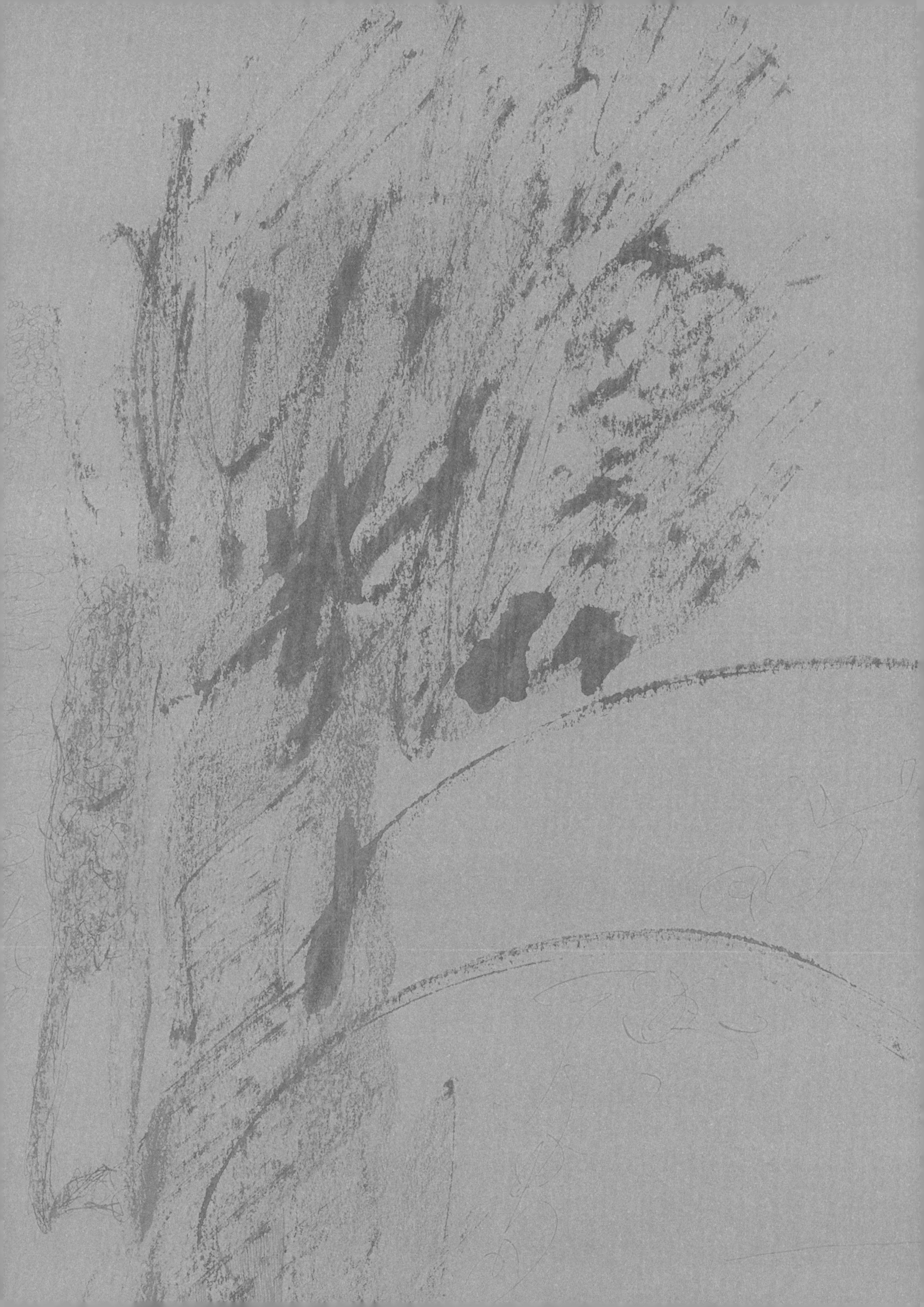

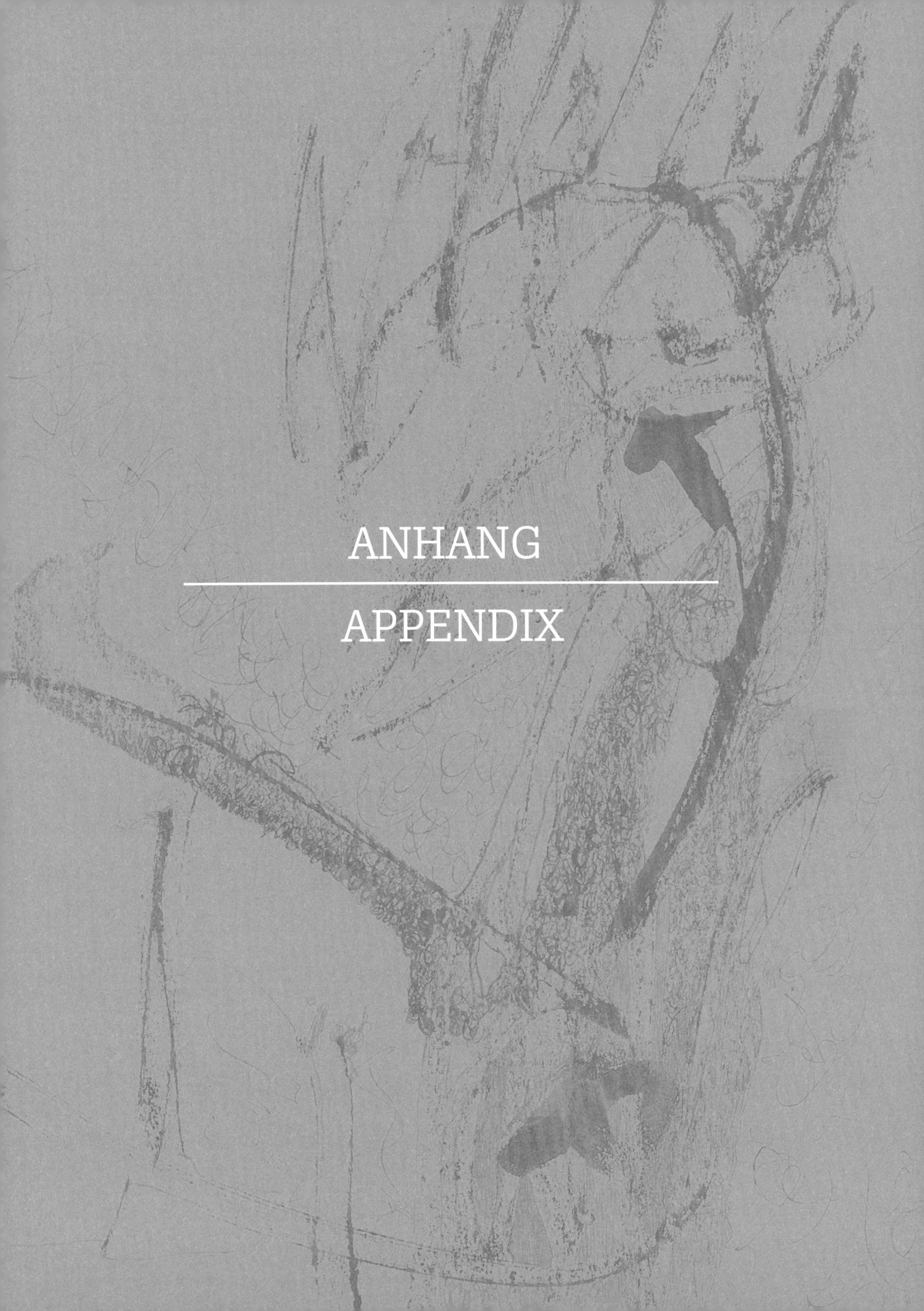

ANHANG

APPENDIX

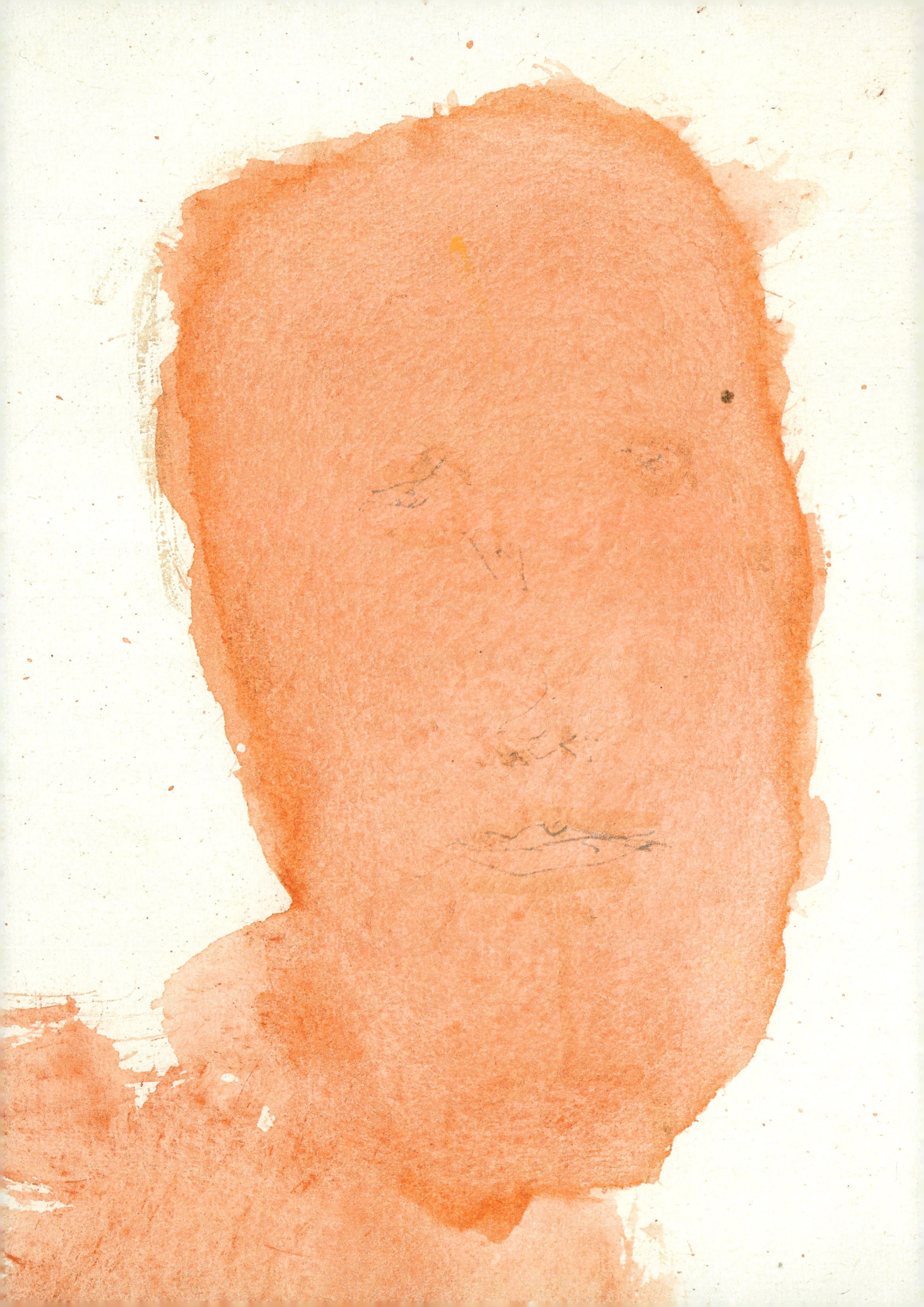

Biografie

1926–1944

Am 22. November 1926 wird Gerhard Ströch als Sohn eines Baptistenpredigers in Rödichen-Schnepfenthal in Thüringen geboren. Ab 1929 lebt er bis zu seinem Tod in Altenburg, wird 1944 zum Militärdienst eingezogen, kehrt schwer krank nach Altenburg zurück.

1946–1950

Ströch ist zunächst als Schriftsteller und Journalist tätig. Der Bildhauer und Maler Erich Dietz (1903–1990) unterrichtet ihn bis 1948. Bis zu seiner vorzeitigen Exmatrikulation studiert er an der Hochschule für Baukunst und Bildende Kunst in Weimar.

1951

Der Westberliner Galerist Rudolf Springer (1909–2009) wird Ströchs erster Kunsthändler.

1955

Als freischaffender Künstler in Altenburg nimmt er den Künstlernamen Gerhard Altenbourg an.

1956

Das Lindenau-Museum Altenburg erwirbt als erstes Museum Werke des Künstlers.

1959

Altenbourg nimmt mit dem Künstlerbuch *Altenbourg Zehn Reproduktionen* an der documenta 2 in Kassel teil.

1960

Das MoMA in New York erhält die großformatige Zeichnung *Gartenkolonie hinter der Spinnbahn Ende Februar* (Garden Behind the Spinnbahn, End of February), 1956 als Schenkung von der Künstlerin Eve Clendenin.

Biography

1926–44

Gerhard Ströch is born on 22 November 1926 as the son of a Baptist preacher in Rödichen-Schnepfenthal in Thuringia. In 1929 his family moves to Altenburg, where he will live the rest of his life. In 1944 he is called up for military service, returning to Altenburg seriously ill.

1946–50

Ströch begins working as a writer and journalist. The sculptor and painter Erich Dietz (1903–1990) is his teacher until 1948. Ströch studies at the Hochschule für Baukunst und Bildende Kunst (College for Architecture and Fine Arts) in Weimar but is expelled before graduating.

1951

The West Berlin gallerist Rudolf Springer (1909–2009) becomes Ströch's first art dealer.

1955

Ströch works as a freelance artist in Altenburg and takes on the name Gerhard Altenbourg.

1956

The Lindenau-Museum in Altenburg is the first museum to acquire work by him.

1959

Altenbourg takes part in *documenta 2* in Kassel, exhibiting his artist's book *Zehn Reproduktionen* (Altenbourg Ten Reproductions)

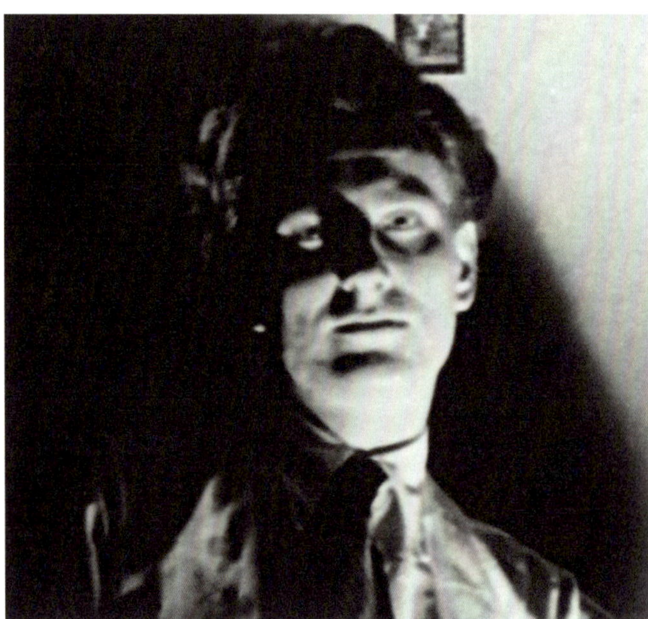

Abb. 1 *Gerhard Altenbourg in Weimar*, Anfang der 1950er-Jahre, Schwarz-Weiß-Fotografie, Privatbesitz, Stiftung Gerhard Altenbourg, Inv.-Nr. SGA F1707
Fig. 1 *Gerhard Altenbourg in Weimar*, early 1950s, black-and-white photograph, private collection, Gerhard Altenbourg Foundation, inv. no. SGA F1707

1961
Altenbourg bezieht in Westberlin ein Gastatelier der Akademie der Künste.

1963
Tod der Mutter; Teilnahme an der Ausstellung *Schrift und Bild* im Stedelijk Museum Amsterdam und in der Staatlichen Kunsthalle Baden-Baden.

1964
Altenbourg wird wegen Zollvergehens zu einer Bewährungsstrafe verurteilt. Da er sich der offiziellen Kunstpolitik der DDR verweigert, wird er bis in die 1980er-Jahre in seinem Wirken behindert.

1966
Altenbourg beteiligt sich an den Ausstellungen *Phantastische Figurationen* im Haus am Waldsee und *Labyrinthe* im Kunstverein Berlin (beide Westberlin). Der Künstler erhält den Burda-Preis für Grafik.

1967
Altenbourg beteiligt sich an der Ausstellung *Ars phantastica* in Nürnberg. Ihm wird der Preis der II. Internationale der Zeichnung in Darmstadt verliehen.

1960
The Museum of Modern Art in New York receives the large-scale drawing *Gartenkolonie hinter der Spinnbahn Ende Februar* (Garden Allotments Behind the Spinnbahn, End of February; 1956) as a gift from the artist Eve Clendenin.

1961
Altenbourg uses a guest studio in West Berlin provided by the Akademie der Künste.

1963
Death of his mother. Takes part in the exhibition *Art and Writing* at the Stedelijk Museum Amsterdam and in the Staatliche Kunsthalle Baden-Baden.

1964
Altenbourg is charged with customs violations and receives a suspended sentence. Since he refuses to comply with GDR official art policies, he is hindered in his career until the 1980s.

1966
Altenbourg takes part in the exhibitions *Phantastische Figurationen* (Fantastic Figurations) at Haus am Waldsee and *Labyrinthe* (Labyrinths) at the Kunstverein Berlin (both in West Berlin). He receives the Burda Prize for Graphic Art.

1967
Altenbourg shows at the exhibition *Ars phantastica* in Nuremberg. He is awarded the prize at the II Internationale der Zeichnung in Darmstadt.

1968
Altenbourg is nominated for the Premio Marzotto but does not travel to Italy. He receives the Will Grohmann Prize in West Berlin. The gallerist Dieter Brusberg (1935–2015) represents the artist, initially in Hanover and then in Berlin.

1969
First major retrospective, *Gerhard Altenbourg. 1947–1969* (with a catalogue raisonné, compiled together with Dieter Brusberg), shown at Haus am Waldsee in the Zehlendorf district of Berlin and subsequently in Baden-Baden, Hanover and Düsseldorf.

1970
Appointed a member of Akademie der Künste in West Berlin and of the Institut für moderne Kunst in Nuremberg.

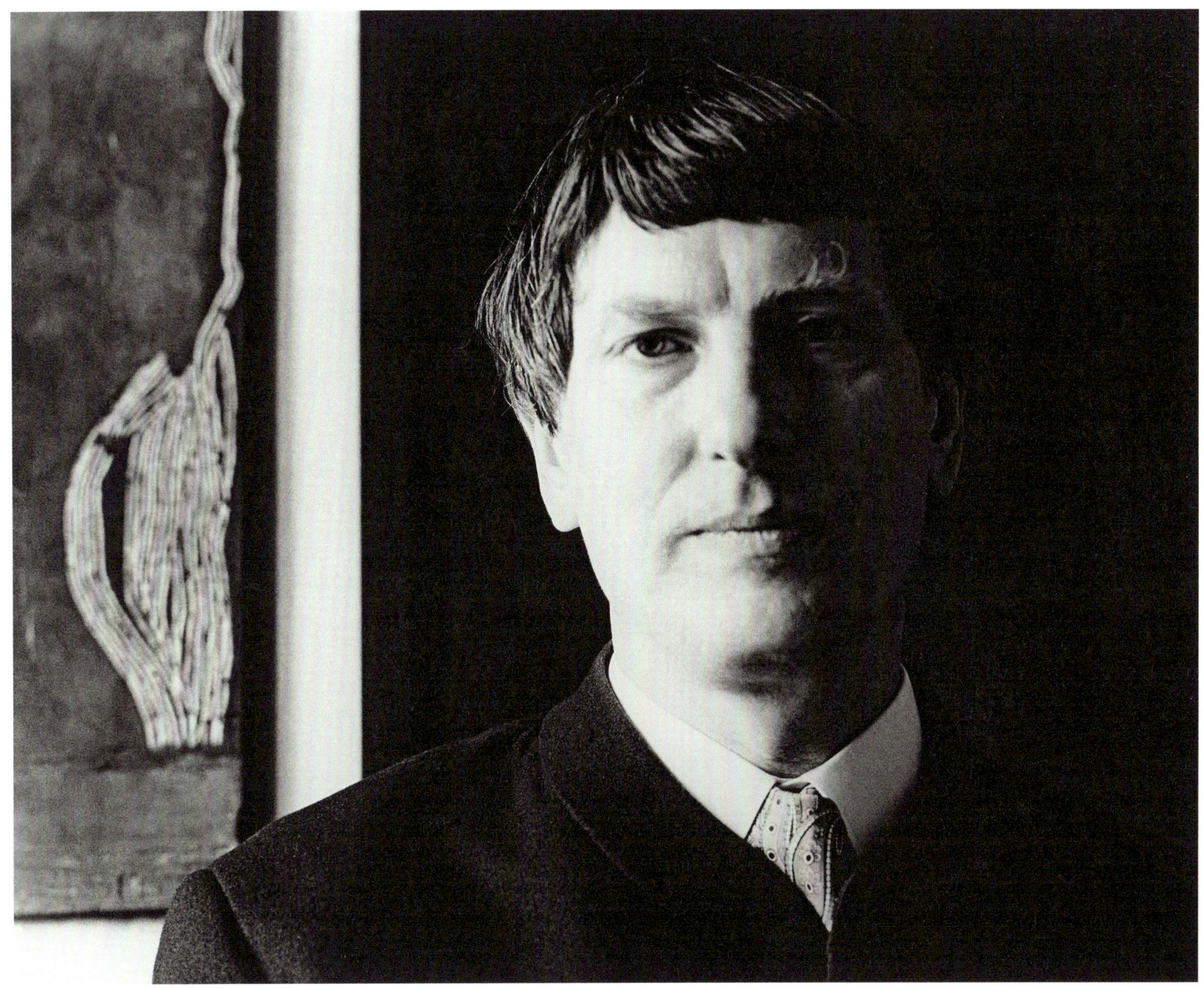

Abb. 2 Lothar Reher, *Gerhard Altenbourg in seinem Ankleidezimmer*, 1971, Schwarz-Weiß-Fotografie, Stiftung Gerhard Altenbourg, Inv.-Nrn. SGA F0835
Fig. 2 Lothar Reher, *Gerhard Altenbourg in His Dressing Room*, 1971, black-and-white photograph, Gerhard Altenbourg Foundation, inv. no. SGA F0835

1968

Altenbourg wird für den Premio Marzotto vorgeschlagen, reist jedoch nicht nach Italien. Ihm wird der Will-Grohmann-Preis in Westberlin verliehen. Der Galerist Dieter Brusberg (1935–2015) vertritt den Künstler zunächst in Hannover, dann in Berlin.

1971

The artist's book *Ich-Gestein* (I-Stone) is published by Propyläen Verlag, featuring large colour plates and texts by Altenbourg and Erhart Kästner.

1976

The exhibition *Gerhard Altenbourg. Holzschnitte* (Woodcuts) at the Museum Schloss Hinterglauchau in Saxony, curated and designed by Altenbourg himself, is closed after a few days and the museum's director, Günter Ullmann, is fired.

1977

Altenbourg exhibits at *documenta 6* in Kassel.

1969

Erste große Werkschau *Gerhard Altenbourg. 1947–1969* (zugleich Werkverzeichnis zusammen mit Dieter Brusberg), die zunächst in Berlin-Zehlendorf im Haus am Waldsee, später in Baden-Baden, Hannover und Düsseldorf zu sehen ist.

1970

Ernennung zum Mitglied der Akademie der Künste in Westberlin und des Instituts für moderne Kunst in Nürnberg.

1971

Das Künstlerbuch *Ich-Gestein* erscheint im Propyläen Verlag mit großen Farbtafeln, Texten von Gerhard Altenbourg und Erhart Kästner.

1976

Die Ausstellung *Gerhard Altenbourg. Holzschnitte* im sächsischen Museum Schloss Hinterglauchau – von Altenbourg selbst zusammengestellt und gestaltet – wird nach wenigen Tagen geschlossen und endet mit der Entlassung des Museumsdirektors Günter Ullmann (geb. 1946).

1977

Altenbourg nimmt an der documenta 6 in Kassel teil.

1979

Die Einzelausstellung *Gerhard Altenbourg. Grafik und Zeichnungen aus drei Jahrzehnten* wird im Kupferstich-Kabinett der Staatlichen Kunstsammlungen Dresden präsentiert.

1981/82

Beteiligung an der Ausstellung *Peinture et gravure en République Démocratique Allemande* im Musée d'art Moderne de la Ville de Paris; Ausstellung in der Galerie Oben und der Galerie Clara Mosch in Karl-Marx-Stadt (Chemnitz).

1982–1984

Teilnahme an der Wanderausstellung *Zeitvergleich – Malerei und Grafik aus der DDR* in Hamburg, Stuttgart, Düsseldorf, München, Nürnberg, Hannover.

1979

The solo exhibition *Gerhard Altenbourg. Grafik und Zeichnungen aus drei Jahrzehnten* (Graphic Art and Drawings from Three Decades) is presented at the Kupferstich-Kabinett of the Staatliche Kunstsammlungen in Dresden.

1981–82

Participates in the exhibition *Peinture et gravure en République Démocratique Allemande* (Painting and Graphic Art in the German Democratic Republic) at the Musée d'art Moderne de la Ville de Paris; exhibition at Galerie Oben and Galerie Clara Mosch in Karl-Marx-Stadt (Chemnitz).

1982–84

Exhibits in the touring exhibition *Zeitvergleich – Malerei und Grafik aus der DDR* (Time Comparison – Painting and Graphic Art from the GDR) in Hamburg, Stuttgart, Düsseldorf, Munich, Nuremberg and Hanover.

1982–86

The artist's book *Wund-Denkmale. Schwebende Labung und Schauer* (Wound-Monument. Floating Sustenance and Shiver) is published in two editions of fifty copies each, in West Berlin (Edition Brusberg) and Leipzig (Reclam Verlag).

1986

Lothar Lang, director of the Staatliches Museum Schloss Burgk, curates the exhibition *Gelegentliches von Gerhard Altenbourg* (Occasional Works by Gerhard Altenbourg) at Schloss Burgk together with the Pirckheimer Society, on the occasion of the artist's sixtieth birthday.

1987–88

Major exhibitions in Bremen, Tübingen, Hanover and Berlin.

1989

The *Schnepfenthaler Suite* (1984–88, 100 drypoint prints) and *Aus dem Hügelgau* (From Hügelgau, 1988, 10 drypoint prints) are published by Edition Brusberg, West Berlin.

1982–1986

Das Künstlerbuch *Wund-Denkmale. Schwebende Labung und Schauer* erscheint in zwei Ausgaben zu je 50 Exemplaren in Westberlin (Edition Brusberg) und Leipzig (Reclam Verlag).

1986

Lothar Lang, Leiter des Staatlichen Museums Schloss Burgk, kuratiert zum 60. Geburtstag des Künstlers zusammen mit der Pirckheimer-Gesellschaft die Ausstellung *Gelegentliches von Gerhard Altenbourg* auf Schloss Burgk.

1987/88

Umfangreiche Ausstellungen in Bremen, Tübingen, Hannover und Berlin.

1989

Die *Schnepfenthaler Suite* (1984–1988, 100 Kaltnadelradierungen) und *Aus dem Hügelgau* (1988, 10 Kaltnadelradierungen) erscheinen in der Edition Brusberg, Westberlin.

1989

Die Internationale Buchkunstausstellung in Leipzig figura 4 verleiht ihm für sein Künstlerbuch *Wund-Denkmale. Schwebende Labung und Schauer* die Goldmedaille. Das Lindenau-Museum Altenburg widmet dem Hauptwerk eine umfassende Ausstellung.

1989

Gerhard Altenbourg stirbt am 30. Dezember 1989 an den Folgen eines Autounfalls in Meißen. Seiner Schwester hinterlässt er das zum Künstlerhaus umgestaltete Elternhaus und seinen umfangreichen künstlerischen Nachlass.

2002

Die Schwester Gerhard Altenbourgs, Anneliese Ströch, gründet die Stiftung Gerhard Altenbourg, die seit ihrem Tod 2013 vom Lindenau-Museum Altenburg betreut und aktuell im Rahmen eines Geschäftsbesorgungsvertrages verwaltet wird.

1989

He wins the gold medal for his artist's book *Wund-Denkmale. Schwebende Labung und Schauer* at figura 4, the International Book Art Exhibition in Leipzig, and the Lindenau-Museum in Altenburg holds a major exhibition on it.

1989

Gerhard Altenbourg dies on 30 December 1989 due to the consequences of a car accident in Meissen. He bequeaths his parents' home, converted into an artist's house, and his extensive artistic estate to his sister.

2002

Gerhard Altenbourg's sister, Anneliese Ströch, founds the Gerhard Altenbourg Foundation, which since her death in 2013 has been overseen, and today administered, by the Lindenau-Museum in Altenburg on the basis of a business management contract.

Verzeichnis der abgebildeten Werke

WVZ Werkverzeichnis
(...) Titel in eckigen Klammern zeigen von Annegret Janda rekonstruierte Titel an
(...) runde Klammern zeigen Übersetzungen an
Klammern innerhalb von in Anführungszeichen gesetzten Beschriftungen zeigen Auslassungen und verkürzte Angaben an

Kat. 1
Ecce homo I (Sterbender Krieger), 1949
Pitt-Kreide, Bleistift auf Rollenpapier, aus zwei Teilen zusammengeklebt, stark unregelmäßig
Blattmaß: ca. 1350 × 880 mm
Auf der Vorderseite sign., dat. und betitelt unten Mi.: »(Titel) 49 GSt«, sign. unten re.: »G. Ströch«, (über: Kinderzeichnung des Künstlers), auf der Rücks. Aufkleber mit Schreibmaschine beschrieben: »Aus dem Zyklus »Ecce homo« von Stephan Kambienna Altenburg in Thür. Braugartenweg 11 Unter(t)itel: »Sterbender Krieger«
WVZ 49/142
Lindenau-Museum Altenburg, Z 1992-12
1992 Ankauf von Astrid und Wilfried Rugo

Kat. 2
Der Gärtner, 1954
Pinsel in Wasserfarben, teilweise weiß unterlegt auf blaugrauem Ingres-Papier
Blattmaß: 630 × 485 mm
Sign., betitelt u. dat. unten Mi.: »(Titel) GSt 54«
WVZ 54/11
Leihgabe der Staatlichen Kunstsammlungen Dresden, Kupferstich-Kabinett, C 2012-51
2012 Ankauf von Heidi und Dieter Brusberg

List of Featured Works

CR Catalogue Raisonné
(...) Titles in square brackets indicate titles reconstructed by Annegret Janda
(...) Round brackets indicate translations
Brackets within text in quotation marks indicate omissions and abbreviated information

Cats. 1
Ecce homo I (Sterbender Krieger) (Ecce Homo I (Dying Warrior)), 1949
Pitt crayon, pencil on roll paper glued together from two parts, very irregular
Dimensions: ca. 1350 × 880 mm
On obverse signed, dated and titled below centre: "(Title) 49 GSt", signed below right: "G. Ströch", (over a childhood drawing by the artist), on reverse label with typewriter writing: "Aus dem Zyklus 'Ecce homo' von Stephan Kambienna Altenburg in Thür. Braugartenweg 11 Unter(t)itel: 'Sterbender Krieger'" (From the cycle "Ecce homo" by Stephan Kambienna Altenburg in Thuringia Braugartenweg 11 Subordinate title: 'Dying Warrior')
CR 49/142
Lindenau-Museum Altenburg, Z 1992-12
1992 purchased from Astrid and Wilfried Rugo

Cat. 2
Der Gärtner (The Gardener), 1954
Brush with watercolour, with partial white highlights on blue-grey Ingres paper
Dimensions: 630 × 485 mm
Signed, titled and dated below centre: "(Title) GSt 54"
CR 54/11
Loan from the Staatliche Kunstsammlungen Dresden, Kupferstich-Kabinett, C 2012-51
2012 purchased from Heidi and Dieter Brusberg

Kat. 3
GING GANZ, 1958
Chinesische Tusche, Aquarellfarben und Kreide auf handgeschöpftem Büttenpapier
Blattmaß: 606 × 169 mm
Betitelt unten li.: (Titel), monogr. u. dat. unten Mi.: »GA 1958 August«
Lindenau-Museum Altenburg, DL 2010-21
WCZ 58/11
2010 drittmittelfinanzierter Ankauf, vormals Sammlung Astrid und Wilfried Rugo

Kat. 4
Achtung!, 1955
Pinsel in Wasserfarben, Feder mit chinesischer Tusche auf Japanpapier
Blattmaß: 710 × 515 mm
Sign. u. dat. unten li.: »GSt 55«, unten re. betitelt: (Titel)
WVZ 55/9
Leihgabe der Staatlichen Kunstsammlungen Dresden, Kupferstich-Kabinett, C 2012-52
2012 Ankauf von Heidi und Dieter Brusberg

Kat. 5
Ein Kinderspiel, 1966
Lithografie durch Lichtübertragung von der Zeichnung (66/62), Druck in München
Bildmaß: 470 × 300 mm, Blattmaß: 608 × 430 mm
Unten betitelt, bez., sign. u. dat.: »(Titel) Altenbourg 1966 (Blindprägung) Archivdruck«
WVZ L 114
Einzelexemplar, Archivdruck
Stiftung Gerhard Altenbourg, SGA 72-L

Kat. 6
Verständigung der Auguren über ein Geschick, 1969
Aquarellfarben und chinesische Tusche auf WSH Watercolor-Papier, England
Blattmaß: 230 × 180 mm
Monogramm. unten Mi.: »GA«, auf der Rücks. unten Mi. betitelt, sign. u. dat.: »(Titel) Altenbourg 1969«
WVZ 69/5
Lindenau-Museum Altenburg, DL 2010-27
2010 drittmittelfinanzierter Ankauf, vormals Sammlung Astrid und Wilfried Rugo

Cat. 3
GING GANZ (WENT COMPLETELY) 1958
China ink, watercolour and chalk on mould-made laid paper
Dimensions: 606 × 169 mm
Titled below left: (Title), monogrammed and dated below centre: "GA 1958 August"
CR 58/11
Lindenau-Museum Altenburg, DL 2010-21
2010 purchased with third party funds, formerly Astrid and Wilfried Rugo Collection

Cat. 4
Achtung! (Attention!), 1955
Brush with watercolour, pen with China ink on Japan paper
Dimensions: 710 × 515 mm
Signed and dated below left: "GSt 55", titled below right: (Title)
CR 55/9
Loan from the Staatliche Kunstsammlungen Dresden, Kupferstich-Kabinett, C 2012-52
2012 purchased from Heidi and Dieter Brusberg

Cat. 5
Ein Kinderspiel (A Child's Game), 1966
Lithograph made by optical transmission from drawing (66/62), printed in Munich
Image: 470 × 300 mm, sheet: 608 × 430 mm
Titled below, annotated, signed and dated: "(Title) Altenbourg 1966 (blind stamp) Archivdruck"
CR L 114
Unique copy, archive print
Gerhard Altenbourg Foundation, SGA 72-L

Cat. 6
Verständigung der Auguren über ein Geschick (Agreement Among the Augurs About a Fate), 1969
Watercolour and China ink on WSH Watercolour Paper, England
Dimensions: 230 × 180 mm
Monogrammed below centre: "GA", on reverse titled, signed and dated below centre: "(Title) Altenbourg 1969"
CR 69/5
Lindenau-Museum Altenburg, DL 2010-27
2010 purchased with third party funds, formerly Astrid and Wilfried Rugo Collection

Kat. 7
Echse mit Blumenstrauß, der kleine Werner, Ungeheuer mit Regenschirm und Applaudierende, 1968
Holzschnitt mit schwarzer Druckfarbe und Temperagrundierung mit Aussparung des Holzschnitts und der Blindprägung auf grauem, marmoriertem Papier
Bildmaß: 87 × 210 mm, Blattmaß: 195 × 280 mm
Sign., dat. und bez. unten Mi.: »Altenbourg 68 (Blindprägung) Archiv«, auf der Rückseite betitelt: (Titel)
WVZ H 111
Archivexemplar
Stiftung Gerhard Altenbourg, SGA 5826-H

Kat. 8
Kwanon mit dem Wiesenblick, 1973
Aquarell- und Temperafarben, Rötel, weiße und schwarze Kreide, Pastell und Bleistift auf Fabriano Roma del Sarto-Büttenpapier, Rückseite kreidegrundiert
Blattmaß: 490 × 353 mm
Sign. u. re.: »Altenbourg«, auf der Rücks. unten Mi. monogramm., dat., betitelt und numm.: »(Titel) GA 73/3«
WVZ 73/3
Lindenau-Museum Altenburg, DL 2010-37
2010 drittmittelfinanzierter Ankauf, vormals Sammlung Astrid und Wilfried Rugo

Kat. 9
Einung, 1978
Geschnittenes und getriebenes Kupferblech, handwerkliche Ausführung Ulrich Schlegel
Objektmaß: 13 × 18 × 5 cm
Re. Mi. monogramm.: »GA«
WVZ 78/28
Einzelstück
Lindenau-Museum Altenburg, DL 2010-97
2010 drittmittelfinanzierter Ankauf, vormals Sammlung Astrid und Wilfried Rugo

Kat. 10
Figuren, 1983
Messingguss (Nachguss)
Objektmaß: 26,5 × 38 × 4,5 cm
Numm. auf der Rücks.: »Ex.: 1/8«
WVZ 57/18
8 Exemplare, Ausführung durch Alfred Schaller, Nr. 1/8
Lindenau-Museum Altenburg, DL 2010-94
2010 drittmittelfinanzierter Ankauf, vormals Sammlung Astrid und Wilfried Rugo

Cat. 7
Echse mit Blumenstrauß, der kleine Werner, Ungeheuer mit Regenschirm und Applaudierende (Lizard with Bouquet of Flowers, Little Werner, Monster with Umbrella and Applauding Figures), 1968
Woodcut with black printer's ink and tempera priming, excluding the woodcut and blind stamp, on grey marbled paper
Image: 87 × 210 mm, sheet: 195 × 280 mm
Signed, dated and annotated below centre: "Altenbourg 68 (blind stamp) Archiv", on reverse titled: (Title)
CR H 111
Archive print
Gerhard Altenbourg Foundation, SGA 5826-H

Cat. 8
Kwanon mit dem Wiesenblick (Kwanon with Meadow-Gaze), 1973
Watercolour and tempera, red, white and black chalk, pastel and pencil on Fabriano Roma del Sarto laid paper, reverse primed with chalk
Dimensions: 490 × 353 mm
Signed below right: "Altenbourg", on reverse monogrammed, dated, titled and numbered below centre: "(Title) GA 73/3"
CR 73/3
Lindenau-Museum Altenburg, DL 2010-37
2010 purchased with third party funds, formerly Astrid and Wilfried Rugo Collection

Cat. 9
Einung (Union), 1978
Cut and embossed copper sheet, technical execution by Ulrich Schlegel
Dimensions: 13 × 18 × 5 cm
Monogram right centre: "GA"
CR 78/28
Unique piece
Lindenau-Museum Altenburg, DL 2010-97
2010 purchased with third party funds, formerly Astrid and Wilfried Rugo Collection

Cat. 10
Figuren (Figures), 1983
Brass cast (replica cast)
Dimensions: 26.5 × 38 × 4.5 cm
Numbered on reverse: "no. 1/8"
CR 57/18
8 casts, executed by Alfred Schaller, no. 1/8
Lindenau-Museum Altenburg, DL 2010-94
2010 purchased with third party funds, formerly Astrid and Wilfried Rugo Collection

Kat. 11
nympha, 1949
Lithografie mit Lithotusche in Schwarz direkt auf den Stein gezeichnet, Druck auf Papier (Horst Arloth)
Bildmaß: 368 × 249 mm, Blattmaß: 500 × 427 mm
Unten li. betitelt: (Titel), unten re. monogramm. und dat.: »GA 49«
WVZ L 27
12 Exemplare, nicht nummeriert
Lindenau-Museum Altenburg, 13263
1958 Ankauf vom Staatlichen Kunsthandel der DDR, Berlin

Kat. 12
Johanna wendet sich lieber ihrem Kater zu, 1956
Aquarellfarben, Stabilo-Stifte und chinesische Tusche auf handgeschöpftem Büttenpapier
Blattmaß 615 × 425 mm
Betitelt, monogramm. u. dat. unten Mi.: »(Titel) GA 56«
WVZ 56/9
Lindenau-Museum Altenburg, DL 2010-14
2010 drittmittelfinanzierter Ankauf, vormals Sammlung Astrid und Wilfried Rugo

Kat. 13
Das Flötenkonzert, 1949
Rückseite/verso (*Das Flötenkonzert*): Lithografie mit Lithotusche in Schwarz auf sauber weggeschliffenem Stein (vermutlich Horst Arloth), Vorderseite/recto (*I. Füßle, Füßlein*): Lithografie mit Lithotusche in Schwarz direkt auf den Stein gezeichnet, mit der ganzen, noch nicht sauber abgeschliffenen Fläche des Steins gedruckt, Druck auf Saaleck-Abzugspost (Arno Fehringer)
Bildmaß verso: 400 × 270 mm, Bildmaß recto: 395 × 290 mm, Blattmaß: 430 × 340 mm
Recto unten betitelt, monogramm. u. dat.: »(Titel) GSt 49«, verso unten li. monogramm., dat., betitelt und numm.: »GSt 49 (Titel) 1/1«
WVZ L 12
Einzelexemplar, 1/1
Stiftung Gerhard Altenbourg, SGA 1512-L

Cat. 11
nympha, 1949
Lithograph directly drawn on stone with lithographic ink, printed on paper (Horst Arloth)
Image: 368 × 249 mm, sheet: 500 × 427 mm
Titled below left: (Title), monogrammed and dated below right: "GA 49"
CR L 27
12 prints, not numbered
Lindenau-Museum Altenburg, 13263
1958 purchased from State Art Trade of the GDR, Berlin

Cat. 12
Johanna wendet sich lieber ihrem Kater zu (Johanna Prefers to Turn to Her Cat), 1956
Watercolour, Stabilo pens and China ink on hand-moulded laid paper
Sheet: 615 × 425 mm
Titled, monogrammed and dated below centre: "(Title) GA 56"
CR 56/9
Lindenau-Museum Altenburg, DL 2010-14
2010 purchased with third party funds, formerly Astrid and Wilfried Rugo Collection

Cat. 13
Das Flötenkonzert (The Flute Concert), 1949
Reverse (*Das Flötenkonzert*): lithograph with lithographic black ink on cleanly sanded stone (presumably Horst Arloth),
Obverse (*I. Füßle, Füßlein*, (I Little Foot, Tiny Foot)): lithograph with lithographic black ink drawn directly on stone, printed together with the entire, not completely sanded surface of the stone, on paper (Arno Fehringer)
Image reverse: 400 × 270 mm, image obverse: 395 × 290 mm, sheet: 430 × 340 mm
Titled, monogrammed and dated on obverse below: "(Title) GSt 49"; monogrammed, dated, titled and numbered on reverse below: "GSt 49 (Title) 1/1"
CR L 12
Unique print, 1/1
Gerhard Altenbourg Foundation, SGA 1512-L

Kat. 14
Seltsamer Musikant, 1950
Lithografie mit Lithokreide in Schwarz direkt auf den Stein gezeichnet, Druck auf Papier (Horst Arloth)
Bildmaß: 40 × 24 mm, Blattmaß: 44 × 37,7 mm
Numm., bez. u. betitelt unten li.: »2/2 Probe (Titel)«, monogramm. u. dat. unten re.: »GA 50«, (wohl spätere) (Blindprägung), bez. o. li.: »Druckerei der Hochschule Bildende Kunst Weimar«
WVZ L 28
2. Probedruck 2/2
Lindenau-Museum Altenburg, G 1991-171
1991 Ankauf von Hans-Peter Schulz (Galerie am Sachsenplatz), Leipzig

Kat. 15
Jungfrauen platzen männertoll (Wagner), 1950
Feder und Litho-Tusche in Schwarz (Druck Horst Arloth)
Bildmaß: 341 × 168 mm; Blattmaß: 433 × 304 mm
Bez. unten li.: »3/3 Probedruck«, betitelt unten li.: »Jungfraun (sic!) platzen männertoll (Wagner)«, sign. u. dat. unten: »GSt 50«
WVZ L 35
2. Version (Zustand des 2. Steins), Probedruck, 3/3
Lindenau-Museum Altenburg, G 1997-246
1997 Schenkung aus der Sammlung Gisela und Hans-Peter Schulz

Kat. 16
Ammonon Gillitge, 1949
Schwarze Tusche auf unregelmäßig zugeschnittenem, gelblichem Karton
Blattmaß: 393 mm × 430 mm
Betitelt, dat. u. sign. unten halbre.: »(Titel) 1.4.50 GSt«
WVZ 50/19
Stiftung Gerhard Altenbourg, SGA 183-Z

Kat. 17
Sie verließen das Schiff; Chaos auf der Wanderschaft, 1949
Frottage, schwarze Tusche auf dünnem Zeichenpapier
Blattmaß: 485 × 670 mm
Sign., betitelt u. dat. unten re.:
(»Titel« und später hinzugefügt:) »Altenbourg 49«
WVZ 49/158
Stiftung Gerhard Altenbourg, SGA 142-Z

Cat. 14
Seltsamer Musikant (Strange Musician), 1950
Lithograph drawn directly on stone with lithographic black chalk, printed on paper
(Horst Arloth)
Image: 400 × 240 mm, sheet: 440 × 377 mm
Numbered, annotated and titled below left: "2/2 Probe (Title)", monogrammed and dated below right: "GA 50", (presumably later) (blind stamp), annotated above left: "Druckerei der Hochschule Bildende Kunst Weimar"
CR L 28
2nd trial proof 2/2
Lindenau-Museum Altenburg, G 1991-171
1991 acquired from Hans-Peter Schulz (Galerie am Sachsenplatz), Leipzig

Cat. 15
Jungfrauen platzen männertoll (Wagner) (Maidens Burst Man-Mad (Wagner)), 1950
Pen and lithographic black ink (printed by Horst Arloth)
Image: 341 × 168 mm; sheet: 433 × 304 mm
Annotated below left: "3/3 trial proof", titled below left: "Jungfraun [*sic*] platzen männertoll (Wagner)", signed and dated below: "GSt 50"
CR L 35
2nd version (state of second stone),
trial proof, 3/3
Lindenau-Museum Altenburg, G 1997-246
1997 gift from the collection of Gisela and Hans-Peter Schulz

Cat. 16
Ammonon Gillitge, 1949
Black India ink on irregularly cut, yellowish cardboard
Dimensions: 393 mm × 430 mm
Titled, dated and signed below mid-right: "(Title) 1.4.50 GSt"
CR 50/19
Gerhard Altenbourg Foundation, SGA 183-Z

Cat. 17
Sie verließen das Schiff; Chaos auf der Wanderschaft (They Left the Ship; Chaos on the Wanderings), 1949
Frottage, black India ink on thin tracing paper
Dimensions: 485 × 670 mm
Signed, titled and dated below right: "(Title)" and added later: "Altenbourg 49"
CR 49/158
Gerhard Altenbourg Foundation, SGA 142-Z

Kat. 18
Da sitzen sie in ihrer Frühlingsfrühe die Gedanken, 1977
Farbholzschnitt mit braun-schwarzer und hellblauer Druckfarbe auf Merian Ingres-Büttenpapier in Hellgrau
Bildmaß: 183 × 135 mm, Blattmaß: 218 × 152 mm
Unten Mi. sign. u. dat.: »Altenbourg (Blindprägung) 1977«, a. d. Rücks. monogramm., numm., bez. u. betitelt: »GA (Titel) IV/VIII Künstlerdruck«
WVZ H 196
2. Zustand, 3. Druckreihe, 8 Exemplare, Nr. 4/8
Stiftung Gerhard Altenbourg, SGA 3476-H

Kat. 19
Die Hörner, 1972
Geschmiedetes Eisen, handwerkliche Ausführung: Ulrich Schlegel
Objektmaß: 40 × 11 × 5,8 cm
Auf der Stellfläche des Sockels sign., dat. u. numm.: »Altenbourg 72 (Blindprägung) Ex. 1/4«
WVZ 72/39
4 Exemplare, 1/4
Lindenau-Museum Altenburg, DL 2010-95
2010 drittmittelfinanzierter Ankauf, vormals Sammlung Astrid und Wilfried Rugo

Kat. 20
War da, 1963
Holzschnitt mit schwarzer Druckfarbe auf Zeichenpapier
Bildmaß: 270 × 175 mm, Blattmaß: 346 mm × 230 mm
Unten li. bez. u. numm.: »1/1 Probedruck«, unten Mi. sign., dat. u. betitelt: »(Titel) (Blindprägung) Altenbourg 61«, mit Widmung für Heinrich Mock: »Mit dem Jarry-Wort »merdre« alles Gute 1962 Gerhard«
WVZ H 63
1. Zustand Probedruck 1/1
Lindenau-Museum Altenburg, G 1996-30
Schenkung von Dr. Heinrich Mock

Kat. 21
Der uralte Moby, 1961
Zinkblech, montiert auf Birkenholzplatte, MUSSINI-Ölfarbe
Objektmaß: 29,8 × 44 cm, Zinkblech: 24 × 55,5 cm
Monogramm. unten Mi.: GA, auf der Rücks. oben betitelt, dat. u. sign.: »(Titel) 1961 Altenbourg«
WVZ 61/26
Leihgabe aus Privatsammlung

Cat. 18
Da sitzen sie in ihrer Frühlingsfrühe die Gedanken (The Thoughts, They Sit There in Their Spring Morning), 1977
Colour woodcut with brown-black and light blue printer's ink on Merian Ingres laid paper in light grey
Image: 183 × 135 mm, sheet: 218 × 152 mm
Signed and dated below centre: "Altenbourg (blind stamp) 1977", on reverse monogrammed, numbered, annotated and titled: "GA (Title) IV/VIII Künstlerdruck"
CR H 196
Second state, third printing, eight prints, no. 4/8
Gerhard Altenbourg Foundation, SGA 3476-H

Cat. 19
Die Hörner (The Horns), 1972
Wrought iron, technical execution: Ulrich Schlegel
Dimensions: 40 × 11 × 5.8 cm
Signed, dated and numbered on the bottom of the pedestal: "Altenbourg 72 (blind stamp) Ex. 1/4"
CR 72/39
4 copies, 1/4
Lindenau-Museum Altenburg, DL 2010-95
2010 purchased with third party funds, formerly Astrid and Wilfried Rugo Collection

Cat. 20
War da (Was There), 1963
Woodcut with black printing ink on drawing paper
Image: 270 × 175 mm, sheet: 346 mm × 230 mm
Annotated and numbered below left: "1/1 Probedruck", signed, dated and titled below centre: "(Title) (blind stamp) Altenbourg 61", with a dedication to Heinrich Mock: "Mit dem Jarry-Wort 'merdre' alles Gute 1962 Gerhard" (With Jarry's word "merdre" best wishes 1962 Gerhard)
CR H 63
1st state, trial proof 1/1
Lindenau-Museum Altenburg, G 1996-30
Gift from Dr. Heinrich Mock

Cat. 21
Der uralte Moby (The Ancient Moby), 1961
Zinc sheet mounted on birch panel
MUSSINI oil colours
Dimensions: 29.8 × 44 cm, zinc sheet: 24 × 55.5 cm
Monogrammed below centre: "GA", titled, dated and signed on reverse above: "(Title) 1961 Altenbourg"
CR 61/26
Loan from private collection

Kat. 22
O. T. (Werkzeichnung für zehn Schrankbeschläge), 1968
Bleistift, Rotstift, Spuren von blauem Pauspapier auf Transparentpapier
Blattmaß: 715 × 375 mm
Bez. von o. nach unten: »Rückseite Lampe rechts links neg links rechts Rücke. 7 negativ«
WVZ 68/64
Stiftung Gerhard Altenbourg, SGA 4450-E

Kat. 23
Das Mirakel der Spitzafter, 1972
Bleistift, chinesische Tusche und Aquarellfarben auf Büttenpapier
Blattmaß: 690 × 440 mm
Betitelt, sign. u. dat. unten Mitte: »(Titel) Altenbourg 72«
WVZ 72/30
Lindau-Museum Altenburg, DL 2010-35
2010 drittmittelfinanzierter Ankauf, vormals Sammlung Astrid und Wilfried Rugo

Kat. 24
Verklärte Eingebung, 1974
Bleistift, Aquarell- und Temperafarben auf Fabriano Roma Michelangelo-Büttenpapier, Rückseite kreidegrundiert
Blattmaß: 218 × 155 mm
Monogramm. unten halbli.: »GA«, sign. u. betitelt auf der Vorderseite/recto unten M.: »(Titel) Altenbourg«
WVZ 74/4
Lindenau-Museum Altenburg, DL 2010-39
2010 drittmittelfinanzierter Ankauf, vormals Sammlung Astrid und Wilfried Rugo

Kat. 25
Ritter ohne Furcht, 1977
Gouachen, Aquarellfarben und Bleistift auf Richard de Bas »Papier à fleurs« in Braun
Blattmaß: 590 × 235 mm
Betitelt dreiviertelhoch re.: »(Titel)«; unten halbre. sign. u. dat.: »Altenbourg 77«
WVZ 77/10
Leihgabe aus der Sammlung Drechsel

Cat. 22
Untitled (Werkzeichnung für zehn Schrankbeschläge) (Technical Drawing for Ten Closet Fittings), 1968
Pencil, red pencil, traces of blue tracing paper on transparent paper
Dimensions: 715 × 375 mm
Annotated from top to bottom: "Rückseite Lampe rechts links neg links rechts Rücke. 7 negativ"
CR 68/64
Gerhard Altenbourg Foundation, SGA 4450-E

Cat. 23
Das Mirakel der Spitzafter (The Miracle of the Pointed Anus), 1972
Pencil, China ink and watercolour on laid paper
Dimensions: 690 × 440 mm
Titled, signed and dated below centre: "(Title) Altenbourg 72"
CR 72/30
Lindenau-Museum Altenburg, DL 2010-35
2010 purchased with third party funds, formerly Astrid and Wilfried Rugo Collection

Cat. 24
Verklärte Eingebung (Transfigured Inspiration), 1974
Pencil, watercolour and tempera on Fabriano Roma Michelangelo laid paper, primed with chalk on reverse
Dimensions: 218 × 155 mm
Monogrammed below mid-left: "GA", signed and titled on obverse below centre: "(Title) Altenbourg"
CR 74/4
Lindenau-Museum Altenburg, DL 2010-39
2010 purchased with third party funds, formerly Astrid and Wilfried Rugo Collection

Cat. 25
Ritter ohne Furcht (Fearless Knight), 1977
Gouache, watercolour and pencil on Richard de Bas "Papier à fleurs" in brown
Dimensions: 590 × 235 mm
Titled three-quarters above right: "(Title)", signed and dated below mid-right: "Altenbourg 77"
CR 77/10
Loan from the Drechsel Collection

Kat. 26
Werkzeichnung für das Relief *Ringelreih und Wonnetraum: da schlägt dein Herz im Zisternenlaub*, 1979
Bleistift, Einstiche, auf der Vorderseite/recto: Linien vom Durchpausen auf Transparentpapier
Blattmaß: 231 × 35 mm
Betitelt halbhoch li.: (Titel), dat., monogramm. u. bez. unten Mi.: »1979 GA Kupfer Handwerk Ulrich Schlegel, Zeitz Montierung: Flur im Altenbourg-Haus«
WVZ 79/43
Stiftung Gerhard Altenbourg, SGA 4493-E

Kat. 27
Ringelreih und Wonnetraum: da schlägt dein Herz im Zisternenlaub, 1979
Geschnittenes und getriebenes Kupferblech, handwerkliche Ausführung Ulrich Schlegel
Objektmaß: 22,5 × 35 × 5 cm
O. li. monogramm.: »GA«
WVZ 79/34
Ausstattungsstück aus dem Künstlerhaus von Gerhard Altenbourg
Stiftung Gerhard Altenbourg, SGA 5951-A

Kat. 28
Vogelähnliches Tongefäß, 1958
Rotbrauner Ton, innen dunkelbraun glasiert, ein wenig mit weißer Ölfarbe bemalt
Höhe: 55 cm
Sign. a. d. Unterseite des Fußes: »GA«, zudem ist eine Waage als Signet von Annemarie Hase eingeritzt
WVZ 58/41
Stiftung Gerhard Altenbourg, SGA 4888-A

Kat. 29 sowie
Abb. 1–3 im Beitrag von Marit Heuß
Salutation, 1960
Künstlerbuch aus 20 Seiten mit elf Zeichnungen in Aquarellfarben und acht handgeschriebenen Gedichten von Gerhard Altenbourg auf Specхthausen-Büttenpapier
Gesamtmaß: 230 mm × 180 mm
Bez. (in Auszügen): vor S. 1: »hâte de tenir dans mes mains la joie de tiennes René Char«, S. 3: »Salutation Gedichte und Aquarelle von Altenbourg«, S. 5: »Zärtlich ist das Blau der Stunde (…)«, S. 7: »Schlangenhaft umwunden (…)«, S. 9: »O diese Dunkelheiten (…)«, S. 11: »Heil mich Frau ja heil mich (…)«, S. 13: »Ich lebe durch das Anderssein (…)«, S. 15: »Wo sich auch das Auge breitet (…)«, S. 17: »Immerdar begraben sein (…)« , S. 19: »Einmal beschenkt und tausendmal (…)«, S. 20 bez. u. sign.: »Die Gedichte entstanden 1960 Geschrieben wurde das Buch im August 1960 Die Aquarelle entstanden

Cat. 26
Technical drawing for the relief *Ringelreih und Wonnetraum: da schlägt dein Herz im Zisternenlaub* (Circle Dance and Bliss Dream, Your Heart Beats in Cistern Leaves), 1979
Pencil, punctures on obverse: lines from tracing on transparent paper
Dimensions: 231 × 350 mm
Titled middle left: (Title), dated, monogrammed and annotated below centre: "1979 GA Kupfer Handwerk Ulrich Schlegel, Zeitz Montierung: Flur im Altenbourg-Haus"
CR 79/43
Gerhard Altenbourg Foundation, SGA 4493-E

Cat. 27
Ringelreih und Wonnetraum: da schlägt dein Herz im Zisternenlaub (Circle Dance and Bliss Dream, Your Heart Beats in Cistern Leaves), 1979
Cut and wrought copper sheet
Technical execution Ulrich Schlegel
Dimensions: 22.5 × 35 × 5 cm
Monogrammed above left: "GA"
CR 79/34
Decorative piece from Gerhard Altenbourg's house
Gerhard Altenbourg Foundation, SGA 5951-A

Cat. 28
Vogelähnliches Tongefäß (Bird-Like Clay Vessel) 1958
Red-brown clay, glazed inside in dark brown, slightly painted with white oil
Height: 55 cm
Signed on the underside of support: "GA", incised image of scales as the signet of Annemarie Hase
CR 58/41
Gerhard Altenbourg Foundation, SGA 4888-A

Cat. 29 and
figs. 1–3 in essay by Marit Heuß
Salutation, 1960
Artist's book with 20 pages and 11 drawings in watercolour and eight handwritten poems by Gerhard Altenbourg on Spechthausen laid paper
Overall dimensions: 230 mm × 180 mm
Annotated (excerpts): before p. 1: "hâte de tenir dans mes mains la joie de tiennes René Char" (can't wait to hold in my hands the joy of yours), p. 3: "Salutation Gedichte and Aquarelle von Altenbourg" (Salutation Poems and Watercolours by Altenbourg), p. 5: "Zärtlich ist das Blau der Stunde (…)" (Tender is the blue of the hour), p. 7: "Schlangenhaft umwunden (…)" (curled around snake-like), p. 9: "O diese Dunkelheiten (…)" (O these darknesses), p. 11: "Heil mich Frau ja heil mich (…)" (Heal me woman, yes heal me), p. 13: "Ich lebe durch

in der gleichen Zeit Das Buch wurde geschaffen als Huldigung für Frau Eva Schwalbe Gerhard Altenbourg«, S. 21 sign.: »Altenbourg« (Blindprägung)
WVZ 60/27
Einzelexemplar, gebunden von Werner Lorenz
Lindenau-Museum Altenburg, Dauerleihgabe der Sparkassen-Kulturstiftung Hessen-Thüringen, DL 2015-1/1-20
Vormals Sammlung Annmarie Kramer und Ingeborg Schwalbe

Kat. 30
Altenbourg Zehn Reproduktionen und zwei Originalzeichnungen, 1958/59
Künstlerbuch; 28 Seiten mit zwei Zeichnungen in Aquarellfarben und acht handgeschriebenen Gedichten von Gerhard Altenbourg auf Spechthausen-Büttenpapier, hrsg. von Galerie Springer
Gesamtmaß (Papp-Schuber): 320 × 230 mm, (Buch): 315 × 220 mm
Leineneinband mit je einem aufgeklebten Aquarell außen auf der Vorder- und Rückendecke, in einem Pappschuber, Buchbinderarbeiten von Werner Lorenz
Sign., numm. u. dat., S. 27: »26 Altenbourg 1958« (Blindprägung) gewidmet und dat.: »Für Anneliese 1959« (Gedicht) auf dem Papp-Schuber numm. u. sign.: (Blindprägung) »Altenbourg Nr. 26«
WVZ 59/3
50 nummerierte und signierte Exemplare, Exemplar Nr. 26/50
Stiftung Gerhard Altenbourg, SGA 4595-Kb

Kat. 31
Im Kopf ein pfiffiges Luder; schau, schau, 1988
Blatt 87 der *Schnepfenthaler Suite*, 1989
Kaltnadelradierung in Bordeauxrot auf Hahnemühle-Büttenpapier
Plattenmaß: 187 × 185 mm, Blattmaß: 545 × 395 mm
Unten Mi. sign., dat., monogramm., u. betitelt: (Blindprägung) »Altenbourg 1988 GA (Titel)«, bez. unten re.: »Drucker-Exemplar«
R 165
Einzelblatt, Druckerexemplar
Lindenau-Museum Altenburg, G 1997-231
1997 Ankauf aus der Sammlung Gisela und Hans-Peter Schulz

das Anderssein (...)" (I live through being other), p. 15: "Wo sich auch das Auge breitet (...)" (Where the eye can see), p. 17: "Immerdar begraben sein (...)" (Forever be buried), p. 19: "Einmal beschenkt und tausendmal (...)" (Once gifted, a thousand times), p. 20 annotated and signed: "Die Gedichte entstanden 1960 Geschrieben wurde das Buch im August 1960 Die Aquarelle entstanden in der gleichen Zeit Das Buch wurde geschaffen als Huldigung für Frau Eva Schwalbe Gerhard Altenbourg" (The poems were written in 1960, the book was written in August 1960, the watercolours were made at the same time, the book was made as a homage to Ms. Eva Schwalbe, Gerhard Altenbourg), p. 21 signed: "Altenbourg" (blind stamp)
CR 60/27
Unique copy, binding Werner Lorenz
Lindenau-Museum Altenburg, permanent loan from the Sparkassen-Kulturstiftung Hessen-Thüringen, DL 2015-1/1-20
Formerly in the collection of Annmarie Kramer and Ingeborg Schwalbe

Cat. 30
Altenbourg Zehn Reproduktionen und zwei Originalzeichnungen (Altenbourg Ten Reproductions and Two Original Drawings) 1958–59
Artist's book; 28 pages with two drawings in watercolour and eight handwritten poems by Gerhard Altenbourg on Spechthausen laid paper, published by Galerie Springer
Overall dimensions (cardboard slipcase): 320 × 230 mm, (book): 315 × 220 mm
Cloth binding with a watercolour glued to the outside front cover and one to the back cover, in a cardboard slipcase, binding by Werner Lorenz
Signed, numbered and dated, p. 27: "26 Altenbourg 1958" (blind stamp) dedicated and dated: "Für Anneliese 1959" (poem) numbered and signed on the cardboard slipcase: (blind stamp) "Altenbourg no. 26"
CR 59/3
50 numbered and signed copies, copy no. 26/50
Gerhard Altenbourg Foundation, SGA 4595-Kb

Kat. 32
Janus und die Kinder der Zeit, 1955
Tempera- und Aquarellfarben auf grauem Italienisch-Ingres-Papier
Blattmaß: 484 × 625 mm
Betitelt unten M.: (Titel), monogramm. u. dat. unten re.: »GA 55«
WVZ 55/74
Lindenau-Museum Altenburg, Z 16666
1956 Ankauf direkt vom Künstler

Kat. 33
Spiel auf zweierlei Ebenen, 1956
Aquarellfarben, chinesische Tusche, Rötel, blaue Tinte und Kreide auf rosafarbenem Ingres-Papier
Blattmaß: 485 × 625 mm
Monogramm. u. dat. unten li.: »GSt 55«, betitelt unten re.: (Titel)
WVZ 56/14
Leihgabe der Staatlichen Kunstsammlungen Dresden, Kupferstich-Kabinett, C 2012-53
2012 Ankauf von Heidi und Dieter Brusberg

Kat. 34
Variatio delectat, 1968
Aquarell- und Temperafarben, Ölfarben und Kreide auf Hahnemühle-Büttenpapier, Rückseite kreidegrundiert
Blattmaß: 606 × 500 mm
Betitelt unten li.: (Titel), unten rechts: »Altenbourg 68«
WVZ 67/1
Leihgabe aus der Sammlung Drechsel

Kat. 35
Der Bunker, 1956
Kreide, Rötel, chinesische Tusche und Aquarellfarben auf Büttenpapier
Blattmaß: 420 × 595 mm
Betitelt unten li.: (Titel), monogramm. u. dat. unten re.: »GA 56 Jan.«
WVZ 56/2
Lindenau-Museum Altenburg, Z 2015-54
1996 Schenkung von Suse und Werner Pfäffle

Kat. 36
Kraule Emmachen, Emmachen Kraule, 1967
Chinesische Tusche, Rötel, Pastellkreiden, Aquarellfarben und Bleistift auf Hahnemühle-Büttenpapier
Blattmaß: 685 mm × 554 mm
Sign., dat. und betitelt unten halbre.: »(Titel) Altenbourg 1967«
WVZ 67/10
Lindenau-Museum Altenburg, Z 2015-62
1996 Schenkung von Suse und Werner Pfäffle

Cat. 31
Im Kopf ein pfiffiges Luder; schau, schau (In the Head a Clever Hussy; Look, Look), 1988
Sheet 87 from *Schnepfenthaler Suite*, 1989
Drypoint etching in Bordeaux-red on Hahnemühle laid paper
Plate dimensions: 187 × 185 mm, sheet: 545 × 395 mm
Signed, dated, monogrammed and titled below centre: (blind stamp) "Altenbourg 1988 GA (Title)", annotated below right: "Drucker-Exemplar"
CR R 165
Single sheet, printer's proof
Lindenau-Museum Altenburg, G 1997-231
1997 purchased from the collection of Gisela and Hans-Peter Schulz

Cat. 32
Janus und die Kinder der Zeit (Janus and the Children of Time), 1955
Tempera and watercolour on grey Italian Ingres paper
Dimensions: 484 × 625 mm
Titled below centre: (Title), monogrammed and dated below right: "GA 55"
CR 55/74
Lindenau-Museum Altenburg, Z 16666
1956 purchased directly from artist

Cat. 33
Spiel auf zweierlei Ebenen (Game on Two Levels), 1956
Watercolour, China ink, red pencil, blue ink and chalk on pink Ingres paper
Sheet: 485 × 625 mm
Monogrammed and dated below left: "GSt 55", titled below right: (Title)
CR 56/14
Loan from the Staatliche Kunstsammlungen Dresden, Kupferstich-Kabinett, C 2012-53
2012 purchased from Heidi and Dieter Brusberg

Cat. 34
Variatio delectat, 1968
Watercolour and tempera, oil and chalk on Hahnemühle laid paper, reverse primed with chalk
Sheet: 606 × 500 mm
Titled below left: (Title), below right: "Altenbourg 68"
CR 67/1
Loan from the Drechsel Collection

Kat. 37
Hinüber und Herüber, 1958
Chinesische Tusche, Rötel, Bleistift auf Büttenpapier
Blattmaß: 780 × 606 mm
Betitelt, sign. u. dat.: »(Titel) GA 58«
WVZ 58/22
Lindenau-Museum Altenburg, Z 2015-57
1996 Schenkung von Suse und Werner Pfäffle

Kat. 38
in Honigmondtracht, 1970
Aquarell- Temperafarben und Bleistift auf Büttenpapier
Blattmaß: 270 × 650 mm
Unten Mi. monogramm.: »GA«, auf der Rücks. betitelt, sign. u. dat.: »(Titel) Altenbourg 1970«
WVZ 70/15
Lindenau-Museum Altenburg, DL 2010-31
2010 drittmittelfinanzierter Ankauf, vormals Sammlung Astrid und Wilfried Rugo

Kat. 39
Wenn der janusköpfige nachtbeheimatete Vogel in den wahnwitzigen Mittag gleitet in das Waldnest unter den Tälerschwingen, in Leidensglück, getigert und fessellos, 1980
Seite 75 aus: *Gerhard Altenbourg. Wund-Denkmale. Schwebende Labung und Schauer*, 1980, hrsg. Galerie Brusberg, Hannover 1982 (Edition Brusberg)
Farbholzschnitt in Rotbraun und Grün
Künstlerbuch *Gerhard Altenbourg Wund-Denkmale. Schwebende Labung und Schauer*. 126 Seiten mit Texten, 28 Farbholzschnitten und einer beigelegten Originalarbeit, lose in eine Kassette eingelegt als gefaltete Doppelblätter, darauf Farbholzschnitte und farbig gedruckte Gedichte, Texte und Titelzeiten von Gerhard Altenbourg, die Kassette mit je einem Holzschnitt auf Vorder- und Rückendeckel, handwerkliche Ausführung und Druck der Holzschnitte durch Tobias Lorenz
Plattenmaß: 205 × 262 mm, Blattmaß: 315 × 330 mm
WVZ Künstlerbuch: 82/92, Holzschnitt: H 248, VI. Zustand, 50 nummerierte und signierte Exemplare, Exemplar Nr. 2/50
Lindenau-Museum Altenburg, DL 2010-106/75
2010 drittmittelfinanzierter Ankauf, vormals Sammlung Astrid und Wilfried Rugo

Cat. 35
Der Bunker (The Bunker), 1956
Chalk, red pencil, China ink and watercolour on laid paper
Sheet: 420 × 595 mm
Titled below left: (Title), monogrammed and dated below right: "GA 56 Jan."
CR 56/2
Lindenau-Museum Altenburg, Z 2015-54
1996 gift from Suse and Werner Pfäffle

Cat. 36
Kraule Emmachen, Emmachen Kraule (Crawl Emmachen, Emmachen Crawl) 1967
China ink, red pencil, pastels, watercolour and pencil on Hahnemühle laid paper
Sheet: 685 mm × 554 mm
Signed, dated and titled below mid-right: "(Title) Altenbourg 1967"
CR 67/10
Lindenau-Museum Altenburg, Z 2015-62
1996 gift from Suse and Werner Pfäffle

Cat. 37
Hinüber und Herüber (Back and Forth), 1958
China ink, red pencil, pencil on laid paper
Sheet: 780 × 606 mm
Titled, signed, and dated: "(Title) GA 58"
CR 58/22
Lindenau-Museum Altenburg, Z 2015-57
1996 gift from Suse and Werner Pfäffle

Cat. 38
in Honigmondtracht (In Honeyed Moon Costume), 1970
Watercolour, tempera and pencil on laid paper
Sheet: 270 × 650 mm
Monogrammed below centre: "GA", titled, signed and dated on reverse: "(Title) Altenbourg 1970"
CR 70/15
Lindenau-Museum Altenburg, DL 2010-31
2010 purchased with third party funds from the collection of Astrid and Wilfried Rugo

Kat. 40
Flügel der Morgenröte, 1981
Aquarellfarben, chinesische Tusche, Pitt- und Lithokreide auf gelblichem Velinpapier
Rückseite Titanweiß und Gouache
Blattmaß: 610 × 265 mm
Sign. u. dat. unten halbli.: »Altenbourg 1981«, betitelt unten re.: (Titel)
WVZ 81/33
Lindenau-Museum Altenburg, DL 2010-50
2010 drittmittelfinanzierter Ankauf, vormals Sammlung Astrid und Wilfried Rugo

Kat. 41
Auch ein Mikrophon, 1973
Aquarell- und Temperafarben, chinesische Tusche, Bleistift, Lithokreide und Rötel auf schwach grünem Japanpapier
Blattmaß: 722 × 500 mm
Unten li. betitelt: (Titel), sign. u. dat. unten Mi.: »Altenbourg 73«
WVZ 73/33
Lindenau-Museum Altenburg, Z 2015-64
1996 Schenkung von Suse und Werner Pfäffle

Kat. 42
Huldigung für Quirinius Kuhlmann, 1963
Aquarell- und Druckfarben und chinesische Tusche auf Schoellershammer-Büttenkarton
Blattmaß: 520 × 373 mm
Unten halbre. monogramm. u. dat.: GA 63, auf der Rückseite sign. u. betitelt: »Huldigung für Quirinus Kuhlmann Altenbourg«
WVZ 63/13
Lindenau-Museum Altenburg, Z 2015-59
1996 Schenkung von Suse und Werner Pfäffle

Kat. 43
Der Zeiten Wind, der Tage Raunen, 1984
Bleistift, Sibirische Reißkohle, Rötel, Aquarellfarben, Litho-, Pastell- und Pitt-Kreide, Sepia und chinesische Tusche auf Fabriano Roma Michelangelo-Büttenpapier
Blattmaß: 675 × 485 mm
Dat. unten li.: »1984«(Blindprägung), betitelt unten halbli.: (Titel), auf der Rückseite sign. u. monogramm. unten Mi. um Werkverzeichnisnummer ergänzt: »Altenbourg GA 84/55«
WVZ 84/55
Lindenau-Museum Altenburg, Z 2015-66
1996 Schenkung von Suse und Werner Pfäffle

Cat. 39
Wenn der januskӧpfige nachtbeheimatete Vogel in den wahnwitzigen Mittag gleitet in das Waldnest unter den Tälerschwingen, in Leidensglück, getigert und fessellos
(When the Two-Faced Nocturnal Bird Glides into the Mad Midday in the Forest Nest Beneath the Valley-Wings, in Blissful Suffering, Striped and Unbound), 1980
page 75 from: *Gerhard Altenbourg. Wund-Denkmale. Schwebende Labung und Schauer* (Wound-Monument. Floating Sustenance and Shiver) 1980, published by Galerie Brusberg, Hanover, 1982 (Edition Brusberg)
Colour woodcut in red-brown and green
Artist's book *Gerhard Altenbourg Wund-Denkmale. Schwebende Labung and Schauer.* 126 pages with texts, 28 colour woodcuts and an enclosed original work, separately placed in slipcase as folded double leaf, on it colour woodcut and poems printed in colour, texts and title pages by Gerhard Altenbourg, slipcase with a woodcut on front cover and one on back cover, Technical execution and printing of woodcuts by Tobias Lorenz
Plate dimensions: 205 × 262 mm, sheet dimensions: 315 × 330 mm
CR artist's book: 82/92, woodcut: H 248, 6th state, 50 numbered and signed prints, copy no. 2/50
Lindenau-Museum Altenburg, DL 2010-106/75
2010 purchased with third party funds, formerly Astrid and Wilfried Rugo Collection

Cat. 40
Flügel der Morgenröte (Wings of Dawn), 1981
Watercolour, China ink, Pitt crayon and lithographic pencil on yellowish vellum paper
Reverse titanium white and gouache
Dimensions: 610 × 265 mm
Signed and dated below mid-left: "Altenbourg 1981", titled below right: (Title)
CR 81/33
Lindenau-Museum Altenburg, DL 2010-50
2010 purchased with third party funds, formerly Astrid and Wilfried Rugo Collection

Cat. 41
Auch ein Mikrophon (Also a Microphone) 1973
Watercolour and tempera, China ink, pencil, lithographic pencil and red pencil on light green Japan paper
Dimensions: 722 × 500 mm
Titled below left: (Title), signed and dated below centre: "Altenbourg 73"
CR 73/33
Lindenau-Museum Altenburg, Z 2015-64
1996 gift from Suse and Werner Pfäffle

Kat. 44
Dem geheimen Flug entgegen, 1978
Graphit, chinesische Tusche, Aquarellfarben, Bleistift, Pitt-, Litho- und Wachsmalkreide auf Richard de Bas-Handbüttenpapier
Blattmaß: 780 × 570 mm
Betitelt, sign., u. dat. unten li.: »(Titel) Altenbourg 1978«, monogramm. unten halbre.: »GA« (Blindprägung)
WVZ 78/21
Lindenau-Museum Altenburg, DL 2010-45
2010 drittmittelfinanzierter Ankauf, vormals Sammlung Astrid und Wilfried Rugo

Kat. 45
Sunem, 1984
Aquarellfarben, chinesische Tusche, Litho- und Pitt-Kreide und Rötel auf Fabriano Roma Michelangelo-Büttenpapier
Blattmaß: 485 × 670 mm
Sign. unten li.: »Altenbourg«, unten Mi.: (Blindprägung), betitelt, dat. u. monogramm. unten halbre.: »(Titel) 1984 GA«
WVZ 84/105
Lindenau-Museum Altenburg, Z 2015-67
1996 Schenkung von Suse und Werner Pfäffle

Kat. 46
Knurrbarts brüchiges Schweigen im Wind, 1989
Chinesische Tusche, Aquarellfarben, Bleistift, Pastell-, Pitt- und Lithokreide, Sepia, Rötel, sibirische Reißkohle auf handgeschöpftem Büttenpapier
Blattmaß: 420 × 603 mm
Sign. unten Mi.: »GA Altenbourg« (Blindprägung), dat. unten re.: »1989«, auf der Rückseite unten Mi. betitelt, sign., dat. u. um Werkverzeichnisnummer ergänzt: »(Titel) GA Altenbourg 1989 89/24«
WVZ 89/24
Leihgabe aus Privatsammlung

Kat. 47
O. T. (Wie ägyptische Gottheiten bekrönt), undatiert
Aquarellfarben, Pulverfarbe und Pitt-Kreide auf Büttenpapier
Blattmaß: 334 × 460 mm
Unbez., unbet., unsign., unten Mi. (Blindprägung)
WVZ 90/N 343
Lindenau-Museum Altenburg, DL 2010-84
2010 drittmittelfinanzierter Ankauf, vormals Sammlung Astrid und Wilfried Rugo

Cat. 42
Huldigung für Quirinius Kuhlmann (Homage for Quirinius Kuhlmann), 1963
Watercolour, printing ink and China ink on Schoellershammer handmade paperboard
Dimensions: 520 × 373 mm
Monogrammed and dated below mid-right: "GA 63", signed and titled on reverse: "Huldigung für Quirinus Kuhlmann Altenbourg" (Homage for Quirinus Kuhlmann Altenbourg)
CR 63/13
Lindenau-Museum Altenburg, Z 2015-59
1996 gift from Suse and Werner Pfäffle

Cat. 43
Der Zeiten Wind, der Tage Raunen (The Wind of the Times, the Murmuring of the Days), 1984
Pencil, Siberian pressed charcoal, red pencil, watercolour, lithographic pencil, pastel and Pitt crayons, sepia and China ink on Fabriano Roma Michelangelo laid paper
Dimensions: 675 × 485 mm
Dated below left: "1984" (blind stamp), titled below mid-left: (Title), on reverse signed and monogrammed below centre, with catalogue raisonné number: "Altenbourg GA 84/55"
CR 84/55
Lindenau-Museum Altenburg, Z 2015-66
1996 gift from Suse and Werner Pfäffle

Cat. 44
Dem geheimen Flug entgegen (Towards the Secret Flight), 1978
Graphite, China ink, watercolour, pencil, Pitt, lithographic and wax crayons on Richard de Bas handmade laid paper
Dimensions: 780 × 570 mm
Titled, signed, and dated below left: "(Title) Altenbourg 1978", monogrammed below mid-right: "GA" (blind stamp)
CR 78/21
Lindenau-Museum Altenburg, DL 2010-45
2010 purchased with third party funds, formerly Astrid and Wilfried Rugo Collection

Kat. 48
O. T. (Zwei alte Schachteln), undatiert
Aquarellfarben und chinesische Tusche auf handgeschöpftem Büttenpapier
Blattmaß: 330 mm × 460 mm
Sign. unten li.: »Altenbourg« (Blindprägung)
WVZ 90/N 342
Lindenau-Museum Altenburg, DL 2010-83
2010 drittmittelfinanzierter Ankauf, vormals Sammlung Astrid und Wilfried Rugo, Düsseldorf

Kat. 49
O. T. (Zwei verbunden durch die kleine Eva), undatiert
Chinesische Tusche und Pitt-Kreide auf Maschinenbütten
Blattmaß: 637 × 732 mm
Bez.: unten Mi.: (Blindprägung)
WVZ 90/N 514
Stiftung Gerhard Altenbourg, SGA 365-N

Kat. 50
O. T. (Luftgeist, lächelnd), 1984
Pinselabstreifungen mit Tempera- und Aquarellfarben und Bleistift auf vergilbtem Zeichenkarton
Blattmaß: 221 × 208 mm
Unten li. monogrammiert: »GA« (Blindprägung), unten re. sign. u. dat.: »Altenbourg 1984«
WVZ 84/115
Stiftung Gerhard Altenbourg, SGA 225-Z

Kat. 51
O. T. (Flirt mit dem Steckenpferd), undatiert
Aquarellfarben, Gouache und chinesische Tusche auf Zeichenkarton
Blattmaß: 298 × 211 mm
Bez.: unten Mi.: (Blindprägung)
WVZ 90/N 298
Stiftung Gerhard Altenbourg, SGA 446-N

Kat. 52
Krebse schmecken gut, 1985
Pinselabstreifungen mit Tempera- und Aquarellfarben, Graphit- und Bleistift auf vergilbtem Zeichenkarton
Blattmaß: 213 × 298 mm
Betitelt o. Mi.: (Titel), dat. unten li.: »1985 (Blindprägung)«, monogramm. unten Mi.: »GA«, sign. unten re.: »Altenbourg«
WVZ 85/60
Stiftung Gerhard Altenbourg, SGA 312-Z

Cat. 45
Sunem, 1984
Watercolour, China ink, lithographic and Pitt crayon and red pencil on Fabriano Roma Michelangelo laid paper
Dimensions: 485 × 670 mm
Signed below left: "Altenbourg", below centre: (blind stamp), titled, dated and monogrammed below mid-right: "(Title) 1984 GA"
CR 84/105
Lindenau-Museum Altenburg, Z 2015-67
1996 gift from Suse and Werner Pfäffle

Cat. 46
Knurrbarts brüchiges Schweigen im Wind (Knurrbart's Fragile Silence in the Wind), 1989
China ink, watercolour, pencil, pastel, Pitt and lithographic crayons, sepia, red pencil and Siberian pressed charcoal on handmade laid paper
Dimensions: 420 × 603 mm
Signed below centre: "GA Altenbourg" (blind stamp), dated below right: "1989", titled, signed, dated and catalogue raisonné number added on reverse below centre: "(Title) GA Altenbourg 1989 89/24"
CR 89/24
Loan from private collection

Cat. 47
Untitled (Wie ägyptische Gottheiten bekrönt) (Crowned Like Egyptian Gods), no date
Watercolour, powder paint and Pitt crayon on laid paper
Dimensions: 334 × 460 mm
Not annotated, titled or signed, below centre: (blind stamp)
CR 90/N 343
Lindenau-Museum Altenburg, DL 2010-84
2010 purchased with third party funds, formerly Astrid and Wilfried Rugo Collection

Cat. 48
Untitled (Zwei alte Schachteln) (Two Old Biddies), no date
Watercolour and China ink on mould-made laid paper
Dimensions: 330 mm × 460 mm
Signed below left: "Altenbourg" (blind stamp)
CR 90/N 342
Lindenau-Museum Altenburg, DL 2010-83
2010 purchased with third party funds from the collection of Astrid and Wilfried Rugo, Düsseldorf

Kat. 53
Turbulentes Künstlerfest, 1955
Kreide und Aquarellfarben auf horizontal gefaltetem Papier
Blattmaß: 415 × 315 mm
Monogramm. u. dat. unten li.: »GA 55 Juli/August«, unten re. betitelt: (Titel)
WVZ 55/35
Lindenau-Museum Altenburg, Z 2015-52
1996 Schenkung von Suse und Werner Pfäffle

Kat. 54
Tiefsee-Jahrmarkt, 1948
Fett- und Pastellkreide und Stabilo-Stifte auf altem Kupferdruckpapier
Blattmaß: 1140 × 745 mm
Betitelt unten li.: (Titel), monogramm. u. dat. unten re.: »48 GSt«
WVZ 48/93
Lindenau-Museum Altenburg, DL 2010-3
2010 drittmittelfinanzierter Ankauf, vormals Sammlung Astrid und Wilfried Rugo

Kat. 55
Wunderliche Zusammenziehung, 1950
Schwarze Tusche auf Papier
Blattmaß: 390 × 345 mm
Sign. unten li.: »Altenbourg«, betitelt unten halbli., dat. unten halbre.: »26.7.50«, unten re. später monogramm. u. dat.: »GA 50«
WVZ 50/75
Lindenau-Museum Altenburg, DL 2010-9
2010 drittmittelfinanzierter Ankauf, vormals Sammlung Astrid und Wilfried Rugo

Kat. 56
Mekönkchen, 1969
Farbholzschnitt mit roter schwarzer, grüner, orangener Druckfarbe auf Spechthausen-Büttenpapier
Bildmaß: 440 × 340 mm, Blattmaß: 480 × 350 mm
Unterhalb betitelt, bez., sign. und dat.: »(Titel) Altenbourg 1969 (Blindprägung) Archiv«
WVZ H 131
Komposition aus zwei Drucken der beiden äußeren Holzstöcke, Archivexemplar
Stiftung Gerhard Altenbourg, SGA 2779-H

Cat. 49
Untitled (Zwei verbunden durch die kleine Eva) (Two Linked by Little Eve), no date
China ink and Pitt crayon on manufactured laid paper
Dimensions: 637 × 732 mm
Annotated below centre: (blind stamp)
CR 90/N 514
Gerhard Altenbourg Foundation, SGA 365-N

Cat. 50
Untitled (Luftgeist, lächelnd) (Airy Spirit, Smiling), 1984
Brush wipings of tempera and watercolour and pencil on yellowish drawing board
Dimensions: 221 × 208 mm
Monogrammed below left: "GA" (blind stamp), signed and dated below right: "Altenbourg 1984"
CR 84/115
Gerhard Altenbourg Foundation, SGA 225-Z

Cat. 51
Untitled (Flirt mit dem Steckenpferd) (Flirt with the Hobby Horse), no date
Watercolour, gouache and China ink on drawing board
Dimensions: 298 × 211 mm
Annotated below centre: (blind stamp)
CR 90/N 298
Gerhard Altenbourg Foundation, SGA 446-N

Cat. 52
Krebse schmecken gut (Crabs Taste Good), 1985
Brush wipings with tempera and watercolour, graphite and pencil on yellowed drawing board
Dimensions: 213 × 298 mm
Titled above centre: (Title), dated below left: "1985" (blind stamp), monogrammed below centre: "GA", signed below right: "Altenbourg"
CR 85/60
Gerhard Altenbourg Foundation, SGA 312-Z

Cat. 53
Turbulentes Künstlerfest (Turbulent Artists' Party), 1955
Chalk and watercolour on horizontally folded paper
Dimensions: 415 × 315 mm
Monogrammed and dated below left: "GA 55 Juli/August", titled below right: (Title)
CR 55/35
Lindenau-Museum Altenburg, Z 2015-52
1996 gift from Suse and Werner Pfäffle

Kat. 57
Glossen um eine Figur, die ich das gesichtlose Mekönkchen nenne, 1969
Farbholzschnitt mit roter schwarzer, grüner, gelbgrüner, orangener Druckfarbe auf Spechthausen-Büttenpapier
Bildmaß: 438 × 336 mm, Blattmaß: 481 × 352 mm
Unterhalb betitelt, sign., dat., beschr. u. numm.: »(Titel) Altenbourg 1969 (Blindprägung) 17/50«
WVZ H 131
5. Komposition, 50 Exemplare, Exemplar Nr. 17/50
Lindenau-Museum Altenburg, G 1997-184
1997 Ankauf aus der Sammlung Gisela und Hans-Peter Schulz

Kat. 58
Formvariationen, 1951
Schwarze Tusche auf Zeichenpapier
Blattmaß: 281 mm × 368 mm
Betitelt, sign. und dat. unten li.: »(Titel) GSt 51«
WVZ 51/12
Stiftung Gerhard Altenbourg, SGA 161-Z

Kat. 59
O. T. (Das groteske Schattenbild), undatiert
Ölfarbe und weiße Kreide auf einem Druckbogen mit Fehldrucken Altenburger Spielkarten
Blattmaß: 730 × 720 mm
Bez. u. bedruckt von anderer Hand: »Aufl. 977a Kärtchen (unlesbar) 19.000 Be M 12-15 Lippold März 1960«
WVZ 90/N 331
Stiftung Gerhard Altenbourg, SGA 369-N

Kat. 60
Gierig witternd die Trauben, 1973
Farbholzschnitt mit roter und fleckiger schwarzer Druckfarbe auf Spechthausen-Büttenpapier
Bildmaß: 340 × 240 mm, Blattmaß: 600 × 420 mm
Betitelt, bez., sign., dat. u. numm.: »(Titel) (Blindprägung) Altenbourg 1973 6/6d«
WVZ H 170
8 Versionen vom Druck des 2. Druckstocks für *Ariadne*, diese aus einer Folge von sechs nummerierten Exemplaren mit den Druckfarben Rot und fleckiges Schwarz, 6/6d
Stiftung Gerhard Altenbourg, SGA 4366-H

Cat. 54
Tiefsee-Jahrmarkt (Deep Sea Fair), 1948
Grease and pastel crayons and Stabilo pens on old copper engraving paper
Dimensions: 1140 × 745 mm
Titled below left: (Title), monogrammed and dated below right: "48 GSt"
CR 48/93
Lindenau-Museum Altenburg, DL 2010-3
2010 purchased with third party funds, formerly Astrid and Wilfried Rugo Collection

Cat. 55
Wunderliche Zusammenziehung (Miraculous Contraction), 1950
Black ink on paper
Dimensions: 390 × 345 mm
Signed below left: "Altenbourg", titled below mid-left, (Title), dated below mid-right: "26.7.50", later monogrammed and dated below right: "GA 50"
CR 50/75
Lindenau-Museum Altenburg, DL 2010-9
2010 purchased with third party funds, formerly Astrid and Wilfried Rugo Collection

Cat. 56
Mekönkchen, 1969
Colour woodcut with red, black, green and orange printing ink on Spechthausen laid paper
Image: 440 × 340 mm, sheet: 480 × 350 mm
Titled, annotated, signed and dated below: "(Title) Altenbourg 1969 (blind stamp) Archiv"
CR H 131, composition made from two prints from both of the outer woodblocks, archive print
Gerhard Altenbourg Foundation, SGA 2779-H

Cat. 57
Glossen um eine Figur, die ich das gesichtlose Mekönkchen nenne (Glosses on a Figure I Call the Faceless Mekönkchen), 1969
Colour woodcut with red, black, green, yellow-orange and orange printing ink on Spechthausen laid paper
Image: 438 × 336 mm, sheet: 481 × 352 mm
Titled, signed, dated, annotated and numbered below: "(Title) Altenbourg 1969 (blind stamp) 17/50"
CR H 131
5th composition, 50 prints, copy no. 17/50
Lindenau-Museum Altenburg, G 1997-184
1997 purchased from the collection of Gisela and Hans-Peter Schulz

Kat. 61
Ariadne, 1973
Farbholzschnitt mit Druckfarben in Schwarz, Rot, Gelb, Blau und Grün auf Papier d'Arches
Bildmaß: 437 mm × 687 mm, Blattmaß: 565 × 760 mm
Unten li. betitelt, bez. u. numm.: »20/20 Farbandruck Ariadne«, unten Mitte sign. u. dat.: »Altenbourg« (Blindprägung), dat. unten re.: »1973«
WVZ H 170
13. Version, 20 Exemplare gedruckt von Werner und Tobias Lorenz, Nr. 20/20
Lindenau-Museum Altenburg, G 1992-105
1992 Ankauf von der Galerie am Sachsenplatz, Leipzig

Kat. 62
Portrait Prof. Klemm, 1956
Aquarell- und Temperafarben auf Japanpapier, Kreide grundiert
Blattmaß: 715 × 510 mm
Betitelt, monogramm. und dat. unten re.: »(Titel) GA 56«
WVZ 56/76
Stiftung Gerhard Altenbourg, SGA 68-Z

Kat. 63
O. T. (Roter Kopf), undatiert
Aquarellfarben, chinesische Tusche und Bleistift auf Zeichenkarton
Blattmaß: 298 × 213 mm
Bez.: unten li.: (Blindprägung)
WVZ 90/N 506
Stiftung Gerhard Altenbourg, SGA 497-N

Kat. 64
O. T. (Das Damenbildnis mit dem grünen Häubchen), undatiert
Bleistift, Aquarellfarben und Gouache auf oval zugeschnittenem Büttenpapier
Blattmaß: 233 × 170 mm
Unbez., undat., unsign.
WVZ 90/N 279
Lindenau-Museum Altenburg, DL 2010-82
2010 drittmittelfinanzierter Ankauf, vormals Sammlung Astrid und Wilfried Rugo

Kat. 65
Der Angler, 1949
Pastellkreide auf schwarzem Karton
Blattmaß: 215 × 286 mm
Betitelt unten li., sign. u. dat. unten re.: »GSt 49«
WVZ 49/168
Stiftung Gerhard Altenbourg, SGA 146-Z

Cat. 58
Formvariationen (Form Variations), 1951
Black ink on drawing paper
Dimensions: 281 mm × 368 mm
Titled, signed and dated below left: "(Title) GSt 51"
CR 51/12
Gerhard Altenbourg Foundation, SGA 161-Z

Cat. 59
Untitled (Das groteske Schattenbild) (The Grotesque Shadow Picture), no date
Oil and white chalk on printing sheet with misprints of Altenburg playing cards
Dimensions: 730 × 720 mm
Annotated and printed in another hand: "Aufl. 977a Kärtchen (unlesbar) 19.000 Be M 12-15 Lippold März 1960" (Edition 977a small cards (illegible) 19.000 Be M 12-15 Lippold March 1960)
CR 90/N 331
Gerhard Altenbourg Foundation, SGA 369-N

Cat. 60
Gierig witternd die Trauben (Greedily Smelling the Grapes), 1973
Colour woodcut with red and blotchy black printing ink on Spechthausen laid paper
Image: 340 × 240 mm, sheet: 600 × 420 mm
Titled, annotated, signed, dated and numbered: "(Title) (blind stamp) Altenbourg 1973 6/6d"
CR H 170
8 versions of print of the second woodblock for *Ariadne*, this from a succession of 6 numbered prints with red and blotchy black printing ink, 6/6d
Gerhard Altenbourg Foundation, SGA 4366-H

Cat. 61
Ariadne, 1973
Colour woodcut with printing ink in black, red, yellow, blue and green on Arches paper
Image: 437 mm × 687 mm, sheet: 565 × 760 mm
Titled, annotated and numbered below left: "20/20 Farbandruck Ariadne", signed and dated below centre: "Altenbourg" (blind stamp), dated below right: "1973"
CR H 170
13th version, 20 copies printed by Werner and Tobias Lorenz, no. 20/20
Lindenau-Museum Altenburg, G 1992-105
1992 purchased from the Galerie am Sachsenplatz, Leipzig

Kat. 66
O. T. (Aufmarsch der vier Großkopfigen), undatiert
Gewalzte Bahnen von Druckfarben, Pitt-Kreide und Bleistift auf gelblichem Velinpapier
Blattmaß: 328 × 267 mm
Bez.: unten re.: (Blindprägung)
WVZ 90/N 384
Lindenau-Museum Altenburg, DL 2010-88
2010 drittmittelfinanzierter Ankauf, vormals Sammlung Astrid und Wilfried Rugo

Kat. 67
O. T. (Rötel und Bläuchen im Rosenhag), undatiert
Tempera-, Aquarellfarben und Lithokreide auf Richard de Bas-Handbüttenpapier
Blattmaß: 783 × 575 mm
Bez.: unten li.: (Blindprägung)
WVZ 90/N 104
Stiftung Gerhard Altenbourg, SGA 361-N

Kat. 68
O. T. (Einsam im Gestöber), undatiert
Graphitstift, Pinselabstreifungen mit Aquarellfarben, auf vergilbtem Zeichenkarton
Blattmaß: 212 × 300 mm
Bez.: unten li.: (Blindprägung)
WVZ 90/N 562
Stiftung Gerhard Altenbourg, SGA 394-N

Kat. 69
O. T. (Nachdenken über das Rinnen der Zeit), undatiert
Bleistift und Aquarellfarben auf vergilbtem Zeichenkarton
Blattmaß: 301 × 210 mm
Unten re.: (Blindprägung), bez. o. re.: »1) graubraune Papiere für (daneben Skizze) Pergament+Leinwand 3 × 3) Tempera einpinseln«, bez. a. li. Blattrand: »Altenbourg Rinnen«
WVZ 90/N 519
Stiftung Gerhard Altenbourg, SGA 505-N

Cat. 62
Portrait Prof. Klemm (Portrait of Prof. Klemm), 1956
Watercolour and tempera on Japan paper, primed with chalk
Dimensions: 715 × 510 mm
Titled, monogrammed and dated below right: "(Title) GA 56"
CR 56/76
Gerhard Altenbourg Foundation, SGA 68-Z

Cat. 63
Untitled (Roter Kopf) (Red Head), no date
Watercolour, China ink and pencil on drawing board
Dimensions: 298 × 213 mm
Annotated below left: (blind stamp)
CR 90/N 506
Gerhard Altenbourg Foundation, SGA 497-N

Cat. 64
Untitled (Das Damenbildnis mit dem grünen Häubchen) (The Portrait of a Woman with the Green Bonnet), no date
Pencil, watercolour and gouache on ovally cut laid paper
Dimensions: 233 × 170 mm
Not annotated, dated or signed
CR 90/N 279
Lindenau-Museum Altenburg, DL 2010-82
2010 purchased with third party funds, formerly Astrid and Wilfried Rugo Collection

Cat. 65
Der Angler (The Fisherman), 1949
Pastel crayon on black board
Dimensions: 215 × 286 mm
Titled below left, signed and dated below right: "GSt 49"
CR 49/168
Gerhard Altenbourg Foundation, SGA 146-Z

Cat. 66
Untitled (Aufmarsch der vier Großkopfigen) (March of the Four Big Heads), no date
Printing ink applied with paint rollers, Pitt crayon and pencil on yellowish vellum paper
Dimensions: 328 × 267 mm
Annotated below right: (blind stamp)
CR 90/N 384
Lindenau-Museum Altenburg, DL 2010-88
2010 purchased with third party funds, formerly Astrid and Wilfried Rugo Collection

Kat. 70
O. T. (Dem Weidegott gewidmet), undatiert
Bleistift, Aquarellfarben und Gouache auf Zeichenpapier
Blattmaß: 210 × 297 mm
Unsign., bez. o. re.: (Titel); »Der Windhauch aus dem nächtlich schweigenden, dem Busch Ein Hauch aus dem Schweigen Fräulein Spätfrüh anrührlich Demut und Geduld nebbich (schade!) Was fürchtest Du? gescheckte Tiere? Trinke einen Portwein, er hilft Dir gewiß, Deine Seele spränge Bocksprünge. Ich wollte, du nähmest das Hindernis mit Vergnügen«, unten re.: (Blindprägung)
WVZ 90/N 311
Stiftung Gerhard Altenbourg, SGA 453-N

Kat. 71
O. T. (Baumnymphen), undatiert
Bleistift und Aquarellfarben auf Zeichenpapier
Blattmaß: 297 × 211 mm
Unbez., unsign., unten Mi.: (Blindprägung)
WVZ 90/N 303
Stiftung Gerhard Altenbourg, SGA 451-N

Kat. 72
O. T. (Mit Altenbourg im Profil), undatiert
Bleistift, Pinselabstreifungen mit Tusche und Aquarellfarben auf Zeichenkarton
Blattmaß: 298 × 212 mm
Unten li.: (Blindprägung), unten Mi. sign.: »Altenbourg«
WVZ 90/N 295
Stiftung Gerhard Altenbourg, SGA 443-N

Kat. 73
O. T. (Zettel, träumend), undatiert
Bleistift, Aquarellfarben, Gouache und chinesische Tusche auf Zeichenpapier
Blattmaß: 295 × 213 mm
Bez. o. re.: »Zahlenkolonnen«
WVZ 90/N 273
Stiftung Gerhard Altenbourg, SGA 437-N

Cat. 67
Untitled (Rötel und Bläuchen im Rosenhag) (Rötel and Bläuchen in the Rose Arbour), no date
Tempera, watercolour and lithographic crayon on Richard de Bas handmade laid paper
Dimensions: 783 × 575 mm
Annotated below left: (blind stamp)
CR 90/N 104
Gerhard Altenbourg Foundation, SGA 361-N

Cat. 68
Untitled (Einsam im Gestöber) (Alone in a Flurry), no date
Graphite pencil, brushstrokes with watercolour on yellowed drawing board
Dimensions: 212 × 300 mm
Annotated below left: (blind stamp)
CR 90/N 562
Gerhard Altenbourg Foundation, SGA 394-N

Cat. 69
Untitled (Nachdenken über das Rinnen der Zeit) (Reflecting on the Passage of Time), no date
Pencil and watercolour on yellowed drawing board
Dimensions: 301 × 210 mm
Below right: (blind stamp), annotated above right: "1) graubraune Papiere für (daneben Skizze) Pergament+Leinwand 3 × 3) Tempera einpinseln" (grey-brown paper for (adjacent sketch) parchment and canvas 3 × 3) brush in tempera)
Annotated at left edge: "Altenbourg Rinnen"
CR 90/N 519
Gerhard Altenbourg Foundation, SGA 505-N

Cat. 70
Untitled (Dem Weidegott gewidmet) (Dedicated to the God of Pasture), no date
Pencil, watercolour and gouache on drawing paper
Dimensions: 210 × 297 mm
Unsigned, annotated above right: (Title); "Der Windhauch aus dem nächtlich schweigenden, dem Busch Ein Hauch aus dem Schweigen Fräulein Spätfrüh anrührlich Demut und Geduld nebbich (schade!) Was fürchtest Du? gescheckte Tiere? Trinke einen Portwein, er hilft Dir gewiß, Deine Seele spränge Bocksprünge. Ich wollte, du nähmest das Hindernis mit Vergnügen" (The breath of wind from the night silence, the bush A breath from the silence Miss Late-Morning Touching humility and patience *nebbish* (what a pity!) What are you afraid of? Spotted animals? Drink a glass of port, it will surely help you, your soul will leap. I wish you would take the obstacle with pleasure), below right: (blind stamp)
CR 90/N 311
Gerhard Altenbourg Foundation, SGA 453-N

Kat. 74
O. T. (Gespräch mit dem Moorgeist), undatiert
Aquarellfarben, Gouache und chinesische Tusche auf Zeichenpapier
Blattmaß: 211 × 298 mm
Unbez., unsign.
WVZ 90/N 272
Stiftung Gerhard Altenbourg, SGA 436-N

Kat. 75
O. T. (Die bucklige Alte im Gespräch mit dem Luftgeist), undatiert
Pinselabstreifungen mit Gouache, Rötel, Pitt-Kreide und Bleistift auf vergilbtem Zeichenkarton
Blattmaß: 213 × 300 mm
Bez.: unten li.: (Blindprägung)
WVZ 90/N 544
Stiftung Gerhard Altenbourg, SGA 529-N

Kat. 76
O. T., Werkzeichnung für Beschläge auf Fensterrahmen, undatiert
Bleistift auf Transparentpapier
Blattmaß: 130 × 455 mm
Bez. Mi. re.: »Knauf Kasten: Material Kupfer«
WVZ 90/N 469
Stiftung Gerhard Altenbourg, SGA 4463-E

Kat. 77
O. T., Schriftblatt mit mehreren Skizzen für Gitter am Künstlerhaus und im Garten von Gerhard Altenbourg, undatiert
Bleistift, chinesische Tusche und Pinselabstreifungen mit Aquarellfarben auf Zeichenkarton
Blattmaß: 301 × 210 mm
Bez., nicht dat., nicht sign.: »(...) Entwurf aus einem Stück für Klosett-Fenster, Parterre (...) Hussel, Berlin (...) hat (...)«
WVZ 90/N 437
Stiftung Gerhard Altenbourg, SGA 5708-N

Cat. 71
Untitled (Baumnymphen) (Dryads), no date
Pencil and watercolour on drawing paper
Dimensions: 297 × 211 mm
Not annotated or signed, below centre: (blind stamp)
CR 90/N 303
Gerhard Altenbourg Foundation, SGA 451-N

Cat. 72
Untitled (Mit Altenbourg im Profil) (With Altenbourg in Profile), no date
Pencil, brush wipings with India ink and watercolour on drawing board
Dimensions: 298 × 212 mm
Below left: (blind stamp), signed below centre: "Altenbourg"
CR 90/N 295
Gerhard Altenbourg Foundation, SGA 443-N

Cat. 73
Untitled (Zettel, träumend) (Zettel, Dreaming), no date
Pencil, watercolour, gouache and China ink on drawing paper
Dimensions: 295 × 213 mm
Annotated above right: "Zahlenkolonnen"
CR 90/N 273
Gerhard Altenbourg Foundation, SGA 437-N

Cat. 74
Untitled (Gespräch mit dem Moorgeist) (Conversation with the Bog Spirit), no date
Watercolour, gouache and China ink on drawing paper
Dimensions: 211 × 298 mm
Not annotated or signed
CR 90/N 272
Gerhard Altenbourg Foundation, SGA 436-N

Cat. 75
Untitled (Die bucklige Alte im Gespräch mit dem Luftgeist) (The Hunchbacked Old Woman in Conversation with the Airy Spirit), no date
Brush wipings with gouache, red pencil, Pitt crayon and pencil on yellowed drawing board
Dimensions: 213 × 300 mm
Annotated below left: (blind stamp)
CR 90/N 544
Gerhard Altenbourg Foundation, SGA 529-N

Cat. 76
Untitled, technical drawing for fittings on window frames, no date
Pencil on transparent paper
Dimensions: 130 × 455 mm
Annotated middle right: "Knauf Kasten: Material Kupfer"
CR 90/N 469
Gerhard Altenbourg Foundation, SGA 4463-E

Kat. 78
über dem großen Monogramm: In den Wellen der Nacht, 1975
Holzschnitt in Dunkelbraun auf Fabriano Roma Michelangelo-Büttenpapier
Bildmaß: 136 × 209 mm, Blattmaß: 165 × 247 mm
Unten li. numm. u. unten Mitte: »2/4«(Blindprägung), sign. u. dat. unten rechts: »Altenbourg 1975«, auf der Rückseite betitelt unten li.: (Titel) und Widmung unten re.: »für Lutz Grösel«
WVZ H 187
6. Komposition, vier nummerierte Exemplare, Nr. 2/4
Lindenau-Museum Altenburg, G 1997-197
1997 Ankauf aus der Sammlung Gisela und Hans-Peter Schulz

Kat. 79
Gerhard Altenbourgs Schlüssel zum Arbeitszimmer im Künstlerhaus, zwischen 1960–1979
Messing, gebläuter Stahl, tauschiert, handwerkliche Ausführung Schlosserei Fritz Haase und Ulrich Schlegel
Objektmaß: ca. 9,8 × 5,7 × 0,6 cm
Unbez.
WVZ 90/N 474
Einzelstück aus einem Set von 18 Schrank- und Zimmerschlüsseln für das Künstlerhaus von Gerhard Altenbourg
Stiftung Gerhard Altenbourg, SGA 5370-01

Für Kat. 3, 6, 8, 9, 10, 12, 19, 23, 24, 38, 39, 40, 44, 47, 48, 54, 55, 64, 66 gilt:
Die Werke von Gerhard Altenbourg, ehemals Sammlung Rugo, wurden 2010 durch den Förderkreis *»Freunde des Lindenau-Museums« e.V.* für das Lindenau-Museum Altenburg mit Mitteln der Bundesrepublik Deutschland (Miteigentümerin zu 21,5 %), der HERMANN-REEMTSMA-STIFTUNG, der Kulturstiftung der Länder, dem Freistaat Thüringen, der Ernst Siemens Kunststiftung sowie dem Freundeskreis »Freunde des Lindenau-Museums Altenburg« e. V. erworben.

Cat. 77
Untitled, sheet with several sketches for fences at the artist's house and garden by Gerhard Altenbourg, no date
Pencil, China ink and brushstrokes with watercolour on drawing board
Dimensions: 301 × 210 mm
Annotated, not dated, not signed: "(…) Entwurf aus einem Stück für Klosett-Fenster, Parterre (…) Hussel, Berlin (…) has (…)" (sketch for bathroom window, ground floor)
CR 90/N 437
Gerhard Altenbourg Foundation, SGA 5708-N

Cat. 78
über dem großen Monogramm: In den Wellen der Nacht (Over the Large Monogram: In the Night's Waves), 1975
Woodcut in dark brown on Fabriano Roma Michelangelo laid paper
Image: 136 × 209 mm, sheet: 165 × 247 mm
Numbered below left and below centre: "2/4" (blind stamp), signed and dated below right: "Altenbourg 1975", titled on reverse below left: (Title) and dedication below right: "für Lutz Grösel"
CR H 187
6th composition, four numbered copies, no. 2/4
Lindenau-Museum Altenburg, G 1997-197
1997 purchased from the collection of Gisela and Hans-Peter Schulz

Cat. 79
Gerhard Altenbourgs Schlüssel zum Arbeitszimmer im Künstlerhaus (Gerhard Altenbourg's Key to the Studio in His House), between 1960 and 1979
Brass, blued steel, damascened, technical execution Fritz Haase and Ulrich Schlegel's locksmith shop
Dimensions: ca. 9.8 × 5.7 × 0.6 cm
Not annotated
CR 90/N 474, unique piece from a set of 18 closet and room keys for Gerhard Altenbourg's house
Gerhard Altenbourg Foundation, SGA 5370-01

For cats. 3, 6, 8, 9, 10, 12, 19, 23, 24, 38, 39, 40, 44, 47, 48, 54, 55, 64, 66:
The works by Gerhard Altenbourg from the former Rugo collection were purchased in 2010 by the "Freunde des Lindenau-Museums" e. V. association on behalf of the Lindenau-Museum Altenburg with funds from the Federal Republic of Germany (21.5% co-owner), the Hermann Reemtsma Stiftung, the Cultural Foundation of the German States, the Free State of Thuringia, the Ernst Siemens Kunststiftung and the Association of "Freunde des Lindenau-Museums" e. V.

Literaturverzeichnis (Auswahl)

Altenbourg, Gerhard: Gezweig im Haar eines Tages, 1967, in: Brusberg, Dieter (Hrsg.): Gerhard Altenbourg. Werk-Verzeichnis 1947–1969, unter Mitarbeit von Annegret Janda, zugl. Ausst.-Kat. Berlin/Baden-Baden/Hannover/Düsseldorf, Hannover 1969, S. 43.

Altenbourg, Gerhard: Klar dem Nächtlichen verschwistert, 1971, in: Altenbourg, Gerhard: Ich-Gestein: Arbeiten aus zwei Jahrzehnten, Berlin/Frankfurt a. M./Wien 1971, (Anhang:) handschriftlicher, paginierter und als Faksimile gedruckter Text von Gerhard Altenbourg, S. 1–6.

Altenbourg, Gerhard: Narbenrisse beim Durchstreifen jener Hügellandschaft, 1969, in: Brusberg, Dieter (Hrsg.): Gerhard Altenbourg. Werk-Verzeichnis 1947–1969, unter Mitarbeit von Annegret Janda, zugl. Ausst.-Kat. Berlin/Baden-Baden/Hannover/Düsseldorf, Hannover 1969, S. 34 f.

Altenbourg, Gerhard: Näherung. Ein Vorgang als ein Bericht über diese Jahre, 1986, in: Brusberg, Dieter (Hrsg.): Gerhard Altenbourg: das einsschauende Ausschauen; Köpfe u. Szenen 1949–1986, zum 60. Geburtstag von Gerhard Altenbourg, Ausst.-Kat. Galerie Brusberg, Berlin, Berlin/Hannover 1986, S. 7 f.

Altenbourg, Gerhard: Versuch einer Merkmal-Fixierung, 1962, in: Altenbourg, Gerhard: Tatauierte Litaneien. Aufrisse und Weg-Spindeln, Berlin/Paris (Privatdruck) 1962, S. 5–17, enth. in: Janda, Annegret: Gerhard Altenbourg. Monographie und Werkverzeichnis, 3 Bde., Bd. 2, 1959–1976, Köln 2007, S. 50 f.

(Altenbourg, Gerhard)/Ahrend, Thorsten/Stiftung Gerhard Altenbourg (Hrsg.): Gerhard Altenbourg, Wald minotaurisch. Gedichte, mit einem Nachwort von Wulf Kirsten, Göttingen 2019.

Selected Bibliography

Altenbourg, Gerhard, "Gezweig im Haar eines Tages", 1967, in Brusberg, Dieter (ed.), *Gerhard Altenbourg. Werk-Verzeichnis 1947–1969*, with the collaboration of Annegret Janda, also exh. cat. Berlin/Baden-Baden/Hanover/Düsseldorf (Hanover, 1969), p. 43.

Altenbourg, Gerhard, "Klar dem Nächtlichen verschwistert", 1971, in Altenbourg, Gerhard, *Ich-Gestein: Arbeiten aus zwei Jahrzehnten* (Berlin/Frankfurt am Main/Vienna, 1971), (appendix:) handwritten, paginated text by Gerhard Altenbourg printed in facsimile, pp. 1–6.

Altenbourg, Gerhard, "Narbenrisse beim Durchstreifen jener Hügellandschaft", 1969, in Brusberg, Dieter (ed.), *Gerhard Altenbourg. Werk-Verzeichnis 1947–1969*, with the collaboration of Annegret Janda, also exh. cat. Berlin/Baden-Baden/Hanover/Düsseldorf (Hanover, 1969), pp. 34f.

Altenbourg, Gerhard, "Näherung. Ein Vorgang als ein Bericht über diese Jahre", 1986, in Brusberg, Dieter (ed.), *Gerhard Altenbourg: das einschauende Ausschauen; Köpfe u. Szenen 1949–1986*, for the 60th birthday of Gerhard Altenbourg, exh. cat. Galerie Brusberg, Berlin (Berlin/Hanover, 1986), pp. 7f.

Altenbourg, Gerhard, "Versuch einer Merkmal-Fixierung", 1962, in Altenbourg, Gerhard, *Tatauierte Litaneien. Aufrisse und Weg-Spindeln* (Berlin/Paris, private printing, 1962), pp. 5–17, contained in Janda, Annegret, *Gerhard Altenbourg. Monographie und Werkverzeichnis*, 3 vols. (Cologne: Wienand, 2004–10), vol. 2 1959–1976, pp. 50f.

(Altenbourg, Gerhard)/Ahrend, Thorsten/Stiftung Gerhard Altenbourg (eds.), *Gerhard Altenbourg, Wald minotaurisch. Gedichte*, with an afterword by Wulf Kirsten (Göttingen, 2019).

(Altenbourg, Gerhard/Kästner, Erhard:) Das dritte Auge. Ein Dialog der Freunde Gerhard Altenbourg und Erhart Kästner. Mit einem Geleitwort von Eduard Beaucamp und Texten von Dieter Brusberg, Dieter Hoffmann, Roland Jäger, Werner Schmidt und Bernard Schultze, Frankfurt a. M./Leipzig 1992.

(Altenbourg, Gerhard/Lang, Lothar:) Gerhard Altenbourg/Lothar Lang – Briefwechsel 1965–1988, bearb. u. komm. v. Katrin Roth, hrsg. von Christa Grimm, Leipzig 2008.

(Altenbourg, Gerhard/Mennekes, Friedhelm:) Im Gespräch (Interview mit Friedhelm Mennekes), in: Grinten, Franz Joseph van der/Mennekes, Friedhelm: Abstraktion und Kontemplation. Auseinandersetzung mit einem Thema der Gegenwartskunst, Stuttgart 1987, S. 234–241.

(Altenbourg, Gerhard)/Sparkassen-Kulturstiftung Hessen-Thüringen (Hrsg.): Salutation. Ein Künstlerbuch von Gerhard Altenbourg. Texte von Julia M. Nauhaus. Leipzig 2016.

Altenbourg, Gerhard: Betrachtungen vom Arbeitstisch aus, 1966, in: Lang, Lothar (Hrsg.): Die Handzeichnung. Kunstkabinett am Institut für Lehrerweiterbildung. Berlin-Pankow 1967, S. 2 f.

Barbarino, Christin: Das Buchkunstwerk von Gerhard Altenbourg, Berlin 2018.

Blume, Dieter: Ein Engel im Atelier. Zu Gast bei Gerhard Altenbourg, hrsg. v. Roland Krischke, Göttingen 2021.

Brusberg, Dieter/Ströch, Anneliese (Hrsg.): Gerhard Altenbourg – Der Gärtner. Eine Monografie in Bildern, Berlin 1996.

Dieckmann, Friedrich: Ausflug zu Altenbourg. Ein Reisebericht, in: Brusberg, Dieter/Ströch, Anneliese (Hrsg.): Gerhard Altenbourg – Der Gärtner. Eine Monografie in Bildern, Berlin 1996, S. 12–29.

Dwars, Jens-Fietje (Hrsg.): Mit Salut & Flügelschlag. Der Briefwechsel zwischen Gerhard Altenbourg und Horst Hussel, Bucha bei Jena 2016.

Fischer, Sören: Bütten, Japanpapier, Karton. Zum Papier als Objekt und Ort bei Gerhard Altenbourg, in: Maaz, Bernhard/Günther, Daniela/Fischer, Sören (Hrsg.): terra Altenbourg. Die Welt des Zeichners, Ausst.-Kat. Kupferstich-Kabinett, Staatliche Kunstsammlungen Dresden, Berlin/München 2014, S. 150–162.

(Altenbourg, Gerhard/Kästner, Erhart,) *Das dritte Auge. Ein Dialog der Freunde Gerhard Altenbourg und Erhart Kästner*. With a foreword by Eduard Beaucamp and texts by Dieter Brusberg, Dieter Hoffmann, Roland Jäger, Werner Schmidt and Bernard Schultze (Frankfurt am Main/Leipzig, 1992).

(Altenbourg, Gerhard/Lang, Lothar,) *Gerhard Altenbourg/Lothar Lang – Briefwechsel 1965–1988*, ed. and annotated by Katrin Roth, ed. Christa Grimm (Leipzig, 2008).

(Altenbourg, Gerhard/Mennekes, Friedhelm,) "Im Gespräch" (interview with Friedhelm Mennekes), in Grinten, Franz Joseph van der/Mennekes, Friedhelm, *Abstraktion und Kontemplation. Auseinandersetzung mit einem Thema der Gegenwartskunst* (Stuttgart, 1987), pp. 234–41.

(Altenbourg, Gerhard)/Sparkassen-Kulturstiftung Hessen-Thüringen (eds.), *Salutation. Ein Künstlerbuch von Gerhard Altenbourg*. Texts by Julia M. Nauhaus (Leipzig, 2016).

Altenbourg, Gerhard, "Betrachtungen vom Arbeitstisch aus", 1966, in Lang, Lothar (ed.), *Die Handzeichnung*. Kunstkabinett am Institut für Lehrerweiterbildung (Berlin-Pankow, 1967), pp. 2f.

Barbarino, Christin, *Das Buchkunstwerk von Gerhard Altenbourg* (Berlin, 2018).

Blume, Dieter, *Ein Engel im Atelier. Zu Gast bei Gerhard Altenbourg*, ed. Roland Krischke (Göttingen, 2021).

Brusberg, Dieter/Ströch, Anneliese (eds.), *Gerhard Altenbourg – Der Gärtner. Eine Monografie in Bildern* (Berlin, 1996).

Dieckmann, Friedrich, "Ausflug zu Altenbourg. Ein Reisebericht", in Brusberg, Dieter/Ströch, Anneliese (eds.), *Gerhard Altenbourg – Der Gärtner. Eine Monografie in Bildern* (Berlin, 1996), pp. 12–29.

Dwars, Jens-Fietje (ed.), *Mit Salut & Flügelschlag. Der Briefwechsel zwischen Gerhard Altenbourg und Horst Hussel* (Bucha bei Jena, 2016).

Grinten, Franz Joseph von der/Mennekes, Friedhelm: Abstraktion und Kontemplation. Auseinandersetzung mit einem Thema der Gegenwartskunst, Stuttgart 1987, S. 234–241.

Hocke, Gustav René: Malerei der Gegenwart. Der Neo-Manierismus. Vom Surrealismus zur Meditation, Wiesbaden/München 1975.

Janda, Annegret: Altenbourg im »Hügelgau«, in: Brusberg, Dieter (Hrsg.): Gerhard Altenbourg. Werk-Verzeichnis 1947–1969, unter Mitarbeit von Annegret Janda, zugl. Ausst.-Kat. Berlin/Baden-Baden/Hannover/Düsseldorf, Hannover 1969, S. 12–15.

Janda, Annegret: Gerhard Altenbourg. Monographie und Werkverzeichnis, 3 Bde., Bd. 1, 1937–1958; Bd. 2, 1959–1976; Bd. 3, 1977–1989, Köln 2004, 2007, 2010.

Janda, Annegret: Gerhard Altenbourg. Chronik eines Künstlerlebens im 20. Jahrhundert. Zweiter Teil: 1959–1976, in: Janda 2007, S. 8–25.

Kirsten, Wulf: Nachwort, in: (Altenbourg, Gerhard)/ Ahrend, Thorsten/Stiftung Gerhard Altenbourg (Hrsg.): Gerhard Altenbourg, Wald minotaurisch. Gedichte, mit einem Nachwort von Wulf Kirsten, Göttingen 2019, S. 89–94.

Kulturstiftung der Länder/Lindenau-Museum Altenburg (Hrsg.): Gerhard Altenbourg. Die Sammlung Rugo im Lindenau-Museum Altenburg, Berlin 2024 .

Lang, Lothar (Last, Ludwig): Ironie bei Altenbourg, in: Brusberg, Dieter (Hrsg.): Gerhard Altenbourg. Werk-Verzeichnis 1947–1969, unter Mitarbeit von Annegret Janda, zugl. Ausst.-Kat. Berlin/Baden-Baden/Hannover/Düsseldorf, Hannover 1969, S. 15 f.

Lang, Lothar: Annotation zum Holzschnitt-Werk von Gerhard Altenbourg, in: Schmidt, Werner /(Ullmann, Günter) (Hrsg.): Gerhard Altenbourg: Holzschnitte, Ausst.-Kat. Museum Schloss Hinterglauchau, Glauchau 1976, S. 6.

Lang, Lothar: Malerei und Graphik in der Deutschen Demokratischen Republik, Leipzig 1983.

Fischer, Sören, "Bütten, Japanpapier, Karton. Zum Papier als Objekt und Ort bei Gerhard Altenbourg", in Maaz, Bernhard/Günther, Daniela/Fischer, Sören (eds.), *terra Altenbourg. Die Welt des Zeichners*, exh. cat. Kupferstich-Kabinett, Staatliche Kunstsammlungen Dresden (Berlin/Munich, 2014), pp. 150–62.

Grinten, Franz Joseph van der/Mennekes, Friedhelm, *Abstraktion und Kontemplation. Auseinandersetzung mit einem Thema der Gegenwartskunst* (Stuttgart, 1987), pp. 234–41.

Hocke, Gustav René, *Malerei der Gegenwart. Der Neo-Manierismus. Vom Surrealismus zur Meditation* (Wiesbaden/Munich, 1975).

Janda, Annegret, "Altenbourg im 'Hügelgau'", in Brusberg, Dieter (ed.), *Gerhard Altenbourg. Werk-Verzeichnis 1947–1969*, with the collaboration of Annegret Janda, also exh. cat. Berlin/Baden-Baden/Hanover/Düsseldorf (Hanover, 1969), pp. 12–15.

Janda, Annegret, *Gerhard Altenbourg. Monographie und Werkverzeichnis*, 3 vols., vol. 1, 1937–1958; vol. 2, 1959–1976; vol. 3, 1977–1989 (Cologne, 2004, 2007, 2010).

Janda, Annegret, "Gerhard Altenbourg. Chronik eines Künstlerlebens im 20. Jahrhundert. Zweiter Teil: 1959–1976", in Janda 2007, pp. 8–25.

Kirsten, Wulf, "Nachwort", in (Altenbourg, Gerhard)/ Ahrend, Thorsten/Stiftung Gerhard Altenbourg (eds.), *Gerhard Altenbourg, Wald minotaurisch. Gedichte*, with an afterword by Wulf Kirsten (Göttingen, 2019), pp. 89–94.

Kulturstiftung der Länder/Lindenau-Museum Altenburg (eds.), *Gerhard Altenbourg. Die Sammlung Rugo im Lindenau-Museum Altenburg* (Berlin, 2024).

Lang, Lothar (Last, Ludwig), "Ironie bei Altenbourg", in Brusberg, Dieter (ed.), *Gerhard Altenbourg. Werk-Verzeichnis 1947–1969*, with the collaboration of Annegret Janda, also exh. cat. Berlin/Baden-Baden/Hanover/Düsseldorf (Hanover, 1969), pp. 15f.

Lang, Lothar, "Annotation zum Holzschnitt-Werk von Gerhard Altenbourg", in Schmidt, Werner/(Ullmann, Günter) (eds.), *Gerhard Altenbourg: Holzschnitte*, exh. cat. Museum Schloss Hinterglauchau (Glauchau, 1976), p. 6.

Maaz, Bernhard: Terra Altenbourg. Die Beharrung auf dem Ich, in: Maaz, Bernhard/Günther, Daniela/ Fischer, Sören (Hrsg.): terra Altenbourg. Die Welt des Zeichners, Auss.-Kat. Kupferstich-Kabinett, Staatliche Kunstsammlungen Dresden, Berlin/München 2014, S. 8–42.

Mössinger, Ingrid/ Milde, Brigitta: »…nahezu lautlose Schwingungs-Symbiose.« Die Künstlerfreundschaft zwischen Franz Mon und Carlfriedrich Claus. Briefwechsel 1959–1997. Visuelle Texte. Sprachblätter. Ausst.-Kat. Kunstsammlungen Chemnitz – Museum am Theaterplatz, Chemnitz, Bielefeld/Berlin 2013.

Nauhaus, Julia M.: Gerhard Altenbourgs Künstlerbuch Salutation, in: (Altenbourg, Gerhard)/Sparkassen-Kulturstiftung Hessen-Thüringen (Hrsg.): Salutation. Ein Künstlerbuch von Gerhard Altenbourg. Texte von Julia M. Nauhaus. Leipzig 2016, S. 5–15.

Penndorf, Jutta: »Ein Gehen der Wege, ein Schweben…«, in: Janda, Annegret: Gerhard Altenbourg. Monographie und Werkverzeichnis, 3 Bde., Bd. 2, 1959–1976, Köln 2007, S. 26–31.

Penndorf, Jutta (Hrsg.): Altenbourgs Garten. Schattengewächse und Mittagshelligkeiten, Altenburg 2022.

Prinz, Ursula: Chronologie, in: Gachnang, Johannes (Hrsg.): Der gekrümmte Horizont. Kunst in Berlin 1945–1967, Ausst.-Kat. Akademie der Künste, Berlin, Berlin 1980, S. 11–30.

Schmidt, Werner: Gerhard Altenbourg. Zeichnungen und Graphik aus drei Jahrzehnten, in: Gerhard Altenbourg. Zeichnungen und Graphik aus drei Jahrzehnten, Ausst.-Kat. Kupferstich-Kabinett, Staatliche Kunstsammlungen Dresden, Dresden 1979, S. 1–3.

Zweite, Armin: »Im Erinnern ist die Wirklichkeit, im Ungreifbaren das Hiersein«. Altenbourgs Verhältnis zur Tradition – eine Anmerkung, in: ders. (Hrsg.): Gerhard Altenbourg. Im Fluß der Zeit, Ausst.-Kat. K20-Kunstsammlung am Grabbeplatz, Düsseldorf / Kupferstich-Kabinett, Staatliche Kunstsammlungen Dresden / Staatliche Graphische Sammlung, München, München 2003, S. 17–28.

Lang, Lothar, *Malerei und Graphik in der Deutschen Demokratischen Republik* (Leipzig, 1983).

Maaz, Bernhard, "Terra Altenbourg. Die Beharrung auf dem Ich", in Maaz, Bernhard/Günther, Daniela/ Fischer, Sören (eds.), *terra Altenbourg. Die Welt des Zeichners*, exh. cat. Kupferstich-Kabinett, Staatliche Kunstsammlungen Dresden (Berlin/Munich, 2014), pp. 8–42.

Mössinger, Ingrid/Milde, Brigitta, *"…nahezu lautlose Schwingungs-Symbiose." Die Künstlerfreundschaft zwischen Franz Mon und Carlfriedrich Claus. Briefwechsel 1959–1997. Visuelle Texte. Sprachblätter*, exh. cat. Kunstsammlungen Chemnitz – Museum am Theaterplatz, Chemnitz (Bielefeld/Berlin, 2013).

Nauhaus, Julia M., "Gerhard Altenbourgs Künstlerbuch Salutation", in (Altenbourg, Gerhard)/Sparkassen-Kulturstiftung Hessen-Thüringen (eds.), *Salutation. Ein Künstlerbuch von Gerhard Altenbourg*. Texts by Julia M. Nauhaus (Leipzig, 2016), pp. 5–15.

Penndorf, Jutta, "Ein Gehen der Wege, ein Schweben…", in Janda, Annegret, *Gerhard Altenbourg. Monographie und Werkverzeichnis*, 3 vols., vol. 2, 1959–1976 (Cologne, 2007), pp. 26–31.

Penndorf, Jutta (ed.), *Altenbourgs Garten. Schattengewächse und Mittagshelligkeiten* (Altenburg, 2022).

Prinz, Ursula, "Chronologie", in Gachnang, Johannes (ed.), *Der gekrümmte Horizont. Kunst in Berlin 1945–1967*, exh. cat. Akademie der Künste, Berlin (Berlin, 1980), pp. 11–30.

Schmidt, Werner, "Gerhard Altenbourg. Zeichnungen und Graphik aus drei Jahrzehnten", in *Gerhard Altenbourg. Zeichnungen und Graphik aus drei Jahrzehnten*, exh. cat. Kupferstich-Kabinett, Staatliche Kunstsammlungen Dresden (Dresden, 1979), pp. 1–3.

Zweite, Armin, "'Im Erinnern ist die Wirklichkeit, im Ungreifbaren das Hiersein'. Altenbourgs Verhältnis zur Tradition – eine Anmerkung", in idem (ed.), *Gerhard Altenbourg. Im Fluß der Zeit*, exh. cat. K20-Kunstsammlung am Grabbeplatz, Düsseldorf/Kupferstich-Kabinett, Staatliche Kunstsammlungen Dresden/Staatliche Graphische Sammlung, Munich (Munich, 2003), pp. 17–28.

Ausstellungskataloge

1966
Phantastische Figuration: Altenbourg, Bellmer, Oelze, Ausst.-Kat. Haus am Waldsee, Berlin, Berlin 1966.

Deutsche Gesellschaft für Bildende Kunst/Akademie der Künste (Hrsg.): Labyrinthe: Phantastische Kunst vom 16. Jahrhundert bis zur Gegenwart, zusammengestellt von Eberhard Roters, Ausst.-Kat. Kunstverein und Akademie der Künste, Berlin / Staatliche Kunsthalle Baden-Baden / Kunsthalle Nürnberg, Berlin 1966.

1967
Lang, Lothar (Hrsg.): Die Handzeichnung. Kunstkabinett am Institut für Lehrerweiterbildung. Berlin-Pankow 1967.

Albrecht-Dürer-Gesellschaft e.V. (Hrsg.): Ars phantastica – deutsche Kunst des Magischen Realismus, Phantastischen Realismus und Surrealismus seit 1945, Ausst.-Kat. Schloss Stein, Nürnberg, Nürnberg 1967.

1968
Premio Marzotto (…). La pittura figurativa in Europa (…) Valdagno 1968.

1969
Brusberg, Dieter (Hrsg.): Gerhard Altenbourg. Werk-Verzeichnis 1947–1969, unter Mitarbeit von Annegret Janda, zugl. Ausst.-Kat. Berlin/Baden-Baden/Hannover/Düsseldorf, Hannover 1969.

1973
Magie, Dämonie und Groteske in der Kunst des 19. und 20. Jahrhunderts, Ausst.-Kat. Galerie Pels-Leusden, Berlin, Berlin 1973.

1976
Schmidt, Werner/(Ullmann, Günter) (Hrsg.): Gerhard Altenbourg: Holzschnitte, Ausst.-Kat. Museum Schloss Hinterglauchau, Glauchau 1976.

1979
Gerhard Altenbourg. Zeichnungen und Graphik aus drei Jahrzehnten, Ausst.-Kat. Kupferstich-Kabinett, Staatliche Kunstsammlungen Dresden, Dresden 1979.

1980
Gachnang, Johannes (Hrsg.): Der gekrümmte Horizont. Kunst in Berlin 1945–1967, Ausst.-Kat. Akademie der Künste, Berlin, Berlin 1980.

Exhibition Catalogues

1966
Phantastische Figuration: Altenbourg, Bellmer, Oelze, exh. cat. Haus am Waldsee, Berlin (Berlin, 1966).
Deutsche Gesellschaft für Bildende Kunst/Akademie der Künste (eds.), *Labyrinthe: Phantastische Kunst vom 16. Jahrhundert bis zur Gegenwart*, compiled by Eberhard Roters, exh. cat. Kunstverein und Akademie der Künste, Berlin/Staatliche Kunsthalle Baden-Baden/Kunsthalle Nürnberg (Berlin, 1966).

1967
Lang, Lothar (ed.), *Die Handzeichnung*. Kunstkabinett am Institut für Lehrerweiterbildung (Berlin-Pankow, 1967). Albrecht-Dürer-Gesellschaft e.V. (eds.), *Ars phantastica – deutsche Kunst des Magischen Realismus, Phantastischen Realismus und Surrealismus seit 1945*, exh. cat. Schloss Stein, Nuremberg (Nuremberg, 1967).

1968
Premio Marzotto (…). La pittura figurativa in Europa (…) (Valdagno, 1968).

1969
Brusberg, Dieter (ed.), *Gerhard Altenbourg. Werk-Verzeichnis 1947–1969*, with the collaboration of Annegret Janda, also exh. cat. Berlin/Baden-Baden/Hanover/Düsseldorf (Hanover, 1969).

1973
Magie, Dämonie und Groteske in der Kunst des 19. und 20. Jahrhunderts, exh. cat. Galerie Pels-Leusden, Berlin (Berlin, 1973).

1976
Schmidt, Werner/(Ullmann, Günter) (eds.), *Gerhard Altenbourg: Holzschnitte*, exh. cat. Museum Schloss Hinterglauchau (Glauchau, 1976).

1979
Gerhard Altenbourg. Zeichnungen und Graphik aus drei Jahrzehnten, exh. cat. Kupferstich-Kabinett, Staatliche Kunstsammlungen Dresden (Dresden, 1979).

1980
Gachnang, Johannes (ed.), *Der gekrümmte Horizont. Kunst in Berlin 1945–1967*, exh. cat. Akademie der Künste, Berlin (Berlin, 1980).

1986
Brusberg, Dieter (Hrsg.): Gerhard Altenbourg: das einsschauende Ausschauen; Köpfe u. Szenen 1949–1986, zum 60. Geburtstag von Gerhard Altenbourg, Auss.-Kat. Galerie Brusberg, Berlin, Berlin/ Hannover 1986.

Museum der Bildenden Künste Leipzig (Hrsg.): Gerhard Altenbourg. Zeichnungen und Graphik, Ausst.-Kat. Museum der Bildenden Künste Leipzig / Kupferstich-Kabinett, Staatliche Kunstsammlungen Dresden, Leipzig 1986.

1988
Kunsthalle Bremen (Hrsg.): Gerhard Altenbourg, Arbeiten 1947–1987, Ausst.-Kat. Kunsthalle Bremen / Kunsthalle Tübingen / Sprengel Museum Hannover / Akademie der Künste Berlin, Berlin 1988.

1989
Dieter Brusberg (Hrsg.): Gerhard Altenbourg. »Schnepfenthaler Suite« und »Aus dem Hügelgau«. Kaltnadelradierungen. Zur Ausstellung der Kaltnadelradierungen, Mischtechniken und Zeichnungen. (Galerie Brusberg, Berlin, Galerie Berlin, Staatlicher Kunsthandel der DDR) Berlin 1989 .

1994
Janda, Annegret (Hrsg.): – sah ichs wie Feuer glänzen um und um –. Werkverzeichnis der Metallarbeiten und zugehörigen Zeichnungen von Gerhard Altenbourg, Ausst.-Kat. Grassimuseum, Museum für Kunsthandwerk Leipzig, Berlin 1994.

Gleisberg, Dieter (Bearb.): Gerhard Altenbourg. Frühe Lithographien und Zeichnungen, Ausst.-Kat. Alte Leipziger Lebensversicherungsgesellschaft AG, Leipzig, Leipzig 1994.

2001
Lindenau-Museum Altenburg/Saarland-Museum Saarbrücken (Hrsg.): Silence: silence, silence: Gerhard Altenbourg; die Sammlung Wilfried und Astrid Rugo, Ausst.-Kat. Lindenau-Museum Altenburg / Saarland-Museum Saarbrücken, Altenburg 2001.

Schmidt, Hans-Werner/Museum der Bildenden Künste Leipzig (Hrsg.): Janus im Flüstern Pans. Gerhard Altenbourg, Ausst.-Kat. Lindenau-Museum Altenburg / Saarland-Museum Saarbrücken, Leipzig 2001.

1986
Brusberg, Dieter (ed.), *Gerhard Altenbourg: das einsschauende Ausschauen; Köpfe u. Szenen 1949–1986*, for the 60th birthday of Gerhard Altenbourg, exh. cat. Galerie Brusberg, Berlin (Berlin/Hanover, 1986).
Museum der Bildenden Künste Leipzig (eds.), *Gerhard Altenbourg. Zeichnungen und Graphik*, exh. cat. Museum der Bildenden Künste Leipzig/Kupferstich-Kabinett, Staatliche Kunstsammlungen Dresden (Leipzig, 1986).

1988
Kunsthalle Bremen (eds.), *Gerhard Altenbourg, Arbeiten 1947–1987*, exh. cat. Kunsthalle Bremen/Kunsthalle Tübingen/Sprengel Museum Hannover/Akademie der Künste Berlin (Berlin, 1988).

1989
Brusberg, Dieter (ed.), *Gerhard Altenbourg. "Schnepfenthaler Suite" und "Aus dem Hügelgau". Kaltnadelradierungen.* Zur Ausstellung der Kaltnadelradierungen, Mischtechniken und Zeichnungen. (Galerie Brusberg, Berlin, Galerie Berlin, Staatlicher Kunsthandel der DDR) (Berlin, 1989).

1994
Janda, Annegret (ed.), *– sah ichs wie Feuer glänzen um und um –. Werkverzeichnis der Metallarbeiten und zugehörigen Zeichnungen von Gerhard Altenbourg*, exh. cat. Grassimuseum, Museum für Kunsthandwerk Leipzig (Berlin, 1994).

Gleisberg, Dieter (ed.), *Gerhard Altenbourg. Frühe Lithographien und Zeichnungen*, exh. cat. Alte Leipziger Lebensversicherungsgesellschaft AG, Leipzig (Leipzig, 1994).

2001
Lindenau-Museum Altenburg/Saarland-Museum Saarbrücken (eds.), *Silence: silence, silence: Gerhard Altenbourg; die Sammlung Wilfried und Astrid Rugo*, exh. cat. Lindenau-Museum Altenburg/Saarland-Museum Saarbrücken (Altenburg, 2001).

Schmidt, Hans-Werner/Museum der Bildenden Künste Leipzig (eds.), *Janus im Flüstern Pans. Gerhard Altenbourg*, exh. cat. Lindenau-Museum Altenburg/ Saarland-Museum Saarbrücken (Leipzig, 2001).

2003
Zweite, Armin (ed.), *Gerhard Altenbourg. Im Fluß der Zeit*, exh. cat. K20-Kunstsammlung am Grabbeplatz, Düsseldorf/Kupferstich-Kabinett, Staatliche Kunstsammlungen Dresden/Staatliche Graphische Sammlung, Munich (Munich, 2003).

2003
Zweite, Armin (Hrsg.): Gerhard Altenbourg. Im Fluß der Zeit, Ausst.-Kat. K20-Kunstsammlung am Grabbeplatz, Düsseldorf / Kupferstich-Kabinett, Staatliche Kunstsammlungen Dresden / Staatliche Graphische Sammlung, München, München 2003.

2009
Friedrich, Thomas/Mössinger, Ingrid (Hrsg.): Gerhard Altenbourg. Horst Hussel. Werke im Museum Gunzenhauser, Ausst.-Kat. Kunstsammlungen Chemnitz, Chemnitz 2009.

2010
Zilch-Döpke, Ilse (Hrsg.): Altenbourg Angesehen. Künstler und Autoren zu Altenbourg, Ausst.-Kat. Europäischen Akademie Berlin / Heck-Art-Haus des Vereins für Kunst Chemnitz / Röntgen-Museum Neuwied, Berlin 2010.

2014
Nauhaus, Julia M./Lindenau-Museum Altenburg (Hrsg.): Erzgebirge, Hügel-Grund, Artemis-Land. Altenbourgs Landschaften, Ausst.-Kat. Lindenau-Museum Altenburg, Altenburg 2014.

Maaz, Bernhard/Günther, Daniela/Fischer, Sören (Hrsg.): terra Altenbourg. Die Welt des Zeichners, Auss.-Kat. Kupferstich-Kabinett, Staatliche Kunstsammlungen Dresden, Berlin/München 2014.

2015
Beloubek-Hammer, Anita (Hrsg.): Gerhard Altenbourg. Das gezeichnete Ich. Neuerwerbung der Sammlung Solgärd und Rolf Walter und Bestand des Berliner Kupferstichkabinetts, Ausst.-Kat. Kupferstichkabinett, Staatliche Museen zu Berlin, Petersberg 2015.

2016
Krischke, Roland/Lindenau-Museum Altenburg (Hrsg.): Altenbourg in Altenburg: die Stiftung Gerhard Altenbourg, Ausst.-Kat. Lindenau-Museum Altenburg, Altenburg 2016.

2021
Bußmann, Frédéric/Milde, Brigitta (Hrsg.): Nähe und Distanz. Carlfriedrich Claus und Gerhard Altenbourg im Dialog, Ausst.-Kat. Kunstsammlungen Chemnitz, Dresden 2021.

2009
Friedrich, Thomas/Mössinger, Ingrid (eds.), *Gerhard Altenbourg. Horst Hussel. Werke im Museum Gunzenhauser*, exh. cat. Kunstsammlungen Chemnitz (Chemnitz, 2009).

2010
Zilch-Döpke, Ilse (ed.), *Altenbourg Angesehen. Künstler und Autoren zu Altenbourg*, exh. cat. Europäische Akademie Berlin/Heck-Art-Haus des Vereins für Kunst Chemnitz/Röntgen-Museum Neuwied (Berlin, 2010).

2014
Nauhaus, Julia M./Lindenau-Museum Altenburg (eds.), *Erzgebirge, Hügel-Grund, Artemis-Land. Altenbourgs Landschaften*, exh. cat. Lindenau-Museum Altenburg (Altenburg, 2014).

Maaz, Bernhard/Günther, Daniela/Fischer, Sören (eds.), *terra Altenbourg. Die Welt des Zeichners*, exh. cat. Kupferstich-Kabinett, Staatliche Kunstsammlungen Dresden (Berlin/Munich, 2014).

2015
Beloubek-Hammer, Anita (ed.), *Gerhard Altenbourg. Das gezeichnete Ich. Neuerwerbung der Sammlung Solgärd und Rolf Walter und Bestand des Berliner Kupferstichkabinetts*, exh. cat. Kupferstichkabinett, Staatliche Museen zu Berlin (Petersberg, 2015).

2016
Krischke, Roland/Lindenau-Museum Altenburg (eds.), *Altenbourg in Altenburg: die Stiftung Gerhard Altenbourg*, exh. cat. Lindenau-Museum Altenburg (Altenburg, 2016).

2021
Bußmann, Frédéric/Milde, Brigitta (eds.), *Nähe und Distanz. Carlfriedrich Claus und Gerhard Altenbourg im Dialog*, exh. cat. Kunstsammlungen Chemnitz (Dresden, 2021).

Autorinnen und Autoren

Manuela Büchting studierte Freie Kunst an der Universität der Künste, Braunschweig, und Documentary Media an der Ryerson University, Toronto (Kanada). Es folgten ein Work-Study-Programm im Bereich Publishing am Banff Centre (Kanada) und ein Volontariat Kulturelle Bildung bei der ALTANA Kulturstiftung. Von 2015 bis 2022 arbeitete sie als Referentin für Kunstvermittlung am Museum Sinclair-Haus bei der Stiftung Kunst und Natur, Bad Homburg. Seit 2022 arbeitet sie als Kunst- und Kulturvermittlerin für die Altenburger Museen. Darüber hinaus ist sie Wildnis- und Naturpädagogin und zertifizierte Stadtnaturführerin. Sie arbeitet verstärkt zu den Themen Nachhaltigkeit, Outreach und künstlerische Forschung.

Dr. Sören Fischer studierte Kunstgeschichte, Klassische Archäologie und Germanistik an den Universitäten von Münster, Perugia und Mainz. Von 2009 bis 2012 war er wissenschaftlicher Mitarbeiter am Institut für Kunstgeschichte der Johannes Gutenberg-Universität Mainz, anschließend wissenschaftlicher Volontär bei den Staatlichen Kunstsammlungen Dresden, danach Co-Kurator für das dortige Kupferstich-Kabinett und zwischen 2014 und 2019 wissenschaftlicher Mitarbeiter des Sakralmuseums St. Annen der Städtischen Sammlungen Kamenz. Seit November 2019 leitet er die Graphische Sammlung am Museum Pfalzgalerie Kaiserslautern.

Dr. Marit Heuß ist Privatdozentin und wissenschaftliche Mitarbeiterin im Fachbereich Neuere deutsche Literatur und Literaturtheorie am Institut für Germanistik der Universität Leipzig. Sie hat Germanistik und Kunstgeschichte in Dresden studiert und wurde 2019 zum Thema »Peter Handkes Bildpoetik« promoviert. Zu ihren Forschungsschwerpunkten zählen österreichische Gegenwartsliteratur, Kunstliteratur, Lyrik nach 1945 (Schwerpunkt u. a. Sarah Kirsch, Wolfgang Hilbig), Dichternachlässe und Editionsphilologie.

Authors

Manuela Büchting studied fine arts at the Braunschweig University of Art and documentary media at Ryerson University, Toronto. Afterwards she participated in a work-study programme in publishing at the Banff Centre in Canada and an internship in cultural education at the ALTANA Kulturstiftung. From 2015 to 2022 she worked as a specialist for art education at the Museum Sinclair-Haus of the Stiftung Kunst und Natur, Bad Homburg. She has worked as an art and culture educator for the Altenburger Museen since 2022. She is also a wildlife and nature educator and a certified urban-nature guide. She increasingly works in the areas of sustainability, outreach and artistic research.

Dr Sören Fischer studied art history, classical archaeology and German studies at the universities in Münster, Perugia and Mainz. From 2009 to 2012 he was research assistant at the Institute for Art History at the Johannes Gutenberg Universität Mainz, afterwards research trainee at the Staatliche Kunstsammlungen Dresden and co-curator for the Kupferstich-Kabinett in Dresden. From 2014 to 2019 he was a research associate at the Sakralmuseum St. Annen in the Städtische Sammlungen Kamenz. He has been director of the Graphic Arts Collection of the Museum Pfalzgalerie Kaiserslautern since November 2019.

Dr Marit Heuß is a lecturer and research assistant in the department of modern German literature and literary theory at the Institut für Germanistik at Leipzig University. She studied art history and German language and literature in Dresden and earned a PhD with a dissertation on Peter Handke's visual poetics. Her research focuses on contemporary Austrian literature, writing on art, poetry after 1945 (focussing on Sarah Kirsch and Wolfgang Hilbig, among others), the literary estates of poets and textual scholarship.

Steffen Krautzig studierte Neuere Deutsche Literatur und Kunstgeschichte an der Technischen Universität Dresden und der Freien Universität Berlin. Zwischen 2010 und 2023 war er im Kunstpalast, Düsseldorf, tätig, zuletzt leitete er stellvertretend den Bereich Kulturelle Bildung mit einem Schwerpunkt zur analogen und digitalen Kunstvermittlung. 2019 kuratierte er die Ausstellung *Utopie und Untergang. Kunst in der DDR*, u. a. mit Werken Gerhard Altenbourgs, und war Herausgeber des gleichnamigen Katalogs. Seit 2023 ist er als Referent bei der Bundeszentrale für politische Bildung, Bonn, tätig.

Dr. Roland Krischke studierte Romanistik, Slawistik, Philosophie und Germanistik in Heidelberg, Münster, Wien und Frankfurt am Main. Er war u. a. im Museum Haus Cajeth, Heidelberg, im Landesmuseum Mainz, in der Max-Slevogt-Galerie auf Schloss Villa Ludwigshöhe in Edenkoben sowie als Direktor Kommunikation und Bildung der Stiftung Schloss Friedenstein Gotha tätig. Von 2014 bis 2016 arbeitete er als Verleger. Seit November 2016 ist er Direktor des Lindenau-Museums Altenburg, seit 2017 Vorstandsvorsitzender der Stiftung Gerhard Altenbourg und seit 2020 Direktor der Altenburger Museen. Er kuratierte zahlreiche Ausstellungen und publiziert zur Kunst-, Literatur- und Kulturgeschichte.

Dr. Silvia Schmitt-Maaß (geb. Carmellini) studierte Kunstgeschichte, Klassische Archäologie und italienische Literatur an den Universitäten in Marburg und Florenz. Sie absolvierte ein Volontariat am Kunstpalast, Düsseldorf, arbeitete anschließend für die Stiftung Schloss und Park Benrath. Vor ihrem Stellenantritt als wissenschaftliche Mitarbeiterin am Lindenau-Museum Altenburg mit besonderem Schwerpunkt auf dem Werk der Stiftung Gerhard Altenbourg im Sommer 2022 war sie wissenschaftliche Mitarbeiterin am Projekt »Welfenbildnisse – Bildnisse der Welfen« an der Universität Osnabrück.

Steffen Krautzig studied modern German literature and art history at the Dresden University of Technology and the Freie Universität Berlin. He worked at the Kunstpalast, Düsseldorf, from 2010 to 2023, most recently as deputy director of the department for cultural education, with an emphasis on analogue and digital art education. In 2019 he curated the exhibition *Utopie und Untergang. Kunst in der DDR* (Utopia and Decline: Art in the GDR), which included works by Gerhard Altenbourg, and was editor of the eponymous catalogue. Since 2023 he has worked as a specialist for the Federal Agency for Civic Education in Bonn.

Dr Roland Krischke studied Romance languages, Slavic languages, philosophy and German studies in Heidelberg, Münster, Vienna and Frankfurt am Main. He worked at the Museum Haus Cajeth in Heidelberg, the Landesmuseum Mainz, the Max Slevogt Galerie at Schloss Villa Ludwigshöhe in Edenkoben and was director of communications and education for the Stiftung Schloss Friedenstein Gotha. From 2014 to 2016 he was active as a publisher. He has been the director of the Lindenau-Museum Altenburg since November 2016, chairman of the board of the Gerhard Altenbourg Foundation since 2017 and director of the Altenburger Museen since 2020. He has curated numerous exhibitions and publishes on topics in the history of art, literature and culture.

Dr Silvia Schmitt-Maaß (born Carmellini) studied art history, classical archaeology and Italian literature at the universities in Marburg and Florence. She completed a traineeship at the Kunstpalast, Düsseldorf, afterwards working for the Stiftung Schloss und Park Benrath. She was a research assistant at the project *Welfenbildnisse – Bildnisse der Welfen* at the Universität Osnabrück, before taking up her position in the summer of 2022 as research assistant at the Lindenau-Museum Altenburg, with a special emphasis on the Gerhard Altenbourg Foundation.

Bildnachweis / Image Credits

Foto | Photo: punctum/Bertram Kober
© Lindenau-Museum: Kat. | Cats. 1, 8–10, 12, 19, 23–24, 30, 35–38, 40–43, 45–48, 53, 55, 64, 66
Foto | Photo: Digitalisat Lindenau-Museum Altenburg
© Lindenau-Museum Altenburg: Beitrag | Text by R. Krischke: Abb. | Figs. 1, 2; Beitrag | Text by S. Schmitt-Maaß: Abb. | Figs. 1–3, 7; Beitrag | Text by M. Heuß: Abb. | Figs. 1–3; Beitrag | Text by S. Fischer: Abb. | Fig. 8; Beitrag | Text by S. Krautzig: Abb. | Figs. 3, 5, 6; Beitrag | Text by M. Büchting: Abb. | Figs. 1–6; Vita | Biography: Abb. | Fig. 1, Kat. | Cats. 3, 5–7, 11, 13–18, 20–22, 25–29a–d, 31–32, 34, 39, 44, 46–47, 49–51, 56–60, 63–79
© Museum Bochum: Beitrag | Text by S. Schmitt-Maaß: Abb. | Fig. 6
© Claus Bach: Beitrag R. Krischke: Abb. 2; Beitrag S. Krautzig: Abb. 3
© Deutsche Fotothek / Christian Borchert: Beitrag | Text by R. Krischke: Abb. | Fig. 3
© Foto | Photo: Lothar Schnepf; Kolumba, Köln: Beitrag | Text by S. Schmitt-Maaß: Abb. | Fig. 5
© Egbert Kasper: Beitrag | Text by S. Fischer: Abb. | Fig. 4
© Kupferstich-Kabinett, Staatliche Kunstsammlungen Dresden / Foto | Photo: Herbert Boswank: Beitrag | Text by S. Fischer: Abb. | Figs. 1a, 1b, Kat. | Cats. 2, 4, 33
© Nachlass Ulrich Lindner / Foto | Photo Ulrich Lindner: Beitrag | Text by R. Krischke: Abb. | Fig. 4, Beitrag | Text by S. Krautzig: Abb. | Figs. 1, 2
© Historisches Archiv der Stadt Köln mit Rheinischem Bildarchiv, rba_d058584 / Foto | Photo: Sabrina Walz / © Kunststiftung Museum Ludwig; Beitrag | Text by S. Fischer: Abb. | Fig. 5
© Villa Merkel / Gabriela Oberkofler, Esslingen, Graphische Sammlung: Beitrag | Text by S. Fischer: Abb. | Figs. 6a, 6b
© Gabriela Oberkofler: Beitrag | Text by S. Fischer: Abb. | Fig. 7
© Museum Pfalzgalerie Kaiserslautern / Foto | Photo Sebastian Rug: Beitrag | Text by S. Fischer: Abb. | Fig. 3
© Nachlass Lothar Reher / Foto Lothar Reher: Vita | Biography: Abb. | Fig. 2
© bpk / Sprengel Museum Hannover / Michael Herling / Aline Gwose: Beitrag | Text by S. Krautzig: Abb. | Fig. 4
© bpk / Städel Museum: Beitrag | Text by S. Schmitt-Maaß: Abb. | Fig. 4
© Verlag Brinkmann & Bose Berlin / Foto | Photo: Ubu Gallery, New York: Beitrag Text by S. Fischer: Abb. | Fig. 2
© VG Bild-Kunst, Bonn 2026 für die Werke folgender Künstler | for works by the following artists: Hans Bellmer, Bernard Schultze, Max Ernst
© Stiftung Gerhard Altenbourg, Altenburg / VG Bild-Kunst, Bonn 2026 für die Werke von | for the works by Gerhard Altenbourg

Wir haben uns intensiv bemüht, alle Inhaber und Inhaberinnen von Abbildungsrechten ausfindig zu machen. Personen und Institutionen, die weitere Rechte an verwendeten Abbildungen beanspruchen, werden gebeten sich nachträglich mit dem Herausgeber in Verbindung zu setzen. | Every effort has been made to identify all holders of image reproduction rights. Individuals and institutions who claim further rights to images used in this publication are asked to contact the publisher.

Die Geltendmachung der Ansprüche gem. § 60h UrhG für die Wiedergabe von Abbildungen der Exponate/Bestandswerke erfolgt durch die VG Bild-Kunst | Claims pursuant to § 60h of the German Copyright Act (UrhG) for the reproduction of images of exhibits/collection works are asserted through VG Bild-Kunst.

Impressum / Colophon

Diese Publikation erscheint anlässlich der Ausstellung *Der fantastische Gerhard Altenbourg – Ausstellung zum 100. Geburtstag* des Lindenau-Museums Altenburg im Prinzenpalais des Residenzschlosses Altenburg vom 12. Mai bis 16. August 2026.

This publication has been published on the occasion of the exhibition *The Fantastic Gerhard Altenbourg – 100th Birthday Exhibition* of the Lindenau-Museum Altenburg in the Prinzenpalais of the Residenzschloss Altenburg from 12 May to 16 October 2026.

Herausgeber | Editor
Roland Krischke für das | for the Lindenau-Museum Altenburg

Konzeption | Concept
Silvia Schmitt-Maaß

Redaktion | Editorial Team
Karoline Schmidt

Bildnachweise | Image Credits
Anna Lutz, Silvia Schmitt-Maaß

Übersetzungen aus dem Deutschen | Translations from the German
David Sánchez Cano

Deutsches Lektorat | German Copy-Editing
Lutz Stirl

Englisches Lektorat | English Copy-Editing
James Copeland

Gestaltung, Satz und Produktion | Graphic Design, Typesetting and Production
Sophie Friederich

Lithografie | Lithography
Reproline Mediateam Achter, Unterföhring

Projektmanagement Hirmer Verlag | Project Management Hirmer Publishers
Judith Kárpáty

Druck und Bindung | Printing and Binding
Beltz Grafische Betriebe GmbH, Bad Langensalza

Papier | Paper
150 g/qm Munken Lynx

Schriften | Typefaces
ITC Avant Garde Gothik, Oso Serif

Bibliografische Information der Deutschen Nationalbibliothek: Die Deutsche Nationalbibliothek verzeichnet diese Publikation in der Deutschen Nationalbibliografie; detaillierte bibliografische Daten sind im Internet über https://www.dnb.de abrufbar.

Bibliographic information published by the Deutsche Nationalbibliothek: The Deutsche Nationalbibliothek lists this publication in the Deutsche Nationalbibliografie; detailed bibliographic data are available online at https://www.dnb.de.

ISBN 978-3-7774-4773-5

Printed in Germany

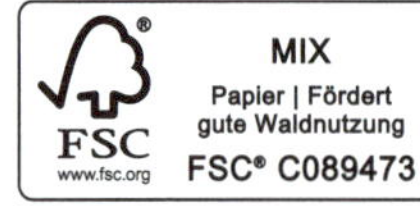

HIRMER VERLAG
Geschäftsführerin | Managing Director: Kerstin Ludolph
Bayerstraße 57–59
80335 München | Munich

www.hirmerverlag.de
www.hirmerpublishers.com
www.hirmerpublishers.co.uk

Cover Vorderseite | Cover Image
Detail / detail Kat. / cat. 41
Cover Rückseite | Back Cover Image
Detail / detail Kat. / cat. 16

Detailabbildungen der Seiten (Kat.) | Detailed Images of Pages (Cat.):
2, 3 (65); 4 (66); 5 (46); 6 (54); 8 (52); 10 (2); 14 (77); 26 (1); 42 (4); 56 (18); 66 (29); 82 (29); 90 (40); 102 (32); 107 (35); 122 (49); 130 (49); 132 (50); 137 (53); 140 (56); 150 (59); 166 (75);174 (63); 215 (15); 216 (24)

Altenburger Museen

LINDENAU-MUSEUM ALTENBURG

In Kooperation mit | In cooperation with Stiftung Gerhard Altenbourg | Gerhard Altenbourg Foundation

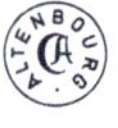

STIFTUNG GERHARD ALTENBOURG

Das Lindenau-Museum Altenburg wird gefördert von/ The Lindenau-Museum Altenburg is sponsored by

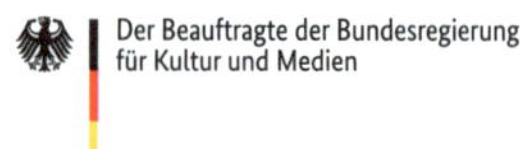

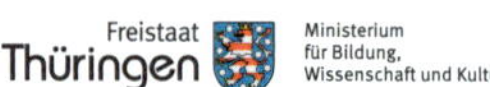

Partner

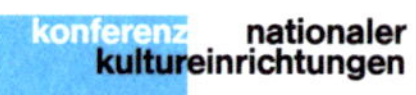

Wir treten ein für ein/ We stand for a

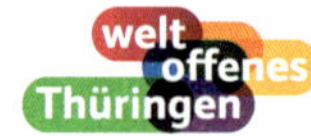

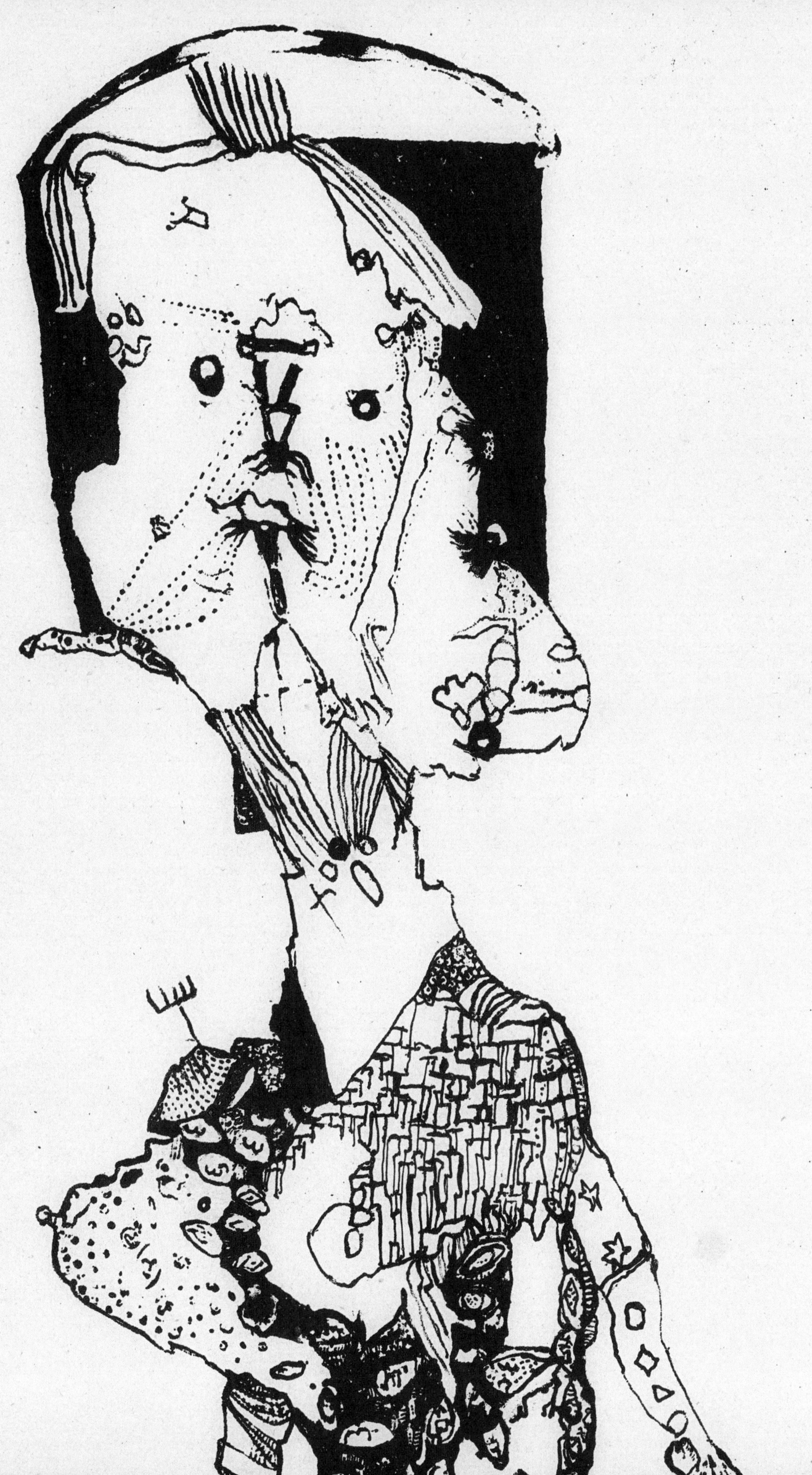

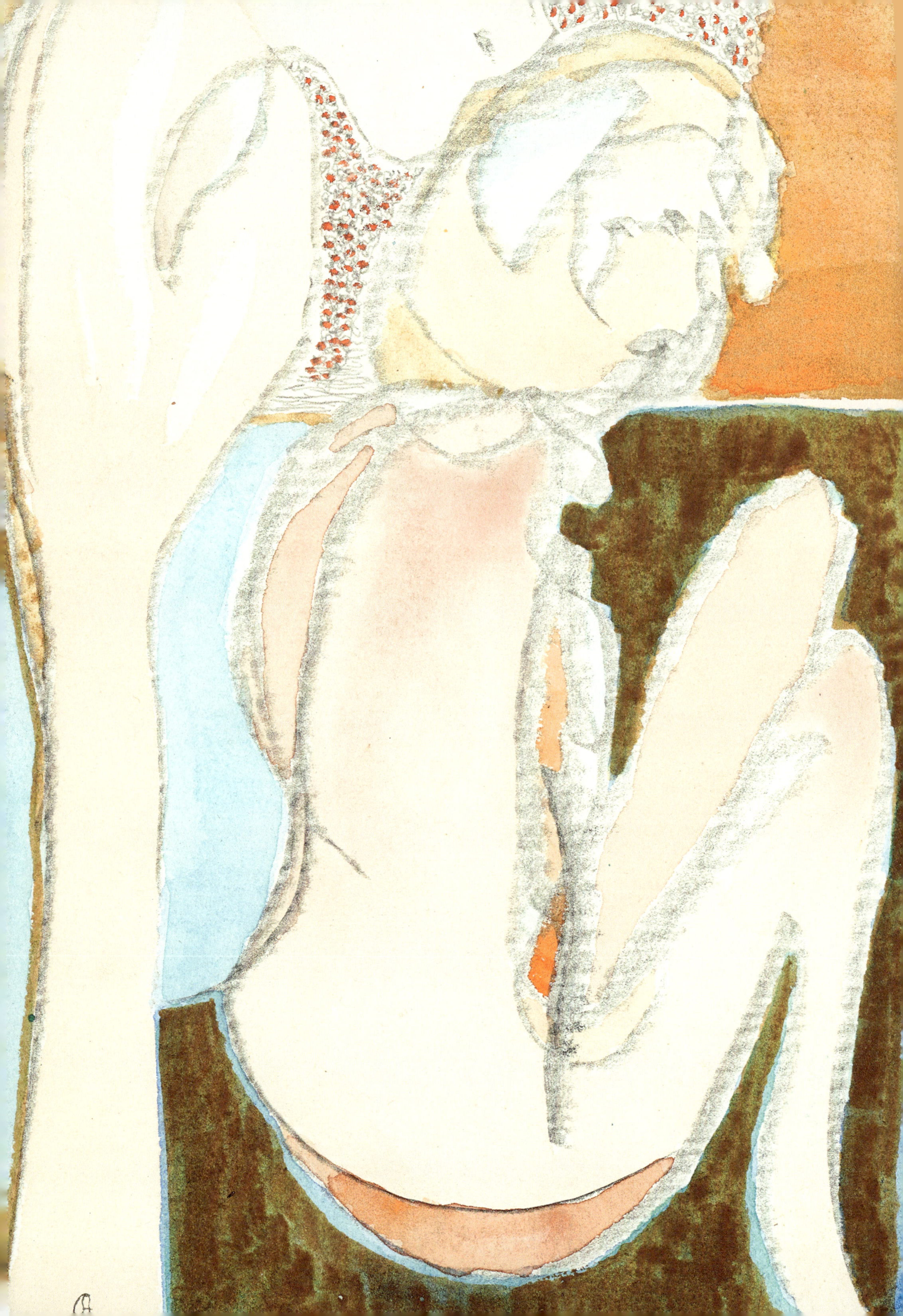